The Phonology of Tone and Intonation

Tone and Intonation are two types of pitch variation, which are used by speakers of many languages in order to give shape to utterances. More specifically, tone encodes morphemes, and intonation gives utterances a further discoursal meaning that is independent of the meanings of the words themselves. In this comprehensive survey, Carlos Gussenhoven provides an up-to-date overview of research into tone and intonation, discussing why speakers vary their pitch, what pitch variations mean, and how they are integrated into our grammars. He also explains why intonation in part appears to be universally understood, while at other times it is language-specific and can lead to misunderstandings.

The first eight chapters concern general topics: phonetic aspects of pitch modulation; typological notions (stress, accent, tone, and intonation); the distinction between phonetic implementation and phonological representation; the paralinguistic meaning of pitch variation; the phonology and phonetics of downtrends; developments from the Pierrehumbert–Beckman model; and tone and intonation in Optimality Theory. In chapters 9–15, the book's central arguments are illustrated with comprehensive phonological descriptions – partly in OT – of the tonal and intonational systems of six languages, including Japanese, French, and English.

Accompanying sound files can be found on the author's web site:
http://www.let.kun.nl/pti

Carlos Gussenhoven is Professor and Chair of General and Experimental Phonology at the University of Nijmegen. He has previously published *On the Grammar and Semantics of Sentence Accents* (1994), *English Pronunciation for Student Teachers* (co-authored with A. Broeders, 1997), and *Understanding Phonology* (co-authored with Haike Jacobs, 1998).

Research Surveys in Linguistics

In large domains of theoretical and empirical linguistics, scholarly communication needs are directly comparable to those in analytical and natural sciences. Conspicuously lacking in the inventory publications for linguists, compared to those in the sciences, are concise, single-authored, non-textbook reviews of rapidly evolving areas of inquiry. Research Surveys in Linguistics is intended to fill this gap. It consists of well-indexed volumes that survey topics of significant theoretical interest on which there has been a proliferation of research in the last two decades. The goal is to provide an efficient overview and entry into the primary literature for linguists – both advanced students and researchers – who wish to move into, or stay literate in, the areas covered. Series authors are recognized authorities on the subject-matter as well as clear, highly organized writers. Each book offers the reader relatively tight structuring in sections and subsections and a detailed index for ease of orientation.

Previously published in this series
A Thematic Guide to Optimality Theory *John J. McCarthy*
ISBN 0 521 79194 4 hardback
ISBN 0 521 79644 X paperback

The Phonology of Tone and Intonation

CARLOS GUSSENHOVEN

University of Nijmegen

CAMBRIDGE
UNIVERSITY PRESS

PUBLISHED BY THE PRESS SYNDICATE OF THE UNIVERSITY OF CAMBRIDGE
The Pitt Building, Trumpington Street, Cambridge, United Kingdom

CAMBRIDGE UNIVERSITY PRESS
The Edinburgh Building, Cambridge, CB2 2RU, UK
40 West 20th Street, New York, NY 10011–4211, USA
477 Williamstown Road, Port Melbourne, VIC 3207, Australia
Ruiz de Alarcón 13, 28014 Madrid, Spain
Dock House, The Waterfront, Cape Town 8001, South Africa

http://www.cambridge.org

First published 2004

Printed in the United Kingdom at the University Press, Cambridge

Typefaces Times Roman 10/12 pt. and Franklin Gothic   *System* LATEX 2_ε [TB]

A catalogue record for this book is available from the British Library

Library of Congress Cataloging-in-Publication Data
Gussenhoven, Carlos, 1946-
The phonology of tone and intonation / Carlos Gussenhoven.
p. cm. – (Research surveys in linguistics)
Includes bibliographical references and index.
ISBN 0-521-81265-8 – ISBN 0-521-01200-7 (pb.)
1. Tone (Phonetics)   2. Intonation (Phonetics)   3. Grammar, Comparative
and general–Phonology.   I. Title.   II. Series.
P223.G87   2004
414′.6 – dc22   2003065202

ISBN 0 521 81265 8 hardback
ISBN 0 521 01200 7 paperback

Voor Karel en Otto

Contents

Contents

Figures

Map

Tables

Preface

The question of how the delicate pitch variations that humans can produce are employed in language has been one of the most fascinating topics in phonological and phonetic research at least since Joshua Steele's *Essay towards establishing the Melody and Measure of Speech* (Steele 1775), but has developed a particularly fruitful momentum in the past two decades. This book is an account of my current understanding of this issue.

Lexical pitch variations and intonational pitch variations are phonologically represented as tones, like H(igh) and L(ow), which form a string of elements running parallel to the string of vowels and consonants. Like vowels and consonants, tones may delete, assimilate, or change their value in particular contexts. They are organized temporally with reference to prosodic constituents, such as the mora, the phonological phrase, and the intonational phrase. Studying the phonology of tone and intonation can sharpen one's understanding of phonetics and phonology in a relatively brief time. The greater variation in the realization of tones, together with their relative sparsity compared with the denser occurrence of vowels and consonants, encourages a comprehensive view of the trajectory from underlying representation to phonetic surface form. As a result, the difference between phonology and phonetics as well as that between underlying phonology and surface phonology can more readily be appreciated.

The theory of intonational structure presented in this book owes a great deal to the work of Janet Pierrehumbert, whose 1980 thesis on American English intonation in effect provided the theoretical framework it has adopted, which work itself was intellectually indebted to Gösta Bruce's 1976 thesis on Stockholm Swedish. I was 'around' at the time Janet Pierrehumbert's thesis came out, but it took me a while to realize that its greatest significance was not in the details of the analysis of American English, which is very elegant, though nothing to sweep the board, but its conception of the relation between phonology and phonetics, and that it was – indeed – a model of how phonology works in general.

It is hoped that the book will stimulate theoretical and descriptive research in tonal phonology. Possibly, the order 'theoretical and descriptive' places the wrong emphasis here: 'descriptive and theoretical' better expresses the fact that the number of languages that have been described in terms of the metrical–autosegmental model, a term we owe to Bob Ladd (1996), is still limited. An important advantage of a well worked-out theory is that direct comparisons can be made across languages. Accurate and theoretically responsible descriptions provide the basis for theoretical innovation and improvements in our understanding of the nature of the object we study. There is a vast literature on tonal systems in the languages of Africa and Asia, but in spite of many years of dialectological research in Europe, the prosodic systems of varieties of well-known European languages are to all intents and purposes undescribed, while the same is true of most languages spoken elsewhere in the world.

Chapter 1 provides essential phonetic background information for empirically oriented students of prosody. Chapters 2 and 3 deal with basic typological categories like 'tone', 'stress', 'intonation', and 'accent'. Chapter 4 discusses the place of intonation in language. As implied above, an explicit formulation of the distinction between phonological representation and phonetic realization was a key feature of Pierrehumbert's 1980 thesis, and it accounts in no small measure for the recent progress in the field. Together with chapters 5 and 6, chapter 4 lays out the implications of the distinction. More so than has perhaps been realized, it is crucial to an understanding of the issue of the apparent universality of paralinguistic meaning. Chapters 5 and 6 attempt to explain how people know what the paralinguistic meanings of pitch variation are. These chapters also discuss the typical structural interpretations of these effects in specific languages.

Three general chapters follow: chapter 7 sets out the phonological configurations encountered in languages; while chapter 8 summarizes the ways that sentence prosody has been, or can be, dealt with in Optimality Theory.

An emphasis on the distinction between what is representational and what is due to the phonetic implementation naturally focuses our attention on the prosodic contrasts in languages. The language descriptions in chapters 9 to 15 provide illustrations of how phonological accounts capture sets of contrasting forms. These descriptions, which reproduce and expand on earlier analyses, are each biased towards specific aspects of prosodic structure, some of which are approached within an Optimality Theoretic framework. Basque and Japanese illustrate how tonal structures combine intonational and lexical tone in a situation where both are reasonably non-complex. Swedish and Norwegian provide examples of Germanic languages with a lexical tone contrast that is confined to the stressed syllable of the word. Language change is the focus of the next chapter, where the interaction between lexical and intonational tones is charted diachronically in a group of dialects spoken in Germany, the Netherlands, and Belgium. We continue with a chapter on French that provides an illustration of how a complex pattern of variation in accent distributions can be brought under control by the variable ranking of constraints. In that same chapter, a tonal grammar is presented which shows how French is more complex than, say, Norwegian, but much less complex than English, which is treated in chapter 15. This chapter and chapter 14 are of interest because of the way in which the theoretical positions defended in the preceding chapters are applied to what must be the most thoroughly investigated language in the world. I have not resisted the temptation to introduce new elements in the description of these languages, despite the status of the book as a research summary. Given my background, the bias towards intonation in the choice of languages dealt with in these last chapters is hopefully forgivable.

1 July 2003   Carlos Gussenhoven
Nijmegen, The Netherlands

Acknowledgements

I first became acquainted with the topic of this book through a course called *Tone and Intonation* taught by Gillian Brown at the University of Edinburgh in 1968, where I spent my year abroad as a student of English. Between then and now, I have had many opportunities to learn from others, whether they were teachers, colleagues, students, or authors. I am very grateful to Christine Bartels for suggesting that I should write a book on intonation when she was still working for Cambridge University Press, for I don't think I would have done it without her encouragement. More recently, I have benefited greatly from the interaction with the co-ordinators of the ESF Network *Tone and Intonation in Europe* (2001–2004). I am also indebted to numerous people who posed questions and supplied corrections at workshops and conferences over the past years. I have asked a number of people to read drafts of selected passages of this book and incorporated their responses in the final text in various ways. None of them is, of course, responsible for the way I have done this and in particular any errors are mine only. For these responses I would like to thank Daniel Bühring, Aoju Chen, Yiya Chen, Nick Clements, Paul de Lacy, Gorka Elordieta, Rachel Fournier, Sónia Frota, Martine Grice, Larry Hyman, Haike Jacobs, René Kager, Gjert Kristoffersen, Haruo Kubozono, Aditi Lahiri, Jörg Peters, Brechtje Post, Henning Reetz, Stéphane Robert, Tomas Riad, Sotaro Kita, Annie Rialland, Jørgen Rischel, Joe Salmons, Lisa Selkirk, Hubert Truckenbrodt, Leo Wetzels, Keiko Yoshioka, as well as an anonymous reviewer engaged by the publisher. I would also like to thank those who were kind enough to record examples whose F_0 tracks are reproduced in the book: Joumard Alban, Arantzazu Elordieta, Eukene Elordieta, Stephanie van Elven, Nanna Haug Hilton, Hedy Kamara, Eric Kellerman, Sotaro Kita, Aditi Lahiri, Madeleine Lambrechts-Doecet, Yoshihisa Miura, Mariko Sugahara, Stéphane Tardy, Fumiko Uchiyama, Anne Wichmann and Nicole Verberkt. I am grateful to Femke Deckers and Wilske Driessen for producing these graphics with the help of the PRAAT program. These speech files, as well as representative speech files for the numbered examples throughout the book, are available at www.let.kun.nl/pti I thank Gorka Elordieta, Sónia Frota, Matt Gordon, Esther Grabe, Judith Haan, Linda Heümans, Vincent van Heuven, Minjoo Kim, Bert Remijsen, Chilin Shih and Henning Reetz for various kinds of help in obtaining recordings and figures, as well as several generations of students for their useful comments.

I worked on the book mainly in Nijmegen, where I was able to draw on the expertise of many colleagues, in particular Joop Kerkhoff and Toni Rietveld, but also spent time elsewhere. I enjoyed the generous hospitality of Aditi Lahiri during several fruitful periods spent at the University of Constance. Additionally, I spent four weeks at the University of Massachusetts Amherst and six weeks at the Institute for the Study of Languages and Cultures of Asia and Africa of the Tokyo University of Foreign Studies in 2000, and I thank Shigeki Kaji and Lisa Selkirk for their kind and effective efforts to make my life both useful and pleasant during those times.

Permission to reproduce figures was obtained from Esther Grabe (figure 1.7); the Regents of the University of California (figure 4.11); S. Karger AG (figure 5.4., originally *Phonetica*, vol. 11. p. 181, figure 3); Kingston Press Services (figures 4.6, 4.8, 4.9, and 5.4, originally *Language and Speech*, vol. 42, pp. 286, 287, 289, figures 1, 2, and 3, respectively, and vol. 43, pp. 195, 198, figures 2 and 3, respectively); Cambridge University Press (figures 5.2, 6.2, 6.5, 7.1, and 10.3); MIT Press (figures 5.3, 6.4 panel a, and 10.2), ESCA (figure 6.1); Bill Poser (figure 6.3); Shigeki Kaji (figure 6.4, panel b); Algemene Vereniging Taalwetenschap (figure 6.8); Gösta Bruce (figure 11.1). I thank the Netherlands Organization for Scientific Research for financial support.

Abbreviations

AL	Analogical Lengthening
C$_\text{ON}$	constraint hierarchy (Optimality Theory)
CR	Compound Rule
DAT	digital audiotape
ERB	Equivalent Rectangular Bandwidth
ES	extra-sentential constituent
E$_\text{VAL}$	evaluation procedure (Optimality Theory)
F_0	fundamental frequency
G$_\text{EN}$	Generator (Optimality Theory)
Hz	hertz
IAD	Initial Accent Deletion
IO	Input–Output (Optimality Theory)
ip	Intermediate Phrase
MHG	Middle High German
ms	millisecond
NP	noun phrase
OCP	Obligatory Contour Principle
OO	output–output (Optimality Theory)
OSL	Open Syllable Lengthening
OT	Optimality Theory
PA	pitch accent
PP	prepositional phrase
RMS	Root Mean Square
RP	Received Pronunciation (Standard English accent in England)
s	second
S	root sentence (also: matrix sentence)
ST	semitone
SOV	Subject-Verb-Object

SVO	Subject-Object-Verb
ToBI	Tones and Break Indices
ToDI	Transcription of Dutch Intonation
VP	verb phrase
VOT	voice onset time
XP	syntactic phrase
XP'	maximal syntactic phrase

Symbols

[1]	Accent 1
[2]	Accent 2
´	high tone; primary stress
`	low tone; secondary stress
ˆ	falling tone
ˇ	rising tone
( )	accentual phrase or any other constituent below ϕ
[ ]	phonological phrase
{ }	intonational phrase
⟨ ⟩	utterance
'	primary stress
ˌ	secondary stress
*	violation (Optimality Theory)
*!	fatal violation (Optimality Theory)
☞	winning candidate (Optimality Theory)
☞!	incorrectly selected winner (Optimality Theory)
*X	ungrammatical X; do not have X (Optimality Theory)
T*	accent marking tone
T-	Intermediate Phrase boundary tone
T%	intonational phrase boundary tone
!T	downstepped tone
T_x	boundary tone of constituent x
α	accentual phrase
ι	intonational phrase
Ⓣ	floating tone
μ	mora
ϕ	phonological phrase
σ	syllable
υ	utterance
ω	phonological word

1

Pitch in Humans and Machines

1.1 Introduction

In this first chapter, some phonetic information is given which will be required for an active engagement in research in the area of tone and intonation. For further information on the articulatory, acoustic, and technological facts, handbooks like Laver (1990), Ladefoged (1996), Johnson (1997), Rietveld and van Heuven (1997), Reetz (1999) should be consulted.

1.2 Frequency of vocal fold vibration, fundamental frequency (F_0), and pitch

Pitch is the auditory sensation of tonal height. We have this sensation when listening to the difference between [s] and [ʃ], for instance, but in speech, it is most precise when it reflects the periodicity in the acoustic signal. Periodicity amounts to repetitions of the same pattern of vibration, each such repetition being a *period* and corresponds to a closing-and-opening action of the vibrating vocal folds. The actual shape of the speech signal during a period determines the sound quality (the vowel quality, say) that we perceive. In panel (a) of figure 1.1, 25 milliseconds (ms) from the speech waveform produced by a woman are shown. During that time, just over six periods were produced, representing as many vibratory cycles of the vocal folds. These are two muscles, situated halfway down the larynx, which run front to back from the inside of the thyroid (the shield cartilage sticking out in the front of the neck) to the two arytenoids, which are located above the cricoid. In a relaxed state, there tends to be a slit between the vocal folds, known as the glottis, through which we breathe. The slit can be widened to a triangular opening by rolling the arytenoids away from each other, allowing increased air intake or escape. They can also be brought more closely together, to a point where their edges will be pushed up by the air pressure below them during the exhalation phase, prising the glottis open. The subsequent drop

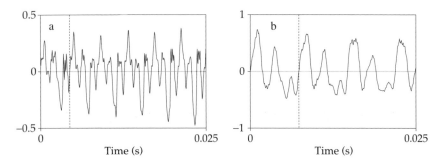

Fig. 1.1 Sections of 25 ms from the speech waveform during vocal fold vibration produced by a woman (panel a) and produced by a man (panel b). The vertical dotted lines mark of the end of the first period, which is 4.42 in panel (a) and 7.28 ms in panel (b).

in air pressure between the vocal folds, which is due to the rapid flow of air through the glottis (the Bernoulli effect), will cause them to be sucked together again, after which the subglottal pressure will again push them up, and apart, and so on. Vocal fold vibration is the alternation between these opening and closing events.

The opening action of the vocal folds is normally slower than the snappier closing action. Each closing action has an effect which is comparable to that of the flick of a finger against the throat: a brief shock wave is set up, which hits the walls of pharynx and mouth. If this happens more than forty times a second, we stop hearing the flicks as separate events, and instead perceive a continuous event: pitch. The faster these waves follow each other, i.e. the higher the frequency of vibration of the vocal folds, the higher will be the number of periods per second, commonly known as the *fundamental frequency*, or F_0 ('F-zero'), of the acoustic signal, and the higher the resulting pitch. The beginning of the graph in panel (a) coincides with a point in time during which the air pressure is neither raised nor lowered as compared to the surrounding air pressure, a zero-crossing. The first period ends at the dotted vertical line, which has been drawn through a zero-crossing. The duration of this period is 4.42 ms. As can be seen, the waveform during this period contains three positive peaks, of which the second and third clearly reveal further smaller peaks within them. These higher frequencies ride on the crest of the F_0, and in this case cause it to be heard as a mid front vowel. Each of the six closing actions of the vocal folds that are responsible for the six periods in panel (a) of figure 1.1 is thus comparable to what happens when you flick a finger against the skin of the neck, near the larynx. When this is done while holding the larynx closed and holding the mouth in the position for some vowel, [ɛ] in this case, a popping noise is produced, which rapidly fades away.[1]

F_0 is usually expressed in Hz (or hertz), the number of periods per second. The F_0 corresponding to the first period in panel (a) is 1,000 (ms) divided by

4.42 ms, the period, or 226 Hz. In panel (b) of figure 1.1, 25 ms from a speech waveform produced by a man are shown. Its shape during the period corresponds to that of high back vowel, [u]. As will be clear, only about 3.5 periods fit into this time span. The first period is 7.26 ms long, and the F_0 is therefore 138 Hz. Rates of vibration in male speakers average around 125 Hz while those in female speakers, whose larynxes are much smaller in the front to back dimension than those of men, average around 225 Hz (cf. Holmberg, Hillman, and Perkell 1988).

1.3 Pitch tracks

Several techniques are available for recording the pitch of utterances (Hermes 1993; Reetz 1996: 83ff.). They can be based on the articulation, the acoustics, or the perception. By definition, the best source for obtaining a record is the listeners' perception, since pitch is a perceptual sensation. Unfortunately, listeners lack the appropriate conceptualizations and vocabulary to report their sensations, and are typically incapable of saying even whether a given pitch change represents a fall or a rise. Things become very much simpler if the voiced parts of the speech signal are divided up into sections of some 30 ms, and static pitch judgements are obtained for each of these, as recorded on a scale from low to high. The evidently laborious nature of this procedure is not its only drawback. It is still unreliable because of the inaccurate way in which people report their pitch sensations, a drawback which can only be overcome with the help of a careful experimental design allowing averaging over many trials. Not surprisingly, this method of reporting pitch variation is rarely, if ever, used.

An effective way of measuring the vocal fold vibration is by running a weak electric current between two electrodes placed on the skin on either side of the larynx, so that the vocal folds lie between them. Because the impedance for the electric signal emitted by the first electrode is increased when the vocal folds open, the opening actions can be read off the electric signal reaching the second electrode (Fourcin and Abberton 1971). While it generally records vocal fold vibration rates accurately, this method can be used only in laboratory conditions.

Most commonly, records are obtained from the speech signal. There are many ways in which the F_0 of a signal can be established automatically, which are commonly referred to as 'pitch trackers' (even though they measure the fundamental frequency). The evaluation of their merits is virtually a field of study in itself (cf. Reetz 1999, who refers to Hess 1983, Hermes 1993, and Reetz 1996). Because they are implemented as computer algorithms, pitch trackers need to work with digitized forms of the signal. Digitization of the continuous speech waveform is performed by determining a single value at regular intervals, as shown in panel (a) in figure 1.2. The number of times per second that a measurement of the waveform is recorded is the *sampling rate*. A musical CD-Rom contains 44.100 measurements per second, and thus has a sampling rate of 44.1 kHz, a DAT-recording stores the signal at a 48 kHz sampling rate, while many speech scientists make do with a sampling rate 16 kHz. Panel (b) shows

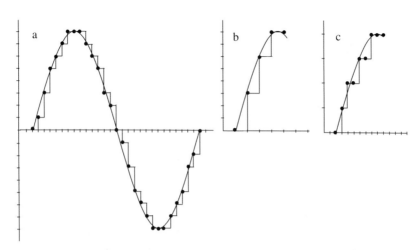

Fig. 1.2 A continuous speech waveform and a digitized waveform (panel a), and digitized waveforms with a lower sampling rate (panel b), and a lower quantization accuracy (panel c).

part of the same waveform sampled with half the sampling rate of that in panel (a), as is evident from the calibration marks on the time axis and the corresponding durations of the 'steps'. As a result, the first upward excursion which in panel (a) is represented by seven values (including the first sample with zero excursion), is represented by only four values in panel (b). A second parameter determining the reproduction quality of the digitized signal is the accuracy with which the value of each sample is stored, or *quantized*. The lower the accuracy, expressed in bits,[2] the larger the rounding errors, and the greater the jumps from one sample to the next will be. This is illustrated in panel (c). Due to the larger rounding errors, instead of the seven values of panel (a), there are effectively only five values, even though the signal is sampled at the same rate. Larger jumps lead to more *quantization noise*. A 16-bit accuracy is a good choice for music, while 8-bit accuracy is not uncommon in speech research.

It stands to reason that in order to preserve a period in a digitized signal, at least two values for that period must be recorded. If the sampling rate were to equal the signal frequency, the information would be reduced to a single value. This is the reason why the sampling rate must be (preferably more than) twice the highest signal frequency we wish to preserve. Signal frequencies that lie between half the sampling rate and the sampling rate give rise to 'false' periods. This 'aliasing' effect is comparable to the visual effect of spoked wheels turning backwards in cinefilms. This is why all signal frequencies above half the sampling rate are filtered out before digitization. A sampling rate of 16 kHz is therefore way below what would be required for hifi equipment, since younger people may perceive frequencies of up to 20 kHz. However, it is usually good enough for speech, where no significant phonetic information is found above 8 kHz.

Once the signal is represented as a digital file, automatic F_0 detection can begin. Broadly, a division can be made between algorithms that operate directly on the digitized speech signal and those that take a spectral analysis as input. Algorithms that work directly on the signal employ some form of *autocorrelation*. The series of values within an analysis window, whose duration might be chosen to fall well above the period to be detected, is established, to represent the window's starting position. As the window is moved through the speech waveform, sample by sample, the string of values encountered at each step is correlated with those of the starting position. Clearly, the sections of the waveform within the window encountered at each step are not likely to resemble that in the starting position at all closely, except when the window begins at an equivalent point in a following period. At that point, the sections will be very similar, resulting in a high positive correlation between the strings of values. Alternatively, the duration of the window is gradually increased from a starting duration well below the estimated period duration, and the values in each of the incremented windows is correlated with the values in the next section having the same duration. Again, when the duration of the window equals the duration of the period, the correlation will be relatively high, reflecting the fact that the values in the two periods are now very similar. In practice, the choice of pitch tracker is determined by circumstance and convenience: their evaluation is typically beyond the competence of a phonologist.

1.4   Interpreting pitch tracks

The results of a pitch tracker can be plotted against time to provide a visual representation of the F_0 variation in the utterance. The x-axis gives time, usually in milliseconds (ms), the y-axis F_0, commonly reported in hertz (Hz). It is sometimes felt that a linear representation of the number of periods per second gives a biased view of the auditory impression of pitch changes. For instance, a difference between 600 Hz and 650 Hz seems smaller than one between 100 and 150. Two measures that have been claimed to give a better auditory representation are the semitone scale (ST) and the Equivalent Rectangular Bandwidth (ERB) scale. According to Hermes and van Gestel (1991), of the three scales this scale represents auditory impressions in intonation most closely. In practice, the choice here is hardly ever a problem, since within the usual F_0 range in speech, ERB and Hz values are very similar (Rietveld and van Heuven 1997: 210). In this book, Hz scales are used.

1.4.1   Tracking errors

Pitch trackers make mistakes. A pitch tracker may mistake voiceless friction for voicing, and irregular measurement points may therefore show up during fricatives and releases of affricated plosives. Conversely, it may interpret irregularly

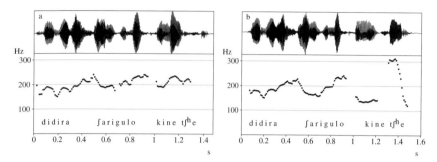

Fig. 1.3 Incorrectly detected voicing during the fricative part of an affricate and incorrectly detected voicelessness during creaky [e] in the last syllable of Bengali 'My sisters (also) BOUGHT the saris' (panel a) and a correctly analysed contour for an interrogative pronunciation of the same sentence, 'Did my sisters buy the saris?' (panel b).

voiced signals as voicelessness. Of course, the researcher can always inspect the waveform and measure the period(s) he or she is interested in so as to calculate the corresponding F_0 by hand. Both problems appear in the pitch track in figure 1.3. Incorrectly detected voicing during the aspirated affricate tʃʰ occurs at 1.3 s, while incorrectly detected voicelessness during creaky [e] occurs at 1.4 s. The F_0 of this vowel is actually around 120 Hz, but no record was made. Finally, there may be periodic background sounds that are picked up by the pitch tracker, causing it to report spurious F_0 values. For comparison, consider the contour in panel (b), which represents a different intonation pattern, and where the tʃʰe has been correctly analysed as voicelessness followed by a steep fall on [e].

Even if the detection of voicing and voicelessness is correct, the pitch tracker may fail to analyse the voiced signal correctly. When the voice becomes creaky, as it often does at lower pitches, the algorithm may be confused by peaks in the signal that do not correspond to the vibratory action of the vocal folds. If these appear halfway through the period, they may be interpreted as peaks created by the opening actions of the vocal folds, leading to fundamental frequency measurements that are twice that of the 'real' fundamental frequency (*doubling errors*). Similarly, the algorithm may miss every second periodicity peak, 'believing' these peaks determine the sound quality rather than the periodicity (*halving errors*). Such 'octave jumps' are usually easy to detect: the pitch track shows a sudden change to a value half or double that of the immediately preceding value, while there is no auditory impression that corresponds to this jump. The pitch track in figure 1.4 shows a halving error in the last part of the vowel [ɪ]. A corrected version with different analysis settings, obtained by trial and error, appears in panel (c) of figure 2.2. Among other things, pitch trackers allow the user to choose the range of possible frequencies to be detected. If the actual F_0 of the speech file falls outside the upper or lower limits of the analysis band, mistakes are inevitable. Safe ranges are usually 75–400 Hz for male speakers

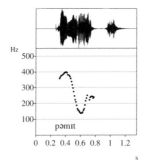

Fig. 1.4 Halving error in last part of the stressed vowel of *permit?* (verb). The pitch continues upwards to 480 Hz, but the F_0 tracker shows a record around 240 Hz.

and 100–600 Hz for female speakers. Children may produce more than 600 Hz. (I have not corrected the graphic results of the pitch analyses reproduced in this book.) Errors other than octave jumps will also occur.

1.4.2 Consonantal effects on F_0

The articulation of segments will interfere with the production of vocal fold vibration. First, if all is well, pitch trackers will report no F_0 during glottal closures or voiceless consonants like [p,s,χ,m̥], there being no vocal fold vibration. Due to their oral constrictions, voiced obstruents, too, particularly plosives like [b,d,g], may impede the airflow needed to keep the vocal folds vibrating, slowing the vibration down or stopping it altogether. By contrast, sonorant consonants and vowels allow the air coming in from the lungs to escape via the nostrils or the opened lips to prevent air pressure from building up in the mouth, and the vocal fold vibration is therefore uninhibited during these sounds. Because our pitch perception in language normally factors such effects out, what is subjectively the same pitch contour may look rather different depending on the consonants in them. This is illustrated in panel (a) in figure 1.5, which gives F_0 tracks of the same intonational fall produced on the segmental structures [ata], [ada], and [ana].

The production of a voiceless consonant requires an active gesture of the arytenoids opening the glottis, but the cricothyroid muscle is also active (Löfqvist, Baer, McGarr, and Story 1989). This may cause the vocal folds to be somewhat tighter than during relaxed vibration. The effect is typically still present during the vibration for the following vowel, causing the fundamental frequency after voiceless consonants to be higher than after voiced consonants. A particularly clear example of the effect is shown in panel (b) of figure 1.5, where a consonantal 'pitch perturbation' occurs after the [ks] of *niks* in the Dutch utterance *Ik kan gewoon niks anders* 'I can't do anything else.' There is a raised F_0 after the [ks] of *niks*. Again, the auditory impression is that of a smoothly falling pitch

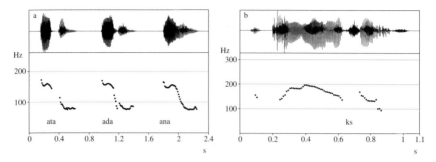

Fig. 1.5 Pitch falls in VCV-structures with a voiceless obstruent, a voiced obstruent, and a sonorant consonant for C, respectively (panel a), and an F_0 perturbation after [ks] in Dutch (panel b).

contour. Although this is generally hard to detect in F_0 tracks, a small effect must also exist *before* obstruents. Some lowering occurs for both voiced and voiceless consonants, but the lowering is greater before voiced consonants (Silverman 1984; Silverman 1990). The F_0 in the section of the vowel immediately preceding [t] and [d] was shown to influence the perception of the voicing of the consonant in German and English (Kohler 1990): higher F_0 in the preceding vowel increased the chance that [t] was perceived in a task in which listeners could choose between [t] and [d].

Further effects are due to phonation type (Laver 1980). Breathy voice induces low pitch, although the mechanism is not entirely clear (Hombert, Ohala, and Ewan 1979). During breathy voice, more air escapes per opening action than is needed to keep the vibration going, the excess air being used to create friction in the glottal aperture. The combination of friction and vibration must be easier to obtain at lower frequencies. Laryngealized voice may be conducive to high pitch, since the vocal folds need to be stiffened to produce it. However, there is also the converse fact that creaky voice, a form of laryngealization which is produced with slacker vocal folds, is easier to obtain at lower frequencies (Kingston 2003).[3]

1.4.3   Vocalic effects on F_0

The articulation of vowels may also affect the tenseness of the vocal folds, and so interfere with the rate of vocal fold vibration. The most plausible explanation is that high vowels like [i,u] are pronounced with the tongue high in the mouth, causing the hyoid, the horseshoe-shaped bone to which the tongue root is attached, to pull up the forward part of the larynx, the thyroid, to which the vocal folds are attached. As a result, higher vowels will on average be pronounced with higher vibration rates than lower vowels, like [a]. The component in the F_0 which is due to the correlation between vowel height and F_0 is known as *intrinsic pitch*, but, as Reetz (1999) suggests, 'intrinsic F_0' would be a better term. The difference is larger in stressed than in unstressed syllables (Silverman 1990).

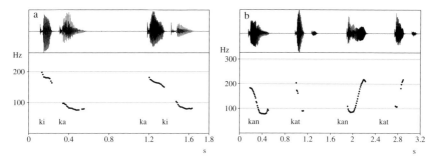

Fig. 1.6 The effect of intrinsic F_0 in acoustically different, but perceptually identical F_0 contours on [kika] and [kaki] (panel a), and fade-out reversals in [ken] compared with the same contours cut short by [t] in [kat] (panel b).

Panel (a) in figure 1.6 shows two subjectively identical pitch contours on [kika] and [kaki], respectively. However, the first syllable in the second word has lower F_0. Indeed, we do not normally hear intrinsic pitch as pitch. When [a] has the same fundamental frequency as [i], we hear it as higher than [i], and we thus factor out the effect in perception (Silverman 1985). In practice, intrinsic pitch need not cause any problems when relating the pitch track to our auditory impression of the pitch contour. However, when setting up experiments involving pitch, vowel height may have to be controlled for.

1.4.4 End-of utterance effects

Utterances ending in sonorant consonants (e.g. [m,r,l,w]) or vowels may end with a reversal of the F_0 in the last part of the utterance, where the signal fades out, a phase which may be detectable to the pitch tracker, but is ignored in human perception. There appears to be no discussion in the literature, but it would seem reasonable to assume that it is due to a relaxation of the muscles controlling the frequency of vibration of the vocal folds. Panel (b) in figure 1.6 shows a fall and a rise on the syllable [kɑn], with what might be called a fade-out reversal on each, i.e. a weak rise after the fall and a weak fall after the rise. When the same contours are spoken on the syllable [kɑt], the pitch movement occurs inside a high-intensity part of the signal. Here, the segment [t] cuts short movements, a phenomenon known as *truncation* or *curtailment*. (The pitch tracker had some problems in measuring the central portion of the vowels, as is evident from the gaps.)

Some languages truncate more drastically than others (Grabe 1998b). In German, final falls on rhymes consisting of a short vowel and a voiceless obstruent (e.g. *Schiff* 'ship') are quite drastically truncated, often leaving just a level portion. By comparison, the syllable with a long vowel, *schief* 'slanted'), or a disyllable like *Schiefer* (proper name), have contours that fall. Importantly, to the native ear, these intonation patterns are identical. In equivalent conditions in British English

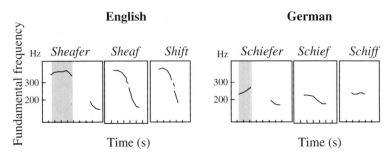

Fig. 1.7 Representative F_0 traces of falls in British English and German on a pre-final syllable, on a final syllable with a long vowel, and a final syllable with a short vowel followed by an obstruent. The shaded area indicates the stress vowel of a disyllabic word. German truncates falls on final rhymes like -*iff*, but English does not (cf. *shift*). From Grabe (1997: 163).

(e.g. *shift*), the contour is hardly different from what is found in segmentally more favourable conditions, like *Sheafer, Sheaf*, as shown in figure 1.7, from (Grabe 1998b). It is thus not only gaps that may 'distort' the visual picture but also early curtailments of the vocal fold vibration, something that may occur before final voiceless obstruents.

1.5   Experimentation

Our understanding of the prosodic structure of languages has greatly benefited from production and perception experiments. Production experiments may use either scripted or unscripted speech. Scripted speech is produced on the basis of written material which is read out or acted out in some fashion; while unscripted speech relies on spontaneous speech, elicited with the help of the Map Task or similar methods (Anderson *et al.* 1991). Such 'games' typically involve two speakers, who are drawn into conversations which stimulate the production of linguistic structures that the researcher is interested in, either because the speakers are invited to talk about items that have names exemplifying those structures or because communicative situations are created that are likely to lead to the production of particular intonation contours.

Perception experiments may use either natural stimuli, selected sections of naturally spoken speech, or stimuli in which the F_0 contour has been created artificially. Since 1995, an efficient technique has been available which performs such F_0 manipulation directly on the waveform (Moulines and Verhelst 1995). It replaces earlier techniques by which the specification of the F_0 component was altered after the signal had been analysed into the F_0 component and a number of spectral components, and a new signal was 'resynthesized' with the help of the components which included the altered values. The direct techniques reproduce shorter or longer versions of the periods detected in the signal by a procedure known as PSOLA (Pitch-Synchronous OverLapAdd). If the deviation from the original F_0 is not too great, there is barely any loss in the naturalness of the signal; larger deviations may lead to effects that may remind one of the croaking of a frog.

1.6 Conclusion

The study of linguistic pitch variation is empirically supported by F_0 measurements produced by computer programs known as 'pitch trackers'. The F_0 is reported as a graph, often printed synchronously with the speech waveform, so that the reader can relate the F_0 to the segments in the utterance. The visual appearance of an F_0 track will be determined by the measurement scale, and may contain pitch-tracker errors. In addition, there would appear to be four ways in which segmental conditions interfere with the fundamental frequency. First, consonants may affect fundamental frequency during their articulation, due to gaps and curtailments caused by voiceless consonants and to brief decreases during the oral strictures of voiced obstruents. Second, the effects of the voicelessness gesture is typically detectable as increased fundamental frequency in the following vowel, causing vowels after voiced obstruents to have lower F_0 than vowels after voiceless obstruents. To a lesser extent, this is also true for vowels before obstruents. Third, vowel height is positively correlated with fundamental frequency, which is probably due to the ligatures connecting the hyoid and the larynx, causing a raised tongue body to pull up the thyroid and so tighten the vocal folds. Fourth, relaxation of the muscles controlling glottal vibration rates may cause a reversal of F_0 direction in low-intensity fade-outs of utterances.

For most people, it is not too difficult to develop an awareness of pitch variation, and the F_0 track may help the uninitiated to develop such awareness, if account is taken of the factors discussed above.

Notes

1. Of course, being human, we cannot produce sequences of physically identical periods during vocal fold vibration, which is why reference is often to *quasi-periodic(ity)*.
2. One bit equals one binary digit. Two bits will allow the expression of four values: 00, 01, 10, and 11, or 0, 1, 2, and 3. The number of values per number of bits equals 2 to the power of the number of bits. Thus, with three bits, 2^3 or 8 values can be expressed, and so on.
3. Kingston argues that this is probably the explanation of the dual fate of stem-final glottal stops in Proto-Athabaskan (see section 3.6).

2

Pitch in Language I: Stress and Intonation

2.1 Introduction

A consideration of the ways in which pitch variation functions in language brings up a number of concepts that provide the basis for a broad prosodic typology. *Stress* is without a doubt the most widely researched prosodic concept. Section 2.2 aims to clarify what it is, how it is realized, and how it relates to tone and F_0. Tone languages, which use pitch for distinguishing words, are discussed in chapter 3. Languages without lexical tone are referred to as 'non-tonal languages' or 'intonation-only languages'. In section 2.3, *intonation* is treated as the use of phonological tone for non-lexical purposes, or – to put it positively – for the expression of phrasal structure and discourse meaning. In the discussion of intonation, the notion *accent* is introduced as a location where intonational tones are located.

The notions 'stress', 'tone', 'accent', and 'intonation' all refer to suprasegmental aspects of the phonological structure, but they are in fact rather different. Many phonologists would argue that all languages have phonological stress in the sense of foot structure, even though the phonetic salience of stressed syllables will vary considerably from language to language, to the extent that some languages have no observable phonetic stress. Probably all languages have structural intonation. However, only about half have lexical tone, while for many languages it will not make sense to speak of 'accent'.

2.2 Stress

In Francis Ford Coppola's film *The Conversation* (1974), a conversation carried on by two people in a busy square is surreptitiously recorded with the help of three microphones (partly long-distance directional). One of the crucial utterances in that recording, as heard in the laboratory by the surveillance agent (a stellar performance by Gene Hackman) is *He'll KILL us if he gets the chance*,

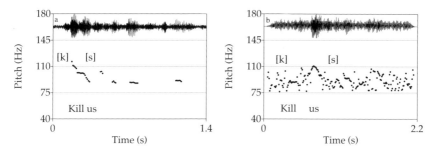

Fig. 2.1 F$_0$ tracks of *(He'll) KILL us if he gets the chance* (panel a) and *He'll kill US if he gets the chance* (panel b) from Francis Ford Coppola's *The Conversation*. The words *kill* and *us* are different in the two utterances. The second utterance has considerable background noise. The analyses were done with the 'To Pitch' program in the PRAAT package, using an analysis window of 60–150 Hz.

pronounced with a somewhat subdued, but clear stress on *kill* and a less prominent one on *chance*. The plot of the story hinges on a reversal of the roles of murderer and victim: it turns out that the utterance had in reality been *He'll kill US if he gets the chance*. The conversation had amounted to a plot by the two participants to murder the man referred to as *he*, but by mishearing the location of stress the surveillance agent had naturally suspected him of wanting to kill *them*, the participants in the conversation. After the murder has taken place, it turns out that the reason why the agent had so fatally misheard the sentence was that the volume controls of the three original recordings had been set so as to blank out the stress on *us* and create one on *kill*. An adjustment of the volume of the three playback recorders could in fact bring back the intended interpretation.

This film illustrates one of the most widespread misconceptions about the prosodic structure of English, one which was held within the field of linguistics itself well into the 1960s. It is the incorrect intuition that stress amounts to a louder pronunciation of the word or syllable it is found on. Among phoneticians, the myth was dispelled in the 1950s, when it was shown that the perception of stress was effectively influenced by F$_0$ features and duration (Fry 1955; Fry 1958; Fry 1964; Mol and Uhlenbeck 1956; Bolinger 1958) (see further below). However, increases in overall intensity, of the sort that are obtained by turning up the volume of some electronic playback machine, are totally ineffective, a point Mol and Uhlenbeck (1956) made explicitly. Not surprisingly, different utterances were used in *The Conversation*. Figure 2.1 shows their waveforms and F$_0$ tracks. The F$_0$ track in panel (a) shows how a falling contour was used on *kill*, while that in panel (b) shows a pitch peak on *us*, which word is also longer in this utterance.

A second misconception, one which originated from the above perception experiments, is that stress is realized by F$_0$. While it is true that F$_0$ patterns provide powerful cues to the location of stressed syllables in many languages, the presence and shape of these F$_0$ contours are independent of a word's stress pattern and instead depend on the intonational grammar of the language (Hayes

1995; Sluijter 1995; Ladd 1996). From a structural point of view, stress is a property of the rightmost or leftmost syllable of a prosodic constituent, the foot. The prototypical foot is a sequence of two syllables one of which is strong (S, or stressed) and the other weak (W, or unstressed) (Selkirk 1980; Hayes 1995). S–W feet are *trochees*, W–S feet are *iambs*, and any one language employs either one or the other. The stressed syllable in the foot is both unique and obligatory: any additional syllables are (also) unstressed, and a monosyllabic foot has, by definition, a stressed syllable. Examples of English feet are given in (1). As in Hayes (1995), parentheses mark out the feet in a 'metrical grid', in which stressed syllables (x) are distinguished from unstressed syllables (.), and one stressed syllable is identified as having the *main stress* (also *primary stress*, *word stress*), as indicated by an extra 'x' in the higher line (Halle and Vergnaud 1987; Hayes 1995).

(1)   x   x   x
           x   .   x   x . .
      a. (manner)   b. (man)   c. (manager)
           x   x   x
           x . x   x . x .   x . x .
      d. (mani)(cure) e. (alli)(gator) f. (Mani)(toba)

A general principle of biological mechanics must be held responsible for the rhythmic, pulse-like behaviour of many types of sustained muscular activity, and thus also for the fact that languages tend to alternate syllables pronounced with greater and lesser precision. Feet are typically binary, and some theories exclude monosyllabic feet (Burzio 1994) or ternary feet (Hayes 1995), analysing them somehow as binary structures with empty or extra structural elements. As said, the phonetic consequences of phonological stress will vary across languages (Berinstein 1979; Hayes 1995), but can often be found in the energy distribution across the frequency spectrum, in the duration, and in the accuracy with which articulatory targets are reached (section 2.2.1). These consequences may be phonologized, as will be briefly illustrated. The role of pitch will be clarified in section 2.2.3.

2.2.1 The phonetic correlates of stress

Stress is a property of syllables (Hayes 1995: 49). The difference between stressed and unstressed syllables may be detected in a number of phonetic measures.

- Vowels in stressed syllables have a fairly even intensity distribution across the frequency spectrum, while vowels in unstressed syllables tend to have lower intensities for the higher frequencies, thus displaying a downward slope towards the higher end of the spectrum (Sluijter 1995). This difference in *spectral tilt* has only recently been diagnosed as a feature distinguishing the two types of syllable. It appears to be caused mainly by the more abrupt closure of the glottis during vocal fold vibrations in stressed syllables (Sluijter and van Heuven 1997; Sluijter 1995: 125).

- Due to a reduced effort to pronounce vowels in unstressed syllables, their quality is likely to be more centralized and less rounded (more schwa-like) than that of stressed syllables. In English, this is true for vowels before consonants. In prevocalic position, reduction due to lack of stress amounts to raising and consonantal glide formation, as in the first syllable of English *piano* or the medial syllable in *India*, both of which vary between [i] and [j].
- Consonants and vowels in stressed syllables tend to be longer than those in unstressed syllables.

These three differences can be related to the greater articulatory care with which stressed syllables are treated (de Jong 1995). While not all languages show the phonetic effects of foot structure in this way, it would be entirely unexpected to find a language that realized stressed syllables in phonetically conflicting ways.

The motivation for assuming that languages without phonetic stress do nevertheless have foot structure is based on morphological processes that impose foot-sized constraints on the length of morphemes, as happens in Japanese (Poser 1990). For instance, the shortened version of a name which appears before the suffix *tyan* must be a single foot. Because a foot consists of two short vowels or one long one, proper names are either disyllabic or monosyllabic in these 'hypochoristics': *humiko* appears as *humityan*, but *syuusuke* and *keiko* as *syuu-tyan* and *keityan*, while in the case of *taroo* the second syllable is shortened in *tarotyan*. Also, in many Japanese compounds and loan words, the location of lexical tone is predictable in a way that is reminiscent of stress placements in the world's languages, suggesting that in these cases the tone goes to the stressed syllable (Haraguchi 1991: 12). Thus, while Japanese has no stress in the phonetic sense (Beckman 1986), it does have foot structure. At the other extreme, we find languages like English, where the phonetic correlates of stress have been phonologized, and are very salient.

In tone languages, which are discussed in chapter 3, the effect of stress can also be seen in the care with which lexical tones are pronounced. In Trique, for instance, a language with five contrasting tones, the three lowest tones are pronounced lower, and the two highest tones higher in stressed syllables than in unstressed syllables (Longacre 1952).

2.2.2 Phonological effects

Vowel quality

The number of different vowels that are possible in stressed syllables is often higher than in unstressed syllables, reflecting the reduction of the phonetic space as used by reduced vowels. Depending on the variety, and not counting schwa or syllabic [r], Standard English has between nineteen (Southern British English, or RP) and thirteen (California English) vowels (Giegerich 1997; Hammond 1999:

Ladefoged 1999: 43ff.), but only stressed syllables can have the full set. According to Bolinger (1981), unstressed syllables display only a three-way contrast, as shown in (2) (letters corresponding to the unstressed vowels concerned are in italics; syllabic consonants may appear instead of schwa).[1]

(2)

	LOW	FRONT	BACK
a. PREVOCALIC	–	rad*i*o	us*u*al
b. PRECONSONANTAL	*a*bout	*e*nough	K*u*wait
c. WORD-FINAL	vill*a*	man*y*	fell*o*w

Such restrictions are likely to figure in many languages, but need not. Dutch is similar to English in many respects, but has considerably fewer restrictions on the appearance of vowels in unstressed syllables (Gussenhoven 2003).

Duration and quantity

As said, the prototypical foot is disyllabic, and if this were the only relevant factor, languages would shape their words to have perfectly alternating occurrences of stressed and unstressed syllables: there would be a ti-túm (iambic) or a túm-ti (trochaic) rhythm which goes right-to-left or left-to-right through the word. However, the longer phonetic duration of stressed syllables may lead to distributional correlations between stressed syllables and long vowels. Contrastive duration of vowels or consonants, i.e. quantity contrasts, occur in many languages. There are two possible implications. First, the rhymes of stressed syllables may have a minimum length of two segments (e.g. [at], [ai]) or a long vowel (e.g. [aː]). In such languages, vowels in open stressed syllables will lengthen. For instance, the vowel in an open penultimate syllable of the phonological phrase is lengthened in Italian as well as in many Bantu languages, like Chicheŵa (Kanerva 1989; Downing 1996) (see section 8.5.1). This dependence of length on stress will typically strengthen the alternating rhythm. The second implication holds that languages disallow bisegmental rhymes in unstressed syllables, an implication which may lead to a-rhythmic patterns. The term 'heavy' generalizes across long-vowelled open syllables and closed syllables. Seminole/Creek, an iambic language which parses a word like [(pomó)(saná)] 'our otter' into two regular iambs, will have an a-rhythmic pattern in [(táːs)(hó)(kitá)] 'to jump+DUAL', because the first syllable, which contains a long vowel underlyingly, refuses to be unstressed, and thus cannot form an iamb with [ho] (Hayes 1995: 65). Since the iambs start counting on the right, both the first and the second syllables form feet by themselves.[2] These two implications are known as 'Stress-to-Weight' and 'Weight-to-Stress', respectively. When languages display both implications, there is a perfect correlation between long rhymes and stress, as in my own analysis of Dutch (Gussenhoven 2003).

Quantity and weight are expressed in moras (Hyman 1985). A commonly accepted analysis is given in (3) (Hayes 1989). It splits off the onset consonant(s), which are prosodically inactive, from the segments in the rhyme. However, the rhyme includes a mora structure: a vocalic rhyme with a single mora, as in (3a), will be short and thus 'light', while two moras represent a long vowel, as in (3b).

(3)

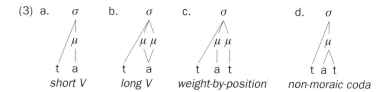

a. σ — t a — short V
b. σ — t a — long V
c. σ — t a t — weight-by-position
d. σ — t a t — non-moraic coda

When a language requires bimoraic syllables to be stressed, it is 'quantity-sensitive' (Hayes 1980). In many languages it is immaterial whether the second mora is filled by a vowel (as in (3b)) or a consonant, as in (3c), since either type attracts stress, the coda consonant is moraic. Such a consonant was said to have 'weight by position' by Hayes (1989). In some quantity-sensitive languages, however, only long vowels attract stress, in which case closed syllables with short vowels are represented as in (3d), causing them to be prosodically equivalent to (3a).[3]

2.2.3 The role of fundamental frequency

A phonetic property not discussed in the above section is F_0. Yet, when it was first realized that stress is not correlated with overall intensity, it was on the basis of a demonstration that the most powerful cue for the perception of stress is F_0. In a classic series of experiments, Fry demonstrated that the contrast between the members of such English word pairs as *pérmit* (Noun) and *permít* (Verb) is most easily signalled by the location of a pitch fall. In addition, duration had an effect, while listeners were more confident if the quality of the stressed vowel was less schwa-like. The explanation for this powerful effect of pitch is that in many contexts, one of which is when the word is spoken in isolation, the stressed syllable is provided with an intonational *pitch accent*, a tone or tone complex like H* ('high') or L*H ('low–high').

Stressed syllables will thus serve as the location for the tones that make up the intonation contour. This mediating role of stress was spelled out by Dwight Bolinger (Bolinger 1958): a stressed syllable is a syllable that has the *potential* for being pitch-accented. The presence of the pitch accent depends on the position of the word in the intonational structure and on contextual factors ('information structure', see chapter 9); but a sure-fire context in which a pitch accent will appear is a citation pronunciation, a one-word utterance. In figure 2.2, panel (a) shows the F_0 registrations of a sequence of citation pronunciations of *pérmit* and *permít*, in which the difference in the location of the F_0 fall is clearly visible. The fall on *mit* in the noun is somewhat truncated. Panel (b) shows the noun *pérmit* in the compound *work permit*, in which there is no longer any appreciable

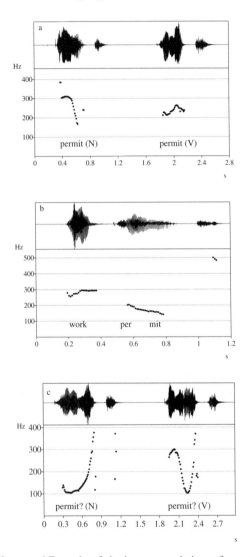

Fig. 2.2 Waveforms and F_0 tracks of citation pronunciations of *permit* (Noun), *permit* (Verb) (panel a) and of the compound *work permit* (panel b), and of interrogative pronunciations of *permit* (Noun) and *permit* (Verb) (panel c).

F_0 movement, because, in English compounds, there is no pitch accent on the second constituent. However, it is still the case that in this second constituent *permit*, the first syllable has the word stress.

A second point Bolinger made was that even if we restrict ourselves to one-word utterances, there is no single F_0 feature that can be associated with stress. This is because English pitch accents come in different kinds. One of these consists of a rising F_0 movement, as shown in panel (c). There is now an F_0 fall at the end of the first syllable, but the main stress is unambiguously on the second. Clearly, native speakers do not perceive stress in terms of some invariable F_0 feature; rather, their perception amounts to a hypothesis about the complete prosodic structure of the utterance, which includes a choice of intonation pattern. In the case of panel (c), their hypothesis will not take the F_0 fall as a pitch accent, but interpret it as the downward slope of a movement to the beginning of a rising pitch accent on the second syllable.

Phonological theory only caught up with Bolinger's understanding of the issue in the 1970s and 1980s, when Autosegmental Phonology created separate representations for tones (H, L), and stress came to be represented separately from intonation (Leben 1975; Liberman 1975; Goldsmith 1976; Goldsmith 1980; Pierrehumbert 1980). What was earlier seen as the highest degree of stress now amounted to the presence of a pitch accent. Just as bimoricity and stress correlate in the languages of the world, so do tones and stress. As in the case of bimoricity, the correlation is fed both ways: there are languages that put the stress where the tone is; others direct the tone to the stress.

The separation of (intonational) tone and stress has led to a more 'analytical' view of stress. For instance, many phonologists will now agree that 'Compound Stress', a pattern exemplified in *work permit*, does not in fact create any difference in stress at all, but is an accentual pattern that requires the first member to be pitch-accented and the second to be unaccented if the compound is spoken in isolation. (This accent disappears again in a context like *That's MY work permit!*) What were earlier seen as 'degrees' of stress tend now to be seen as discrete categories rather than points on a gradient. In the following section, the gradient and discrete views are briefly contrasted (see also Hayes 1995: 22; Ladd 1996: 46ff.).

2.2.4 'Degrees' of stress in English

In a commonly adopted view, stress is gradient. In that view, it makes sense to say that, just as tone is realized by pitch, stress is realized by a number of phonetic features, like duration and vowel quality, which are partly in a trading relationship. In its most extreme form, this conception implies that stress is infinite, in the sense that there is no principled limit to the degree of stress a syllable can have. At one time, this was expressed through the gradient feature [n stress] (Trager and Smith Jr 1951; Chomsky and Halle 1986). The idea was espoused more recently by Liberman and Prince (1977) in the 'metrical tree' representation (in which every node branches into a strong and a weak node and there is no principled limit to the number of nodes that can exist), as well as in interpretations of the metrical grid in which columns can be infinitely high (Halle and Vergnaud 1987). Conceptions of infinitely gradient stress naturally go together with the notion that phonetically more stress somehow means more of the same thing, and that a single representational device should be used to express these degrees. To put it somewhat crudely, to get the right amount of stress, you need to get an appropriate admixture of those phonetic attributes. It has understandably been hard to demonstrate the existence of any such orderly sequence of stress degrees in the phonetic signal. One response to this problem has been to say that stress is 'relative' (Trager and Smith Jr 1951; Liberman and Prince 1977), that you cannot establish its degree, or presence, unless there are other syllables with different degrees of stress to measure it by. Another, perhaps more useful, response has been to point out that stress is ultimately a location in phonological structure, the left or right edge of a foot, and that the way that position reveals itself in the pronunciation of any language depends on the ways in which that language refers to these locations (Hayes 1995).

The view of stress as a bulk commodity, sketched in the preceding paragraph, contrasts with a compositional view, in which 'degrees of stress' are discretely different, expressed by different phonological entities, and possibly realized by different phonetic features. One version of this view, represented by Bolinger (1958, 1981) and Vanderslice and Ladefoged (1972), is summarized in (4). Here, the first cut is between unstressed and stressed syllables, or, for Bolinger (1958), syllables that will never be pitch-accented and those that may be. Stressed syllables then divide into accented (i.e. pitch-accented) syllables, given in capitals, and unaccented syllables.

(4) 'Degree of stress'	Position in structure	Phonetic correlates, and example
Unstressed	Weak syllable in a foot	Qualitative and durational reduction, steep spectral tilt e.g. *po-* and *-to* in *potato*.
Stressed unaccented	Strong syllable in a foot	Vowels without qualitative and durational reduction. Less-steep spectral tilt e.g. *caul-* and *flow-* in *cauliflower*, in the utterance *I LIKE cauliflower*.
Accented	Stressed syllable with an intonational pitch accent	Strong syllable in foot, and so like stressed, but additionally with pitch configuration heard as 'sentence accent'. e.g. *caul-* in the utterance *I like CAULiflower*.

The question is whether these three degrees of stress are enough to explain the facts of English. In general, languages typically distinguish primary from secondary stressed syllables. The primary stress in an English word is defined by the syllable that receives the last intonational pitch accent when spoken in isolation. A secondary stress *after* the main stress, like *-ga-* in *álligàtor* is never pitch-accented. The distinction between primary and secondary stress must somehow be indicated in the representation, because the occurrence of post-primary (unaccentable) stressed syllables is not fully predictable. By the side of *álligàtor* (not *àlligátor*), there is *tàpióca*.

In addition to blocking the association of a pitch accent, a syllable with secondary stress might be phonetically different from one with primary stress *even in the absence of a pitch accent* on the latter. This is true for Dutch. The minimal pair in (5) illustrates the point: each word has two feet, ordered primary–secondary in (5a) and secondary–primary in (5b).

(5) a. [ˈkaː.mə.ˌraːtjə] *camera* + *tje* 'camera+DIM'
    b. [ˌkaː.mə.ˈraːtjə] *kameraad* + *tje* 'comrade+DIM

When these words are pronounced *without* an intonational pitch accent, which occurs when they are used as the second constituent in a compound, as in *FILM-cameraatje* 'little film camera' and *FILMkameraadje* 'little movie pal', the durations of the stressed syllables [kaː] and [raː] are not the same across the two words (Gussenhoven 1993). In either case, but most clearly in the case of [kaː], the syllable with primary stress is longer than that with secondary stress (Rietveld, Kerkhoff, and Gussenhoven 2003). Additional evidence for the distinction is provided by the way in which a particular intonation contour, the 'vocative chant', is pronounced in compounds like (5) (Gussenhoven 1993). This contour, which for speakers of English is readily evoked by the spelling *Jo-ohn!*, consists of two or more level pitches. When used on polysyllabic expressions, levels continue through unstressed syllables, but not through syllables with secondary stress. What this means is that the distinction between secondary stress and primary stress must be phonologically represented independently of the presence of a pitch accent.

The evidence for the same distinction in English is not as strong. Hayes (personal communication 1992) suggests that there is a durational difference in cases like *I didn't SAY 'ex-Rays'* versus *I didn't SAY 'x-rays'*. An investigation of this issue might consider separating in word-internal situations, as when *Burmese* [ˌbɜː.ˈmiːz] is compared with *Hermes* [ˈhɜː.ˌmiːz], and word-combinations, as in Hayes's example. Also, it may make a difference if the two syllables are not adjacent, as in *òverhául* (Verb) versus *óverhàul* (Noun), or, for a multi-word example, in the well-known *'No', said the Spanish teacher*, where *Spanish teacher* could be either the compound *SPANish teacher* in isolation, i.e. a teacher of Spanish, or the noun phrase *Spanish TEACHer*, i.e. a teacher who is Spanish (cf. Schmerling 1974: 27).[4]

Duration is not the only parameter which might reveal a difference. In Gussenhoven (1991a), I suggested that there might be a systematic difference in the way the final rise in interrogative intonations is pronounced on final unaccented stressed syllables. Imagine that (6a,b) are pronounced with a pitch accent for *SAY*, low pitch for *Bur-/Her-*, followed by a final rise (the 'fall–rise' contour). The final syllable of *Hermes* might now be fully high-pitched, while that in *Burmese* might have a pitch rise. If this is a real difference, the timing of intonational pitch movements that do not mark accent would be sensitive to the distinction between primary and secondary stress.

> (6) a. Had you already SAID Burmese?
>   b. Had you already SAID Hermes?

Assuming that there is a distinction between the two types of stress in English, as evidenced by durational differences and possibly F_0 differences, the middle category in (4) must be split into 'unaccented primary stress' and 'unaccented secondary stress'. This compromises the fully compositional view of the table in (4) to the extent that there is a three-step gradient 'unstressed – secondary stressed – primary stressed', the second and third of which have greater duration than, respectively, the first and second.

Finally, English words frequently have two pitch accents, one on the main stress and one on a *preceding* secondary stress, like *sar* in *sàrdíne*, *Cal-* in *Càlifórnia*, or *-so-* in *assòciátion* (Pike 1945; Hayes 1995; Gussenhoven 1991a; Beckman 1986; Shattuck-Hufnagel 1995). Such words can be pronounced with the same intonation as any two-accent phrase can, such as *The FIRST TIME* (see chapter 14).

2.3 Intonation

Languages use pitch variation contrastively for the expression of discoursal meaning and for marking phrases. One of the important points developed in Ladd (1996) is that intonation is structural, just as lexical tone is structural, or morphological paradigms are. In principle, an intonation contour has two structures: a morphological one, which identifies the morphemes and thus gives the meaning of the contour; and a phonological one, which gives its tones. This 'duality of structure' is further discussed in chapter 4, together with other diagnostics of the structural status of intonation.

Intonational tones appear either on (or near) accented syllables, in which case they are (intonational) pitch accents, or at the edges of prosodic constituents, like the intonational phrase, in which case they are boundary tones (Pierrehumbert 1980; Pierrehumbert and Beckman 1988). Pitch accents are tones like H^* and L^* or tone complexes like H^*L and LH^*. The bitonal ones have either a leading tone before the T^* or a trailing tone after T^*, whereby the starred tone associates with an accented syllable.[5] Such syllables, a subset of the stressed syllables, are assumed to be marked with a feature 'accent', which means that they require a pitch accent. Their location is determined by a variety of factors in English, and other languages will share these factors with English. There are first of all lexical rules, like those that determine the main stress and thus the accent location in a citation pronunciation of, say, *piANo*, and the Compound Rule, which removes this accent in the second constituent of *GRAND piano*. These lexical rules do not exist in French, for example (see chapter 13). Phrasal phonology subsequently imposes rhythmic distributions, as in *a VEry nice PICture*, where the accent on *nice* is absent because it is too close to the other accents ('clash', see section 7.4 and chapters 13 and 14). A third factor is focus, or information structure, which will cause further accent deletions on words that represent known information (see also section 5.7.1). The latter kind of rule is often absent in languages spoken on the northern shores of the Mediterranean, like Italian and Greek. Utterances will contain at least one accented syllable, which is usually indicated by capitalization, as has been done here.

Example (7) illustrates these concepts. The sentence consists of two intonational phrases, each with one accent. In the first intonational phrase, or ι, *report* is unaccented because it is the second element in a compound, while *incident* in unaccented because it is meant to be known to the listener: the context of (7) is in fact the incident concerned. In the second ι, the only lexical word is *mentioned*. The rest are function words, which typically remain unaccented. As for the tones, both ιs begin with a boundary L-tone, superscripted for the ι they come with. Although English also has initial H_ι, this is the neutral choice. The first ι ends in H_ι, typically used for ιs that are non-final in the sentence, and the second in L_ι, typically used in final ιs. The pitch accent is bitonal H*L, where the trailing L is responsible for the fall immediately after the accented syllables. The stylized tonal targets and the contour illustrate how this structure is pronounced. Details of association of intonational tones are given in chapter 7, while chapter 15 presents the full tonal grammar of English. At this point observe how only the T* is associated to a syllable, and that therefore most syllables are tonally underspecified (cf. section 3.3.6).

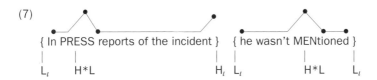

(7)

{ In PRESS reports of the incident } { he wasn't MENtioned }

L_ι H*L H_ι L_ι H*L L_ι

The final boundary H_ι will remain on the right hand boundary of the ι when it is shortened, as in (8) (cf. Ladd 1996: 44).

(8)

{ In the PApers } ...

L_ι H*L H_ι

In (9a), the accented syllable is final in the ι, which causes the pitch accent and the boundary tone to be realized on the same syllable: a complex contour arises on -*port*. In a final ι, its meaning will be that of a reminder, or of a confirmatory question. In (9b), the pitch accent has changed to L*H. Now the meaning is that of a (surprised) question. This is the same interrogative contour as used on 'permit (Noun) and on the second syllable of *per*'mit (Verb) in panel (c) of figure 2.2, the declarative contour of panels (a) and (b) is the same as that used on *mentioned* in (7). Finally, we could now add syllables again by replacing *rePORT* with *PRESS reports of the incident* to show the separation L*H and H$_\iota$. Thus, more so than in the case of lexical tone, the pitch on the syllable associated with intonation tone is highly dependent on the context. Assuming H*L L$_\iota$, a syllable like *press* has falling pitch if it is ι-final but high pitch otherwise, while with H*L L$_\iota$, it will have high pitch in *Pressing them*, falling pitch in *Pressing* and falling-rising pitch in *Press*.

(9) a.   b.

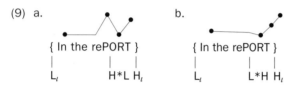

In addition to informational (or 'discoursal') meanings, intonation has been claimed to have emotional or attitudinal meaning. In chapter 5, it will be argued that interpretations like 'surprise', 'friendliness', 'authoritativeness' are typically not due to intonational morphemes, but arise during the phonetic implementation of the pitch contour, and are as such non-structural. They form part of a wider class of *paralinguistic* vocal, facial, and manual gestures which may accompany speech. In chapter 4, a principled distinction will be drawn between the linguistic and paralinguistic use of pitch variation, while chapter 5 attempts to explain how the paralinguistic pitch features come to have the (universal) meanings they have.

Notes

1. As Bolinger points out, the unstressed vowels in *many*, *fellow* contrast with vowels in secondary stressed syllables in *teepee* and *NATO*, which words are rhythmically like *insect* /'ɪnˌsɛkt/ rather than *inner* /'ɪnə/.
2. Left-to-right footing would have produced the equally a-rhythmic *[(taːs)(hoki)(ta)].
3. In a widely accepted foot typology, the trochaic foot has been redefined as a moraic trochee, as opposed to a syllabic trochee. A moraic trochee consists either of a single heavy syllable or two light syllables. In Hayes's theory, there are no 'moraic iambs'.
4. There have been durational investigations which failed to find a distinction (Huss 1975; Faure 1980). Huss (1978) did measure durational differences between post-nuclear

realizations of pairs like *ímpòrt – impórt*, but listeners did not recognize the words. Arguably, too, in pairs like these, the first syllable of the verb is unstressed, rather than secondarily stressed.

5. A third tone type, the 'phrase accent', has been claimed to be intermediate in behaviour between pitch accents and boundary tones (Pierrehumbert 1980; Beckman and Pierrehumbert 1986; Grice, Ladd, and Arvaniti 2000). See further, chapter 7.

3

Pitch in Language II: Tone

3.1 Introduction

All languages use vowels and consonants in the representation of their words,[1] and a large number, referred to as 'tone languages', also employ tone for this purpose. In this chapter, the question of how pitch variation is used in language is continued from chapter 2 with a discussion of lexically contrastive tone patterns. Some background is provided in section 3.2, while in section 3.3 the notion *Tone Bearing Unit* is introduced and the autosegmental representations it implies. While rejecting the idea that there is a meaningful class of 'accent languages' (in the way that a class of 'tone languages' can be defined), we define *accent* as a location for a (lexical or intonational) tone contrast, following its use in the same sense in section 2.3 (section 3.5). Observe that the notion is distinct from pitch accent, which is a tone or a complex of tones occurring in the location designated as 'accented'. When 'accent' is compared with the notion 'word melody', both can be seen as devices that explain distributional restrictions of tones. In a final section, the combined use of intonational and lexical tone is briefly illustrated.

3.2 Tone languages

The earliest distinction within the group of tone languages is between those that just have *level tones*, which require the syllable to reach a certain pitch height, and those that also have *contour tones*, which require the syllable to be said with a pitch movement. Pike (1948) termed these 'register tone languages' and 'contour tone languages', respectively. Additionally, tone contrasts have a *paradigmatic* dimension, the number of tonal contrasts possible on a given syllable, and a *syntagmatic* dimension, the number of positions in a word where these contrasts are used. As for the first dimension, many tone languages just have a binary level contrast, and the symbols H (high) and L (low) – shorthand notations for the two

26

values of a binary feature like [±Hightone] – therefore often suffice to describe them. The number of level tone contrasts may, with increasing rarity, reach three, four, or five (Maddieson 1978). A three-way contrast occurs in Yorùbá (Laniran 1990), a four-way contrast in Mambila (Connell 2000), and a five-way contrast in Benčnon (Wedekind 1983), which language additionally has a contour tone, a rise. Admittedly, the lowest level tone of Benčnon may be somewhat falling and the highest somewhat rising, but these features seem to be there to improve distinctiveness ('enhancement', see chapter 5, section 5.3). Benčnon may well hold the world record for the number of contrasting phonologically level tones. The highest tone in the five-level tone system of Trique only co-occurs with the next highest on a word-final syllable, where the tones may generally form contours. As a result, a minimal quintuplet with five-level tones is systematically ruled out (Longacre 1952). Clearly, to represent these contrasts more is needed than a binary feature. The introduction of a further binary feature [±upper] increases the number of contrasts to be expressed to four, but no consensus exists on what is the best feature system (Hyman 2001b). The number of contrasts including contour tones may go up to eight, as in Iau (West Papua) or more (Bateman 1990). Sagart (1999) estimates the range for Chinese languages to be from three to ten, with tonal complexity increasing as one goes from northwest to southeast. Establishing the number of contrasts can be difficult, because in many cases there are segmental correlates, with some tones only appearing before glottal stops, for instance, or voice quality correlates, with some tones combining with breathy voice and others with creaky voice. The latter type of variation is known as 'register' variation.[2] More discussion of representational issues is postponed till section 3.3.4.

   Along the syntagmatic dimension, languages vary in the number of positions in which a tone contrast can be made. The densest case was earlier taken to define the notion 'tone language' by Pike (1948: 3), for whom a tone language was 'a language having lexically significant, contrastive, but relative pitch on each syllable'. He explicitly excluded languages restricting tonal contrasts to specific syllables, like Norwegian and Japanese, but reserved judgement on what the best typology would eventually be (1948: 14). Languages with a contrast on every syllable, for which Voorhoeve (1973) introduced the term 'unrestricted tone language', are in fact relatively rare, and most tone languages are thus 'restricted' in this sense. 'Restricted' tone distributions can often be usefully described in terms of 'word melodies', whereby a number of tone patterns are abstracted from the number of syllables in the word, as discussed in section 3.3.2; or 'accent', whereby a single melody is abstracted from its location in the word, as discussed in section 3.5.

   Below, the formal representation of tone (H,L) is discussed. Informal notations vary per subdiscipline. In a widely used notation system introduced by Africanists, lexical tone is indicated by typographical accents over the vowel, as in (1). A tonal interpretation is given in the third column.[3]

(1)	´	high	H
	`	low	L
	ˆ	falling	HL
	ˇ	rising	LH
	~	falling–rising	HLH
	∽	rising–falling	LHL
	-	mid	M

Sinologists frequently use the system introduced by (Chao 1930), which comes in two forms. One is the use of 'letters' showing the pitch trajectory, and the other is the use of minimally two digits from 1 (low) to 5 (high), as in the second and third columns of (2) for the four Mandarin tones. A tonal interpretation is given in the fourth column. These tone letters are also used in work on American languages, where the scale is reversed such that 1 is the highest tone. (The rise in (2c) may be due to an utterance-final boundary tone. See also (14).)

(2)	a. ma^{55}	˥	H	'mother'	(Tone 1)
	b. ma^{35}	˧˥	LH	'hemp'	(Tone 2)
	c. ma$^{21(4)}$	˨˩˦	L(H)	'horse'	(Tone 3)
	d. ma^{51}	˥˩	HL	'scold'	(Tone 4)

More than half of the languages in the world are tone languages (cf. Yip 2002: 1; Crystal 1987: 172). Dense concentrations are found in South East Asia and Japan, Africa, and the Americas. Many of the languages spoken in New Guinea (East Papua and the Indonesian province of West Papua) are tone languages (Donohue 1997; Cahill 2000), while there are a few languages with lexical tone in Europe, specifically the Swedish–Norwegian dialect continuum, Lithuanian, what is now called Serbian, Slovene, the Central Franconian and Limburg dialects of German and Dutch, some varieties of Basque, and languages in the Caucasus (van der Hulst 1999), as well as sporadically in the Pacific (Rivierre 2001). Most descriptive and theoretical work has been done on the languages in Africa, Mexico, South East Asia, and Japan, while less attention has been given to the languages of Caucasus, the Amazon, and the eastern Indonesian archipelago. For more information, including maps showing tonal areas, see Yip (2002).

3.3 Autosegmental representations of tone

Autosegmental phonology represents tones on a separate tier from the rest of the representation: the tones are autonomous segments, or autosegments. One class of arguments for this mode of representation over one in which the speech stream is analysed as a single train of segment-sized slices centres on the mutual independence of the element in the segmental representation, syllables in (3), and the tone. If only representations like (3a) were needed, tone would form an integral part of the syllable, or the vowel in it: they would share each other's fate in deletions and insertions. In allowing (3b,c), the theory predicts that a tone can disappear while the vowel it occurred on remains, or vice versa. Representation (3b) is that of a contour tone, which frequently arises at the edges of words or phrases, while the continuation of a tone's pitch value on an adjacent Tone Bearing Unit (TBU) can be represented as in (3c), a multiple association of a tone.

(3) a.   b.   c.

        one-to-one   *contouring*   *multiple association*

3.3.1 The Tone Bearing Unit

One issue arising in an autosegmental representation is the number of tone contrasts per syllable, and the related question of how tones distribute themselves over a word. The 'Tone Bearing Unit', or TBU, is the element in the segmental structure to which tone associates. Imagine two dialects A and B, both of which have the word (4a), but where dialect A has (4b), dialect B has (4c).

(4) a. tàtá   b. tà:tá   c. tǎ:tá
      Dialects A, B   Dialect A   Dialect B

Dialect A has the same tone pattern on the two words, high tone on the first syllable, low tone on the second. At first sight, one might say that dialect B has different tone patterns on its two words, low–high on (4a) and rise–high on the second word (4c). However, in dialect B, too, the patterns of (4a) and (4b) could be said to be the same, provided we distribute the tones over the moras instead of the syllables. Since the first syllable is bimoraic in (4c), LH will occur on the first syllable, creating a rise; the second syllable then has high tone through the multiple association of H. This is seen in (5), which representations match the words in (4). Each tonal association leads to a 'tonal target', indicated by bullets, which are interpolated to give the contour, here as elsewhere given in a stylized form (Bruce 1977; Pierrehumbert 1980).

(5)

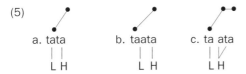

     a. tata   b. taata   c. ta ata
       L H   L H   L H

Many tone languages are like dialect B, while others, like Kikuyu, are like dialect A. Languages with the mora as the TBU often require tone-bearing moras to be [+sonorant]. In such cases, a short vowel is a single TBU, a long vowel or diphthong is two TBUs, and a sonorant consonant in the coda is a TBU, like [m,n,l,r,w], but [k,b,f] or [z], for instance, will not bear tone. The reason for the restriction to *sonorant* consonants is that the consonantal stricture for obstruents, in particular stops, inhibits airflow, needed for the process of vocal fold vibration, which makes them unsuitable for the execution of pitch variation. For instance, the Dutch dialect of Venlo has a binary tone contrast in stressed syllables, but while syllables containing one sonorant mora can have stress, they cannot have the tone contrast. Examples of syllables that can have the contrast are presented in (6a), all of which have minimally a long vowel, a diphthong, or a short vowel plus sonorant consonant. Those in (6b) either have a second mora containing an obstruent or have no second mora, [m] forming the onset of the second syllable in [ɪ.mə].

> (6) a. Tone contrast possible: [ɔː, ɑm, eːk, ɛin]
>   b. Tone contrast impossible: [ɑt, ɛf, ɪ.mə]

Thus, languages vary not only in whether the syllable or the mora counts as the unit to which tone is assigned but will also vary in the further conditioning of the mora or syllable. In restricted cases, they may require the TBU to be in a stressed syllable, or in some domain-final syllable. At the liberal extreme, there are languages like Tiv, in which voiced obstruents can bear tone (Pulleyblank 1986), and Luganda, where the first half of a geminate consonant may be a TBU, as in [òmùsáddʒá] 'man' (Larry Hyman, personal communication 2003).

3.3.2 Word melodies

Imagine a language with two level tones, H and L, and two contour tones, LH and HL, where the contour tones only occur on monosyllabic words; moreover, in polysyllabic words, the restriction holds that if the first syllable is high-toned, the remainder of the word is low-toned, and vice versa, as shown in (7).

> (7) a. tâ   tátà   tátàtà   tátàtàtà
>   b. tǎ   tàtá   tàtátá   tàtátátá

How could we avoid listing these distributional restrictions as in the sentence above (7), and instead describe the situation in a way that somehow *explains* these restrictions? The wrong move would be to assume that the rightmost word in (7a), for instance, is represented as in (8). Instead, we can assume the grammar contains two tone 'melodies', HL and LH, one of which is part of the representation of any given word. When combining with a monosyllabic word, both tones associate with the one TBU, but if there are two, each tone has its own TBU, and if there are more TBUs than tones, the last one associates with all following syllables. This is shown for LH in (9a) and in (9b) for HL.

> (8) tátàtàtà
> | | | |
>   H L L L

(9) a. tǎ　　 tàtá　　 tàtátá　　 tàtátátá　　 b. tâ　　 tátà　　 tátàtà　　 tátàtàtà

     /\　　 | |　　 | |/　　 | |/　　　　　　 /\　　 | |　　 | |/　　 | |/

     L H　 L H　 L H　　 L H　　　　　 H L　 H L　 H L　　 H L

To give a real example, the tone pattern of the Etung noun [èkát] 'leg', in which
L is associated with the first syllable and H with the second (10a), is the same as
that of [nǒŋ] 'how' (10b), where both L and H are associated with one syllable
(Edmondson and Bendor-Samuel 1966). Multiple association arises in a word like
[bìsóŋé] 'spoon', which again has the same LH-melody, but where the number of
tones is smaller than the number of TBUs (10c). In addition to LH, Etung has the
word melodies H (e.g. ékúé 'forest', kpá 'first'), L (e.g. kpè 'even', èjỳrì 'dress')
and LHL (e.g. m̀búà 'goat', ètʃî 'head'), LLH (e.g. òròbé 'bean', èbǐn 'farm',
HHL (e.g. ésébè 'sand', ébêk 'eagle').

(10) a. èkát　　　 b. nǒŋ　　　 c. bìsóŋé

     | |　　　　　 /\　　　　　 | |/

     L H　　　　 L H　　　　 L H

The extraction of the word melodies from the words in the language allows us to
explain a number of distributional restrictions of complex tones. To return to the
hypothetical language in (7a,b), if we assumed representations like (8), we would
have to state explicitly that contour tones only occur on monosyllabic words, or
that a tone on the second syllable of any word is never followed by a different
tone in the same word. Similarly, for Etung, we would have to state that the rise
only appears on monosyllabic words or on the final syllable of disyllabic words,
and so on.

Association Convention(s)

Postulating a word melody implies the availability of a mechanism to distribute the tones over the word. The representations in (10) are obtained by
associating tones and TBUs from left to right, with contouring on the rightmost
TBU and multiple association of the rightmost tone. A language that behaves in
this way is Kukuya, which has L, H, LH, HL, and LHL word melodies. Only
in the case of LH is a special provision required to create the pattern L–L–H
in trimoraic words (as opposed to L–H–H) (Hyman 1987). Another language
that is describable in this way is Mende (Leben 1973), although it has a number
of deviant patterns. When not all tone patterns can be described with the help
of a single association algorithm, lexical associations need to be included, as in
Mende (cf. Dwyer 1978; Zhang 2000). Indeed, Leben (1978) incorporated words
with pre-linked H-tones in Mende, i.e. words with tones associated in the lexicon. When the number of pre-linked words is larger, rival analyses without word
melodies become plausible. The separation of words and word melodies can be
maintained longer if sequences of like tones may occur in melodies, as in the
case of Etung's LLH. (The constraint banning sequences of like tones from word
melodies, the Obligatory Contour Principle, is discussed in the next section.)

Left-to-right association of one tone to one TBU plus rightmost contouring and spreading has been regarded as the default type of melody association, and is enshrined as the ASSOCIATION CONVENTION (Goldsmith 1976). However, this pattern is by no means universal (Hyman and Ngunga 1994): word melodies may have different patterns of association. In Kikuyu, the first tone always associates to the first *two* syllables; for the rest, it is like Mende. Kairi, spoken in West Papua, has the four word melodies H, LH, HL, and LHL, as illustrated on pá 'pulverize', pǎ 'split', p_e 'by, with', and pǎ` 'kind of tree'. Here, the two rightmost tones contour on the last syllable regardless of word length (Newman and Petterson 1990), as illustrated in (11).

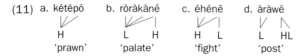

(11) a. kétépó   b. ròràkàně   c. éhéné   d. àràwê
          H   L   H   H   L   L   HL
       'prawn'   'palate'   'fight'   'post'

The Nakamura dialect of Japanese (spoken on the island of Okinoshima) has three word melodies: HLH, where L associates with all syllables except the first and last; LHL, where H associates with all syllables except the first and the last; and H–LH, where the complex LH associates with the last syllable, as illustrated in (12a,b,c), respectively (Uwano 1999).

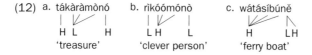

(12) a. tákàràmònó   b. rìkóómónò   c. wátásíbúně
          H L   H   L H   L   H   LH
       'treasure'   'clever person'   'ferry boat'

3.3.3 Obligatory Contour Principle

It has often been assumed that word melodies obey the *Obligatory Contour Principle* (OCP). The OCP holds that adjacent like tones are banned. In fact, sequences of like tones can contrast with multiply associated tones, as they do in Kishambaa (Odden 1986). The second H in (9b) is realized at mid pitch, an effect known as Downstep, to be discussed in section 6.3.3.

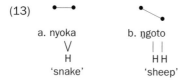

(13)
          a. nyoka   b. ŋgoto
               V | |
               H   H H
           'snake'   'sheep'

Since the OCP is not obeyed universally, the decision to allow HHL and LLH among Etung's word melodies becomes viable. The OCP is, however, widely attested in the world's languages, not just for tones but for many other phonological features as well. A quite drastic case is that of Bengali intonation contours, in which every tone differs from its neighbour, and violations are corrected by tone deletion (Hayes and Lahiri 1991b). Within Optimality Theory, a constraint whose effect is discernable only on some occasions is entirely to be expected (see chapter 8).

3.3.4 Tone contrasts

As will be clear from the above sections, Pike's (1948) contrast between level and contour tones is readily accommodated in autosegmental representation. For instance, the four tones of Mandarin are represented as in (14) (Duanmu 2000; Yip 2002: 180). The H in (14) is an utterance tone, since it is not present when the word is non-final.

(14)

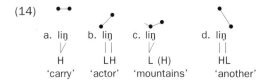

a. liŋ	b. liŋ	c. liŋ	d. liŋ
H	LH	L (H)	HL
'carry'	'actor'	'mountains'	'another'

A further distinction may be made. Contour tones have been argued to be of two kinds (Yip 1989). One type arises as a result of TBU-deletions ('stability') or of contouring on final syllables for lack of further syllables. Such 'tone clusters' differ from 'tone contours' much in the way that diphthongs in Hawaiian, which are combinations of identifiable monophthongs, differ from diphthongs in, say, Dutch, where the separate elements of /ɛi/ are not to be identified with the monophthongs /ɛ/ and /i/, respectively. For instance, the first element of /ɛi/ is currently more open in the speech of younger speakers, while the monophthong /ɛ/ is closer than in the speech of older speakers. They are therefore undergoing separate developments, which suggest that they belong to separate phonemes. In addition to analogous considerations for contour tones, Yip (1989) argues that, unlike tone clusters, contour tones may spread as units, as in the case of a fall which spreads as such in Danyang Chinese. Accordingly, she proposes a tonal root node between tones and the syllable or mora, such that (15a) is a tone cluster, but (15b) a tone contour. In the usual case, tones spread from root node to root node, but in the less usual Danyang case, the root node spreads from syllable to syllable. Likewise, contour tones whose elements are not equatable with level tones will have representations like (15b). Yip's contrast has been adopted for intonational pitch accents by Grice (1995b) (see section 7.3.1).

(15)

a. σ

b. σ   Tonal root tier

H L   H L   Tone tier

As noted earlier, multiple contrasts may exist among level tones. There have been a number of proposals for distinguishing four or five level tones, which are surveyed in Fox (2000: 200ff.) and Yip (2002: 42). The acceptance of a generally applicable feature system appears to be hindered by the fact that different languages group tones differently for the purposes of various generalizations. Thus, a mid tone (M) that in one language shares certain properties with L-tones will in other languages behave like H-tones (see also section 6.3.6). The language-specific nature of feature analyses is illustrated by [±murmur], recently proposed by Duanmu (2000). A [−murmur,+High] tone is higher than a [+murmur, +High] tone, and [−murmur,−High] is higher than [+murmur,−High], but the F_0-relation between [+murmur,+High] and [−murmur,−High] is undetermined and may vary with language or context. While the feature can be used to express the connections between certain tones and voice quality in South East Asian languages, like that between Mandarin Tone 3 and creaky voice, not all languages have such contrast-enhancing voice quality differences between their tones. Hyman (1993) merges the representation of contour tones with the representation of mid tones by introducing a further tier between the tonal root node and the tone tier, the tonal tier. The TBU and the tonal root node dominate cluster contours and unit contours just as in (15), while H and L that are dominated by a branching tonal node characterize a single mid tone.

Yip's tonal root tier of (15) and the tonal tier of Hyman (1993) are among a number of proposals introducing tiers besides the regular tone tier. A 'register' tier has been used by Yip (1980) to account for contrasts between high falls and low falls in Chinese languages, like Cantonese. Both would be HL, but in one case the syllable is specified as [+Upper] and in the other as [−Upper]. Snider (1999) introduced a register tier for the description of upstep (see section 6.3.7) in tone languages, while Inkelas and Leben (1990) used it for the description of interrogative intonation in Hausa. A related form of representation is the tonal tree, used by Clements (1983) for the description of downstep in tone languages and by Ladd (1990a) for register shifts in English. It is not clear that the phenomena described by these devices are in all cases phonological rather than phonetic (see chapter 4 and section 6.6.1). A complete survey of proposals up to 1999 is given by Bao (1999) with reference to Chinese languages.

No intonation-only language has been argued to have more than a binary tone contrast. The tone languages that are dealt with in chapters 9 to 12 have just a single lexical tone contrast.

3.3.5   Toneless and tonal morphemes

The creation of multiple associations is known as *spreading*. Apart from the association of word melodies in underived words, spreading typically occurs when toneless suffixes are added to stems that have tone. The pronunciation of the suffix can be explained by the spreading of the last stem tone to the empty TBU of the suffix, as shown in (16a), where the dotted line expresses the establishment of the new association. In Siane, which has the three contrasting word melodies H, L, and LH, suffixes receive the last tone in this way, as shown by màfókáfó 'taro+ERGATIVE', from màfó 'taro' (James 1994). In fact, the existence of toneless morphemes in a tonal language is evidence that tone and TBUs are represented separately. The reverse case, morphemes that consist only of tone, is not uncommon in African languages, an example being the Bambara definite noun suffix given in (16b). Such morphemes are sometimes called 'floating tones'. This usage competes with the meaning of a tone which remains unassociated in the representation, a mode of existence which is independent of the tone's morphemic status. For the former meaning I will use the term 'tonal morpheme', while the term 'floating tone' is reserved for the situation in (16c). In chapter 6 the existence of floating tones will be motivated.

(16) a. m]$_{Stem}$ m]$_{Affix}$ b. [   ]$_{Noun}$ L]$_{Definite}$ c. m   m

          | ⟍ | |

          T   H L H

      spreading   *tonal morpheme*   *floating tone*

3.3.6 Empty TBUs

As became clear in the above sections, not every TBU is specified for tone in the lexicon. Languages can roughly be placed on a gradient of tonal density. A language exploiting the full range of positions for a binary tone contrasts is Sikaritai, in which every syllable of every word and affix is marked either H or L (Donohue 1997). This situation appears to be rare, however. Even Mandarin, which has tone on every syllable of every root, has word-final 'neutral', i.e. toneless, syllables (Duanmu 2000). Moving further towards the sparser end of the spectrum, Dagaara contrasts H and L in stressed syllables only, tone being predictable elsewhere (Anttila and Bodomo 2000).

A further dimension comes into view when we ask ourselves the question whether, and if so when, TBUs that are empty in the underived forms get to have tones associated to them. Often, this occurs in the lexicon as part of the derivational phonology as illustrated in (16a). In other cases, this may happen only after the words have been put in the sentence (see also section 4.3.1), while in other cases still, no tone is specified at all ('phonetic underspecification', see section 7.2.4). Yorùbá is an example of a language with 'late' M. On the surface, it has a three-way contrast between high, mid, and low tone. However, the mid tone is in fact no tone at all, since unlike H and L, M behaves as if it is not there. For one thing, while H and L readily spread to create HL or LH contours on single syllables, no contour tones with M occur with any regularity. If the reasonable assumption is made that contour tones must have at least two specified nodes, this fact follows without further ado. The reason why an M-tone must nevertheless be specified at a certain point is that contrasts between M and MH do arise when a sentence-level H is introduced (Laniran 1990: 13). In other languages, however, one of the 'tones' may in fact be the phonetic realization of a lexically toneless syllable, as happens in Chichewâ, where F_0 peaks occur fairly precisely in syllables associated with H-tones, but F_0 troughs do not, and are better accounted for by assuming they occur midway between peaks, suggesting they are just F_0 slumps between targets of H-tones (Myers 1998) (see Hyman 2001a for a survey of tonal underspecification in Bantu languages). Phonetic underspecification of syllables without word stress is the typical situation in European languages with lexical tone, like Swedish (chapter 11).

3.4   Other sequential restrictions

In addition to word melodies and toneless morphemes, languages may have contextual restrictions on the number of contrasts. Chinese languages frequently disallow particular sequences of contrasting tones. Tone 3 in Mandarin cannot appear after Tone 3 within a phrasal domain: instead of 3 3, 2 3 is used. As a result, disyllabic words only have 12, not 16, possible tone patterns (disregarding neutral tone). Such *tone sandhi* occurs in many Chinese languages (Chen 2000). In Wenzhou, a Wu dialect, there are six contrasting word tones, but only 14 of 36 possible disyllables actually exist (Chen 2000: 478). Historically, tone sandhi must have originated in allophonic variants of tones which came to resemble other tones of the language and were subsequently equated with them. Today these replacements often appear arbitrary. The Mandarin Tone Sandhi can be seen as the repair of a violation of the Obligatory Contour Principle, created by the sequence of two L-tones (Yip 2002). In fact, at least for some speakers, there may be a subtle difference between a lexical disyllable 2 3 and a 2 3 that comes from a lexical 3 3, suggesting that the sandhi might still be allophonic (Peng 2000). A clearly lower rise than Tone 2 is used for the first Tone 3 in 3 3 in the Hailar dialect (Feng 1999). Tone sandhi may take on more complex forms when (a subset of) the tones of a language replace each other, a phenomenon known as a 'tone circle' or 'tone clock' (Iwata 2001).

3.5   Accent

The term 'accent' is here used to mean a place marker for the insertion of a tone or word melody (Hyman 1978; Goldsmith 1976; Gussenhoven 1991a; van der Hulst 1999). If a tone language with a free distribution of H and L on all syllables, as illustrated in (17), were to lose the pattern represented by (17c), the new dialect could be analysed as an accentual language, as shown in (18). Instead of listing the tone pattern for every word, as in the older dialect (17), the underlying representation could just mark the TBU of the word which is to receive a H, the accented TBU, marked with an asterisk. Any other TBUs would get L-tone 'by default'. The tonal grammar would be rather different, since instead of underlying representations with a tonal specification for every TBU, the new dialect marks some words with an accent on one of its syllables. The only surface difference is the absence of pattern (17c) in the new dialect.

(17) a. tá   b. tà   c. tátá   d. tàtà   e. tátà   f. tàtá

(18) a. tǎ   b. ta   d. tata   e. tǎta   f. tatǎ

Many Bantu languages can be interpreted either as accentual or tonal (Clements
and Goldsmith 1984b). In an accentual analysis, a word like [tátàtà] might have
the representation (19a) instead of (19d). On the surface, (19a) would be provided
with (19b), as in (19c), where the starred tone associates with the accented TBU.
L will associate with the next mora, with each tone subsequently spreading to
adjacent empty TBUs.

(19)

   a. tatᵃ̌tata   b. H*L   c. tatᵃ̌tata   d. tatatata
              | | ＼| ∥
                                H*L   H L

Goldsmith (1976) proposed an accentual analysis of Tonga (Bantu). Tonga nouns
consist of a stem preceded by the nominal marker [i] and a noun class prefix.
Tonally, there are three classes of disyllabic stems, as illustrated in (20). All three
nouns end in low pitch, but, depending on which stem is chosen, the low pitch
begins on the last syllable (20a), the penultimate syllable (20b), or the initial
syllable (20c) (from Goldsmith 1984).

(20) a. í+mó+ómbè   'calf'
     b. í+mó+òmbè   'edge'
     c. ì+mà+tòŋgò   'ruins'

This three-way contrast can be described by assuming that stems either come
with a HL melody, in which case the L-tone is either on the first or on the
second syllable, or have no tone. Instead of including the HL melody in the
underlying representation of stems that have it ('accented words'), it suffices to
mark a syllable: either their first, [ŏmbe] 'edge', or the second, [ombě] 'calf'.
Unaccented stems have no star: [toŋgo] 'ruins'. In the HL word melody, the
L is marked out as the tone that goes to the syllable with the star: HL*. To
describe the low-toned unaccented words, Goldsmith assumes that unaccented
words receive a default accent on the first syllable of the complex word, and that
the initial floating H-tone is deleted, causing all syllables to have low pitch. (A
rival analysis here would be that unspecified syllables get L-tone by default.)

(21) a. í mó ómbè   b. í mó òmbè   c. ì mù tòŋ gò
        ＼| ＼| ∥   ∠
        H L*   H L*   HL*
       'calf'   'edge'   'ruins'

3.5.1 Assigning and deleting accent

The inclusion of a contrastive place marker for tone in the lexicon and the resulting
distinction between accented and unaccented noun stems embodies the claim

that the language learner only needs to register whether a given word is accented and, if so, on which syllable. A strong indication that an accentual analysis of a language's tonal system is correct is the existence of 'accent rules', morpho-syntactic regularities in the location of the accent, enforcing either its presence ('accent assignment') or its absence ('deaccentuation' or 'accent deletion'). For instance, morphological processes may require the stem to have a tone or a tone complex like HL on the syllable immediately before an affix ('pre-accenting suffix'). Typically, there are restrictions on the number of such accents in the word, such that only the leftmost or only the rightmost is retained. An example that has pre-accenting suffixes and an upper limit of one accent per word, the rightmost, is given in (22), which illustrates the Japanese pre-accenting suffix -ke ('the X family'). Since the accent assigned by the suffix survives, the difference between accented (22a, b) and unaccented (22c) words is neutralized (Poser 1984).

(22) a. hǎra   harǎke   'The Hara family'
     b. ǎndoo   andǒoke   'The Andoo family'
     c. matumoto   matumotǒke   'The Matsumoto family'

Japanese accented words have a pitch fall from the accented syllable which is absent in unaccented words. An accentual analysis will have a star on the syllable on which the melody H*L is to be inserted (Haraguchi 1991). By contrast, tonal analyses will include HL (or H, with L being supplied later) in the appropriate location of the underlying words, and allow the morphology to assign and delete the actual tones (Poser 1984; Pierrehumbert and Beckman 1988). Of course, whichever way we look at it, Tonga and Japanese are tone languages. For this reason, Hyman (2001b) avoids making the presence of tone in the lexicon a crucial criterion for a 'tone language'. In his definition, a language has tone if 'an indication of pitch enters into the lexical realization of at least some morphemes'.

An analysis that combines the abstraction of word melodies and the abstraction of accent is given by Uwano (1999) for the Japanese dialect of Ibukujima. Uwano calls the word melodies 'registers' and the accent a 'kernel', and I take the liberty of paraphrasing his description here. Words have the melodies H ('high', (23a)), LH ('rising', (23b)), and HL ('falling' (23c)), each of which may occur on monosyllables. In polysyllables, H of LH goes to the last syllable, leaving any syllables to the left for L. H of HL associates with the first two syllables in words with three or more syllables, leaving any further moras for L. This falling pattern falls to mid pitch, indicated by the overstrike. In unaccented words, these are the only available patterns.

(23) a. íwátórí 'chicken'
     b. kìbìbàtàké 'millet field'
     c. átámākāū 'number of persons'

In accented words, these melodies are confined to the part of the word to the left of a fall to low pitch, which begins on the accented syllable. In final accented syllables, which only occur in LH-words and in monosyllabic H-words, the fall occurs inside the syllable, instead of after it. In LH-words, the leftmost syllable that can be accented is the second, and in HL words, the third. Examples of polysyllabic words with 'earliest' positions of the accent are given in (24a,b,c) for a high, rising, and falling word, respectively. The accented syllables appear to have L*, which spreads right to any post-accentual syllables.

(24) a. ícyòòyàkù 'digestive'
     b. kìnóbòrì 'tree climbing'
     c. sádógāsìmà 'Sadogasima (place name)'

3.5.2 Accent without a subgroup of unaccented words

Rules deleting or assigning tone(s) may sometimes be usefully formulated in terms of 'accent' even in the absence of a division of the lexicon between 'accented' and 'unaccented' words. A language may have a single lexical tone whose distinctiveness resides in its location. Somali nouns either have an H-tone on the last mora or on the last mora but one, as shown in (25). Since long vowels have two moras, an H-tone can only appear on the penultimate syllable if the final syllable is monomoraic, as in (25c,d). The contrast is used for the expression of gender (25a) and number (25b,c,d), while there are many constructions that cause the removal of the H-tone (Hyman 1981).

(25) a. náil   'lamb-MASC'   naíl   'lamb-FEM'
     b. doofáar   'pig'   doofaár   'pigs'
     c. kálax   'ladle'   kaláx   'ladles'
     d. Soomaáli 'Somali man'   Soomaalí 'Somali people'

Arguably, no principled choice can be made for Somali between an analysis including accentual rules or one with tonal rules, since * and H are equivalent. An accentual analysis would be somewhat less avoidable if every location in which tone can appear could have either of two, lexically determined, tones, as happens in Kaure (West Papua), where either H or HL occurs in the stressed syllable, whose location is largely unpredictable (Donohue 1997). Another example is Barasana, spoken in Brazil, which can be analysed as having words with accent on the first or on the second mora. The difference with Somali is that in either position either H or HL occurs, giving a four-way word prosodic contrast: H on first mora, H on second mora, HL on first mora, HL on second mora. Association is left-to-right, with spreading for the rightmost tone, and optional contouring on a lengthened syllable if HL occurs on the last mora. The initial toneless mora in words with accent on the second mora gets L by default (Gomez-Imbert and Kenstowicz 2000; Gomez-Imbert 2001). The motivation for an accentual analysis can be based on the existence of processes that delete all tones, like the Nominal Compound Rule. Instead of sixteen prosodic patterns, four times four, only four exist, as determined by the prosodic pattern of the first constituent. The tones on the second constituent are deleted, as illustrated for four examples in (26). The words are given as pronounced in isolation; optional lengthening has been applied in (26c,d) (Gomez-Imbert 2001).

(26) a. héá   'fire'   bùjá   'cotton'   héá búá   'lighting cloth'
        H, 1st   H, 2nd   H, 1st

     b. héè   ancestor   rìkáà   'fruit'   héè rìkà   'tree fruits'
        HL, 1st   HL, 2nd   HL, 1st

     c. gìbó   'foot'   cùdíró   dress'   gìbó cúdíró 'dress'
        H, 2nd   H, 2nd   H, 2nd

     d. gìhéè   'garden   mímí   'humming'   gìhémìmì   'humming.
        HL, 2nd bird'   H, 1st   HL, 2nd   bird (spec.)'

The analysis of the first low-toned syllable as toneless can be amply motivated, among other things on the basis of a tone-copying rule which treats both H and HL as single entities, regardless of whether they occur on the first or second mora. For instance, certain possessive pronouns copy H or HL to the following noun. Crucially, it is immaterial whether H is associated with the first or the second mora of the possessive pronoun, while the insertion of the copied tone occurs on the lexically determined mora of the noun. For instance, HL of [ĩn ʾã] 'their' is copied onto the second mora of [òkáré] 'language', because this noun has its lexical tone on the second mora, so as to give [ĩn ʾã òkárè] 'their language'. This process reveals that Barasana analyses surface H(H), HL(L), LH(H), LHL(L) as the melodies H and HL, plus accent on the first or second mora.

3.5.3   On the prominence of accent

In most of the above cases there has been no implication that the accented syllable is somehow prominent independently of the prominence it acquires through the presence of the tone. Duration and amplitude of an accented syllable of Tokyo Japanese only marginally exceed those of an otherwise equivalent unaccented syllable, for instance (Beckman 1986: 145ff.).[4] Moreover, when the accent is deleted, i.e. when a lexically accented syllable does not get associated with tone (cf. *Ha-* in (22a)), it is no different from any other unaccented syllable. However, there is a general tendency for concentrating phonological contrasts in stressed syllables (cf. Beckman 1997). This is true for vowel quality (see section 2.2.2) but also for tone. In some languages tone is restricted to the syllable with main stress, but many less straightforward situations exist. The cohabitation of tone and stress may arise in two ways. In Norwegian and Swedish, for instance, tone occurs where stress is, but in the Japanese dialect of Maeno, stress arises where tone is. In this dialect, the syllable to which the tone complex is associated is bimoraic, causing the vowel to lengthen if there is no coda consonant (Matsumori 2001). It seems reasonable to suppose, as does Matsumori, that the tone complex attracts stress, and hence bimoricity. This is shown by (27b–c) and (27d) (the latter already has a bimoraic syllable due to the coda [n]), where in the absence of tone, stress defaults on the penultimate syllable (cf. (27a)), a typologically common location for word stress.

(27) a. tjikja:ra   'power, force'
     b. kagamí: 'mirror'
     c. katá:na-nu 'sword-NOMINATIVE'
     d. gúnzja-katji 'to the whale' (whale-towards)

A further restriction occurs in languages that require the tone-bearing stressed syllable to be in a particular location. Word stress in Ma'ya is final or penultimate; if it is final, the tone on that syllable can be H, L, or LH; if the stress is penultimate, L-tone invariably appears on the stressed syllable and H on the last syllable (Remijsen 2002). The Curaçao variety of Papiamentu illustrates a tone contrast on the penultimate stressed syllable. Word stress is final, penultimate, or antepenultimate. If it is penultimate, either L or H can appear on the stressed syllable, but in the other stress positions only H can appear (Römer 1991; Rivera-Castillo 1998). Minimal triplets will thus exist for disyllables, like ['mà:tá] 'to kill', ['má:tà] 'plant', [ma'tá] 'killed'. Swedish, like Papiamentu, has final, penultimate, or antepenultimate stress, and has a tone contrast on the stressed syllable if it is non-final. Central Carrier has exceptionless final stress, but some words are characterized by a sequence of a high and a low syllable. The low-toned syllable either occurs inside the word or is the first syllable of the next word. There is thus a three-way contrast, no fall, fall from penult, and fall from final syllable, as reported by Eunice Pike (van der Hulst and Smith 1988).

The important point here is that stress is analytically independent of tone, and thus of accent. The independence is underlined by the fact that tone (and thus accent) can be contrastively located *within* the stressed syllable. If we assume, with Lorentz (1995), that in Somali stress falls on the syllable containing the last mora but one, which makes the syllable with the H-tone stressed (also Giorgio Banti, personal communication, April 2001), the plural–singular contrast causes accent to shift from the last syllable to the penultimate if the last syllable is short, but shifts within the stressed syllable if it is long. Accent can be on a mora, as in Barasana and Somali. By contrast, stress, as we have seen in section 2.2, is a property of the syllable.

3.5.4 Is there a class of 'accent languages'?

Phonologists may occasionally doubt the usefulness of the category 'tone language' as defined in section 3.2, and point to the gradient nature of lexical tonal marking (cf. van der Hulst and Smith 1988). Rather more, including myself, will doubt the usefulness of a group of 'accent languages', or more specifically languages that have one tonal contrast per word or phrase, since such languages do not obviously form a typologically coherent class (Hyman 2001a). It would group Tokyo Japanese with Somali and the Dutch dialect of Maastricht (Gussenhoven and Aarts 1999), to mention three tonally disparate languages. A case might be made for the subclass of languages that restrict its tone contrast(s) to stressed syllables, like Norwegian, Lithuanian, and Maastricht (Kristoffersen 2000; Halle and Vergnaud 1987), which Hermans (1985) referred to as having 'metrically bound tone'. These contrast with Tokyo Japanese and Northern Biskaian Basque, which have a single tonal contrast which is not metrically bound (Pierrehumbert and Beckman 1988; Hualde, Elordieta, Gaminde, and Smiljanić 2002). However, the metrically bound class is disparate to the extent that further subclasses could be distinguished, like Venlo Dutch (Gussenhoven and van der Vliet 1999), which allows the contrast in syllables with primary stress as well as in word-final syllables with secondary stress.

   Moreover, the decision to isolate the location for inserting tones from the tones to be inserted is more evident for some languages than for others (Clements and Goldsmith 1984b). 'Accent', like 'word melody', is an analytical notion, and cannot be measured. These concepts are thus different from stress, which is typically an observable phenomenon, and different also from tone, whose existence is equally measurable. McCawley (1978) gives a third reason why the notion 'accent language' is awkward, namely that a language may well be accentual at the lexical level, but tonal at the phrasal level.

3.6   Tonogenesis

Languages may lose lexical tone or acquire it. Tone appears to be an areal feature: it frequently occurs in genetically unrelated languages spoken by geographically contiguous speech communities, a point well illustrated by Africa and South East Asia (Nettle 1998; Svantesson 2001: 7). Within the latter area, languages from five language families are spoken, with only two of these being entirely contained within it. In other words, geographical contiguity is a better predictor of tone than genetic affiliation. The typical way in which a language acquires tone, therefore, must be because of its propagation through borrowing, through the imitation of one's neighbours, while tone loss might similarly typically occur in communities that are adjacent to non-tonal languages. It also suggests that *tonogenesis*,[5] in the sense of the creation of a tone contrast where there was none before in one's own or in neighbouring languages, may be relatively rare. Like all phonological change leading to novel representations, tonogenesis occurs when, in the course of constructing a phonological grammar, children interpret some surface feature as tone which in the parental language had some other representation.

   A frequent type is based on F_0 perturbations after consonants. Normally, these are not perceived as pitch differences, but as qualitative features on the conso-nants: a [t] with lowered F_0 in the following 50 ms of voicing will sound more like [d] than one with raised F_0 in the same stretch of speech (Kohler 1990). However, the F_0 can be perceived as pitch. This is shown by the fact that tone contrasts can often be traced back to a difference in voice onset time (Matisoff 1973; Hombert

1978; Hombert, Ohala, and Ewan 1979; Maddieson 1984). The first account of tonogenesis on the basis of consonantal effects is Haudricourt's analysis of the origin of the six tones of Vietnamese (Haudricourt 1954). A less complex case is presented by two small clusters of Austronesian languages spoken in a central section and in the southeastern tip of New Caledonia, which are surrounded by – in this case literally – an ocean of non-tonal languages.[6] Cèmuhî, in the central section, earlier had a contrast between voiceless geminate and voiceless singleton obstruents in initial position, which developed into, respectively, high tone and mid tone. The more vigorous voicelessness gesture required for the geminates was associated with higher pitch. At some point, children must have considered the pitch difference to provide a more salient phonological contrast than that between voiceless unaspirated singletons and voiceless unaspirated geminates. Word-initially, the latter contrast will frequently be inaudible (Kraehenmann 2001).

Phonation types like breathy voice and glottalized voice may also be the source of a tone contrast. Breathy voice may lead to low tone, as it did in Punjabi, where breathy voiced consonants lost the breathy specification and the following vowel acquired low tone ([bʱa] → [bà]) (Hombert, Ohala, and Ewan 1979). Glottalized voice, which is likely to occur near glottalized consonants, typically leads to high tone, due to the tenseness of the vocal folds during tight phonation, but may also have a lowering effect, due to the fact that creaky voice, a manifestation of glottalization with irregular phonation, naturally goes with low vibration rates, as suggested by Kingston (Ms). He proposes that these two effects may be responsible for the fact that in some Athabaskan languages, like Chipewayan, post-vocalic glottalization gave rise to H-tone, while in others, like Navajo, it led to L-tone (Leer 1999).

Tonogenesis is normally interpreted as referring to the creation of *lexical* tone. Seoul Korean presents a case of segmentally induced genesis of a *postlexical* tone (see section 4.3.1): if the phrase begins with an aspirated or tense obstruent, like [tʰ, t'], it begins with H rather than L, which would occur if the phrase begins with a different segment, like a vowel, sonorant, or [t] (Jun 1993).

3.6.1 Propagation of tone within and across languages

Once a tone contrast arises in some phonological context, tones may get distributed in phonetically convenient positions. For instance, H-tone may get located on sonorant segments that are adjacent to voiceless obstruents, while L-tone may arise next to voiced contexts. Similarly, low vowels may attract L-tone, while high vowels may attract H-tone, in sympathy with 'intrinsic pitch'. In Awid Bing vowel-initial words have L-tone, except when the vowel is [i], which has H-tone (Cahill 2000). After [a] was raised to [ɛ] in Cèmuhî a new [a] developed from two adjacent vowels as a result of the deletion of intervocalic consonants. Cèmuhî, which by that time already was a tone language, interpreted the merging vowel as a short [a] with L-tone (Rivierre 2001).[7] Similarly, the presence of tone in the broader linguistic environment may lead to the creation of tone in natural contexts in a non-tonal language. Ramsay gives an account of the development of tone in Middle Korean, meanwhile lost from the modern standard, in which there are a large number of segmental correlations, each of which might conceivably be the locus of true tonogenesis, that is tonogenesis *de novo*. However, at the time, Chinese was a prestigious language in Korean society, and it is conceivable that lexical tone was introduced via the robustly tonal Chinese language, and subsequently came to be used in phonetically 'favourable' contexts (Ramsay 2001), a case of contact-tonogenesis.

The point can be illustrated with the help of U, a Mon-Khmer language which has four tones, H, L, HL, and LH (Svantesson 2001). Svantesson's reconstruction involves tonal reinterpretations of three segmental effects on F_0. First, in closed syllables, H-tone developed before voiceless codas and L-tone before voiced ones; in the case of long vowels, these tones appeared on the second mora, and a tone with the opposite value occurred on the first mora. This gives H, as in (28a), and L, as in (28b), on short vowels, and LH, as in (28c), and HL, as in (28d), on long vowels. Subsequently, HL lost its L if the onset was voiceless (cf. (28e)), leaving falling tone only between voiced onset and voiced coda. Thus, both voicelessness of the coda and voicelessness of the onset promoted the occurrence of high tone. Second, in open syllables with voiceless onsets, H-tone occurs on high vowels, as in (28f), and low tone elsewhere, as in (28g). Thus, high vowels and voicelessness of the onset promoted high tone. Subsequently, open syllables with voiced onsets developed HL, regardless of vowel height (28h), and at some stage, long vowels shortened, giving the four contrasting lexical tones on segmentally identical structures. The words in the first column are from a related nontonal language, Lamet.

(28)	Lamet	U	
a.	kat	át	'cold'
b.	ŋạl	ŋàw	'fire'
c.	laat	lāt	'to fear'
d.	jaạm	jâm	'to cry'
e.	poon	phón (*phôn)	'four'
f.	siʔ	nchí	'louse'
g.	soʔ	sào	'dog'
h.	mịiʔ	mî	'you'

The U tone contrasts did not develop as a reinterpretation of segmental contrasts, since the language did not lose the voicing contrast in onset position. (It replaced voiceless with aspirated voiceless and voiced with plain voiceless.) Neither did it neutralize vowel height, and it only partly neutralized coda voice. Like Middle Korean, U illustrates the distribution of tone in segmentally favourable contexts, where it arose through diffusion from neighbouring tone languages.

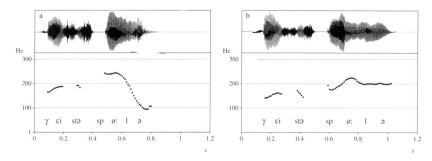

Fig. 3.1 Waveforms and F$_0$ tracks of 'Are you going to rinse' (panel a) and 'Are you going to play' (panel b) in the dialect of Maastricht. From Gussenhoven and Aarts 1999.

3.6.2 Lexical tone and intonation

Most tone languages will have some form of structural intonation. Frequently, even tonally quite dense tone languages have intonational boundary tones, causing questions to end at higher F$_0$ than statements.[8] Often, the balance between lexical tone and intonational tone is more even, as in Japanese (chapter 10). A tonal minimal pair from one of the dialects dealt with in chapter 12 is given in (29), which is from the dialect of Maastricht. In (29a), the word for 'rinse' has no lexical tone, while the segmentally identical word for 'play' in (29b) has a lexical H-tone. Both words have an intonational pitch accent H*, which together with the final L$_\iota$, represents an interrogative intonation contour. The word for 'go-2SG' has a lexical H, but is not (intonationally) accented. In spite of the F$_0$ difference, then, (29a) and (29b) have the same intonation contour.

(29)

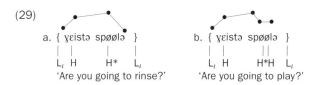

a. { ɣɛistə spøølə }
   │ │   │   │
   L$_\iota$ H   H*   L$_\iota$
   'Are you going to rinse?'

b. { ɣɛistə spøølə }
   │ │   ││ │
   L$_\iota$ H   H*H   L$_\iota$
   'Are you going to play?'

The example also illustrates that the context determines the precise realization of a tonal target, regardless of whether the tone is lexical or intonational. Specifically, in (29b), H and L$_\iota$ influence each other so that each tone has a mid target, as shown in panel (b) of figure 3.1. Further examples of such allophonic effects will be found throughout chapters 9–15.

3.6.3 Tonal or non-tonal?

Hyman's definition of a tone language can be pushed a little further by considering three typologically special cases. First, languages may have non-distinctive word-based tone. Arguably, because the pitch feature is non-distinctive, these should not be classed as tone languages. For instance, Noon predictably has an H-tone on the penultimate syllable of every word (Soukka 2000). While the tone's location will crucially mark word boundaries, it does not play a contrastive role in the phonological specification of the word.

Second, in addition to specifying lexical items, tone may be used morphologically and syntactically. Morphological use of tone occurs when a whole word class or a derivational category is marked by tone, and syntactic use of tone occurs when particular phrases or clauses are characterized by tone, like the H-tone in Yorùbá that appears between subject and VP (Laniran 1990). Conceivably, there are languages that only have morphological tone. However, it would be surprising to find a language that restricted (non-discoursal) tone to marking syntactic constructions; if there were such a 'syntactic' tone language, it would form a separate class between tone languages and intonation-only languages. It would not use tone to make up the representation of words, yet use it for other than discoursal purposes, and thus not be an intonation-only language.

Finally, a case can be made for lexically specified tone in intonation-only languages. Clearly, pitch accents and boundary tones constitute an 'intonational lexicon' from which speakers make semantically and phonologically appropriate choices for every accented syllable and intonational phrase (Liberman 1975). Additionally, intonation-only languages may have tonal specifications in the 'segmental' lexicon for particles which invariably appear with a particular intonation contour, like Dutch sentence-final [hɛ], which expresses an appeal for agreement, as in *Leuk, hè'? '*Nice, isn't it?'. It is unaccented, but always appears with H_l after the pitch accent H*L on a preceding word, as shown in (30a) (cf. Kirsner and van Heuven 1996). This fact needs to be specified in the lexicon.[9] Similarly, Bengali has a number of focus-governing particles like (30b) which come with their own pitch accent (Lahiri and Fitzpatrick-Cole 1999). Although they must be lexically specified for tones, these tones crucially constitute morphemes in their own right, and, unlike lexical tone, do not form part of the representation of the segmentally represented morphemes. These toned particles are thus polymorphemic expressions, like idioms or compounds with unpredictable meanings.

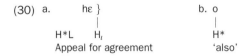

(30) a.   hɛ }   b. o
             | |
       H*L   H$_l$ H*
       Appeal for agreement   'also'

A different matter altogether is that probably all language communities have (non-phonemic) paralinguistic items whose pitch patterns are invariable, like American English [ʌʔɔ̀ː] to indicate an unpleasant surprise event. Of course, such items do not make a language tonal.

3.7   Conclusion

Our consideration of the question how pitch functions in language brought up a number of challenging typological questions. Stress was characterized as a phonological position: the strong syllable of a foot (Selkirk 1980; Hayes 1989). The tentative assumption has been made that all languages have feet, but that the phonetic difference between stressed and unstressed syllables is greater in some languages than in others. If there is a difference, however, a stressed syllable will be longer and less reduced than an unstressed syllable in otherwise equivalent circumstances. The connection between pitch and stress is established through tone: stressed syllables, like final syllables, are attractive locations for (lexical or intonational) tones.

We have followed Hyman (2001a) and others when drawing a typological distinction between languages with and languages without lexical tone, calling the former 'tone languages'. The term is used regardless of the density of lexically contrastive tones on words, as it seems difficult to draw a dividing line between languages with contrastive tone on (almost) all syllables and languages with tone contrasts in more restricted locations in the word. Standard Chinese and Swedish are thus both tone languages by this definition.

Accent was defined as a marker for the insertion of tone (cf. Goldsmith 1976; Hyman 1978; Hyman 2001a; Gussenhoven 1991a; Yip 2002, as well as van der Hulst 1999, who additionally allows the accent position to be filled with other elements than tone, like duration). The notion 'accent' was argued to be of the same class as the notion 'word melody', and both terms refer to analytical abstractions of the location of a tone contrast (accent) and strings of tones (word melodies) from the word-based tonal patterns on the basis of distributional restrictions. As such, the treatment distances itself from a definition of accent as 'prominence', as used in Beckman (1986), Downing (forthcoming), and Fox (2000). The term 'stress accent' was introduced by Beckman (1986) to refer to the situation in which the F_0 features co-occur with durational and other features to create prominence of a syllable, as in English. Beckman opposed it to 'pitch accent', which refers to the situation that exists in Japanese, where the F_0 features alone are responsible for signalling prominence. 'Accent' in this usage is thus equivalent to 'phonological prominence', and the labels 'stress' and 'pitch' indicate the way in which the prominence is achieved phonetically (cf. also Fox 2000). The term is not always easy to apply, however. In Limburg Dutch dialects, where both the intonational pitch accent and the lexical tone occur in the stressed syllable, the notion 'stress accent' comprises two different types of tone, since in both cases the pitch features co-occur with the vowel quality and vowel quantity characteristics of stressed syllables. Or again, in Somali, accent is on a mora, while stress, as always, is on a syllable. The notion 'stress accent' would appear to combine the syllabic notion of stress and the (potentially moraic) notion of tone.[10]

Lexical tone and intonational tone frequently combine in the same tone string, as illustrated with the help of an example from the dialect Maastricht. Chapter 7 continues this discussion. The following chapter offers a discussion of the distinction between the structural and phonetic aspects of intonation.

Notes

1. Whistling languages, used by some communities to communicate over larger distances, are not really languages, but reduced forms of conventional, phonologically explicit languages. Silbo Gomero is the best-known case: a whistled form of Spanish used by some of the inhabitants of the island of La Gomera in the Canaries. Whistled speech has been reported in many parts of the world. In some cases, the pitch variations are whistled, in other cases consonantal distinctions are mimicked by whistling (Grimes 2000).
2. The term 'register' is used in many meanings in prosodic studies. In addition to voice quality, it is commonly used to refer to a narrowed (higher or lower) pitch band within which the utterance is spoken, as in section 6.6.1. This meaning also explains its use for a representational device for expressing higher and lower versions of H and L (e.g. 'upper register'), as well as Pike's term 'register language'. The term has been used for the notion 'word melody' (see section 3.5.1) and is commonly used for 'speaking style', as in 'formal register'.
3. The symbols for high and low tone are the same as those which are often used to mark primary and secondary stress, respectively, and care must be exercised when interpreting them.
4. I am not aware of differences in spectral tilt between accented and unaccented syllables in Japanese; however, such differences have been found between 'prominent syllables' as pronounced in contrastively focused and neutral utterances (Campbell 1995).
5. The term 'tonogenesis' was introduced by James Matisoff in Matisoff (1973), with 'tonogenetic' already occurring in Matisoff (1970).
6. The fully tonal Austronesian language Utsat is contiguous with the tonal Sino-Tibetan language Min Nan in the island of Hainan (Maddieson and Pang 1993).
7. Rivierre is not responsible for this interpretation of the historical and synchronic data he presents.
8. The literature on intonation in tone languages is still fairly limited (Mountford 1983; Inkelas and Leben 1990; Laniran 1990; Connell and Ladd 1990; Laniran and Clements 2003).
9. Kirsner and van Heuven (1996) argue that the coincidence ought to follow from the semantics of intonational contour and particle. For other sentence-final particles the coincidence is indeed not absolute. On modal particles and intonation, see also Schubiger (1965); Vismans (1994).
10. This term 'pitch accent' ('prominence realized only by pitch', Beckman 1986, cf. 'stress accent') should not be confused with the same term referring to a 'tone or tone complex inserted in accented position' (Bolinger 1958; Pierrehumbert 1980; Pierrehumbert and Beckman 1988). It is used only in the second meaning in this book.

4

Intonation and Language

4.1 Introduction

When discussing its place in language, Bolinger (1978a) characterized intonation as 'a half-tamed savage'. This raises the question whether we can describe intonation in terms of the same structures with which we analyse the segmental morphology and phonology. We will approach this issue by considering the extent to which a number of design features of language that were proposed by Charles Hockett apply to intonation. We will conclude that intonation is indeed a half-tamed savage, but will draw a sharp dividing line between the tamed half and the untamed half. The difference lies in the discretely represented prosodic structure on the one hand, and the unusually generous scope that speakers have – compared to the latitude they have in the realization of the segmental phonology – in the phonetic implementation of fundamental frequency on the other. A rich communicative world appears to exist in this phonetic implementation component.

Broadly speaking, speakers gain control over aspects of speech production which might at first sight seem automatic, like the gradually declining pitch through the utterance, and use these for communicative purposes. In chapter 5, we will give an account of these paralinguistic meanings. At a further stage, this gradient behaviour may become *grammaticalized*, that is, be incorporated in the discrete structure of the language's morphology and phonology. For example, when we are more than usually concerned to get our message across, we will expend more physical effort on pronouncing the word or words that express it. While in the neutral situation, every word or word group might have a weak rising–falling pitch envelope, in the emphatic case, the words pronounced with more effort would have a larger pitch movement enveloping them. The next step is to use pitch excursion size as a signal for emphasis, whereby the pitch movement may have become divorced from the expenditure of effort. Taking a big step, and begging many questions, this behaviour may become grammaticalized for the expression of focus. Many languages express focus in the prosodic phonology, and often the phonology and morphology appear to have arranged matters such that the focused part is more salient, and is characterized by greater pitch excursions. At this stage, intonation has been tamed.

A crucial difference between meaning expressed in the phonetic implementation and meaning expressed by the intonational morphology is that the latter can – but need not! – be arbitrary. Exploitation of naturally occurring fundamental frequency variation will be in tune with whatever it is that induces the variation in the first place. Hence, greater excursions signal more, rather than less, emphasis. By contrast, form-meaning relations in the grammar are listed, and once forms have become phonologically encoded, they might change, or the meaning might change, so as to create form-meaning relations that go against the original 'natural' meanings. In fact, such cases are by no means rare.

The distinction between the untamed intonation in the phonetic implementation and the tamed intonation in the grammar may be conceptually clear, but it may still be difficult to determine whether a given phonetic difference is due to a difference in phonological representation or to a difference in the phonetic implementation. Section 4.4 discusses this question further, and makes the point that differences in implementation will be constrained by the way the phonetic space is used by the tonal phonology of the language. There, the question is also considered to what extent experiments can help us to decide whether a difference is phonetic or phonological.

4.2 Intonation and the design features of language

It would be hard to say in one or two sentences what intonation is and how it works. There are so many aspects to consider: people use it to express their feelings; it encodes the information structure of the sentence; it appears sensitive to syntactic categories like 'argument' and 'predicate'; it appears to have different phonetic forms in different segmental conditions; it is integrated with lexical tone distinctions in tone languages, and so on. A useful way to start is to try and answer the old question whether intonation is part of the grammar or whether it is an expressive system which is overlaid on language. In the latter case, it is technically a form of animal communication, in which a signal has some meaning, and the intensity of the signal is related to the intensity of the meaning. To get a grip on this issue, we will check off three of the design features that Hockett (1958, 1960) identified as being true for human language. Not all of his design features are true for animal communication, among which are arbitrariness, discreteness, and duality. What will appear from this investigation is that intonation is *both* a form of animal communication, as argued in section 4.2.1, *and* part of the linguistic structure, as argued in section 4.2.2.

4.2.1   Non-linguistic intonation

Lack of arbitrariness

Arbitrariness is the property that there is no connection between the phonological form of a morpheme and its meaning. One of the central tenets in linguistics is that this relation is arbitrary. This fact is underscored by the relatively rare occurrence of words with a non-arbitrary ('iconic') relation between form and meaning, like the English words *boo*, *puff*, and arguably, *scratch*. Yet, many linguists have observed that there seems to be something pervasively non-arbitrary about intonation. When we are excited, our pitch goes up, and when we are depressed we tend to have low pitch with few excursions. When we wish to emphasize a word, we may raise our pitch, in addition to raising our voice in the sense of speaking more loudly. When we want to signal – for real, or more probably in jest – that we need the speaker's protection or deserve his mercy, we instinctively raise our pitch, to create a 'small' voice. Intonational features that are more closely integrated with the linguistic structure, too, may somehow seem natural, such as when a non-final phrase ends with high pitch and a final phrase with low pitch, or when a rising intonation is used to signal a question and a falling intonation a statement, as is the case in many languages (Hermann 1942; Bolinger 1978a). These circumstances make it difficult to maintain that intonational meaning is largely arbitrary (cf. also the discussion in Couper-Kuhlen 1986: 118ff.).

Lack of discreteness

Discreteness is the property that linguistic forms (morphemes, segments, features, etc.) are either present or absent, but, like pregnancy, cannot be a little bit present. The verb form *drew* differs from *draw* in the presence of a morphological feature [PAST], but there is no way that English allows a linguistic expression to be formed that is semantically intermediate between these forms. We cannot generate an expression that means 'recent past', a time-depth intermediate between those of *draw* and *drew*, nor can we legitimately make up a vowel sound that is phonetically in between [uː] and [ɔː]. This is different from the way animal communication works. Bees perform various kinds of dances in their hive to communicate the details of a food source to their fellow bees. There are three dances, which are used for close, intermediate, and distant sources of food, respectively. In addition to this three-way discreteness, two gradient signals are embodied in the dances, indicating the direction of the food source and its quality. The direction is encoded in the orientation of the dance. In the middle-distance dance, the sickle dance, the bee may move across the floor of the hive along a trajectory describing a figure eight whose two loops are curved in the direction of the food source, which is given by the line bisecting the figure into two symmetrical halves, each containing one loop. And the quality is signalled by the enthusiasm with which the bee performs the dance (cf. Dobrovolsky 1997).

In languages like English and Dutch, there is gradience in the way words are emphasized. The height of the pitch peak corresponds to its perceived emphasis (abstracting away from factors like the distance from the beginning of the contour and the pitch height of the beginning of the contour (Gussenhoven, Repp, Rietveld, Rump, and Terken 1997)). The situation described as impossible above, whereby a gradient can be created between two forms, is quite imaginable in the case of different prominence levels. Consider the different interpretations of *He's Iranian* in (1): (1a) is an unemphatic utterance supplying perfectly unsurprising information about Mr. Ersan; while (1b) is a correction of the belief that someone is Turkish. Listeners will choose the latter interpretation in preference to the former as the pitch peak is higher. This was shown by Ladd and Morton (1997) in an experiment in which a range of peak heights were randomly presented to subjects, whose task was to indicate on a 10-point scale which of the two interpretations was more likely for each peak height. Now consider a third interpretation, exemplified by (1c), which utterance serves as a justification of the statement *He will understand Farsi*. These three interpretations could arguably be arranged on a scale of noteworthiness. If we were ask listeners to assign three versions of this sentence, one with a very low peak, one with a very high peak, and one with a peak height intermediate between these to the three interpretations exemplified in (1), then (1a) and (1b) would be distributed as in the real experiment, and the utterance with the intermediate peak would almost certainly be assigned to (1c). On the basis of such results, it could be argued that peak height is both phonetically and semantically gradient.

(1) a. Here is Mr. Ersan. He's IRANIAN.
    b. But the man isn't Turkish! He's IRANIAN!
    c. He will understand Farsi. He's IRANIAN.

Lack of duality

Duality of structure is the property that in addition to the organization of the meaningful elements, there is an organization of the phonological form. At first sight, this property of language is rather unexpected. If man did not have language, and we were asked to design a system of communication for this creature, we would probably begin by collecting a large inventory of signals (de Saussure's *signifiants*), each of which would have a meaning (de Saussure's *signifiés*). We would introduce Hockett's design feature of productivity (the property that signals can be combined to form complex signals) and suggest some combinatory grammar, whereby the expectation would be that each combination, each complex signal, reflected the meanings of the component simplex signals. That is, if *signifiant* [A] means 'bowl' and *signifiant* [B] means 'break', we wouldn't expect [AB] to mean 'ocean', say. Neither would we expect the meaning 'break the bowl' to be expressed by a single *signifiant* [C]. But, strangely enough, in human language this would seem quite common, as shown in (2).

(2) a. [kɔn] 'con, deception' ([A])
   b. [tækt] 'tact, ability to deal with people considerately and successfully' ([B])
   c. [kɔn] [tækt] – 'contact, establishment of connection' ([AB])
   d. [jɔː] – *you are*, i.e. '2nd' + 'be' ([C])

As a representation of the facts of English, or of language, (2) is irresponsibly wide of the mark. This is because it mixes units from different organizational structures. One is that of the meaningful units, which allows us to compose expressions whose meanings are a function of the meanings of the component elements, thus saving us from learning a simplex morpheme for every message we wish to convey. The second is due to the fact that the stuff of which these *signifiants* are made, human vocal sound, is itself organized into units, elements of form without meaning. Every morpheme consists of some configuration of these phonological units. This could be a single phonological feature, as in the case of [+nasal] in Guaraní, which is the morpheme for '1st person', or a tone, like the Bambara definite article, which is L, or a whole segment, in the case of English [ɔː] *awe*, or a polysyllabic structure like [kəˈmiːliən] *chameleon*, or even a structure with two phonological words, like *Rolls Royce*. In spite of these widely different phonological structures, in each of these cases, we are dealing with a single *signifiant*. Looking at it from the other end, the same phonological unit, like the segment [k] in English, will appear as a constituting element in a large variety of morphemes, as in *con*, *tact*, *socket*, etc., without causing these morphemes to be semantically related in any way. Just so, the syllable [tækt] is part of the word *contact*, but also happens to be the phonological form of the word *tact*.

The duality in the structure of intonation, to return to our topic, may be anything but obvious. When a speaker raises his voice in indignation, pronouncing his utterances at a high pitch with little variation, he is clearly using pitch variation to signal meaning, but it will be difficult to see any discrete structure at all, let alone duality of structure.

4.2.2 The case for structure

If intonation does not have arbitrariness, discreteness, or duality of structure, it has no structure beyond the trivial fact that there is a list of morphemes. As such, it is not part of language, and is in fact a form of animal communication by Hockett's criteria. Without wishing to compromise this conclusion, let us now see if we can make the case that intonation is in fact characterized by arbitrariness, discreteness, and duality of structure.

Arbitrary form–function relations

Table 4.1 gives a number of examples of intonation contours that have meanings which contradict the pattern identified as natural in the previous section:

Table 4.1 *Examples of 'unnatural' declarative and interrogative intonation contours*

'Unnatural' declarative intonation contours
H* H$_\iota$ Chickasaw
L* H$_\iota$ Belfast English

'Unnatural' interrogative intonation contours
H* L$_\iota$ Chickasaw
L* H$_\iota$L$_\iota$ Bengali

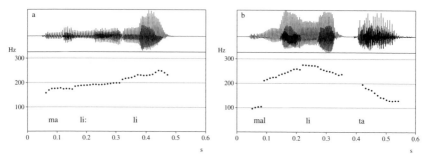

Fig. 4.1 Chickasaw declarative and interrogative intonation contours on [malili] 'S/he runs' (panel a) and [mallita] 'Does s/he jump'? (panel b), with waveforms.

rising patterns for declaratives and falling patterns for interrogatives. The tonal representation for the declaratives in the first columns of table 4.1 describe a high-rise contour for Chickasaw and a low rise in Belfast English. The interrogative contour is falling in Chickasaw, and rising–falling after the accented syllable in Bengali.

Figures 4.1, 4.2, and 4.3 illustrate these statement and interrogative intonation contours. Bengali has a low fall on the last word for neutral declaratives, as shown in panel (a) of figure 4.3, and a post-rise steep fall on the last syllable in interrogatives, as in the contour in panel (b), where the rise starts on the stressed syllable [lom-].[1] These cases illustrate the point stressed by Ladd (1981) that there are many cases of languages that go against the putatively universal pattern of falling statements and rising questions. Evidently, at least some intonation patterns display arbitrary form–function relationships.

Discretely different intonation contours

When two phonetically similar signals are discretely different, we may have the sensation of shifting from one interpretation to the other. To exploit a well-known example from the world of speech technology, we can easily 'hear' a

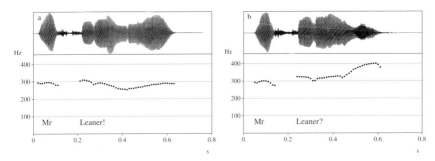

Fig. 4.2 Belfast English declarative (panel a) and interrogative (panel b) intonation contours on *Mr Leaner* in Belfast English, with waveforms.

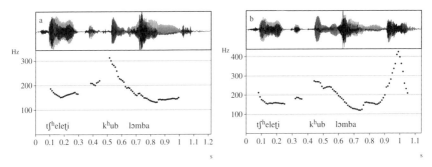

Fig. 4.3 Bengali declarative (panel a) and interrogative intonation (panel a) on [tʃeliti kʰub lɔmba] (boy-PART very tall) 'The boy is very tall' and 'Is the boy very tall?, with waveforms.

low-quality rendering of the phrase *to recognize speech* as *to wreck a nice beach*, and vice versa. Something like this may happen in the case of (3a) (Bolinger 1961: 39). As Bolinger pointed out, this English expression is phonetically similar to (3b), if both are spoken with a fall on the first word and a rise on the second, as shown in the leftmost panels of figure 4.4. However, the expressions are clearly not the same.

(3) a. [A: I've invited John Peck as well]
     B: JOHN Peck?
     [I thought we had agreed to invite only GREGORY Peck]
   b. [A: I've invited John Peck as well]
     B: JOHN PECK?
     [I thought we had agreed NOT to invite John Peck]

Support for the intuition that the two contours are discretely different can be found by changing the segmental structure with which the contours are combined (Gussenhoven 1999a). First, the rise on the syllable *Peck* in (3a) is due to a

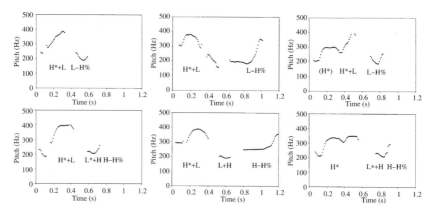

Fig. 4.4 Discretely different British English pitch contours. The leftmost panels show two pronunciations of *John Peck*, one with contrastive accent on *John* and no accent on *Peck* (top panel) and the other with two pitch accents, a fall on *John* and a rise on *Peck* (bottom panel). The middle panels show the same contrast on *John Peck you mean?*, while the rightmost panels do the same for *Jean-Jacques Peck?* From Gussenhoven (1999a).

boundary tone: it is located on *Peck* because this happens to be the last syllable of the expression. However, in (3b), the rise is due to a pitch accent and is located on *Peck* because it is the main stressed syllable of that word. The pitch accent is in fact followed by a boundary rise within that same syllable in (3b), so that it forms a single phonetic movement, obscuring the identity of the separate rises. We can bring out the difference between these phonetically similar contours by supplying unaccented syllables after *Peck* in both cases, as has been done in (4a,b). In (4a), the equivalent of (3a), the rise still occurs on the last syllable (here *mean*), but in (4b), the equivalent of (3b), the two rises are separated, with the lower one appearing on *Peck* and the higher one on *mean*. This can be seen in the middle panels of figure 4.4.[2]

> (4) a. B: JOHN Peck you mean?
>   b. B: JOHN PECK you mean?

Alternatively, we can investigate the phonological status of the prominence on the two instances of *Peck* in (3). If the rise is due to a pitch accent, it will cause an initial accent in a first name like *Jean-Jacques*, due to what is known as 'clash resolution' or 'stress shift' (see chapter 14). That is, the pronunciation would be *JEAN-Jacques*, as opposed to *Jean-JACQUES* (or *JEAN-JACQUES*), in the situation where *Peck* is *un*accented. The resulting contours are shown in the rightmost panels of figure 4.4. The replacement of *John* with *Jean-Jacques* in (5a) does not lead to stress shift, as shown in the top panel, which shows that the rise on *Peck* in (5a) is not an accent. By contrast, we do get stress shift in (5b): as can be seen in the bottom panel, the contour remains more or less the same through *Jean-Jacques*, and so the rise on *Peck* in (5b) must be an accent. On the basis of both kinds of evidence, we can conclude that although contours (3a,b) are very similar phonetically, they are discretely different, and more specifically that (3a) has one pitch accent and (3b) two.

(5) a. B: JEAN/Jean-JACQUES Peck?
    b. B: JEAN-Jacques PECK?

Duality of structure in intonation

    A demonstration that intonation has duality of structure presupposes that we can identify the morphemes in intonation, and that at least some of these morphemes consist of more than one phonological element. Alternatively, we could show that there is some identifiable phonological unit, like a tone or some close-knit group of tones, which encodes two morphemes. However, we have no uncontroversial morphological (semantic) analysis of any intonation system. A much-cited treatment of English intonation, Pierrehumbert and Hirschberg (1990), suggests that the individual tones in bitonal pitch accents may represent separate morphemes, thus ruling out any duality of structure (see also section 7.1). There is, however, an English intonation contour which uncontroversially consists of more than one tone and whose meaning, identified by Ladd (1978), has been generally accepted, the 'vocative chant'. It is easily evoked by imagining a speaker calling to another person by means of a two-level *Jo-ohn!* There are clearly two tones, H* and !H in ToBI (Beckman and Ayers 1994, cf. also chapter 15), which together signal 'routineness'. The two phonological tones are easily discernible. For one thing, we can perceive two distinct phonetic pitches, which effectively break up the syllable *peas* into two halves. For another, each tone begins its realization at a specific location. The first associates with the main stressed syllable, and the second with the following secondary stress, as illustrated by (6b); or, if there is no secondary stress, with the last syllable, as shown in (6a,c). Clearly, then, (6) illustrates duality of structure in that it is one morpheme embodied in two phonological elements.

(6)

    a. Pea-eas!   b. Cu-cumbers!   c. Brocco-li!

4.3 A half-tamed savage

In the preceding sections, we have argued on the one hand that intonation is like animal communication, having gradient signals which do not show internal structure, and on the other that it is like the rest of language in having arbitrary form–meaning relations, discreteness, and duality of structure. The paradox can be solved by assuming that these two conclusions are valid for different components of language. The non-linguistic kind of intonation is to be understood as purposeful variation in the phonetic implementation, while structural intonation is morphologically and phonologically encoded, and is thus part of the grammar.

4.3.1   Intonation as structure

The phonetic implementation component accepts the surface phonological representation as an executable programme for the creation of the appropriate acoustic signal through articulatory gestures. The grammar tells us what such surface representations may look like for any given language and how they are constructed from the intonational and lexical tones. In the model of Lexical Phonology, given in (7), the grammar is divided into a lexical component, where the phonological representation of words is computed and lexical tone exists, and a postlexical component, where intonational morphemes are added and the surface representation is computed. Subsequently, the phonetic implementation can take place (Kiparsky 1982b; Keating 1985; Pierrehumbert 1990).

(7)

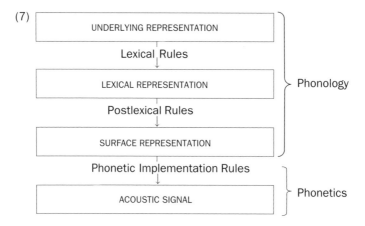

Lexical tone will be included in the *underlying representation* of morphemes, either as tone or as accent. Morphological operations may cause the segmental and tonal representations of words to be adjusted as a result of lexical rules, so as to create *lexical representations* (Pulleyblank 1986). These are the shapes in which words come to the syntax for incorporation in the syntactic structure. This *postlexical structure* will be enriched with intonational tones. Together with any lexical tones, a *surface representation* will be built from the combination of lexical and postlexical tones, which may lead to further structural adjustments (*postlexical phonology*) so as to produce the surface representation. This representation serves as the input to the phonetic implementation, which causes the speaker to activate his articulatory skills so as to produce an appropriate acoustic signal.

By way of illustration, consider the expression *Gaeler pepier?* 'More yellow paper?' from the Dutch dialect of Roermond in (9). It consists of the morphemes *gael* 'yellow', listed with an H-tone in the lexicon, shown in (8a), its comparative suffix *-er*, and the noun *pepier*, which also happens to have a lexical H, as in (8c). The speaker could be a customer of a printing firm responding to an employee's suggestion to choose a darker shade of yellow for the paper on which her business card is to be printed. The focus is on *gaeler* and *pepier* is unaccented. Going through the steps in (7), attachment of *er* to *gael* causes the H-tone in *gael-* to disappear, as a morphologically determined consequence of the comparative formation (Bakkes 1996). As a result, the lexical representation (8b) appears without its lexical H. The word *pepier*, by contrast, which does not undergo any morphological operations, leaves the lexicon with an H on the second mora of the main stressed syllable. Postlexically, the words are combined with the inter-rogative intonation contour L^* $H_\iota L_\iota$, which requires L^* to occur on the stressed syllable of the adjective and $H_\iota L_\iota$ to occur as a boundary sequence at the end of the ι. Importantly, however, the Roermond's postlexical phonology requires that, when occurring on the last mora of the intonational phrase, a lexical tone must be in rightmost position, after the boundary tones (see also section 12.5). This causes the surface phonology, given schematically, to be as in (9). The phonetic implementation will create a low target early in accented *gael*; the pitch will then rise through the unstressed syllables *er pe-* to the beginning of stressed, but unac-cented *pier*, where a falling–rising contour is produced over the syllable rhyme.

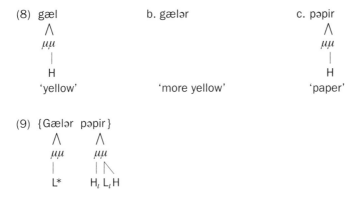

(8) gæl   b. gælər   c. pəpir
      Λ   Λ
      μμ   μμ
      | |
      H   H
   'yellow'   'more yellow'   'paper'

(9) {Gælər pəpir}
      Λ   Λ
      μμ   μμ
      | | \
      L* H_ι L_ι H

The example illustrates the relevance of both lexical and postlexical phonology to tonal structure, as well as the language-specific nature of tonal and intonational systems.

4.3.2 Phonetic implementation

The phonetic implementation of (9) is a very different concept from (9) itself, which representation could be that of a child, a woman, or a man. Strictly speak-ing, we can neither see nor hear the object that (9) stands for, or in any way observe it except indirectly, by inference on the basis of native-speaker behaviour. It is essentially a theory about the cognitive representation of an expression in the mind of a Roermond speaker (reassuringly, one that fits in well with the theory of

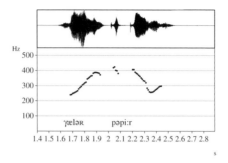

Fig. 4.5 Waveform and F_0 contour of *Gaeler pepier* 'More yellow paper?' in the dialect of Roermond, spoken with an accent on *Gael-* and interrogative intonation.

the larger phenomenon of the entire grammar of the speaker, and with the theory of the still larger phenomenon of human language). By contrast, the results of phonetic implementation are observable in many ways, most obviously as an audible acoustic signal. There is an infinite number of possible implementations of (9), across speakers, but also within any speaker, one of which is given in figure 4.5.

Chapter 5 attempts to give a fuller answer the question in what ways within-speaker variation is under control. Notice at this point that speaker *control* is not the same as speaker *awareness*. The level of awareness in linguistic matters depends on one's natural inclination to think about such things and on one's exposure to opportunities for doing so, like learning to spell or reading a linguistics textbook. Whether a dolphin jumping through a hoop is aware of what it is doing is a hard question to answer, but it is not hard to see that the animal is in control of its actions.

4.3.3 Phonetic implementation or phonological representation?

One of the most persistent issues in intonational research concerns the status of meaningful phonetic differences. Any such difference could in principle result from discretely different representations or from different implementations of the same representation. Our intuition in the case of intonational contrasts is less sharp than in the case of lexical tone contrasts, where the pitch difference is used to distinguish one word from another. For instance, in the Zagreb dialect of Serbo-Croatian, sentence-initial words with initial stress tend to have a wide pitch peak, which is located some 40–80 ms after the end of the first syllable (Smiljanić and Hualde 2000). However, when narrow focus is placed on the word, the peak is located some 100 ms earlier, and falls inside the stressed syllable. That is, when *Màra je jela bananu* 'Mara ate a banana' is a reply to 'What was going on?', the peak occurs in *-ra*, but when it is an answer to 'Who ate a banana?', it falls in *Ma-*. This variation could in principle be due to a tendency for speakers to allow the peak to be late in the neutral case, but to place it more precisely inside the stressed syllable in the narrow-focus case. Alternatively, however, the Zagreb dialect might have two intonational pitch accents, H*+L and L*+H, one meaning 'neutral focus' and the other 'contrastive focus'. The situation would be parallel to that found in Portuguese, which has two pitch accents: one for focused and one for neutral expressions (Frota 1998).

There are certain predictions that each of these possible accounts makes. If the difference is due to a difference in phonetic implementation, it will be gradient in character. Intermediate realizations would be well formed, but judgements about whether narrow focus or neutral focus was intended might be less well defined. If it is a phonological contrast, speakers would wish to assign every intermediate pronunciation either to one type or the other. Producing unambiguous experimental results is not always easy, however, and intuitions by native speakers may not be clear.

In the case of lexical tone contrasts, intuitions are much clearer. In the Belgrade dialect, the early peak and the late peak are realizations of two contrasting lexical tone patterns. The late peak occurs some 30–80 ms into the post-stress syllable for what is known as the 'rising' pattern, while the early peak occurs some 110 ms before it, the 'falling' pattern. There is no doubt that this is a phonological contrast: *Mára* has a late peak and *Mlâda* 'bride' has an early peak, i.e. each tone pattern is part of the lexical identity of different sets of words. There are minimal pairs, like *ríta* 'swamp$_{GEN}$' vs. *rîta* 'rag$_{GEN,PL}$'. Interestingly, the Belgrade dialect also uses peak alignment to express the difference between neutral and narrow focus. In narrow-focus sentences, the peaks were on average 40 ms earlier than in neutral realizations of the same sentences.

It is not implausible that, as Smiljanić and Hualde (2000) suggest, the correct interpretation of these data is that both dialects manipulate pitch alignment for pragmatic reasons in the phonetic implementation, with narrow-focus utterances inviting more precise placements of the pitch peak in the stressed syllable. However, speakers of the Belgrade dialect have less scope to do this, since the variation in peak alignment is employed by the phonology. Speakers of the toneless Zagreb dialect, who need not concern themselves about the preservation of a lexical contrast, make a more liberal use of their phonetic space for the expression of the same pragmatic difference. The interpretation of the Zagreb early peak as a more precise articulation of the same pitch accent is also suggested by the fact that the variation in peak timing is much less if the utterance is a reply to 'Who ate a banana'? than if it is a reply to 'What was going on?' That is, 'narrow focus' (Ladd 1980, see also chapter 9) invites speakers to implement their representations more precisely (see also section 5.7).

The difference between phonetic variation and phonological contrasts was incorporated in the research strategy that led to the intonational grammar of Dutch summarized in 't Hart, Collier, and Cohen (1990). They defined a 'standard pitch movement', the basic element in their grammar, as one that could be substituted for an observed pitch movement without changing the identity of the contour: even though there might be substantial phonetic differences between them, the standardized contour and the original contour were 'perceptually equivalent'. If the contours were to fall short of 'perceptual equivalence', the standardization must have obliterated some phonological contrast. Not only did 't Hart *et al.* thus make the contrast between phonetics and phonology in intonation explicit (although they may not have agreed with this interpretation of their position), they also pioneered experimental approaches to the issue, first in a contour sorting experiment (Collier 1975a), but later with the help of acceptability judgements (de Pijper 1983; Willems 1984; 't Hart, Collier, and Cohen 1990: 53). Acceptability judgements will yield valuable information about the success of a phonetic model, but the relation to the presence of a phonological contrast may be somewhat indirect. Recently, experiments have addressed the issue of discreteness vs. gradience more directly, some of which I discuss in the next section.

4.4   Experimental approaches towards establishing discreteness in intonation

There have been a number of experimental approaches to the question whether a given phonetic difference represents a phonological contrast or a gradient phonetic difference. In most cases, they involve the collection of listener judgements of natural or manipulated stimuli. The first experiment involves the collection of speaker productions on the basis of a number of stimuli.

4.4.1   The imitation task

Pierrehumbert and Steele (1989) ran an experiment in which listeners were asked to imitate a large number of artificial intonation contours. The artificial contours, which consisted of an accentual peak followed by a final rise, differed in the alignment, i.e. the timing of the peak: there were fifteen versions, each 20 ms apart, so that the difference between the earliest and the latest peak was 300 Hz. This stimulus continuum is shown in panel (a) of figure 4.6. The authors argued that if their English subjects were capable of reproducing the continuum in their imitations, the difference must be gradient. However, if subjects were to produce a bimodal distribution of the peak times in their imitations, i.e. were to produce two clearly identifiable clusters of peak alignments, the difference must be categorial, and constitute a phonological contrast between an early peak and a late peak.

The results of the experiment favoured an interpretation whereby speakers could not accurately produce the continuum. The peak alignments in their imitations clustered around two values, one around 150 ms and the other some 300 ms after the beginning of [m]. Panel (b) of figure 4.6 reproduces the data from the speaker with the clearest separation between the two types of imitations. These data thus suggest that the contrast between early and late peaks is discrete

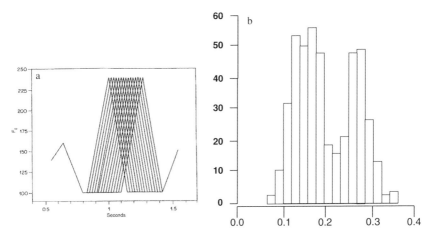

Fig. 4.6 Continuum of fifteen artificial contours for the expression *Only a MILLionaire*, with peak alignments 20 ms apart (panel a) and peak alignments relative to the release of [m] for one speaker's imitations of these fifteen stimuli showing a bimodal distribution (panel b). From Pierrehumbert and Steele (1989).

in American English. In (10), the phonological interpretations of the two pitch accents is given in the analysis presented in chapter 15.

(10) a. {   Only a millionaire }
          | | | |
          L₁   H*L   H*L   H₁

     b. {   Only a millionaire }
          | | | |
          L₁   H*L   L*HL   H₁

4.4.2 The pitch-range task

A different approach was adopted by Gussenhoven and Rietveld (2000). The issue here was the difference between the 'high rise' and the 'low rise' in Dutch. In the low rise, the vowel in the accented syllable is low throughout, or is low during much of the duration of the vowel if the syllable is final, while the high rise has a mid-pitched accented syllable. This sometimes subtle difference is shown in figure 4.7, where panel (a) illustrates two pronunciations of the high rise on the sentence *Ga je naar HILversum, niet naar BreDA?* 'Are you going to Hilversum, not to Breda?' Panel (b) shows a pronunciation with low rises. In the word *Hilversum* the difference is fairly clear from the step up between *Hil-* and *-ver*, but in the final accented syllable only a small difference in pitch level is observed. Pierrehumbert (1980) distinguished these contours in American English as H* H–H% (the high rise) and L* H–H% (the low rise). The purpose

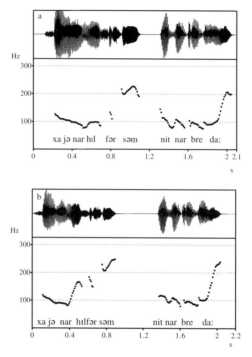

Fig. 4.7 High rises (panel a) and low rises (panel b) on Dutch *Ga je naar Hilversum,
niet naar Breda* 'Are you going to HILversum, not to BreDA?'

of the experiment was to see if the Dutch contrast was categorical by capitalizing
on the fact that expansion of the pitch range, which occurs when people are being
emphatic or surprised, might affect H* and L* differently. In particular, while H*,
like all H-tones, would go up, L* might go down.

In the experiment, two sets of one-accent stimuli were judged by Dutch
listeners, both with artificial contours. One set had nine versions of the low
rise, resulting from combining three values of the beginning of the contour with
three values for the end; while another set had nine versions of the high rise,
similarly obtained by combining three end values and three beginning values.
Source utterances had either final or non-final accent (see figure 4.8).

Inescapably, the results forced the conclusion that the high rise and the low
rise are discretely different contours. As shown in figure 4.9, higher perceived
surprise is associated with lower values for L* and with higher values for all
H-tones, including H*. If the high rise and the low rise were different realizations
of the same phonological contour, differing only in pitch range, listeners would
have treated any pitch range variation in either contour type in the same manner.
That is, we would not expect a raising of the pitch in the accented syllable first to
have negative effects on perceived surprise, and then, as we get to some critical
pitch, to have positive effects.

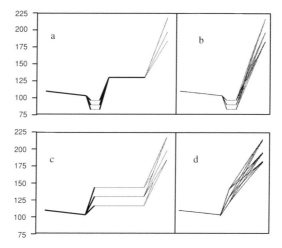

Fig. 4.8 Structure of the 18 artificial contours used in the 'surprise' experiment. From Gussenhoven and Rietveld (2000).

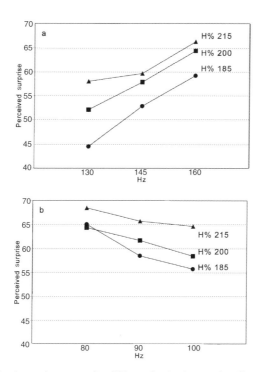

Fig. 4.9 Perceived surprise scores for different beginnings and endings of the high rise (panel a) and the low rise (panel b) in standard Dutch. From Gussenhoven and Rietveld (2000).

4.4.3   The semantic task

There are two techniques that may be less suitable. One is the 'categorical perception' task, discussed in the next section, and one relies on the perception of
semantic differences between phonetically different forms. As Ladd and Morton
(1997) point out, the sole fact that speakers tend to associate one form with one
meaning and the other with another cannot serve as a demonstration that the
difference is representational. This is because the differences of interpretation
may be due to the fact that F_0 variation in the phonetic implementation can be –
and often is – meaningful, and such results are therefore ambiguous.

The issue in the Ladd and Morton experiment was whether there is a phonological entity 'Extra High' in British English, as distinct from plain H. Listeners
were asked to judge whether a given pronunciation of *The alarm went off* reported
an 'everyday occurrence' or an 'unexpected event'. They were more likely to
choose the second interpretation as the F_0 peak over *-larm* was higher. Although
the shift in interpretation was clearly brought about by the increased F_0 peak, it
could be due to a gradient form–function relation, with higher peaks signalling
greater significance (see section 4.2.1).

4.4.4   The categorical perception task

Categorical perception occurs when listeners interpret stimuli from some phonetic continuum as belonging to one phonological category or to another, without
hearing much difference between the stimuli that are interpreted as belonging to
the same category (Liberman, Harris, Hoffman, and Griffith 1957; Liberman,
Cooper, Shankweiler, and Studdert-Kennedy 1967). Two separate tests are
required to establish categorical perception. One is an identification task, in which
listeners are asked to assign randomly presented stimuli from the continuum to
either of two categories. If the English categories are /p/ and /b/, say, the stimuli
would be CV syllables in which the C is a labial stop whose Voice Onset Time
(VOT) is varied so as to create a continuum between canonical realizations of
/p/ and /b/. The results of this experiment should show an abrupt perceptual shift
from /p/ to /b/, rather than a gradual transition, or one with inconsistencies. The
second is a discrimination task, in which listeners hear pairs of stimuli that differ
by one acoustic step on the continuum, and are asked to say whether the members
of each pair are the same or different. The results of this identification experiment
should reveal that discrimination is good at the point where, according to the first
test, listener's perception shifts from one category to the other, but poor within
the two regions of the continuum on either side of the switch-over point. The
ideal result, therefore, is as depicted in figure 4.10, after Newport (1982). Here,
the dashed graph represents the identification scores for, say, /b/. At early VOTs,
identification of /b/ is perfect, while at late VOTs, no /b/s are heard. As will be
clear, the identification function for /p/ is the exact complement. The solid graph

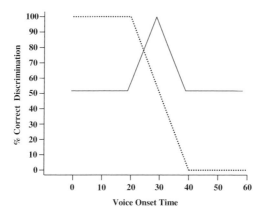

Fig. 4.10 Idealized discrimination function in relation to the idealized identification function for stimuli varying in Voice Onset Time. Adapted from Newport (1982).

gives the discrimination scores: in most cases, people cannot hear any difference between the members of each pair, and so the scores reflect chance (50 per cent). However, near the stimuli where people stop hearing /b/ and start hearing /p/, discrimination improves considerably.[3]

The paradigm was applied to differences in peak alignment in German contours by Kohler (1987), and the results were in reasonable agreement with what might expected if the contrast was categorical. However, it is doubtful if the paradigm can be used for intonational contrasts in general. It was used with less clear-cut results by Remijsen and van Heuven (1999), who illustrate its application to an undoubted intonational contrast in Dutch, that between a final fall ($H^*L\ L_l$) and a final rise ($H^*L\ H_l$). As expected, identification scores for stimuli in which the F_0 of the contour end was varied (see figure 4.11) showed an S-shape. The status of this result by itself is no different from that obtained in a semantic task, in which subjects use a scale to record their responses: it is not clear whether the shift reflects a categorical distinction or a gradient one. The results of the discrimination task were in fact somewhat ambiguous, in that there were two peaks: one at the very low end, where it would not be expected in a 'classic' result; and one near the value where the identification function crosses the 50 per cent mark, which happens when the final pitch is around 120 Hz (cf. the top three graphs in panel (b) of figure 4.11). In addition, there is a peak in the false alarms at the same point in the continuum, which should really be subtracted from the discrimination peak, since it reflects listeners' uncertainty rather than their sensitivity. Moreover, the transition in discrimination function is not particularly abrupt, being spread out over a 20 Hz interval.[4]

Thus, while there is little doubt that the contrast Remijsen and van Heuven investigated is categorical, the categorical perception paradigm does not bring this out convincingly. In cases in which the paradigm has been applied to contrasts that

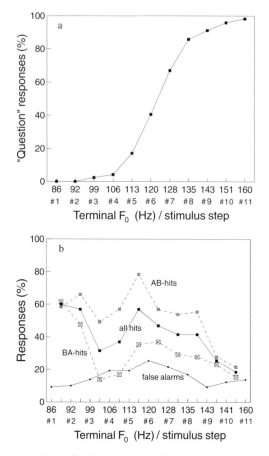

Fig. 4.11 Percentage 'question' responses as a function of final F_0 in Dutch stimuli (panel (a)) and percentage correct discriminations (two orders of presentation, A–B and B–A, separately and summed) and percentage false alarms. From Remijsen and van Heuven (1999).

might on independent grounds be considered gradient, the results have been disappointingly similar. Ladd and Morton (1997) followed up their semantic experiment referred in section 4.4.3 with a classical categorical perception experiment. Their results were not obviously worse than those obtained by Remijsen and van Heuven (1999). Post (2000b: 191ff.) tested three putative and two undoubted categorial contrasts in French, and similarly obtained mixed results. Indeed, even perception of lexical tone has failed to yield results that are comparable to those for voicing contrasts in obstruents (cf. Connell 2000).

Newport (1982) suggested that the categorical perception effect probably depends on the acoustic nature of the contrast. On the one hand, vowel duration differences between (structurally different) long and short vowels can lead to much less abrupt perceptual shifts and much smoother discrimination functions than contrasts between plosives. On the other hand, categorical perception effects have been found for non-linguistic contrasts: the difference between hearing a string being plucked and one being bowed is apparently abrupt (Cutting, Rosner, and Foard 1976). As suggested by Aoju Chen (personal communication 2002), it may be that some intonation contrasts, like peak alignment differences, are more amenable to the paradigm than other differences, like differences in end-points of rises.

4.5 Conclusion

The reason why intonation is somehow 'around the edge of language', to use another characterization of Bolinger's (1964), is that what people normally under-stand by intonation is located in two different components of language. On the one hand, it forms part of the linguistic structure in the ordinary sense. The design features that have been found to be valid for language generally are unambigu-ously also valid for intonation. First, because its phonology and morphology are non-isomorphic, it has duality of structure; second, because the meaning of intonational forms often appear counter-intuitive, it has arbitrary form–meaning relations; and third, because we can have the experience of interpreting ambigu-ous acoustic signals as either one structure or as another, it has discreteness. At the same time, however, intonation can be shown to be a form of animal commu-nication when we consider the way speakers express such meanings as surprise, emphasis, and anger. This part is non-structural, and the way people use pitch to express these meanings is likely to be largely independent of the language they speak. It manifests itself in the phonetic implementation of prosodic structures, when people have the opportunity to express universal meanings simultaneously with the realization of their linguistic structures. This response to the problem of the partly paralinguistic nature of intonation contrasts with earlier ones in which either a largely non-linguistic viewpoint is adopted (e.g. Martinet 1962: 28) or an exclusively linguistic viewpoint (e.g. Ladd 1981), as well as with approaches in which the two aspects are reconciled with each other in a gradient conception of their difference (e.g. Crystal 1969: 128; Lindsey 1985).

Because the structural form–function relations often look as if they might be non-structural and vice versa, there may be uncertainties about the status of phonetic contrasts: two forms could be different because they are (meaningfully different) implementations of the same structure; or because they are imple-mentations of different linguistic expressions. In addition to our intuitions about sameness and difference, there is a role for experimental approaches to this type of question, and a number of research paradigms were discussed and illustrated. A resolution of such questions is obviously of great importance for a proper understanding of the nature of intonational grammars. Before we look at gram-mars, however, the next chapter addresses the question how humans know what the universal, paralinguistic meanings are.

Notes

1. The same interrogative contour was shown in panel (b) of figure 3.1. Roermond Dutch, Greek and Hungarian have similar interrogative contours (Ladd 1996; Gussenhoven 2000b, Varga 2002; Arvaniti and Baltazani 2003).
2. A further test would be needed to show that *mean* in (4) is in fact unaccented. For instance, we could employ additional expansions like *you mean to say*, *you mean to say*, *my darling*, to show that, when we keep the intonation the same, the rise on *mean* 'travels', and is located on the final syllable in each of these expansions, regardless of their length.
3. Discrimination experiments should always include stimulus pairs with identical members, and in practice, the chance level is therefore not 50 per cent, but is determined by the number of 'false alarms', that is, the number of times listeners claim to hear a distinction where there is none.
4. When results per speaker were considered, the transitions appeared more abrupt, and the locations of individual discrimination peaks correlated positively with individual crossover points. This suggests that there is variation in the establishment of the category boundary.

5

Paralinguistics: Three Biological Codes

5.1 Introduction

In chapter 4, we have seen that speakers manipulate their phonetic implementation for communicative purposes in a way that is to some extent independent of the language they speak. In this chapter, it is argued that the knowledge people have of these form–function relations derives from three biologically determined conditions. One is that the organs with which we produce speech, in particular the larynx, vary in size, the second that the production of speech requires energy and that variation in effort is detectable in the signal, and the third is that the supply of this energy occurs in phases, as determined by the breathing process. The exploitation of the connection between F_0 and size of the organism, with smaller larynxes producing higher notes than larger ones, was identified as the Frequency Code by Ohala (1983). Variation in effort is associated with the excursion size of pitch movements, greater effort leading to wider excursions, the Effort Code (Gussenhoven 1999c). Third, the Production Code associates high initial pitch with beginnings and final low pitch with endings of speech events (Gussenhoven 2002).

Before moving on, it must be stressed that speakers do indeed actively control their phonetic implementation, for a variety of purposes. Phonetic implementation is not automatic, such that given the physiological properties of the speaker, the acoustic realization of a linguistic representation is given (Kingston and Diehl 1994). To put the discussion in its right perspective, section 5.2 considers phonetic variation which is *not* under speaker control, while section 5.3 deals with a variety of non-intonational purposes for control in phonetic implementation. Section 5.4 takes a closer look at the notion pitch range, distinguishes pitch register from pitch span, and makes the point that speakers actively control their pitch range. The nature of the universal meanings expressed through pitch variation is dealt with in sections 5.5–5.9.

5.2   Variation beyond the speaker's control

The output of the phonetic implementation will in part be determined by one's anatomy. Most evidently, the vocal tracts of men are longer than those of women (17.5 cm and 14 cm, respectively, cf. Ohala 1983), which difference will affect formant values, with smaller vocal tracts producing higher formants. Importantly, too, the larger and heavier vocal folds of men will produce lower rates of vibration, and hence lower average pitch (Beck 1997). Under equivalent levels of effort, therefore, a male larynx will produce a lower F_0 contour than a female larynx. Xu (1998) has argued that the time between the emission of a neural command for the beginning or end of a pitch movement and its execution by the vocal cords is responsible for the frequently observed phenomenon that pitch peaks tend to occur late in or even after the syllable in which the phonology locates them. If this delay is in fact non-negligible, it may help to account for the widespread finding that pitch movements tend to lag behind the segmental structure. Interestingly, Braunschweiler (2003) finds that intensity peaks tend to precede peaks of H^* accents in German by some 20 ms, suggesting that the F_0 movement comes after the peak in the articulatory gesture for the vowel. In section 5.9, I will argue that peak delay, over and above any automatic effects, is under speaker control.

Another factor which is at least partially outside the speaker's control is his emotional state, and to the extent that it is its phonetic effects will be the same for speakers from different cultures. Bezooijen (1984: 128) shows that Taiwanese and Japanese listeners perform well above chance when identifying sadness, anger, and surprise as deliberately expressed emotions by Dutch speakers. In addition to unavoidable effects, there is also a cultural element in the way we express emotions. Indeed, emotions like contempt and shame were poorly recognized by the non-Dutch listeners. Scherer (2000) similarly demonstrates on the basis of speakers from nine speech communities from three continents that the recognition of emotions is largely, but not entirely, universal.

5.3   Motivations for control in speech production

There are several purposes for which speakers exercise control over their speech production. These include their social aspirations, the care they give to the discriminability of phonological contrasts, and iconic uses of the voice (other than those to be discussed under the Effort Code, the Production Code, and the Frequency Code).

5.3.1   Social aspirations

As emphasized in section 4.3.1, phonological representations do not have unique phonetic implementations. The same representation will give different outputs in different languages or language varieties (Pierrehumbert 1990). The expression *Good heavens!* most probably has the same phonological representation in many varieties of English which nevertheless sound recognisably different. Or again, it is reasonable to assume that the prosodic structure of a citation pronunciation of a Dutch monosyllabic word is identical to that of an equivalent pronunciation in British English, but, on average, the phonetics are different. The British English rising–falling movement (for that is what would be observed) would peak higher (Willems 1984); it will also be longer, in comparable segmental conditions, which is due to the fact that British English adds the effects of 'accentual lengthening' and 'final lengthening', while Dutch does not. First, in both languages, a pitch accent lengthens the accented syllable, and to a lesser extent the post-accentual syllables (Cambier-Langeveld and Turk 1999). Second, both languages lengthen syllables at the ends of prosodic constituents, like the end of the intonational phrase. But only in British English are the two effects additive, resulting in a longer final syllable than in Dutch (Cambier-Langeveld 2000).

Thus, the precision with which people pronounce their representations is responsible for the notion 'native accent'. It might be objected that speaking one's language with a native accent does not constitute an instance of speaker control, as the articulatory behaviour is entirely automatized. A related type of control which is less open to such criticism, because it is unambiguously employed for effect, concerns prestige-related variation. Speakers will vary their pronunciation to their social advantage by choosing the variant with the higher social prestige as frequently as they think they can afford to, given their social position and the status of the hearer, as shown by a large body of sociolinguistic research since Labov (1963). This not only goes for variation in the morpho-syntax, such as when speakers choose to say *loo* rather than *toilet*, or the phonological representation, such as when speakers choose to say [ˈɡæɑːʒ] rather than [ˈɡærɪdʒ] for *garage*, but crucially also when they fine-tune the articulation of their vowels.

5.3.2 Contrast enhancement and contrast preservation

Another type of goal-oriented behaviour draws on the speaker's (tacit!) knowledge of his phonology. Two types can be distinguished: 'enhancement' of phonological contrasts (Stevens, Keyser, and Kawasaki 1986); and something I will refer to as 'contrast preservation'.

Contrast enhancement

Enhancement of phonological contrasts is the recruitment of ancillary phonetic features to aid the perceptual effect of the phonetic feature that is most directly linked to the phonological feature being implemented (Stevens, Keyser, and Kawasaki 1986). For instance, Slis and Cohen (1969) showed that intervocalic voiced and voiceless stops are phonetically different in many more ways than just the state of the glottis. Among other things, a voiceless stop is longer than a voiced one, the preceding vowel tends to be shorter, and the intensity of the plosive burst is higher. The duration difference is due, on the one hand, to the temporal requirements of the gesture for voicelessness, which takes time to execute and to perceive, and, on the other, to the requirement to maintain voicing, which in a closed vocal tract takes place in adverse conditions. (The air pressure in the vocal tract will increase as air is pumped into it through the intermittently open glottis during voicing, but in order to maintain the air flow that drives the vocal fold vibration, lower air pressure must exist above the glottis than below it.) The difference in the duration of preceding vowels assists the hearer in the perception of the voicing of the obstruent, particularly in syllable-final position, where the difference between a voiced and a voiceless plosive is harder to hear: the longer vowel suggests that the following plosive is shorter, and vice versa. The existence of speaker control here is suggested by the fact that languages with more devoicing of the voiced member of the opposition, like British English, tend to have a greater duration difference in the pre-obstruent vowel than languages like French, which retain more voicing in the voiced obstruents, or Arabic, which has barely any duration difference, but also little or no devoicing (Kluender, Diehl, and Wright 1988).

The hypothesis that enhancement is at least partially under speaker control was argued for by Kingston and Diehl (1994) on the basis of the enhancement of voicing contrasts in syllable-initial plosives. As explained in chapter 1, F_0 perturbations lead to higher F_0 immediately before and after voiceless obstruents than before and after voiced obstruents, which difference had been shown to help the identification of the voicing of following obstruents by Kohler (1990). The effect has been explained as a consequence of the vocal fold spreading gesture for the voiceless obstruents. Because the relative stiffness of the vocal folds during the spreading may leak into the voicing phase, an increased vibration rate will result, all else being equal. While this may be so, Kingston and Diehl argue that the effect cannot be entirely automatic. In a language that contrasts voiceless unaspirated with voiceless aspirated plosives or with voiceless geminates (Abrahamson 1999), F_0 after a voiceless unaspirated plosive is relatively low, but in a language that contrasts voiced unaspirated with voiceless unaspirated stops, the F_0 after a voiceless unaspirated plosive is relatively high. In other words, speakers are not at the mercy of the particular voicing properties of the obstruent in question, but adjust the F_0 such that the *more voiced* member has lower F_0: [p] will trigger F_0 lowering if it contrasts with [pʰ], but F_0 raising if it contrasts with [b].

Contrast preservation

Contrast preservation is a related type of behaviour, whereby the speaker suppresses a natural phonetic effect in order not to compromise a contrast that relies on the phonetic variable concerned. An example is the focus-dependent peak alignment variation in the Belgrade dialect, which might jeopardize a lexical tone contrast (see section 4.3.3). Another example concerns vowel duration differences before voiced and voiceless obstruents. Even though Scottish English might at first sight fare well by having a similar difference in vowel duration as exists in other varieties of English between words of the type *bead* and *beat* (i.e. [biːd̥] and [biʈ]), Norval Smith (*voce*) claims the difference is negligible in his own speech. As it happens, there is a phonological vowel duration contrast in pairs like *greed* [ɡrid] – *agreed* [ʌˈɡriːd], and the adoption of an enhancement strategy for voiced and voiceless coda obstruents would in this case compromise the vowel quantity contrast (see also Foulkes and Docherty 1999). Or again, the finding that consonantal perturbations are less persistent in tone languages than in non-tonal languages like English can be explained as due to contrast preservation (Hombert 1978).

5.3.3 Automatic or controlled?

In chapter 4, the point was made that meaningful control in speech production cannot always readily be distinguished from variation due to the occurrence of different phonological forms. At the phonetic end, it may be hard to distinguish speaker control from aspects of the speech signal that are unavoidably due to the speech production mechanism. In addition to the effects due to anatomy and uncontrolled emotion (section 5.2), speakers may choose not to bring some articulatory interaction under control. A case of this kind was made by Whalen and Levitt (1995), who surveyed research results on intrinsic pitch in vowels in thirty-one languages, and found that F_0 was positively correlated with vowel height in all of these. Their conclusion was that the effect is automatic, and not due to enhancement, as claimed by (Diehl 1991), since the effect is apparently omnipresent, and more particularly since there appeared to be no relation between the size of the vowel inventory and the size of the effect. That is, people do not apparently use it to enhance the distinctiveness of vowels that are close together in the vowel space. However, their case is not entirely convincing. First, enhancement of a vowel contrast by boosting the F_0 of the closer vowel and lowering that of the opener one would imply having to fine-tune the entire range of vowel heights, in order not to upset the listener by a 'reversed' intrinsic pitch relation for one vowel and the next vowel up, or down, in the scale of vowel heights. Intrinsic F_0 may therefore not be an efficient way of enhancing vowel height, because the more vowel heights there are and thus the greater the need for enhancement, the smaller will be the latitude for F_0 enhancement. And when there are few vowel heights to be distinguished, their acoustic separation is wide enough to make enhancement by means of pitch a pointless exercise.[1] In other words, there is little motivation for the speaker to interfere in the natural occurrence of intrinsic F_0. But absence of enhancement does not exclude speaker control. There is in fact positive evidence for the control of intrinsic pitch for contrast *preservation*. Connell (2002) has shown that speakers of Mambila suspend intrinsic F_0 differences in order not to compromise its tonal contrasts: Mambila has four contrasting level tones!

5.3.4   Iconic opportunism

Finally, there are ways in which semantic knowledge can be directly exploited in speech production. Many words mean things that can be expressed iconically in the acoustic signal, which happens when a speaker pronounces the English word *long* with a much longer vowel than is warranted by the phonological context. Similarly, some speakers will contrive to pronounce a word like *dull* or *drone* with low level pitch, and conversely, words like *tiny* and *squeak* with high pitch, when used in multi-word sentences. Because objects more often have visual characteristics offering opportunities for imitative expression through manual gestures, this kind of iconic opportunism may be more common in sign language than in spoken language (van der Hulst *voce*, Gussenhoven 1999a).

5.4   Pitch register and pitch span

This section deals with the control of pitch range. There are two main types of pitch-range variation. The first is called 'register' (Cruttenden 1997: 123) or 'pitch level' (Ladd 1996: 260). Variation in the register amounts to the raising and lowering of the contour in the F_0 space. The variation has also been referred to as variation in the 'reference line', where the idea is that there is a constant value for every contour that enters into the calculation of the targets for the Hs and Ls. Thus, male speech has a lower reference line than female speech, while children will have a higher reference line than adults, but their contours could nevertheless be otherwise equivalent. While our pitch register is first of all determined by the size of our vocal folds, we vary it for communicative purposes, such as when we speak with higher than usual pitch to imitate the voice of a child or to express surprised indignation, or when we lower it to suggest confidentiality. (Think of the British English confidentiality marker *'Between you and me and the gatepost* . . . customarily said with lower than usual register.) A choice of pitch register will remain valid for the whole intonational phrase.

The other way in which pitch range is varied concerns the 'pitch span' (Ladd 1996: 260), also referred to as the 'excursion size' ('t Hart, Collier, and Cohen 1990: 75) or 'key' (Cruttenden 1997: 123), and often simply as 'pitch range'. This measure refers to the distance between the highest and the lowest pitches in the contour. When the pitch span is increased, the highs are raised, while the lows stay put or, at least in the case of the realization of L* in Dutch, go down (Gussenhoven and Rietveld 2000). Unlike register variation, variation in pitch span can apply to subparts of the utterance (Ladd and Terken 1995). Cruttenden (1997) distinguishes 'key' as a contour-wide type of variation in pitch span from 'accent range', pitch-span variation which is locally defined by a single pitch accent. Speakers thus not only choose a pitch-span specification for the entire utterance, but – in at least some contours – may independently differentiate the pitch spans of local accentual contours. For instance, *but MATHS is EASy* may be pronounced as a single intonational phrase with two equally high-accent peaks,

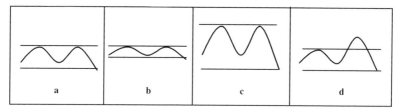

Fig. 5.1 Variations in pitch range relative to the contour in *but MATHS is EAsy* in panel a, higher register (panel b), greater span (panel c), and greater local-accent range (panel d).

but the second may also be spoken with a substantially higher peak than the first, without changing the phonological identity of the contour. Second, different intonational phrases within the same utterance may have different pitch spans. The variation in the span of the peak on *EASy* is independent of the relative pitch spans maintained for the two intonational phrases *WRITing is HARD* and *but MATHS is EASy* when spoken as a single utterance. Figure 5.1 illustrates the effect of a register change, an utterance-wide pitch-span range, and a local pitch-span change in *but MATHS is EASy*.

5.4.1   Control of pitch range

The illustration of speaker control in pitch is based on a well-known data set presented by Liberman and Pierrehumbert (1984). The point is to show that, given some realization of the pitch spans of the two intonational phrases within an utterance, speakers can vary the span of the entire utterance, *while keeping the relative pitch spans of the two intonational phrases constant* (Ladd 1996). That is, speakers can accurately retain a subjectively constant ratio between the heights of the peaks in each intonational phrase in ⟨{*ANna*} {*came with MANny*}⟩. Liberman and Pierrehumbert showed this to be true for two phonologically different contours: one of which was pronounced with a wider pitch span for the first peak, P1, than for the second, P2; and one of which had a P1 that was lower than or equal to P2. As can be seen in the top panel of figure 5.2, in one contour *Anna* has a falling tune and *Manny* a falling-rising one (the 'A–B' contour), while the other (bottom panel) has these tunes in the opposite order (the 'B–A' contour). Figure 5.3 plots the F_0 of the two peaks as measured in a large number of repetitions with different utterance-wide pitch spans by one speaker. Each data point represents two values: one for the highest F_0 in P1; and one for the highest F_0 of P2 in the same utterance. The data points for each contour lie fairly neatly along a straight line, indicating that speakers can calculate the appropriate new values for a given contour when moving the overall pitch span for the utterance to a higher value.

Of course, there are many other phonetic realizations of the 'A–B' and 'B–A' contours, among which those that reverse the relative pitch spans of the peaks.

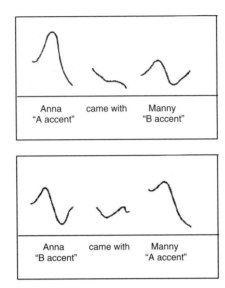

Fig. 5.2 Phonetic implementations of two phonological contours for the sentence *Anna came with Manny*, with different pitch spans for the pitch peak on each accented word. From Liberman and Pierrehumbert (1984).

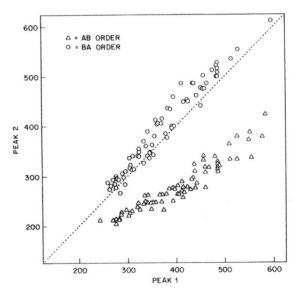

Fig. 5.3 F_0 plots of P1 and P2 for a large number of realizations of two phonological contours for the sentence *Anna came with Manny*, illustrating good control of the relative heights of the peaks. In the 'A–B' order, P1 is perceptually less salient than P2, and in the 'B–A' order, P1 is more salient, and physically higher, than P2. From Liberman and Pierrehumbert (1984).

For example, the contour of panel (a) could have a clearly higher P2 than P1 if it is used as an echo question, a surprised repetition of the hearer's previous statement. The point is therefore not that the contours must have these particular realizations, but that speakers *are capable of* preserving a given choice of pitch span for each intonational phrase, while increasing or decreasing the overall pitch span of the whole utterance (see also Ladd 1996: 64).

We now move on to the question of what universal meanings are expressed with the help of variations in pitch span and pitch register.

5.5 Biological codes in pitch variation

The rate of vocal fold vibration is principally controlled by muscles adjusting the position and tension of the vocal folds. In addition, there are three inherent features of the speech-production mechanism which affect vibration rates. First, smaller larynxes contain lighter and smaller vocal folds, with which faster vibration rates are achieved for a given amount of muscular energy (e.g. Laver 1990). Second, the generation of the air pressure driving the vibratory action is tied to the exhalation phase of the breathing process, and hence becomes available in phases, Lieberman's *breath groups* (1967, 1980). Third, the speech production process may be executed with greater or lesser precision. If the speaker lavishes more care on it, his articulation will be more precise, and his pitch movements will carried out with less undershooting of targets (Lindblom 1990; de Jong 1995). These considerations lie at the basis of three biological codes.

First, the correlation between larynx size and rate of vocal fold vibration is exploited for the expression of power relations. The many ramifications of this connection, which he termed the 'Frequency Code', were dealt with by Ohala (1983, 1984, 1996), and my labels for the other two relations are by analogy with his term. Second, the Effort Code associates wider excursions and a higher incidence of movements with greater effort. Third, the Production Phase Code, or Production Code for short, associates high pitch with the beginning of utterances and low pitch with the end.

Together, the three biological codes explain what is universal about the interpretation of pitch variation. In each case, the general form–function relation acquires a number of more specific interpretations. These can be classed as 'affective', in which case they signal attributes of the speaker; or 'informational', in which case they signal attributes of the message. The specific meanings deriving from these codes may occasionally be in competition, when high (or low) pitch signals a meaning in one code which is the opposite of that signalled by the other code, while similar meanings can be achieved from different pitch characteristics, if these are interpreted in terms of different codes.

Many languages have structural, i.e. morphologically encoded, meanings at their disposal which are the same as the universal meanings to be outlined below. We might consider this the unmarked situation: in the absence of any motivation to the contrary, the intonational morphemes of a language will reflect the universal form–function relations. In such grammaticalizations of the universal codes, the function is morphemic; the form phonological. But, of course, as structural elements, these morphemes are subject to the normal forces of languages change, and as a result languages may possess form–meaning relations in their grammars which go against the universal, biological codes, like interrogative intonation contours that end in falling pitch. This happens so commonly that Ladd (1981) rejected the notion of universal form–meaning relations in intonation, on the ground that if a universal is only in evidence, say, 70 per cent of the time, there is little explanatory power to be derived from it. Crucially, in the present perspective, such 'unnatural' form–function relations must be structural, i.e. discrete. An account of how a group of German dialects changed from a 'natural' rising question intonation to an 'unnatural' falling one is given in chapter 11.

A final preliminary remark to prevent a possible misinterpretation. Biological codes are form–meaning relations which are based on effects of physiological properties of the production process on the signal, but communication by means of these codes does not require that these physiological conditions are actually created. It is enough to create the effects. When we say that the meaning 'emphasis' as signalled by wide-pitch excursions is derived from the Effort Code on the ground that greater effort will typically lead to wider pitch excursions, there is no implication that the speaker who signals emphasis by using the Effort Code actually expends greater effort on his speech production. The only thing he needs to do is choose his pitch range such that he will be understood to be exploiting the relation between excursion size and articulatory effort. Similarly, when using the Production Code to signal the end of a speaking turn, the speaker need not have his exhalation phase end with the end of his utterance, or even produce a more steeply declining overall contour shape, but need only lower the pitch of the last one or two syllables of his utterance, and so on. The indirectness of the relation between actual speaker behaviour and the natural connections between speech production and pitch are underscored by the use of delayed peaks as a substitute for high peaks (Gussenhoven 1999c), and the use of high register as a substitute for wide span, as discussed in section 5.9.

5.6 The Frequency Code

The Frequency Code was proposed by Ohala (1983) as an explanation of the striking similarity across languages in the use of rising or high question intonation and falling or low statement intonation. Essentially, Ohala extended the explanation for the widespread similarities in patterns of avian and mammalian vocalizations in face-to-face competitive encounters to human speech given by Morton (1977). Vocalizations by dominant or aggressive individuals are low-pitched, while those by subordinate or submissive individuals are high-pitched. Lower pitch suggests the organ producing the vocalization is larger. In fact, the exploitation of this correlation in nature is not confined to meaningful variation by individuals. In many species, it is hard-wired in the sexes through dimorphism, the different biological developments of the male and female members of a species. In the front-to-back dimension, the male human larynx is almost twice the size of the female larynx, exactly the dimension which affects the fundamental frequency most. It arises at puberty, the age at which boy becomes man, ready to assume the role of defender or aggressor. To underscore the effect, the male larynx is positioned lower in the throat, causing the vocal tract, the tube leading to the lips, to be some 3.5 cm longer than the female vocal tract. The effect is that formant frequencies are lower in men, again suggesting a larger creature. Other aspects of dimorphism in animals and humans point in the same direction: males may have extra feathers to be erected, antlers, thicker manes, or, in the case of humans, peripheral facial hair, all of which serve to make the creature look more imposing. Ohala (1983, 1984, 1996) claims that we associate pitch with this package of evolutionary meanings, for which reason intonation contours have come to have the distributional bias we observe. The Frequency Code, therefore, is a 'size code': just as effort is here seen to lie behind the meanings to be discussed in section 5.7, so size is the explanatory concept behind the meanings discussed in this section.

5.6.1 Affective interpretations of the Frequency Code

It is tempting to think of the anatomical differences between men and women as just a relic of an earlier evolutionary functionalism, with no relevance for present-day social interaction beyond signalling the sex of the speaker. However, people will project what they perceive as their social role in their voice, and gender roles are no exception. Voice characteristics that are manipulated include type of vocal fold vibration (breathy voice, creaky voice), formant frequencies (as a result of vocal-tract manipulations like lip rounding, nasalization, habitual tongue posture, and pharyngeal constriction), but also fundamental frequency (e.g. Laver 1980). For instance, while men will produce lower average formant frequencies than women as a result of their longer vocal tracts, speech communities vary in the social significance they attach to the gender difference, which suggests that one or both sexes might well exaggerate the effect (Henton 1995; Henton 1999). Henton and Bladon (1988) find that creak is a marker of British male speech, and that at least in some varieties it is used to signal masculinity. Similarly, different speech communities may have different average pitch levels, for one or both sexes. Thus, American men speak at a lower pitch than German men (Scherer 1979), Japanese women speak at a higher pitch than American women (Ohara 1992), and Dutch spoken by Belgian women is higher than Dutch spoken by Dutch women (Bezooijen 1993).[2] Biemans (2000: 157), who also gives a survey of the recent literature (2000: 19ff.), found a positive correlation between five artificial registers superimposed on a set of spontaneous male and female utterances and the scores on a 'femininity' scale, and a negative correlation with the scores on a 'masculinity' scale. That is, raising our register will make us sound more feminine and lowering it will make us sound more masculine.

There are several different affective interpretations of the Frequency Code. 'Feminine' vs. 'masculine' values are associated with 'submissiveness' and 'dominance', respectively. Other meanings include (for higher pitch) 'friendliness' and 'politeness'. A closely related one is 'vulnerability' (for higher pitch) versus 'confidence', which may play out as 'protection', or as its counterparts 'aggression' and 'scathing'. They can be grouped as affective interpretations of the Frequency Code, as they signal properties of speaker. Positive scores for high pitch on semantic scales for 'polite', 'non-aggressive', and 'friendly' are a commonplace finding in perception experiments with intonation. Uldall (1964) found that listeners associated high-ending rises with both 'submissiveness' and 'pleasantness'. In a recent experiment, Rietveld, Haan, Heijmans, and Gussenhoven (2002) found that the scores on four scales measuring affective meanings for eight Dutch intonation contours correlated highly with the mean fundamental frequency of the contours. Even stronger correlations were found between these scores and the mean fundamental frequency of the last quarter of the contours, suggesting that contour endings are used more for this purpose than other parts.

5.6.2   Informational interpretations of the Frequency Code

'Informational' interpretations of the Frequency Code are 'uncertainty' (for higher pitch) vs. 'certainty', and hence 'questioning' vs. 'assertive'. In an experiment with a number of artificial intonation contours superimposed on a phrase which could be interpreted as either Swedish *för Jane* or English *for Jane*, Swedish and American listeners were asked to decide whether each utterance presented to them was meant as a statement or as a question (Hadding-Koch and Studdert-Kennedy 1964). The contours on these utterances consisted of a single rising–falling peak on *Jane* varying in peak height (a high 310 Hz and a super-high 370 Hz) and was combined with seven values for the end pitch, ranging from 130 Hz to 370 Hz. The results for both groups of listeners were that the higher peak attracted more 'Question' judgements than the lower peak, while there was a clear correlation between end pitch and these scores. The variables peak height and end pitch are rather salient ways of manipulating the Frequency Code, and the results reflect this. Figure 5.4 presents the structure of a subset of the stimuli[3] and the results for the Swedish listeners in a graph with end point on the x-axis and percentage 'Question' judgements on the y-axis. The interrupted graphs (for the stimuli with the high peak) cross at a lower value for end pitch than the solid graphs (for the stimuli with the superhigh peak), showing that higher peaks are more likely to lead to the perception of questions: for the same end pitch, the higher peak always leads to more 'Question' judgements.

Interestingly, the results also show the influence of the native language. The two crosses indicate the crossover points for the American listeners. Listener language appears to interact with peak height: Swedish listeners differentiate more

Swedish two-category semantic judgements

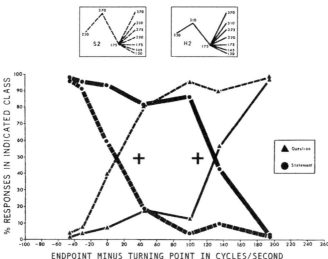

Fig. 5.4 Percentage 'Question' responses (thick graphs) and complementary 'Statement' responses (thin graphs) by Swedish listeners as a function of end pitch (x-axis) and peak height (solid graphs: high peak, interrupted graphs: superhigh peak). The two plus symbols indicate the crossover points for American listeners (high peak: right, superhigh peak: left). From Hadding-Koch and Studdert-Kennedy (1964).

sharply between the superhigh peak and the high peak than do the American listeners, showing a greater influence of this variable in their scores. The difference must be due to the fact that Swedish does not have final rises as a cue for questions, while English does. As we will see in chapter 11, Swedish has essentially a single, falling intonation contour, which may be realized with raised register and/or less deep falls in interrogatives. As a result, Swedish listeners rely more strongly on other cues.[4] Similarly, Japanese listeners are less inclined to hear interrogativity in high-peaked contours that Russian listeners (Makarova 1999b). Indeed, Japanese uses a final rise for questions (Pierrehumbert and Beckman 1988), while Russian employs peak height difference (Makarova 1999a).

When a phonological contour functions both as statement and as question intonation when used on the same syntactic structure, provision can still be made in the phonetic implementation to ensure that the question will be said at a higher pitch than the statement. Such phonetic use of pitch range appears to be common in Chinese languages (Shen 1990; Duanmu 2000).

Grammaticalizations

Grammaticalization of the informational interpretation of the Frequency Code is widespread. A number of ways exist in which raised pitch for questions has been grammaticalized. Languages may suspend downstep (see also

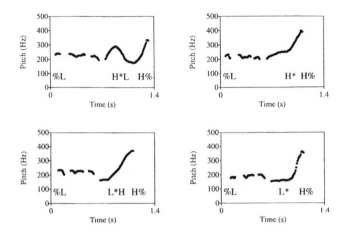

Fig. 5.5 Four phonologically different rising intonation contours in Dutch.

chapter 6), as in the intonation-only language Danish (Gønnum 1983a) or the tone language Twi (Hyman 2001b). Raising of the pitch register is discrete in Jita, a tone language, where in questions the register is raised up to and including the last (lexical) H-tone of the sentence, or, if the sentence consists of L-tones only, the penultimate syllable (Downing 1996). As a result, questions and statements whose last syllable has L-tone have the same low end-points, but differ in pitch height before the last pitch fall, while those whose last syllable has H-tone differ in register throughout the sentence. Phonologically, the difference could be represented by means of an initial H_i. Questions in Malay, not a tone language, similarly begin at a higher pitch than statements (Indirawata Zahid, *voce*), a difference that likewise would appear to be discrete. Most commonly, the end of the sentence is signalled out for phonological interrogativity marking. Over 70 per cent of the languages in the world are estimated to have rising intonation contours, while the use of rising intonation for statements is exceptional (Bolinger 1972). In fact, many languages have more than one rising pattern. Dutch has four phonologically different contours, H*L H_i, or the fall–rise, H* H_i, or the high rise, L*H H_i, the low rise, and L* H_i, the low low rise, as shown in figure 5.5. The same contrasts exist in English.

Grammaticalization of peak height is less common. Bengali has two phonologically different contours showing an intonation-phrase final peak. One signals contrastive declarative focus and the other a yes–no question. Phonologically, the two peaks differ in the status of the H-tone, which belongs to the phonological phrase in the case of the contrastive declarative (H_ϕ), but to the intonational phrase in the case of the interrogative contour (H_i) (see also figure 3.1). The point is that the tone of the intonational phrase is pronounced at considerably higher pitch (Hayes and Lahiri 1991a), in addition to being later.

5.7   The Effort Code

Increases in the effort expended on speech production will lead to greater articulatory precision (de Jong 1995), including a wider excursion of the pitch movement.
Speakers exploit this fact by using pitch-span variation to signal meanings that
can be derived from the expenditure of effort.

5.7.1   An informational interpretation of the Effort Code

A common communicative reason for raising the effort level is the speaker's
concern that his message should come across. Wichmann (2000: 116) found that
the overall pitch range of utterances in British English radio news bulletins correlated with informational salience, as determined independently of the acoustics.
Probably all languages, even those with many tone contrasts, will have sufficient
phonetic space left for expressing degrees of emphasis of this kind.

As many perception experiments with artificial intonation contours have
shown, the higher a pitch peak is, the more prominent it will sound, everything
else being equal (Rietveld and Gussenhoven 1985; Ladd and Morton 1997). Interestingly, however, the roles of pitch-register variation and pitch-span variation
are not the same: perceived prominence is not simply a correlate of peak height.
Rather, it is an estimate of how wide the pitch excursion is, given some choice of
pitch register, and the listener's impression therefore results from an estimate of
the pitch span in relation to an estimated pitch register. The most straightforward
way in which this can be demonstrated is by having listeners judge the prominence of peaks in identical pitch contours superimposed on a male and a female
voice, as reported in Gussenhoven and Rietveld (1998). In this experiment, the
source utterances had been recorded by a woman with a fairly 'deep' voice. They
were provided with artificial spectra by multiplying the first two formants with
a factor of less than 1, so as to create a set of stimuli that sounded as if they
were spoken by a man, as well as by a factor of more than 1, so as to create a set
that sounded as if they were spoken by a woman whose voice was subjectively
more feminine than the original voice. Listeners rated pitch peaks in the artificial
male voice as more prominent than the equivalent pitch peaks in the artificial
female voice, even though the F_0 contours were identical. That is, prominence
judgements are made relative to a hypothesized F_0 reference line, as determined
by the estimate of the speaker's register, and, since the register of a female speaker
will be expected to be higher than that of a male speaker, perceived prominence
in the male stimuli fell considerably short of that in the female stimuli. This effect
can also be found within the same speaker. Gussenhoven, Repp, Rietveld, Rump,
and Terken (1997) found that raising the pitch of the brief stretch of pitch before
the first accent peak decreases the perceived prominence of the peak. This result
can be interpreted as an effect of the raising of the reference line, and shows again
that the perception of emphasis is related to the interpretation of pitch excursion

size, not with height of pitch *per se*.[5] This conclusion will be further modified in section 5.9, which argues that speakers may use *substitute* phonetic features to create particular effects.

Grammaticalization: focus

Common grammaticalizations of the 'significance' interpretation of the Effort Code concern focus. Languages have ways of marking important parts of expressions for focus, or 'information packaging'. Information packaging 'reflects the speaker's beliefs about how the [sentential] information fits the hearer's knowledge store' (Vallduví 1992: 10). In chapters 9–13, a number of issues are raised which I briefly introduce here. First, the size of the significant part of the sentence, the 'focus constituent', will vary. The English expression *In the TALL building* could be a reply to 'Is that where you work?', asked by someone pointing in the general direction of a city's skyline. Here, the focus constituent is *tall*, the concept of buildings being understood from the context. By contrast, *In the TALL BUILDing*, which might be spoken in response to 'Where would you hide if you had to?' in a situation where the addressee had more options for a hide-out besides buildings, the focus constituent is *the tall building*. Ladd (1980: 75) referred to this variation as the difference between 'broad focus', i.e. expression-wide focus, and 'narrow focus', any focus constituent which is smaller than the whole expression. Second, there are different types of focus. The most common type is typically defined as the answer to a question, as in the above example, and is called 'presentational focus' (Zubizarreta 1998; Selkirk 2002) or 'information focus' (Kiss 1998). Languages may have more than one pairing of structural device and focus type. Although English does not typically distinguish 'presentational focus' from 'corrective focus', languages may have different forms. In European Portuguese, a pitch accent expressing presentational focus occurs in (1a), while the pitch accent expressing corrective focus occurs in (1b). Example (1a) could be a reply to 'What about Roberto and Maria?', while (1b) requires a context like 'Have they split up?' (See also Gussenhoven forthcoming.)

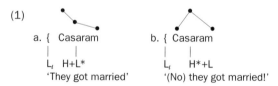

(1)

a. { Casaram
     | |
     L$_i$ H+L*
  'They got married'

b. { Casaram
     | |
     L$_i$ H*+L
  '(No) they got married!'

In fact, 'corrective focus' and 'narrow focus' are sometimes confused in discussions on this topic; both may be referred to as 'contrastive focus'. The difference becomes clear if we were to replace (1a) with *Casaram Roberto y Maria*, where the focus is narrow, i.e. *Casaram*, but not corrective, and the pitch accent on that word would still be H+L*.

A third issue concerns the kind of linguistic device used to express information packaging. It may be expressed in the syntax, by reserving a structural position

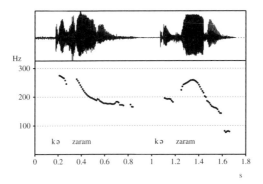

Fig. 5.6 Neutral and contrastive pitch accent on European Portuguese *Casaram.*

for the focus constituent, like the end of the sentence of the position before the verb; or by using focus particles, which are placed in some structural position before or after the focus constituent. Papiamentu uses both devices. As shown in (2b), the focus constituent is topicalized, while a focus particle, *ta*, is appended at the end of the clause that contains a narrow focus constituent (Römer 1991: 8).

(2) a. E kas di glas
          is house of glass
          'The house is made of glass' (neutral focus)
     b. (A: What's the house made of?)
          B: Di glas e kas ta
          of glass is house FOC
          'The house is made of GLASS'

In Wolof, focus is expressed along with verbal aspect in the verbal morphology (Robert 2000). However, for our purposes it is more relevant to consider that many languages express focus in the intonation structure. In such cases, the structural device that is used for this purpose has the effect that the focused information, the focus constituent, is characterized by a relatively wide pitch excursion. While their effects are thus comparable, the structural devices themselves vary. First, West Germanic languages use pitch accents to mark focused parts of sentences, but remove these after the focus ('deaccentuation'). The absence of a pitch accent on *building* in *the TALL building* will cause *tall* to be marked by a wide pitch fall. By contrast, in *the TALL BUILDing* a wide pitch fall would occur in the word *building*. Second, languages may use different pitch accents for narrow or corrective focus and neutral (or broad) focus, as in the case of European Portuguese. In line with the predictions of the Effort Code, the pitch accent marking the more neutral focus will be realized with a smaller pitch excursion on the accented syllable than the corrective or narrow one. In European Portuguese, the corrective accent has a peak in the accented syllable, while the neutral-focus pitch accent has a peak before it, causing the accented syllable to show a mid-to-low fall. This is illustrated in figure 5.6.

A third way to grammaticalize pitch prominence is the suspension of down-step on the focus constituent: in Japanese, prosodic phrasing is sensitive to focus structure, and the most salient consequence of this is that an otherwise automatic lowering of the pitch range cannot take place. Downstep is discussed in chapter 6, and the details of the Japanese case in chapter 10.

Grammaticalization: negation

A different informational use of the Effort Code relies on the *reduction* of the excursion size for the expression of negation. The low and high values are brought together so as to create the impression that the speaker is withdrawing information, the reverse of a significant addition. Phonetic span compression may be used for an English fall–rise on *there* as in *He won't be THERE* to express a gentle negation. In Engenni, a tone language, compression has been grammaticalized: from the VP onwards, high tones are lowered and low tones are raised in negative sentences (Thomas 1978: 67), which may differ from positive sentences only in the use of this feature. While the lowering and raising of the tones is a matter of the phonetic implementation, the context in which it occurs is discrete. This is parallel to downstep, the grammaticalized version of declination (chapter 6).

5.7.2   Affective interpretations of the Effort Code

Affective interpretations of (apparent) speaker effort are 'authoritative', 'insis-tent', and 'enthusiastic' (wide excursions) versus 'lacking in commitment' and 'uninterested'. The wide-span meanings may come close to a meaning signalled by low pitch in the Frequency Code, that of authority due to the metaphor of large size. A positive interpretation of a low degree of effort is given by Brown and Levinson (1987: 267), who explain the use of creak to signal commiseration in Tzeltal as being due to low speech energy implicating calmness and assurance. A further interpretation of wide span is helpfulness: going to some lengths in realizing pitch movements may be indicative of an obliging disposition. Speech addressed to children would frequently appear to have this suggestion of 'a little help' to the listener. Early research into the perception of intonational meaning found that rising–falling and falling–rising contours (representing a 'change of direction') were perceived as 'authoritative' and 'pleasant' by English listeners, illustrating two interpretations of the Effort Code (Uldall 1960; Uldall 1964). Again, there is potential overlap between the Effort Code and the Frequency Code, since wide-span 'obligingness' comes close to the 'friendliness' interpre-tation of high register in the Frequency Code.

Grammaticalization

A grammaticalized 'obligingness' morpheme may have been found by Grabe *et al.* (1997), who investigated the pragmatic effects of high-pitched and low-pitched realizations of the utterance-initial unaccented syllables before the first pitch accent (also known as the 'prehead' or 'onset') in Standard Dutch. High onsets before a low-pitched (L*) accented syllable were more positively evaluated than low onsets. Conversely, low onsets were more positively evaluated before high-pitched (H*) accented syllables than high onsets. In other words, a movement towards the accented syllable, regardless of direction, was seen as reflecting a co-operative speaker attitude, while absence of movement received negative evaluations. The structural solution suggested by Grabe *et al.*, due to John Kingston, is that Dutch has a 'politeness' morpheme consisting of an initial unspecified boundary T_i, whose identity (H_i or L_i) depends on the identity of the following T^*: it must have a value opposite to T^*. Such reversals of tone values for adjacent tones are known as 'polar' rules.

5.8 The Production Code

An additional interpretation of the process of energy generation originates from a correlation between utterances and breath groups: at the beginning of the exhalation phase, subglottal air pressure will be higher than towards its end. A consequence of the fall-off in energy is a gradual drop in intensity and a weak, gradual lowering of the fundamental frequency (Lieberman 1967: 42), known as 'declination' (Cohen and Hart 1967). The communicative exploitation of this effect might be called the Production Phase Code, or Production Code for brevity. The Production Code associates high pitch with the utterance beginnings and low pitch with utterance ends. The significance of declination therefore does not lie in its slope, which has been the focus of a great deal of research, but rather in the variation at utterance edges. Thus, high beginnings signal new topics, low beginnings continuations of topics, while a reverse relation holds for the utterance end, where high endings signal continuation, low endings finality and end of turn. Grammaticalized F_0 variation is commonly found for the utterance end, when an H_i may signal continuation and L_i finality,[6] but might also be found in the use of initial H_i to signal topic change. The Production Code would appear to have informational meanings only.

5.8.1 Descending slope

The central zone of the utterance may show a declining trend. For the purposes of the Production Code, there is no obvious meaning to be attached to this fact, other than that the utterance is progressing. Concomitantly with variation in end-point, variation in slope has been shown to be meaningful in terms of the Frequency Code, in the sense that less steep slopes are used to signal interrogativity. Such use will be in competition with the employment of the variation in end-point for the purposes of the Production Code. In Grønnum's data for Danish (p. 100) the

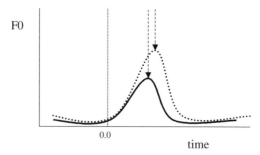

Fig. 5.7 Hypothesized relation between high peaks and late peaks. After Gussenhoven (1999c).

highest versions are employed for interrogativity and the less extreme versions for signalling continuation.

In the present perspective, the significance of the descending slope is that it is commonly grammaticalized as downstep. In a frequent type, H after L is pronounced at a categorically lower pitch than a preceding H, a type that occurs both in tone languages and in intonation-only languages. Downstep may be purely phonological, in which case the information it provides derives from the fact that its context is confined to some prosodic constituent, and thus concerns the phrasing of the utterance (cf. chapter 6). In other cases, there is a morphological effect, such as when languages suspend phonological downstep due to the presence of an H-boundary tone signalling interrogativity, or when downstep on a final H-tone indicates a greater degree of finality. These issues are discussed further in chapter 6, as well as in chapter 9, where in addition to downstep, a grammaticalized form of final lowering is discussed, 'subordination'.

5.9   Substitute phonetic features

This section considers the use of two phonetic variables that appear to be used as substitutes for other phonetic variables when signalling paradigmatic meaning. First, peak delay may replace greater peak height; and, second, higher register may replace wider pitch span.

A higher pitch peak will take longer to reach than a lower one if rate of change is the same. Therefore, higher peaks will tend to be later than lower peaks, as suggested by figure 5.7. Speakers and listeners have tacit knowledge of this mechanical connection, and peak delay can therefore be used as an enhancement of, or even a substitute for, pitch raising.

Indeed, many of the meanings derived from the three biological codes that are associated with high pitch may also be signalled by late peaks. First, late peaks in English sound more prominent than early peaks. The results in Ladd and Morton (1997) indeed show that both higher and later peaks elicit more 'unusual occurrence' interpretations than 'everyday occurrence' interpretations in one-peak realizations of *The aLARM went off*. Although the authors do not make this suggestion, listeners apparently perceive late peaks as if they were higher. In research on the difference between wide focus and narrow focus in the Hamburg dialect of German, Peters (2002) found that narrow focus was realized by later peaks, suggesting again that speakers use it to signal high pitch, in this case to enhance the excursion of the fall for the purposes of the Effort Code. Tellingly, when the accent occurred on utterance-final syllables, narrow focus was realized by *earlier* peaks. The explanation is that high values of the Effort Code cannot be signalled by late peaks on final syllables, because the pitch fall would be truncated, removing the wide excursion, the Effort Code's primary cue.

As for the Frequency Code, there have been reports of languages that use later peaks to mark question intonation and earlier peaks for statements, such as southern varieties of Italian (Grice 1995b; D'Imperio 1997; D'Imperio and House 1997). The difference is generally interpreted as categorical. That is, it is a grammaticalized form of an informational interpretation of the Frequency Code, as signalled by a feature substituting for high pitch. More recently, it has been found that nuclear peaks in Dutch questions are 40 ms later than in declaratives (van Heuven and Haan 2002). Here, the effect is almost certainly phonetic. An affective case for the Frequency Code can be found in the delayed accentual peaks in Japanese that are associated with female speech (Hasegawa and Hata 1994). Finally, the Production Code: Wichmann, House, and Rietveld (1997, 2000) found that the first peak of intonational phrases containing new topics in British English were some 25 ms later than other first peaks. This finding can be related to the Production Code, which links high beginnings to new topics. The high beginning is expressed in the first accentual peak, whose late timing enhances the high pitch.

The universality of late peaks as a cue for question intonation, along with high peaks and high end pitch, was tested in an experiment with Standard Chinese, Dutch, and Hungarian listeners. They were asked to identify the question in pairs of intonation contours superimposed on identical segmental structures (Gussenhoven and Chen 2000). These three languages have different ways of expressing interrogativity prosodically. Standard Chinese raises the pitch register (Shen 1990, Duanmu 2000: 235), presumably an effect produced in the phonetic implementation. Dutch uses final rises, phonologically marked by final H_i, while Hungarian distinguishes earlier accentual peaks in declaratives from later phrase-final (i.e. boundary) peaks in interrogatives (Ladd 1996; Gósy, and Terken 1994). The stimuli consisted of (hypothetical) trisyllabic CVCVCV structures with the stress on the penultimate syllable. The contours, which were similar in structure to the ones used by Hadding-Koch and Studdert-Kennedy (1964), varied in peak height, peak alignment, and end pitch. Unlike the listeners in the 1964 experiment, who judged stimuli in their native language, the listeners were told, quite untruthfully, that they were going to hear sentences from a little-known language spoken on a South Pacific island. Regardless of language background, listeners associated higher peaks and higher end pitch with questions, as in the earlier experiment. There was also an interaction between language group and peak height, which showed that Hungarian speakers were more sensitive to the peak height variable than were the other two language groups, thus paralleling the behaviour of the Swedes *vis-à-vis* the Americans. The interesting additional finding was the effect of peak alignment: all three language groups associated later peaks with questions. These results suggest that humans know both the direct and indirect manifestations of the Frequency Code, regardless of their native language.

Secondly, high register may be used as a substitute for wide span. Chen, Gussenhoven, and Rietveld (2002) showed that Dutch listeners interpret high register as signalling emphasis. Apparently, speakers need not actually return to low pitch for listeners to infer the communication of emphasis (see also next section).

5.10   Language-specific universal meaning?

There are two ways in which the use of the term 'universal' in this chapter has been ill-advised. One is that the term generally refers to the presumed universal presence of *structural* elements in languages, whereas I have used it for form–meaning relations in the phonetic implementation. The second reason why the term may be misleading is that not all languages use the biological codes in the same way. Cross-linguistic differences in the degree to which F_0 peaks signal interrogativity, for instance, have been found in a number of cases, beginning with Hadding-Koch and Studdert-Kennedy (1964). The reason for these differences was not hard to find: grammars may favour or disfavour particular form–meaning relations. To give another example, Chickasaw speakers will be less able to perceive final low pitch as an indication of finality, since the declarative intonation ends in a high rise and the interrogative in a fall to low. However, the universal meanings remain valid even for speakers of Chickasaw, who may add a narrow fall at the end of the declarative rise to indicate finality (Gordon 1999).

In addition to these language-related differences, the exploitation of the three biological codes will to some extent be conventionalized within speech communities, as we have seen in the case of Japanese, where high pitch is used more extensively to signal feminine values (section 5.6.1). That is, communities may choose to use a particular interpretation to different degrees. Thirdly, when mutually incompatible interpretations are in competition, different communities may make different choices. In two studies, mean F_0 of 29 German speakers was found to correlate positively with ratings for personality traits like lack of autonomy, dependability, and likeability; while in the case of 28 American males, mean F_0 correlated positively with dominance, authority, and competence (Scherer 1979). Evidently, the German speakers were understood to be signalling the 'feminine' meanings of the Frequency Code, while the American speakers were understood to be signalling the 'significance' meanings of the Effort Code. It is unclear whether these difference are culturally determined, since we do not know for sure if the phonetics were the same. If the German speakers had a narrower pitch span than the American English speakers (information which is lost when data are represented by the mean F_0 over utterances, as in Scherer 1979), we might interpret the results in part as due to these general differences in contour shape. A clear case of speech communities making different choices from these rival interpretations was presented by Chen, Gussenhoven, and Rietveld (2002). Dutch and British English listeners rated emphasis on the *same* contours, superimposed on Dutch and British English source utterances respectively, as produced by a bilingual speaker. The stimuli varied in pitch register. Interestingly, the Dutch learners perceived more emphasis as the register was higher, but English listeners less. Earlier research had shown that English listeners perceived higher registers as more friendly, while Dutch listeners do not (Chen, Rietveld, and Gussenhoven 1999), and since friendliness and emphasis may be felt to be mutually exclusive meanings, these two speech communities have evidently made different choices from the universally available meanings: emphasis as expressed by pitch register, used as a substitute for pitch span by the Dutch (Effort Code), and friendliness as expressed by high register by the English (Frequency Code).

A final case of competition concerns the availability of different strategies for the expression of emphasis. In the Zagreb variety of Serbocroat, F_0 peaks in initially stressed words occurred in the second syllable when they were spoken in sentences with neutral intonation, but in the first syllable when the focus is on the word in question, a difference of some 100 ms earlier (section 4.3.3). This pattern is the opposite of that found for Hamburg German by Peters (2002). The solution to the paradox is that there are two ways in which the Effort Code can be recruited to express emphasis in F_0 peaks. One, the Hamburg German option, is enhancement of high pitch by late peaks, as discussed in the previous section. The other, the Zagreb Croatian option, is to locate the peak precisely inside the stressed syllable, rather than allowing it to drift rightwards. It presupposes that less effort is involved in allowing peaks to drift rightwards. Indeed, peak delays appear to be greater as there is more space between the accented syllable and the phrase end in English (Pierrehumbert and Steele 1989) or the next accent (Silverman and Pierrehumbert 1990), suggesting that speakers will allow it to drift off where they can afford to do so. In other words, it takes more effort to time a peak inside its associated syllable, i.e. early, just as it takes more effort to have wide excursions. For the other interpretations of late peaks, newness of topic (Production Code), and interrogativity (Frequency Code), this competition does not exist, and early peaks cannot therefore be used to express these meanings.

5.11 Conclusion

Universal meaning in intonation derives from three biological codes, the Frequency Code, the Effort Code, and the Production Code. The codes derive from aspects of the speech production mechanism that affect rate of vocal fold vibration, as by-products of the way the larynx and the pulmonic airstream mechanism are designed. The way in which speakers take charge of these aspects of speech production was seen to fit into a larger picture of speaker control (Kingston and Diehl 1994). Speakers control the phonetic implementation of linguistic expressions for a wide variety of reasons, like social positioning, maximization of the discriminability of phonological contrasts, and the recruitment of iconic uses of the voice to aid the expression of word meanings. The exploitation of the biological codes is a controlled use of pitch variation, whereby speakers need not create the physiological conditions associated with the pitch features from which the meanings derive. In one case, this would be physically impossible, since we cannot alter the size of our larynx to manipulate pitch for the purposes of the Frequency Code. Pitch height in peaks can in part be enhanced or taken over by peak delay, due to the mechanical connection between high peaks and late peaks, while register can be used as a substitute for pitch span.

Table 5.1 presents these connections. Two of the three codes, the Effort Code and the Production Code, are based on the energy used to drive vocal fold vibration; and one, the Frequency Code, is based on the size of the organ in which they are contained, and by extension, on the size of the creature that possesses it (see columns 1 and 2). Column 3 lists the basic form–function relations expressed in each code. Column 4 lists a number of more-specific interpretations. These are divided into affective interpretations, which signal states of the speaker, and informational interpretations, which signal properties of the message.

The informational interpretation of the Effort Code is emphasis, based on the speaker's assumed intention to underscore the importance of the message. Affective interpretations are insistence, enthusiasm, and obligingness. The latter is due to the interpretation of effort as the speaker's desire to appear clear and unambiguous. The Production Code, used for the signalling of phrasing, is due to the effect of energy dissipation in the course of the utterance. Its interpretations are informational only: high beginnings signal newness of topic, low beginnings the opposite; and high endings signal continuation, low endings the opposite. The Frequency Code is widely used for the expression of affective meanings. These include masculinity, dominance/assertiveness, confidence, and protectiveness (low pitch) and femininity, submissiveness/friendliness, insecurity, and vulnerability (high pitch). The informational interpretation is 'certainty', leading to distinctions in what is sometimes referred to as 'sentence mode', the difference between statements and questions.

Column 4 lists grammaticalizations of the paralinguistic meanings in the third column. No grammaticalizations of affective interpretations of the Frequency Code have been identified. In fact, the only case of an affective morpheme was presented for Dutch, which arguably has a polar onset tone signalling 'obligingness' (Grabe, Gussenhoven, Haan, Marsi, and Post 1997). Grammaticalizations of universal meanings are thus typically informational. They refer to the significance of (parts of) the message, as well as to whether the utterance is meant to provide or to solicit information. Following Brazil's discourse treatment of

Table 5.1 *Three biological codes (column 2) and their physiological sources (column 1), examples of their interpretations (column 3), and examples of grammaticalizations (column 4)*

Physiological sources	Biological codes	Universal interpretations	Linguistic interpretations
SIZE	**Frequency Code:** small~big→ high~low	**Affective:** *submissive~authoritative vulnerable~protective friendly~not friendly* **Informational:** *uncertain~certain*	? Question vs. Statement (e.g. H%/L%)
ENERGY (phasing)	**Production Code:** beginning~end→ high~low	**Informational:** At beginning: *new topic~continued topic* At end: *continuation~finality*	Continuation rise vs. final low (H%/L%)
ENERGY (level)	**Effort Code:** less effort~more effort→smaller excursion~ greater excursion	**Affective:** *less surprised~more surprised less helpful~more helpful* **Informational:** *less urgent~more urgent*	Polar onset tone (%T) Focus (various: see text)

intonational meaning (Brazil 1975; Brazil, Coulthard, and Johns 1980), I proposed in Gussenhoven (1983a) that intonational meaning in English was in fact informational in this sense.

The universal form–function relations are often grammaticalized, i.e. encoded in the discrete structures of languages. Since languages change, grammatical form–meaning relations can – and frequently do – arise that run counter to the predictions of the biological codes. Studies of prosodic change have concentrated on word prosodic structure (Fikkert and Jacobs 2003), and accounts of intonational change are rare. In chapter 11, a scenario is given of the development of falling question intonation in German dialects from a hypothesized earlier stage when questions had rising intonation.

The present account of the position of intonation in language (chapter 4 and the present chapter) presupposes a principled distinction between phonetics and phonology, and to the extent that the account is convincing, amounts to a further argument for making that distinction. Without it, we lose the basis on which we distinguish the universal, non-linguistic, gradient system of communication employed in phonetic implementation, and the discrete, linguistic system embedded in the grammar, which is potentially invested with arbitrary meanings.

Notes

1. The absence of enhancement strategies would appear to explain the absence of clear cases of original tonogenesis arising from vowel height, or of the creation of vowel height distinctions from tonal differences (Maddieson 1977: ch. 6). Possibly, vowel height distinction leads to the creation of *extra* tones in a language that already had lexical tone (Wedekind 1983), but even this situation may be rare.

2. Manipulation of the Frequency Code may be evident from correlations between perceptions of masculinity or femininity and the average pitch used by men and women. van Bezooijen *et al.* (1995) found in a paper-and-pencil experiment that Japanese conceptions of the ideal man and the ideal woman are more sharply differentiated than the corresponding Dutch conceptions. Japanese subjects rated the ideal woman as less tall, less strong, less independent, and less arrogant than Dutch subjects, while conversely the ideal man for the Japanese subjects is taller, stronger, more independent, and more arrogant than for the Dutch subjects. Also, average pitch of Japanese women is higher than that of Dutch women, suggesting that pitch is indeed used by speech communities to express social meanings of this kind. Indeed, high pitch carries more prestige in Japanese than in Dutch (van Bezooijen, de Graaf, and Otake 1995).

3. The stimuli also varied in the F_0 of the beginning of the final rise; 175 Hz was the middle of three values.

4. This conclusion is my own. Unexpectedly, the authors conclude that Swedes are more sensitive to final rises in both questions and statements. However, for an interaction of this type, the slopes of the graphs for the Swedish listeners would have to show steeper angles than those for the American listeners, and there is no indication that this is the case. Hadding-Koch and Studdert-Kennedy (1964) also report an effect of the F_0 at the beginning of the final rise, but this finding appears largely dependent on the way they report the final pitch. Instead of values in absolute Hertz, they give differences between end pitch and turning-point (cf. figure 5.4). In fact, the results in their other figures look very similar when absolute end-points are considered.

5. Interestingly, raising the end of the contour had no effect on perceived prominence of the accent peak. This is to be expected if the listener's strategy is to estimate the register from the beginnings of contours. Thus, the listener does not directly respond to mean F_0 excursions. The end of the contour, moreover, is already in use as a finality marker (Production Code).

6. See also Caspers (2003), who finds that *absence* of a boundary tone, corresponding to mid pitch, tends to mark turn-keeping in Dutch.

6

Downtrends

6.1 Introduction

Utterances tend to fall in fundamental frequency, a phenomenon known as 'declination'. The explanation has been sought in falling subglottal pressure (Lieberman 1967; Collier 1975b). After expanding his lungs to take in breath, the speaker will slowly ease up on the tension of the muscles he used for the breath intake (probably the diaphragm, with or without the aid of his chest muscles), so as to slow down the elastic recoil of the lungs and thereby prolong the period of positive pressure below the larynx which is needed for the production of a fluent portion of speech. Unless the speaker uses his muscles to force out the remaining air from his lungs during this slowed down exhalation phase, the pressure below the larynx will drop. Since lower subglottal pressure will lead to slower vocal fold vibration rates, F_0 declination will result.

As with the F_0 dependence on larynx size and articulatory precision discussed in the previous chapter, the effect has a physiological explanation, but many instantiations of the phenomenon are likely be under the control of the speaker (cf. 't Hart, Collier, and Cohen 1990: 136). The number of times that portions of speech bounded by air intakes, termed 'breath groups' by Lieberman (1967), coincide with intonational phrases is low, though much better than chance. In a study on Dutch, Appels (1985) found that 30 out of 70 ι-breaks coincided with the audible intake of air. Strik and Boves (1995) provide a summary of the physiological research into the question whether declination is automatic or under speaker control, and, if under control, whether this is done by manipulating the subglottal pressure or by engaging the laryngeal muscles. They conclude that the answer is difficult to give, as it depends in part on the operational definition of the F_0 downtrend, but that falling subglottal pressure is likely to play a significant role.

If we base ourselves on observations of communicative function, there are ample indications that declination is under speaker control (Grønnum 1992). As explained in section 6.2, there are in fact three separate aspects of the declining trend that we need to consider, even though it will not always be possible to keep them separate. First, there is the overall downsloping pattern, discussed in section (6.3). Second, final lowering is an additional lowering at the utterance end and is discussed in section 6.4. Third, reset, a return to a higher pitch at the beginning of a new utterance, is discussed in section 6.5. The point will be made that the Production Code is typically exploited through final lowering and reset.

As is to be expected, grammaticalized reflexes of declination, final lowering, and reset are found in many languages. The grammaticalization of declination is downstep. In such cases, the pitch drop has a specific phonological or morphological context, and the drop therefore contrasts discretely with its absence. Downstep provides a powerful illustration of the language-specific nature of grammaticalizations, in that the triggering context varies greatly across languages. In the section on downstep, also upstep will be discussed, which is a reflex of the desire to enhance the discrete nature of the step from H and L across a declining utterance, to prevent it from being interpreted as part of the declining trend. It, too, may be grammaticalized. Grammaticalized final lowering occurs in a number of languages; in the examples I have, these also have downstep. Grammaticalized reset is rare, but a case has been made for Dutch, which will briefly be presented in that section.

Phonetic aspects will be discussed in two sections in particular. The 1984 Liberman–Pierrehumbert model for implementing downstep and final lowering in English will be presented in section 6.4, where it naturally fits in with their demonstration that final lowering exists as a separate phenomenon. Section 6.6.3 presents an evaluation of the need for a representation of pitch range or register, an explanation of the abstract register reference line projected by listeners, and a methodological section on the measurement of declination.

6.2   Declination

Declination is the gradual, time-dependent downsloping of the fundamental frequency across points that might be expected to be equal (Cohen and Hart 1967; Ladd 1984). The effect is most straightforwardly observable in pronunciations of sentences with sequences of identical tones. In figure 6.1, the results from two male and two female speakers of Mandarin are given for sentences with sequences of 11 H-tones (Tone 1; the second word has Tone 2, or LH). The dotted graphs indicate the results for the same sentences with an additional final toneless syllable *le*. They show that in this type of structure, there is no effect of final lowering on the last syllable, since the utterances with *le* and those without have identical targets of the last H-tone. In figure 6.2, average F_0 of pronunciations of sentences with 12 consecutive H-tones, M-tones, and L-tones is given for the initial syllable (A) and three last syllables (B, C, and D) by three male and one female speaker of Yorùbá (Connell and Ladd 1990). The comparisons we can now make across

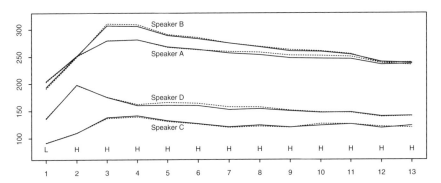

Fig. 6.1 Average F_0 trajectories in all-H utterances by four speakers of Mandarin Chinese, with (········) and without (----) an added toneless syllable (from Shih 1997).

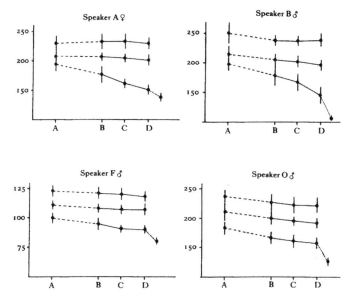

Fig. 6.2 Average F_0 peak values of H-toned syllables from first syllable (A) via the antepenultimate (B) and penultimate (C) syllables to the final syllable (D) in all-H, all-M, and all-L utterances by four speakers of Yorùbá. The added data-point in the all-L graphs indicates the pitch at the end of the last syllable, and thus shows the drop through the last syllable. From Connell and Ladd (1990).

languages and, within Yorùbá, across tones, suggest that declination is under speaker control. A comparison of Mandarin and Yorùbá shows that all-H sequences may be realized differently in different languages. Within Yorùbá, declination is only present in the all-L sentences, where we also see considerable final lowering. In the all-M and all-H sentences, there is neither declination nor final lowering. Equally, identical structures may be pronounced differently in the same language by different speakers, as illustrated for the two-tone language Bambara investigated by Mountford (1983): one speaker has declination in sequences of eight H-tones, but no final lowering, while the other has no declination, but clear final lowering.

The meaningful use of declination in phonetic implementation is illustrated by Thorsen (1978) and Grønnum (1983a, 1992) on the basis of data from scripted speech in Danish. Declination was steepest in terminal declarative sentences, and absent in interrogative renderings of syntactically declarative sentences. Interrogative sentences that were syntactically marked either by subject–verb inversion or by a WH-word, had intermediate slopes, with some speakers staying closer to the type of slope used with the statements, and others staying closer to the level, echo-question condition. The reason why the speakers had the least declination in the 'echo questions' is that there are no syntactic markers of interrogativity in these sentences (cf. also Grønnum 1992, Grønnum 1998). The relation between rate of declination in questions and the presence of morphological markers was confirmed in a large-scale experiment on Dutch (Haan 2002) (see also section 6.6.3).

6.3 Downstep

There is a discrete difference between a downstepped realization of a tone and a non-downstepped one. The phenomenon was first reported for languages spoken in West Africa, when a distinction was drawn between 'terraced-level' tone languages and 'discrete-level' tone languages by Welmers (1959), where 'terracing' is to be equated with 'downstepping' (Stewart 1966). Languages with tone terracing typically have a two-way or three-way tone contrast, with every syllable bearing tone, in which an H-tone is realized at a lower pitch than a preceding H-tone if L intervenes. Each such downstep has a persisting effect on the pitch range of the utterance, so that once a downstep has taken place, any following H-tone will maximally reach the pitch of the preceding downstepped one. A new L will trigger a downstep on the next H, and so on. Since L-tones may follow a roughly similar trend line as the H-tones (though at a lower pitch), a late H may be pronounced at a lower pitch than an early L. A graphic illustration is given in (1).

(1)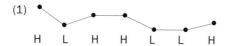
      H   L   H   H   L   L   H

The difference between phonetic declination and phonological downstep is illustrated for Japanese in figure 6.3, from Poser (1984). The effect of downstep is seen in panel (a). In the contour in panel (b), there is no downstep, since the first phrase does not contain the triggering context, the pitch accent HL. Here, the downtrend, which is smaller than in the other contour, is purely due to declination.

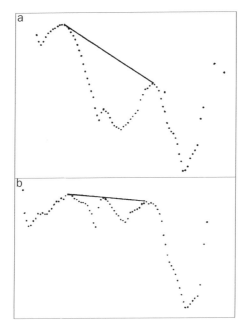

Fig. 6.3 Downstep (upper panel) and declination (lower panel) in Japanese. No F_0 scale: F_0 reaches a higher peak in the contour in the upper panel. From Poser (1984).

6.3.1 Automatic and non-automatic downstep

Until Stewart (1966), downstep after H . . . L, shown graphically in (1), was distinguished as 'downdrift' from the apparently spontaneous occurrence of downstep, indicated as H$^!$H and illustrated in (2), where the second H is downstepped even though there is no apparent L to trigger it. To express the fact that this apparently spontaneous downstep reaches the same pitch as the downstep after H . . . L and has the same effect on following Hs, an observation he credited to Winston (1960), Stewart proposed the terms 'automatic' downstep for the L-induced type (the earlier 'downdrift') and 'non-automatic' downstep for the apparently spontaneous type. The phonetic equivalence of Hs with automatic and non-automatic downstep has been confirmed for Igbo by Laniran (1990) and for Bimoba by Snider (1998).

(2)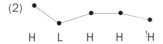

   H   L   H   H $^!$H

Working out a suggestion by Stewart (1966), Clements and Ford (1980) argued on the basis of data from Kikuyu that in that language, non-automatic downstep should be represented as the presence of an L-tone which is not associated with a TBU. In Kikuyu, a language with two phonological tones, some words induce downstep on a following word, while other words do not. After a downstep-inducing word, an H appears as $^!$H, but after other words it remains H. Clements and Ford accounted for the difference between the two types of words by assuming that the downstep-inducing words have a final floating L, as do the second words in the examples in (3). For instance, in [áhɛìré mwàɣáhìɲá L $^!$ɲátá], downstep on the third word is triggered by the second word, giving a surface sequence H $^!$H. This is shown in (3a). In (3b), a L $^!$H sequence is created, because L, too, undergoes downstep in Kikuyu, and if it does is lowered by a step which is equivalent to that for $^!$H.[1] This is shown in (3c). In all three examples, the transition between the first and the second H is free from downstep.

(3)

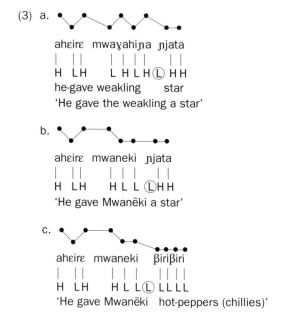

a.
```
aheirɛ mwaɣahiɲa ɲjata
|  ||  | | | |  || 
H  LH  L H L H Ⓛ H H
he-gave weakling   star
'He gave the weakling a star'
```

b.
```
aheirɛ mwaneki ɲjata
|  ||  | | |  ||
H  LH  H L L  ⒧H H
'He gave Mwanẽki a star'
```

c.
```
aheirɛ mwaneki   βiriβiri
|  ||  | | |  ||||
H  LH  H L L Ⓛ L L L L
'He gave Mwanẽki   hot-peppers (chillies)'
```

Kikuyu *only* has non-automatic downstep. This is clear, for instance, from the pronunciation of the verb in (3), in which the last syllable is not appreciably lower than the first. That is, the phonetic implementation module is activated by the floating L, not by associated L. The same is true for Bamileke (Hyman 1979). More commonly, both associated and floating Ls trigger downstep, as is the case in Baule (Ahoua 1996) and Chumburung (Snider 1999), in addition to Igbo and Bimoba.

6.3.2 Independent evidence for floating L

The assumption that a floating L-tone precedes a tone with non-automatic down-step is supported in many languages by cases of synchronic processes creating floating L-tones, as noted by Stewart (1966). Stewart recognized floating Ls as tones with a 'zero tone bearing unit'; Meeussen (1970) referred to these L-tones as 'asyllabic'. In one type, an L-tone is preserved after the deletion of the vowel it was associated with, a phenomenon known as 'tonal stability' (Goldsmith 1976). This is shown for Kanakuru in (4a). Here, [u] is deleted, but its L is preserved, as evidenced by the preservation of the downstep on the next H-toned word. A second type is due to the rightward spreading of a H-tone, as a result of which a L-tone gets displaced from its TBU. The floating L preserves its effect on following H-tones, as shown in (4b) (Clements 1983, citing from Newman 1974).

(4) a. jímù ɗáɗáu → [jím ꜜɗáɗáu]   'We used to play'
    b. kúrè mónó → [kúré ꜜmónó]   'my corn'

Floating L-tones may reveal their presence other than through triggering downstep. In Bambara, where words are either high-toned (e.g. jírí 'tree', só 'house') or low-toned (e.g. mùsò 'woman', sò 'horse'), the definite article is a tonal suffix which just consists of L. Its effect is seen in two ways. First, it triggers downstep on a following H, as in (5); and second, it surfaces in utterance-final syllables, where it forms a fall with H, as shown in (6) (Bird 1966).

(5) a. jírí tέ   'It is not a tree'
    b. jírí ꜜtέ   'It is not the tree'

(6) a. jírí   'a tree'
    b. jírî   'the tree'

There is a third way in which the suffixal floating L of Bambara reveals itself. Quite generally, the final syllable of an L-toned word receives an inserted H before another L-tone. In monosyllabic words, both L and the inserted H occur on the same syllable, forming an LH contour, but in polysyllabic words the final syllable is given over to the inserted H. In (7), this is shown for low-toned words with one, two, and three syllables, respectively.

(7) a. sò   'horse'   sǒ sàbà   'three horses'
    b. mùsò   'woman'   mùsó sàbà   'three women'
    c. nàmàsà   'banana'   nàmàsá sàbà   'three bananas'

Interestingly, H-insertion is also triggered by a floating L-tone. In (8b), where a low-toned word precedes a high-toned word, the effect of the definite suffix L is seen in combination with its downstep-inducing force. Floating L triggers H-insertion on the last syllable of *mùsò*, and then triggers downstep on the H of the auxiliary *bé*. The indefinite version is given in (8a).

(8) a. mùsò bé yàn   'A woman is here'
    b. mùsó ꜜbé yàn   'The woman is here'

While the L triggering downstep may itself be invisible, its presence can thus be independently demonstrated in languages like Bambara. In the next section, we will see that downstep may be triggered by other contexts than a preceding L.

6.3.3 Downstep without preceding L

Many cases of non-automatic downstep undoubtedly have their origin in the preservation of L-tones after some phonological process deprived them of their tone-bearers. However, synchronically, downstep need not be triggered by an L-tone, floating or associated. In many cases, the postulation of an L in the representation would be arbitrary, or even counter-productive. It is not uncommon for languages to downstep H after H, without there being any indication that an L-tone intervenes between them. For instance, in Kishambaa, an H-toned word like *dú* 'only' will be downstepped after another H-toned word, as in *mwáná ¹dú* 'only a child' (Odden 1986). Since Kishambaa has a three-way surface contrast after H-tones, as illustrated by *kúì* 'dog', *ngó¹tó* 'sheep', and *nyóká* 'snake', it is reasonable to assume that the downstep *within* words is triggered in the same way as the downstep *across* words, i.e. by a preceding H. Accordingly, Odden proposes that words like *kúì* have HL, words like *ngó ¹tó* HH, with one H triggering and one undergoing downstep, while words like *nyóká* have a single H. The latter type will undergo downstep only if occurring after another H-tone, but word-internally, there cannot be any action. Thus, *nyóká* triggers downstep in (9a), where *dú* follows it, and undergoes it in (9b), where high-toned *ní* precedes it. In the same contexts, *ngó¹tó* triggers and undergoes downstep in addition to its word-internal downstep. This elegant solution is preferable to a description whereby every H-toned word receives a default L to its right (or, equivalently, to its left) such that all word-internal downstepped tones are preceded by a word-internal floating L. The tone would be, as they say, 'diacritic', i.e. postulated to create an effect, but not independently in evidence.

(9) a. nyóká ¹dú   'only a snake'   ngó¹tó ¹dú   'only sheep'
     b. ní ¹nyóká   'It is a snake'   ní ¹ngó¹tó   'They are/It is a sheep'

In intonation, the pattern of downstepped H after H is exploited in the description of French by Post (2000b) (cf. chapter 13). Helsloot's (1995: 91) 'Pitch Jump' in adjacent accented syllables in Italian poetry, described by her as H* L*, can similarly be interpreted as H* H* being realized as H* ¹H* if occurring on adjacent syllables, as shown in (10). In chapter 13, some arguments are given against an analysis of the equivalent French contour as H* L*.

(10)

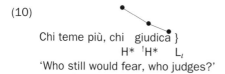

Chi teme più, chi giudica }
                    H* ¹H*   L₁
'Who still would fear, who judges?'

6.3.4 On the status of a downstepped tone

A language with two tones and downstep is distinct from a language with three tones, H, M, and L. That is, the result of downstep is not a phonological mid tone.

For one thing, if a language has a third tone, M, its occurrence will not cause all following Hs to be M, which would be the effect if M were equated with ¹H. The structural nature of the downstep trigger and its discrete effect do not imply that there is a phonological entity [downstepped tone], or a phonological feature [+downstep]. Thus, the H of H-toned Kishambaa words is not first changed to some phonological entity ¹H and then sent to the phonetic implementation module. Rather, in the above transcriptions, the notation ¹H has the status of a phonetic symbol: the !-marked H is implemented as a downstepped tone, because the context for such implementation is present.

This solution (e.g. Clements 1979; Pierrehumbert 1980), correctly expresses that L, H, and ¹H represent only a two-way contrast. Admittedly, taking a strictly local view of a non-initial syllable might lead us to see a paradigmatic system of three terms. However, once we include the left-hand syllable in our window of observation (assuming a situation with tones on all syllables), it will become clear that one of these three is uniquely determined by the preceding context, and that there are therefore only two choices. If we were to take the 'local' view to its logical extreme, we might – inappropriately – argue that on a syllable towards the end of a longer utterance, quite a few tones might have occurred. That is, if the downstepped tone were a phonological entity on the grounds that it would be different from high tone, the question arises as to what kind of entity the next downstepped tone must be (presumably ¹¹H), and so on (cf. Pierrehumbert 1980: 140; van der Hulst and Snider 1993). It is often convenient to use the notation ¹H in transcriptions, but the downstep marker is not included in the transcription, the assumption being that the reader should recognize the context concerned.

6.3.5 Total downstep

The 'implementation' view of downstep may seem to run into difficulties in the case of languages in which the product of downstep is equivalent to an L-tone. To be sure, in many languages this phonetic equivalence does not in fact exist. In languages with H, L, and M, the downstepped H is typically pronounced at a higher pitch than M, as in Ngamambo (Hyman 1986); and in two-tone languages, the downstepped H is usually higher in pitch than L. However, in some languages, like Chumburung and Kikuyu (Clements and Ford 1980; Snider 1999), the product of downstep is phonetically indistinguishable from an L-tone, a phenomenon which was called 'total downstep' by Meeussen (1970). Still, we cannot equate ¹H with L in a language with total downstep: the equation would only be valid when looking at the downstepped tone without its following context. When seen without its preceding context, the tone is an H-tone, since a following L-tone is lower. Moreover, recall that Kikuyu downsteps L-tones after floating L, as shown in (3c). If ¹H is L, then what would a post-downstep ¹L be?

The equivalence of ¹H and L is thus created in the phonetic implementation. The specification of the gesture for a transition from H to L is apparently the same as that between H and ¹H or that between L and ¹L. The idea that there is a single phonetic routine for stepping down within the ι is perhaps supported by the fact that Kikuyu does not create double downsteps in the context H Ⓛ L. Here, the floating L might be expected to create a double downstep on the following L: since it is already lower than H because it is L, Ⓛ might cause a further lowering. This context, which was omitted from (3), is given in (12). It shows how lexically L-toned [βìrìβìrì] has H-tone throughout, while the floating L appears all the way at the end of the utterance. In (12b), it appears after the penultimate syllable of [kèŋàɲi], which has the last L-tone in the underlying representation. In other words, Ⓛ is shifted across a maximal string of L-tones, which themselves are raised to H, a process called DOWNSTEP DISPLACEMENT by Clements and Ford (1980). (Alternatively, Ls after H Ⓛ might be ruled illegal; H could then occupy the empty syllables, squeezing Ⓛ between it and the next H or the utterance end.)

(11)   DOWNSTEP DISPLACEMENT H Ⓛ $L_0^nH \rightarrow H H_0^n$ Ⓛ H

(12)   a.

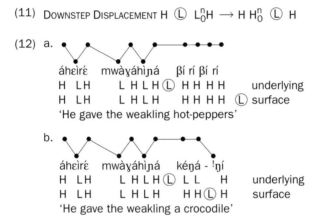

áhɛìrɛ́   mwàɣáhìɲá   βí rí βí rí
H LH   L H L H Ⓛ H H H H   underlying
H LH   L H L H   H H H H Ⓛ surface
'He gave the weakling hot-peppers'

    b.

áhɛìrɛ́   mwàɣáhìɲá   kéɲá - ¹ɲí
H LH   L H L H Ⓛ L L   H   underlying
H LH   L H L H   H HⓁ H   surface
'He gave the weakling a crocodile'

6.3.6   Morphological triggers of downstep

The pervasive grammaticalization of downstep is apparent from the diversity of phonological contexts that trigger it. Besides the two left-hand contexts HL and H discussed above, the variation between no downstep (cf. Welmers's discrete-level tone languages), automatic and non-automatic downstep, and the possibility of a downstepping L, as in Kikuyu and Dinka (Andersen 1987), contexts may vary in other ways. Three-tone languages may, like Moba, or may not, like Yorúbà, downstep M-tones as well as H-tones, or they may allow both L and M to trigger downstep of H, like Ga'anda (cf. Pierrehumbert and Beckman 1988; van der Hulst and Snider 1993).

Morphology may also play a role. Japanese has downstep after accentual HL, but not after a boundary-tone sequence HL (Pierrehumbert and Beckman 1988). Morphological uses of the downstep trigger are common in languages

spoken in Africa. For instance, Kikuyu Noun–Adjective NPs are characterized by the absence of floating L after the noun, regardless of whether an L
appears in the lexical representation. A modal morpheme consisting of floating
L occurs in the same language, termed ASSERTIVE DOWNSTEP (13): verbs used
in positive, non-conditional expressions must be followed by floating L, which
occurs after the first clause-internal constituent if there is one (Clements and Ford
1980).

(13) ASSERTIVE DOWNSTEP: [   ]$_V$ ([   ]$_X$) Ⓛ
                               [+assert]

As a result of (13), an assertive clause has a final floating L when the verb is
clause-final. Unless it is final in the ι, the floating L will induce downstep on the
first word of the next clause. In clause-internal position, the floating L occurs after
the next constituent over, and triggers downstep on any following word within
the ι. As a result, in assertive contexts, the difference between downstep-inducing
nouns and other nouns is neutralized. This is shown in (14a), where [móɣèràniá]
'examiner', which has no floating L underlyingly, appears after an assertive verb
as a downstep-inducing noun, exactly like [moàɣáhìná] 'weakling' in (14b),
which has a floating L lexically. The difference comes out again in (l4c,d), where
the word for 'examiner', but not that for 'weakling', has lost its downstep, since
the verb is no longer assertive.[2]

(14) a. ndɔːnìrɛ́ móɣèrànìá ˈðeínè wáɲómbà
        I-saw examiner inside house
        'Did I see the examiner in the house?'
     b. ndɔːnìrɛ́ mwàɣáhìná ˈðeínè wáɲómbà
        I-saw weakling inside house
        'Did I see the weakling in the house?'
     c. ndjɔ̀níˈrɛ́ móðèrànìá ðeínè wáɲómbà
        I-didn't-see examiner inside house
        'Didn't I see the examiner in the house?
     d. ndjɔ̀níˈrɛ́ɛ mwàðáhìná ˈðeínè wáɲómbà
        I-didn't-see weakling inside house
        'Didn't I see the weakling in the house?'

It is tempting to interpret Kikuyu ASSERTIVE DOWNSTEP as a grammaticalization of final lowering, since positive assertion can be associated with finality,
although the fact that it need not be clause-final speaks against this. A clearer
case of morphemic status of a meaning derived from Production Code is presented by downstep as an intonational morpheme. Van den Berg, Gussenhoven,
and Rietveld (1992) claim this is the case in Dutch, where it adds a finality
meaning: there is no room for further discussion. In this view, a phonological
representation H . . . H*L can be pronounced with or without downstep of the
H*-tone(s) within the ι.[3] Van den Berg *et al.* assume that the morpheme is attached

to the *ι*-node, and is phonologically instantiated as the implementation of downstep over the entire phrase. Thus, to use an example from 't Hart and Collier (1980), (15a) contrasts with (15b) in lacking the downstep morpheme. Downstep in English may exclude the final pitch accent (Ladd 1983c; Gussenhoven 1983c; Truckenbrodt 2002a), and the same is true for Dutch, so that the attachment of a downstep trigger to the *ι* may be analytically too crude. See also sections 15.5.3 and 7.2.1.

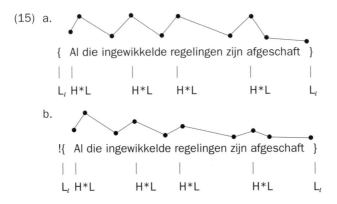

(15) a.

{ Al die ingewikkelde regelingen zijn afgeschaft }

L*ι* H*L   H*L   H*L   H*L   L*ι*

b.

!{ Al die ingewikkelde regelingen zijn afgeschaft }

L*ι* H*L   H*L   H*L   H*L   L*ι*

6.3.7   H-raising (upstep)

Languages with downstep may also have upstep, also known as H-raising. Upstep raises the pitch of an H-tone immediately before an L-tone, and occurs for instance in Bambara (Mountford 1983: 122), Yorùbá (Connell and Ladd 1990) and Kirimi (Hyman 1993). Ergonomically, it could be interpreted as contrast enhancement, in that it facilitates the perception of the L-tone, which is now less easily mistaken for a downstepped H, or even a plain H which has been lowered by declination. From the point of view of the speaker, it can be seen as anticipatory raising, which provides him with more room for the upcoming lowering of the contour (Rialland 2001). This functional interpretation is supported by the fact that in African languages H-raising always co-occurs with downstep (Snider 1990).

H-raising provides further evidence of the reality of floating L-tones, since H is raised before associated and floating Ls alike in some languages, like Kirimi. The process is illustrated graphically in (16), where it is due to an associated L, and (17), where it is due to a floating L. In both cases, the H-tone preceeding L has a higher target than in (1) and (2), respectively. Other languages, like Mankon, have H-rasing only before floating L, not when L is associated.

(16)

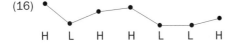

H   L   H   H   L   L   H

(17)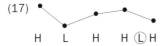

H   L   H   H ⓁH

Typical illustrations from Engenni are given in (18), cited from Hyman (1993), where the up-arrow indicates the occurrence of upstep. The first syllable of (18a) is lower than that in (18b), which is subject to H raising. Moreover, when vowel deletion leaves a floating L, as in (19a), raising nevertheless occurs on the preceding H. It can occur more than once, as shown in (19b), but only if an overt (surface) L-tone intervenes, as illustrated in (19c).

(18) a. ópílópó 'pig meat'

    b. ↑ónù   'mother'

(19) a. /ó vúmù/ → ó ↑vúm ópílópó 'she will dry the pig meat'

    b. ì↑kpílà↑má nà 'the snail'

    c. /ó dírè ẹ̀dà/ → ó ↑dír ẹdà 'she will cook beans' (* ó ↑dír ↑ẹ̀dà)

Phonological contexts for upstep will vary. In Kachru, H-raising occurs *after* floating L, as illustrated in (20), where it occurs twice (Snider 1990). The H after the upstepped syllable returns to non-upstepped pitch, so that the two upstepped Hs have equal pitch.

(20)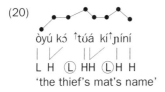

òyú kɔ́ ↑túá kí↑ɲíní

L H Ⓛ HH ⓁH H

'the thief's mat's name'

In Mankon, too, floating L triggers upstep of a following H, if preceded by LH, as illustrated in (21), where floating L is a genitive affix. In the case of Mankon, a following H retains the upstepped pitch, but since a surface L will inevitably intervene before a new upstep context is reached, the language avoids the creation of sequences of adjacent upstepping targets longer than two (Hyman 1993).[4]

(21)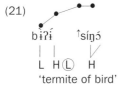

bìʔí   ↑síŋɔ́

L HⓁ H

'termite of bird'

Upstep of H before L may be anticipated by a preceding H, when HHHL is pronounced with increasing F₀ for the H-tones in Yorùbá (Laniran 1990: 75ff.). While recognizing the existence of this type of coarticulation, Clements (1996) claimed that on the basis of the African evidence, cumulative upstep, the mirror image of downstep, does not occur. However, with reference to this claim, Snider (1999: 99ff.) brings up the case of Acatlán Mixtec, which is described by Pike and Wistrand (1974) as having exactly that. This is because it upsteps H after H, as in (22), where the steeply low pitch of the last lexical L will be due to a final L_i (my own addition). Observe that word-internal upstep occurs, too. The case therefore is the mirror image of Kisambaa, which downsteps H after H within and across words.

(22)

{ ko čitu wa ni me e }
  | || | | |||
  H HH H H HL L_i
NEG kisses so 2SG baby
'You don't kiss the baby so much'

Upstep was introduced as an implementation rule into the description of English intonation by Pierrehumbert (1980), who applied it to final H_i after H, a context that has been adopted for many other languages, and L_i after H, which extension is specific to her analysis of English.

6.4 Final lowering

The end of the utterance often gets an extra dose of the lowering, known as final lowering. Liberman and Pierrehumbert (1984) showed its existence as an independent component in English intonation contours by applying a simple downstepping model to multi-accented utterances. Panel (a) in figure 6.4 is based on the mean F₀ of the five peaks of twenty renderings of a list of five berry names by one speaker speaking with wide pitch.[5] The connecting line represents a fit of the first four peaks, based on a model with a decaying exponential (Liberman and Pierrehumbert 1984: 186). This model is given in (23), where P1 is a beginning value in Hz and d a downstep factor between zero and 1. Every peak results from a multiplication of the F₀ of the previous peak by d, which will cause each step down to be smaller than the one before. To express the fact that the steps do not go down beyond a minimum value, a constant r is included to represent the reference line. For instance, if $r = 75$, P1 $= 200$ Hz and $d = 0.5$, then P2 $= ((200 - 75) \times .5) + 75 = 137.5$ Hz, P3 $= 106.25$, P4 $= 90.6$ Hz and P5 $= 82.8$ Hz. A much used value for d is 0.7.

(23) $P_{i+1} = (d \times (P_i - r)) + r$

Values for P1, r, and d were chosen so as to provide the best fit for the first four peaks: the first is near-perfect, the second is marginally below, and the third

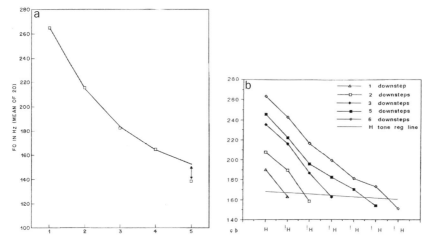

Fig. 6.4 Panel (a): Asymptote predicting the F_0 of five peaks in English utterances containing five berry names, based on a model for the first four peaks, and mean actual F_0 of the five peaks. The double-headed arrow indicates how far the fifth observed peak value is below that predicted on the basis of the downtrend of the first four, from Liberman and Pierrehumbert (1984). Panel (b): Near-linear descending downstepping with anticipatory raising in Dagara utterance with different numbers of downsteps. From Rialland (2001).

marginally above the actual value, while the fourth, too, is very close to the mark. Clearly, 'laboratory speech' of this kind can be modelled by a decaying exponential. However, when the model is used to predict the value of the fifth peak, the predicted value is considerably higher than the actual value. Clearly, the subtraction of a final lowering term from the F_0 of the last peak would improve the model.

6.4.1 On 'preplanning'

The Liberman–Pierrehumbert model has improved our conception of phonetic implementation considerably, and has inspired similar investigations of English and Dutch (Ladd 1988; van den Berg, Gussenhoven, and Rietveld 1992). At the same time, it must not be taken to represent a general model of the implementation of downstepping contours. A claim inherent in (23) is that, given some choice of pitch span and pitch register, a speaker is able to go from one accent to the next by applying d to the preceding $^!$H*, without knowing how many accents will follow, an implication known as 'no preplanning'. At best, this can be taken to mean that preplanning is not *required*, since evidence of control in the execution of downtrends is abundant. In addition to Grønnum's data (1983a) (p. 100) showing that d is chosen for communicative effect, Rialland (2001) demonstrates for different languages that speakers often anticipate the length of the utterance, beginning higher as the utterance is longer, or may minimize d towards the end

of the utterance to prevent the pitch from falling much lower. Her data show that
not all types of implementation are compatible with 'no preplanning'. In Dagara,
each step down is about equal in size, and since declarative utterances tend to end
at the same low pitch, as they often do in languages generally, this means that
speakers begin higher as there are more downsteps in the sentence. This is shown
in panel (b) of figure 6.4. It is interesting to speculate, as does Nick Clements
(personal communication, November 2000), that the asymptotic pattern may be
more common in languages without lexically distinctive downstep, like English,
than in languages with, like Dagara and Kikuyu.

6.4.2   Grammaticalization of final lowering

Variation in final lowering may be grammaticalized distinctly from downstep.
Basque, an SOV language, obligatorily reduces the pitch range of finite verbs
in declarative sentences, discussed as 'subordination' in chapter 9. Kirimi generally has non-total downstep of H, but the last $^!$H (or sequence of $^!$H-tones) *is*
equivalent to L (Hyman 1993). In Ngiti, which contrasts H, M, L, and a contour LM, an L-tone is pronounced as low level pitch, except in utterance-final
position, when there is a low fall (Kutsch Lojenga 1994: 94); no such final falls
occur when the last tone is H or M. Languages may also avoid raising effects
on final syllables. Kikerewe has a general rule of H-Doubling, which spreads an
underlying H-tone to the next syllable, except when this syllable is final in the
utterance (Odden 1997). Final lowering is tied in with downstep in Dinka, which
downsteps H after H L. However, in utterance-final syllables, a final H-tone syllable always undergoes downstep, regardless of the left-hand context (Andersen
1987).

Many of these effects can be phonologically attributed to a final L_ι or L_υ.
This is clearly also the case in Kikuyu, which downsteps an υ-final H-tone
or a sequence of H-tones. Because L and $^!$H are equivalent ('total downstep',
section 6.3.5), this FLATTENING can either be stated as a replacement of H by
L or as the insertion of a floating L-tone before υ-final Hs, as has been done in
(24). In (25a), phonological /kèŋàŋí/ is phonetically realized as low–low–high,
since its H-tone is non-final, but phonological /ɣèðò:kú/ undergoes FLATTENING,
as its H-tone is υ-final, and so does the word for 'crocodile' when pronounced in
isolation, as in (25b), both of these coming out as low–low–low. Interestingly, the
structural context for FLATTENING must be adjacent H L_υ, because when there is
independent evidence for an utterance-final (L), which will occur between H and
L_υ, no flattening occurs, as the intervening floating L-tone destroys the righthand
context for the floating L-insertion. This is shown in (25c), where the floating L
is due to ASSERTIVE DOWNSTEP (13) (see also section 6.3.6).

(24) FLATTENING $\emptyset \rightarrow$ (L) / ___ $H_0^n \, L_\upsilon$

(25) a.

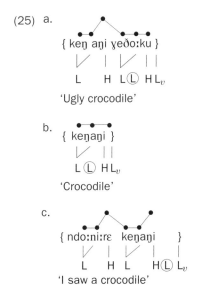

{ keŋ aɲi ɣeðoːku }

L   H LⓁ HL_v

'Ugly crocodile'

b. { keŋaɲi }

L Ⓛ HL_v

'Crocodile'

c.

{ ndoːniːrɛ keŋaɲi   }

L   H L   HⓁ L_v

'I saw a crocodile'

In intonation-only languages, variation in final lowering is often grammaticalized, in which case low endings mark finality, while high or mid-pitched tone
realizations mark non-finality (Production Code). For instance, in Dutch, H_ι is
used to signal continuation (Geluykens and Swerts 1994), while also falls to mid
pitch may have this function (Swerts, Collier, and Terken 1994). Phonologically,
these suspended falls are interpreted as a H*L pitch accent without a final L_ι
(Gussenhoven and Rietveld 1992), while the fall to fully low is H*L L_ι (see also
section 7.3.2 and chapter 15).

6.5 Initial high pitch: reset

The third aspect of declining trends manifests itself in the high beginnings of
utterances, for which the term 'reset' is used. Reset amounts to the interruption of
the downtrend, whether this is just phonetic declination or includes phonological
downstep. For instance, downstep in Japanese and Basque is interrupted by the
start of a new Intermediate Phrase (ip) boundary, while in French, English, and
Dutch it is interrupted by a new ι. Resets may thus be important indications of
phrasing structure.

6.5.1 Interpreting high beginnings

An important issue in studies on reset is the question whether it is just the interruption of downstep, or whether any systematic differentiation in the amount of

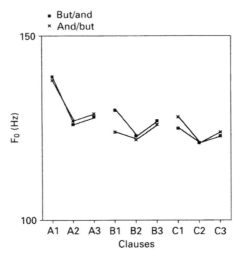

Fig. 6.5 F_0 of accent peaks in 'A and B, but C'-type sentence and in 'A, but B and C'-type sentence. From Ladd (1990).

reset is to be recognized. One motivation for raising the beginning of a phrase is to increase the distance to upcoming lower pitched tones, in which case the speaker's control is exercised for phonological contrast enhancement (see section 5.3.2), as was illustrated for Dagara in panel (b) of figure 6.4. As explained in section 5.8, however, high beginnings are also widely interpreted in terms of the Production Code. The higher the reset, the clearer the break with the preceding utterance will be perceived to be. There are many findings that confirm this, even for Dagara (Rialland 2001). Just as final lowering will affect only the last couple of syllables of the declining domain, so reset need not affect the slope of the entire phrase, and often there is just initial raising, to use Ladd's (1988) term. The English data presented by Ladd (1990b), from one of the four speakers reported in Ladd (1988), show raising only for the initial accent, as shown by the data-points in figure 6.5, which represent the three accents in each of the three subclauses of two minimally different sentences. One is the 'and/but' sentence *Allan is a stronger campaigner, and Ryan has more popular policies, but Warren has a lot more money*; and the other is the 'but/and' sentence which is obtained by switching round *but* and *and* of the first. The conjunction *but* naturally constitutes the right-hand branch of the first, binary-branching node, while *and* introduces the right-hand branch of the node below. Accordingly, the F_0 of the first accent in the *but*-clause may be expected to be higher than that in the *and*-clause, because it introduces a more significant break. As observed by Ladd (1988), it is in fact only the first accent after *but* which is higher than the first accent after *and*, the second and third showing no effect.

The connection between the height of the reset and degree of disjuncture was earlier made by Brazil (1985: 186), who distinguishes three levels of contour

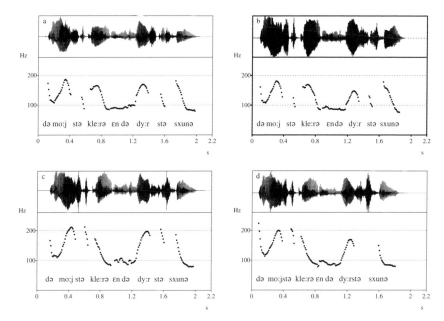

Fig. 6.6 Pronunciations of *De mooiste kleren (en) de duurste schoenen* 'The most beautiful clothes (and) the most expensive shoes' without accentual downstep or phrasal downstep (panel a); with phrasal downstep only (panel b); with accentual downstep only (panel c); and with accentual and phrasal downstep (panel d).

beginning. To my knowledge, no clear evidence for a categorical three-way distinction exists in any language. However, a binary distinction was claimed to exist in Dutch between complete reset, where the pitch goes back to the height reached at the beginning of the previous ι, and what O'Shaughnessy and Allen (1983) called 'partial reset', where it falls below this value (van den Berg, Gussenhoven, and Rietveld 1992). Partial reset was described as 'phrasal downstep', and if downstep applies within the phrase concerned, we have an instance of downstep-within-downstep, or nested downstep (Clements 1983; Ladd 1988; Ladd 1993a). While in English and Dutch regular downstep (referred to as 'accentual downstep' by van den Berg *et al*. 1992), the pitch is lowered at every H* relative to the preceding H within the ι, in phrasal downstep there is a register lowering of the whole phrase relative to the preceding phrase. Significantly, the two types were consistently found to use different downstep factors in four speakers, the accentual downstep from the first H* to the second H* representing a larger interval than the phrasal downstep from the first H* to the first H* of the following phrase. This suggests that the implementation of phrasal downstep does not make use of the same d as accentual downstep. For a two-phrase sentence with more than one accent in each phrase, there are thus four distinct downstepping variants. This has been illustrated in figure 6.6 with the expression *De* MOOI*ste* KLE*ren* *(en) de* DUUR*ste* SCHOE*nen* 'The most beautiful clothes (and) the most expensive shoes.'

Extending Ladd's (1990a) single-factor implementation model, van den Berg, Gussenhoven, and Rietveld (1992) presented a phonetic implementation model including different factors for accentual and phrasal downstep.

6.6   Three phonetic issues

Declination has figured prominently in phonetic research. Three issues are of particular interest to phonologists. One is the extent to which pitch-span and register differences are to be represented phonologically. A second is the perception of an inferred declination line, as revealed through judgements of pitch height and prominence. The third issue, finally, is the extent to which declination can be measured.

6.6.1   Phonological gradience?

The idea that phonetic implementation is subject to purposeful speaker control, as laid out in chapter 4, naturally leads to the assumption that variation in pitch range and register are not represented in the phonology. There have, however, been proposals for the grammaticalization of pitch-range variation by researchers whose work is (or was, at the time) strongly committed to the phonetics–phonology distinction. Such proposals obviously do not espouse the assumption, made throughout in this book, that phonological representations are discrete. For instance, Pierrehumbert and Beckman (1988: 100) tentatively suggested that pitch-range specifications should be supplied in numerical form. In this option, the ι-node is given a value between 0 and 1, say, which is used by the phonetic implementation to create a contour with the corresponding pitch range. Second, tree-based representations are given by Clements (1983), for the description of downstep in tone languages, and Ladd (1990a), for the description of downstep and reset in English. For instance, the difference between the *but* and *and* conditions in figure 6.5 can be captured by a difference in branching of the register tree, although both would be instances of phrasal downstep in van den Berg *et al.* (1992).

Quite apart from the objections that have been raised against particular versions of tonal trees (Clements 1990; van den Berg, Gussenhoven, and Rietveld 1992), the question is whether any such representation is needed or, worse, whether it might not be counter-productive. Since speakers manipulate the phonetic implementation for communicative purposes, they may well reflect morpho-syntactic patterns of branching in the pitch at which they produce an ι, particularly its first accent. In their use of all three biological codes, including the Production Code, speakers intervene in the phonetics of contours in ways that need not be captured in discrete structures. In a related context, Hayes (1994) referred to this type of control as 'the beast' in the speaker, adding that 'the beast knows the grammar'. I am inclined to think that while it makes no sense to say that speakers are 'good at' having phonological representations, it does make sense to believe that some speakers have better control over their phonetic implementation, and thus express the morpho-syntactic constituency more competently during implementation than others, just as they may be better cyclists, or swimmers, or writers. This does not mean that fine-tuning in the expression of morpho-syntactic constituency should not be described, or is of less interest than if it were phonological. The point is merely one about where in language it is located.

A related issue concerns the representation of downstep and upstep. In section 6.3.4, it was argued that what makes the representation of a downstepping or upstepping tone unique is their context, rather than the representation of the tones themselves. However, the position has also been taken that these register shifts are represented more locally, either in terms of a feature [+downstep] (Ladd 1983c) or in terms of elements on a register tier. There have been different conceptions of the register tier (see also section 3.3.4). For Snider (1999), a register tier defines a string of register tones (h,l) that runs parallel to the string of regular H,L tones, both of which are associated with a 'tonal root node'. TBUs associate with this tonal root node, so that every TBU is specified by a register tone and by a regular tone. In (26), an underlying HLH is shown to the left of the arrow. Each TBU is associated with a register tone and a regular tone. Snider assumes that downstep is created by the spreading of the l-tone to the right-hand tonal node, with loss of h. This surface representation, whereby a downstepped H is represented as l,H and a non-downstepped one as h,H, is given to the right of the arrow, together with the phonetic implementation.

(26)

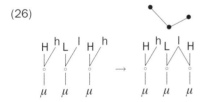

Again, in a conception of an implementation module which is context sensitive, it is not clear how the surface representation of (26) is superior to a plain HLH, given that the implementation module knows what to do. Also, it could be argued that the approach should be extended to a representation of final lowering, which is also tied to a specific context; or to represent the difference between Basque subordination and downstep, the latter of which makes a shallower pitch drop (see section 10.5.2), which decisions would make the representation still more complex. Again, the position taken in section 6.3.4 is that all systematic register changes can be effected in the implementation, provided the context for the raised or lowered tone is unique.

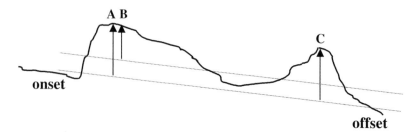

Fig. 6.7 Hypothetical F_0 contour with two projected reference lines. The declination effect is seen by comparing peaks A and C, which differ in F_0, but have equal perceived prominence. The effect of pegging the reference line higher or lower can be seen by comparing peaks A and B.

6.6.2   Perceived declination and the reference line

A number of experiments beginning with Pierrehumbert (1979) have shown that listeners use an abstract declination line when judging the height of the contour. She showed that when judging fundamental frequency peaks for (subjective) pitch height, American English subjects judged later peaks to be higher than earlier peaks, if they have the same fundamental frequency. As it happens, peaks occurring late in the utterance in her stimuli were preceded by other accent peaks, so that the results could either be explained by a time-dependent declination model or by an accent-driven declination model, one much like (23) but with a *d* closer to 1. Later experiments with Dutch listeners, which used one-peak stimuli in which the peak was either on an early or a late word, showed that the effect was due to elapsed time, i.e. was independent of the preceding accent (Gussenhoven and Rietveld 1988).[6] These data suggest that listeners assume some default rate of declination when listening to speech, as illustrated by peaks A and C in figure 6.7 (Ladd 1993b).

   In addition to the rate of declination of this abstract reference, we might wonder how listeners determine how high it is projected, relative to the observed contour. That is, what are the anchor-points in the observed contour which listeners use to peg this reference line? Experiments on Dutch reported in Gussenhoven, Repp, Rietveld, Rump, and Terken (1997) showed that the final pitch (the contour's 'offset') does not affect the perception of prominence of the last accent peak, meaning that the offset is not used to peg the reference line. However, as said in section 5.7, the contour's onset does make a difference: higher onsets (though not as high as would be appropriate for an initial H_i), in particular if they consist of at least three unaccented syllables, lead to less perceived prominence on the first accent peak. This suggests that listeners use the initial portion of the utterance to estimate a reference line and measure the prominence of the peaks accordingly. The effect of different hypothetical estimates is illustrated by peaks A and B in figure 6.7.

A further finding to arise from these experiments is that the abstract reference line is steeper as the first accent peak is higher, confirming the conception of Pierrehumbert (1980: 26), and the model in (23) (Liberman and Pierrehumbert 1984), which predicts larger distances between P_i and P_{i+1} as P_i, is higher.

6.6.3 Measuring declination

Research into downtrends would obviously benefit from a standard way of establishing how steeply a contour declines. As was clear from the results of Strik and Boves (1995), no such standard procedure exists. The problem is only in part one of designing a method for the creation of some declination index; it is also a matter of defining what other aspects of the intonation contour should be factored out before any measuring procedure is started. Studies of declination have been criticized for lumping together different aspects of the overall observable downtrend (Ladd 1984; Pierrehumbert and Beckman 1988: chapter 3). As one of these components, declination is purely the time-dependent downsloping of the contour, from which local downsteps as well as any initial raising and final lowering should be factored out before we can establish that the utterance has declination, as distinct from these other phenomena.

The right way to go will – as always – depend on what the research question is. If the researcher wishes to know whether language X has steeper overall downtrends than language Y, or if in some language statements have overall downtrends but questions overall uptrends, regardless of phonological composition, then obviously separating the various factors would not be desirable, since the interest is after all in these overall effects. However, if the interest is in modelling intonation, or in the speaker's physiological control of downstep versus that of declination, or in a demonstration that these are in fact separate factors, then an attempt must be made to factor out other effects. Unless speech corpora with the relevant annotations become available, the only way to do this is to draw up a carefully composed corpus of sentences in which the different factors are combined orthogonally. If a language allows identical phonological structures to be used for statements and questions, and has downstep, complementary sets of sentences with and without downstep can be constructed, with matching segmental conditions and lengths, which would have to be pronounced as questions and as statements. Further factors, like sentence length, could be added: if a 'long sentence' condition were created by the side of a 'short sentence' condition, the data set would be doubled, etc. Such factorially designed production experiments lie at the basis of much recent knowledge about intonation.

The issue of how to measure downtrends is easily solved in tone languages which permit sequences of identical tones, by simply measuring the (highest) F_0 in sentences containing strings of syllables with identical tones (see figure 6.2). In intonation-only languages such data can be obtained with speech containing repetitions of the same pitch accent. However, such procedures are harder to apply to spontaneous speech, which is likely to contain varying numbers of

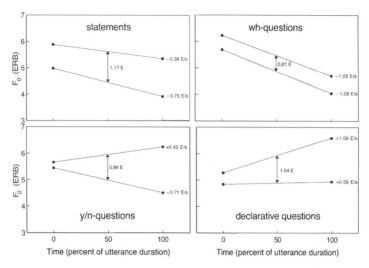

Fig. 6.8 Upper and lower regression lines for four syntactic categories in Dutch, with measures for pitch range. From Haan *et al.* (1997).

up-and-down movements, both in languages with and without lexical tone. Informally, declination has been established by visually fitting a straight line through the F_0 minima, either before or after a stylization. Such eye-balling is unreliable, as different researchers may come up with different slopes for the declination line. Lieberman, Katz, Jongman, Zimmerman, and Miller's (1985) proposal is therefore to draw a 'line of best fit': a regression line, whose position and slope are such as to minimize the distances from the line to the data-points. The drawback of this procedure is that a declining contour with a high final peak or a high final rise will be represented as having a rising line of best fit, even though the intuition is that the contour basically descends. An alternative is to use the regression line as the dividing line between a lower and a higher data set, and to perform new regressions on each of these subsets. This procedure will give a lower trend line and a higher trend line, with the lower trend line corresponding more closely to intuitive notion of declination. Moreover, the information provided by these two lines will be more than the sum of their slopes, as their distance can be a measure of pitch span and their mean of pitch register. I suggested this method to Judith Haan, who adopted it in an investigation of global characteristics of question intonation in Dutch (Haan, van Heuven, Pacilly, and van Bezooijen 1997). They calculated these upper and lower trend lines for scripted speech for four syntactic categories, as shown in figure 6.8: declarative sentences (panel a), wh-questions (panel b), yes–no questions (panel c), and syntactic declaratives read as questions (panel d).[7] These data show that interestingly different results can be obtained, which in principle are comparable across investigators. Again, depending on the research question, it may be desirable to control for tonal structures. If different sentence types show very different mixes of tone types, with L*-tones more frequent in interrogatives for instance, it may not be clear to what extent the trend lines result from behaviour in the implementation or from phonological choices (see also Haan 2002: 141).

6.7 Conclusion

This chapter saw a repeat of the theme of the last. The natural tendency for F_0 to decline during the utterance is in part brought under speaker control, behaviour which may in turn lead to grammaticalized versions of this natural phenomenon. In the case of declination, the confrontation of the phonetic behaviour with the need for categorization by the linguistic mind has led to a wide array of grammaticalizations. For downstep, the prototypical trigger of the phenomenon is an L-tone occurring after an H-tone earlier in the phrase, but there appears to be a great variety of triggering contexts cross-linguistically, which are both phonological and morphological in nature, while also the target of the downstep varies. Declination by itself does not have an obvious communicative function, which is rather concentrated at the beginning and end of the utterance. Indeed, it is *failure* of downstep, i.e. reset, which has a natural function as an indicator of phrasing.

While the beginning and end of the downtrend, discussed as reset (initial raising) and final lowering, reflect phrasing, an additional communicative use concerns the magnitude of disjunctures. Quite delicate degrees of sentence-internal resets can be used to signal the morpho-syntactic structure of the sentence by 'good' speakers. Grammaticalization of final lowering may occur in languages with cumulative downstep, where an extra downstep occurs on some last tone. In such cases, final lowering is no longer gradient and temporally diffuse, but discrete and localized, exactly as is downstep. In addition, grammaticalization may take the shape of discretely different contours for continuation and finality, while grammaticalization of initial raising occurs in Dutch as a categorical distinction between 'complete' and 'partial' reset, i.e. between the presence and absence of phrasal downstep. There may be languages which use initial high boundary tones to mark newness of topic, but I have no examples.

Upstep, or H-raising, was interpreted as a contrast-enhancing type of speaker control. Since the difference between pitch lowerings from H to L and declination or downstep from H to H may be blurred in longer utterances, a phonetic boosting of the phonological difference between H and a following L would appear a sensible measure. This explains why upstep typically combines with downstep. Upstep may be grammaticalized, and in the few cases that were discussed this occurred with varying contexts. Unlike downstep, upstep is rarely cumulative, which is understandable, given that the natural trend line of F_0 contours is descending.

Chapters 5 and 6 discussed a large number of interpretations of the three biological codes: the Frequency Code, the Effort Code, and the Production Code. Speakers control these effects in the phonetic implementation, and may create them in ways that are unrelated to the biological circumstances that inspired

them. The liberty with which speakers can avail themselves of the communicative opportunities provided by the three biological codes will to some extent be
hemmed in by the phonology of their language, as pointed out in the preceding
chapter. As pointed out in section 5.10, conflicting choices may be available
from the biological codes. This occurs not just between the Effort Code and
the Frequency Code, but also between these and the Production Code. One example is the recent use of final rises in declaratives in American and Australian
English, an affective use of the Frequency Code signalling hearer appeal, which
may strike many listeners as an informational use of the same code, i.e. as signalling interrogativity. And former British Prime Minister Margaret Thatcher's
final falls, taken to be used for turn-management by her interrupting interviewers,
were in reality attempts to exploit an affective interpretation of the Frequency
Code, i.e. attempts to sound authoritative (Beattie, Cutler, and Pearson 1982).

Notes

1. In fact, these steps are equivalent to the step down from H to L, as explained in
   section 6.3.5.
2. The negative [di] introduces a word-internal downstep in the verb, which raises L on
   the second syllable to H and places the downstep before the H on the third syllable by
   DOWNSTEP DISPLACEMENT.
3. Ladd (1983b) introduced a phonological feature [downstep] on tones in English; but
   see also section 14.5.3.
4. Mankon has a second upstep context, which likewise requires intervening L-tones to
   be realized on the surface (Hyman 1993).
5. Each berry name may well have been pronounced as a single ι, in which case the
   downsteps represent 'phrasal downstep' (see Ladd 1993a, and section 6.5.1).
6. These experiments employed perceived prominence as the response variable, after
   Rietveld and Gussenhoven (1985), rather than pitch.
7. Haan *et al.* performed the regression analyses on the data with the exclusion of any
   final rises, so as not to bias the results for the questions towards rising trend lines.

7

Tonal Structures

7.1 Introduction

This chapter offers an account of Pierrehumbert's model for the description of
tone and intonation. Her seminal thesis (Pierrehumbert 1980) presented a descriptive framework for intonation which separated the phonological representation
from its phonetic implementation. This made it possible to characterize the notion
'possible prosodic structure' independently of the phonetic details of intonation
contours. Section 7.2 places the model in its historical setting by identifying the
positions in the pre-1980 literature that are intellectually closest to its various
elements. The section ends with a nutshell description of the revised grammar
of American English of Beckman and Pierrehumbert (1986). Section 7.3 discusses the developments that have taken place since the revised 1986 model was
presented in Beckman and Pierrehumbert (1986). Tonal structure is sensitive to
prosodic phrasing because prosodic phrases may begin and end with boundary
tones. Section 7.4 looks at a second effect of phrasing on tone structure, that of
the rhythmic distribution of pitch accents, or the resolution of *stress clash*.

Earlier introductions to intonational phonology are Ladd (1996), who coined
the term 'Autosegmental-Metrical (AM) model' for it, Shattuck-Hufnagel and
Turk (1996), and Beckman (1996). The model is autosegmental because it has
separate tiers for segments (vowels and consonants) and tones (H,L). It is metrical
because it assumes that the elements in these tiers are contained in a hierarchically
organized set of phonological constituents, as depicted in (1), to which the tones
make reference in several ways. The tones, which are organized into pitch accents
and boundary tones, may or may not be associated with TBUs. Representation (1)
gives a possible pronunciation of the English proverb *Too many cooks spoil the
broth*. The example illustrates a commonly adopted set of prosodic constituents
for English. Among these is the intonational phrase (ι), which has initial and final
boundary tones (T_ι). A non-crucial assumption is that in the analysis of English
intonation to be presented in chapter 15, final boundary tones are optional, the

first ι in (1) not having any. As is clear from (1) English has both monotonal and bitonal pitch accents, the starred tone of which associates with the syllable. Instead of these graphically elaborate associations, pitch accents are shown as associating with the vowels in the accented syllable, and boundary tones with the constituent brackets, a notation introduced by Hayes and Lahiri (1991b) (but see section 8.3.4).

As explained in chapter 4, the surface representation (1) is a theory of a mental construct for a speaker of English. This speaker also possesses a phonetic implementation module which, among other things, translates every tone into an F_0 target. The phonetic 'alignment' with the segmental tier, its timing, will to some extent be language-specific, as will its 'scaling', its F_0. As explained in chapter 5, over and above the effects of these implementation rules, the speaker's psychological condition and communicative purpose will influence the overall pitch range.

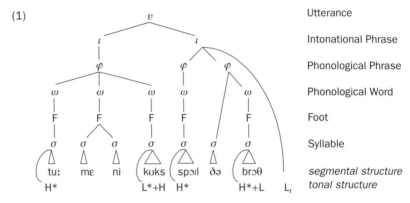

(1)   Utterance
                                                                                 Intonational Phrase
                                                                                 Phonological Phrase
                                                                                 Phonological Word
                                                                                 Foot
                                                                                 Syllable

tu: mɛ   ni   kʊks   spɔɪl   ðə   brɔθ   *segmental structure*
H*   L*+H   H*   H*+L   L$_\iota$ *tonal structure*

This chapter is concerned with the phonological structure. However, a complete analysis of an intonational system will comprise a phonology as well as a morphology. Unlike the tones in the phonology, the elements in a morphological analysis are not given *a priori*. In principle, the ι-wide contour could be a single morpheme, or any single tone or sequence of tones contained within ι could be a morpheme. A whole-contour proposal occurs in Liberman and Sag (1974), where the 'contradiction contour', for example, consists of a two-accent sequence, a position which has not been followed (Bolinger 1986: 245). Morphemes consisting of pitch accents plus boundary tones occur in proposals' intonational meaning in English (Brazil, Coulthard, and Johns 1980; Gussenhoven 1983b; Cruttenden 1997) and Bengali (Hayes and Lahiri 1991a). Pierrehumbert and Hirschberg (1990) propose an analysis in which every tone is a morpheme, a position defended in Bartels (1997). Dainora (2001, 2002) advanced the argument that the relatively high predictability of transitions between pitch accents and following tones in American English suggests that these elements are not morphemically independent. Of course, the same phonological analysis may be compatible with a large number of morphological analyses, just as different views of the morphological structure of a word like *replicate* ([[*re* [*plic*]] *ate*], [[*replic*] *ate*], [*replicate*]?) do not compromise the assumption that its surface phonology is ['rɛplɪˌkeɪt].

7.2 Historical background

The description of American English given in Pierrehumbert (1980) was somewhat revised in Beckman and Pierrehumbert (1986), while the model was consolidated as a general theory of intonational representation in Pierrehumbert and Beckman (1988). In this section, a number of aspects are isolated and related to earlier positions.

7.2.1 Autosegmental-Metrical representation

The idea that there are separate tiers for tones and segmental phonemes was implicit in many descriptions of intonation, inasmuch as pitch features were not considered to be part of the featural composition of segments in the British tradition of intonation description (e.g. O'Connor and Arnold (1973) or the description of Dutch by 't Hart, Collier, and Cohen (1990)). Also, Goldsmith's (1976) autosegmental model had been applied to English intonation before by Goldsmith (1980) (which began as an unpublished MIT paper in 1974), Liberman (1975), and Leben (1975).

The idea that at least one prosodic constituent, the ι, was intonationally defined, had been current in prosodic research at least since Selkirk (1978), and figured in earlier descriptions in the form of the 'tone group' (e.g. O'Connor and Arnold 1973). Prosodic phonology holds that speech is produced in batches of segments that are hierarchically ordered: within any such batch except the lowest a smaller batch can be identified. The gestural integration correlates inversely with rank: syllables are highly integrated articulations, while Utterances may contain noticeable pauses. A widely adopted view of this hierarchy for English includes the syllable (σ), the foot (F), the phonological word (ω, also 'prosodic word'), the phonological phrase (ϕ), the intonational phrase (ι), and the Utterance (υ) (Selkirk 1978; Nespor and Vogel 1986; Hayes 1989). This hierarchy is illustrated in (1).

In the revised theory of Beckman and Pierrehumbert (1986), an additional intonationally defined constituent was introduced for English, the Intermediate Phrase (ip), ranked immediately below ι. This made two degrees of depth available for an intonational boundary. Examples of 'lower' boundaries given by Beckman and Pierrehumbert (1986) are illustrated in (2) and (3), where the square brackets enclose ips and the curly brackets the ι. In (2), the two adjectives are considered to be followed by just an ip-boundary, because the disjuncture with what follows is less complete than that observed for a fully-fledged ι-boundary. In (3), the

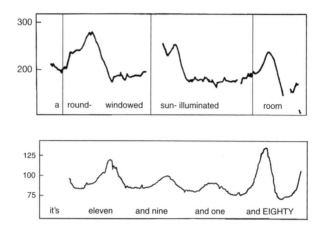

Fig. 7.1 F_0 contours of (2) and (3). From Beckman and Pierrehumbert (1986)

ip-boundary after *nine* is motivated by the high F_0 peak on *eighty*, which is due to an interruption of the downstepping pattern shown by the preceding F_0 peaks on *one* and *nine*. The F_0 contours are given in panels (a) and (b) of figure 7.1, respectively.

(2) { [A round-windowed] [sun-illuminated] [room] }

(3) { [It's eleven and nine and one] [and eighty] }

However, there are many analyses of West Germanic languages, including the description of English in chapters 14 and 15, that do without ip and the 'phrase tone' that has been related to it (van den Berg, Gussenhoven, and Rietveld 1992; Féry 1993; Grabe 1998a; Gussenhoven, Terken, and Rietveld 1999). In those analyses, the internal ip-boundary of (2) would be an ι-boundary, while that in (3) would not be an intonational boundary at all; the exemption from downstep is attributed to fact that it is the last ('nuclear') pitch accent of the ι (Ladd 1983c; Gussenhoven 1983b; Truckenbrodt 2002a).

Work on Japanese, Korean, and Basque led to the inclusion of the Accentual Phrase (α) in those languages, ranked immediately above the ω (Pierrehumbert and Beckman 1988; Jun 1998; Elordieta 1997) and comparable to ϕ (see also chapters 9 and 10).

7.2.2   Pitch accents and boundary tones

The separation into pitch accents and boundary tones harks back to Trager and Smith Jr's (1951) juncture phonemes (# 'falling', – 'sustained', || 'rising'), which existed by the side of the pitch phonemes. A early division between pitch accents and boundary tones can also be recognized in the work in the 1970s and 1980s by Hans't Hart, René Collier, and Antonie Cohen on Dutch ('t Hart, Collier, and

Cohen 1990), as argued by Ladd (1996). They divided up the pitch movements
of Dutch into 'accent-lending' and 'non-accent-lending', but stopped short of
equating the latter with boundary features. An example is given in (4), a non-final
contour, where '1' is an accent-lending rise, 'B' a non-accent-lending fall, 'A' a
steep accent-lending fall, and '2' a non-accent-lending rise. (When two accent-
lending movements appear on the same syllable, only one accent is produced.)

(4)   1&B   1&A   2

We gaan vanavond naar de schouwburg
'We are going to the theatre this evening,...'

The chief motivation in Pierrehumbert (1980) for ending ι with two tones, a phrase
accent (T-) and a boundary tone (T%), was that in many contours two targets can
be identified after the last ('nuclear') pitch accent. For instance, in (5), the L*
pitch accent is followed by a high target at the end of the accented 'Manitowoc,
as well as a final high target, for which H- and H% were postulated, respectively. I
reproduce her contour 2.29 as (5). This example would be natural in a conversation
where someone had just asked the speaker if he knew of any towns with bowling
alleys. In Beckman and Pierrehumbert (1986), T- was reanalysed as a boundary
tone of the ip. As a result, ips ended in T-, and ιs in T-T% in the new analysis,
since the right edge of every ι coincides with that of an ip.

(5)

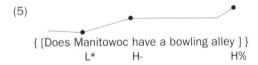

{ [Does Manitowoc have a bowling alley] }
      L*   H-   H%

The decision to postulate two tones after the pitch accent of course depends on the
analysis of the tone string into pitch accents and boundary tones. One of the most
striking differences between the Pierrehumbert model and the earlier descriptions
of British English (Crystal 1969; Halliday 1970; O'Connor and Arnold 1973) is
that Pierrehumbert analysed the contour leading *towards* the accentual target as
the pitch accent, while the British tradition isolated the part leading *off* it. Thus,
in (5), the contour described by L*HH% is a unit, the nuclear tone '(low–to–)high
rise'. This difference in approach is even clearer in the case of contours like (6):
for O'Connor and Arnold, for instance, this contour consists of a (high) fall,
preceded by a low 'prehead' (see (6a)), between which the pitch will necessarily
rise; Pierrehumbert describes it as a rising pitch accent followed by the boundary
tones L- and L%, as in (6b).

(6)

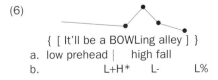

{ [It'll be a BOWLing alley] }
a. low prehead | high fall
b.   L+H*   L-   L%

The British 'off-ramp' analysis was the basis of my own autosegmental description of English and Dutch (Gussenhoven 1983b; Gussenhoven 1988; van den Berg, Gussenhoven, and Rietveld 1992), which analysed (5) as L*H H% and (6) as H*L L%. Pierrehumbert's 'on-ramp' analysis was transferred to the practically oriented transcription system for American English that was derived from the Pierrehumbert model, *Tones and Break Indices*, ToBI (cf. Beckman and Ayers 1994, see chapter 15). This issue has not attracted any empirical research, as far as I am aware (see further section 7.3.1).

7.2.3   Associated and unassociated tones

The Africanists' distinction between associated and unassociated lexical tones was applied by Pierrehumbert (1980) to intonational tones in two ways. The first use of 'floating' tones is based on the role that such tones have as triggers for downstep while remaining without a target themselves (see chapter 6, section 6.3.1). Thus, Pierrehumbert (1980) describes one of the downstepped patterns of English as H*+L H*, whereby the trailing L-tone causes the second H* to be downstepped, without acquiring a low target itself. The non-realization of L in H*+L needs to be specified in the implementation rules, and is thus specific to Pierrehumbert's description of American English.

The second, more generally accepted, use is for tones whose targets are timed with reference to the targets of other tones, rather than to a specific point in the segmental tier. Typically, one tone in a pitch accent, T*, associates with the accented syllable, while the leading or trailing T receives a target which occurs some fixed distance before or after that of T*. As a result, the H of L*+H as used on 'Rigamarole* will occur on *-ma-*, the second syllable after the accented *Rig-*, while in *Stein*, it will be realized on the same syllable as L* (Beckman and Pierrehumbert 1986). In chapter 11, section 11.3, we will see that the timing of the Swedish focus-marking tone depends on the association of preceding lexical tones in the word.

7.2.4   Targets and interpolations

The notion that a contour is an interpolation between points, such that only the beginning and end-points of a movement result from a tonal specification, was inherent in the analyses by Pike (1945) and Trager and Smith Jr (1951), who used numbers to indicate four pitch 'levels'. Pike's (7), for instance, indicates interpolations by means of dashes. In his system, '1' was the highest pitch phoneme, '4' the lowest. The notion of a starred tone was present in that accented levels, which begin a 'primary contour', are marked with the degree symbol. In this case, the representation translates quite readily into Pierrehumbert's (8).

```
(7)  I      wanted to do it,       but I couldn't
     4-       °2-       -4-3/4-        °2-     -4 //
```

(8) I   wanted to do it,   but I couldn't
      H*   L-H%   H* L-L%

From Pierrehumbert (1980) onwards, a distinction has generally been made between interpolation, the creation of phonetic values between the phonetic targets of phonological tones, and specification through spreading. Spreading is illustrated in example (9a), which shows an H-tone spreading to the end of its phrase, from where the contour continues to the initial L of the next phrase. By contrast, in (9b), the H-tone does not spread, and the interpolation thus includes the unspecified syllables before the phrase-initial L. The *locus classicus* is Beckman and Pierrehumbert (1986: 263) (also Pierrehumbert and Beckman 1988: 37ff.), who showed that in a case exactly like this, (9b) is the superior theory for Japanese. This representation predicts that the longer the first phrase is, the less steep is its sloping F_0. Representation (9a) would incorrectly predict that the slope remains high up till the last syllable of the first phrase, regardless of its length. In chapter 10, section 10.7, this case is dealt more fully. The notion of phonetic underspecification was subsequently extended to other features, like nasality (e.g. Cohn 1990).

(9)

a. (ta ta ta ta) (ta …)   b. (ta ta ta ta) (ta …)
     L H   L   L H   L

Other theories identified pitch *movements* as the basic elements instead of the interpolations between level pitches, although the idea of non-specification was present inasmuch as they contained stretchable movements whose duration was determined by the length of the segments over which they were pronounced, like the 'rising head' of O'Connor and Arnold (1973) or the gradually rising pitch movement '4' of 't Hart, Collier, and Cohen (1990).

7.2.5 Lexical and intonational tones in a single tier

The idea that the string of tones contained lexical and intonational tones forms the hallmark of Bruce (1977), who isolated the contribution of the lexical tones of Stockholm Swedish from that of the intonational tones, representing them as a string of pitch levels that were timed with the stresses and phrase ends much as in an autosegmental description (Pierrehumbert 2000; Ladd 2000). Ladd (1983b) characterized this type of description as the Tone Sequence model, to distinguish it from descriptions that superimpose accentual contours on phrasal intonation contours, termed Contour Interaction models by Ladd, as represented by Gårding (1983), Thorsen (1978, 1983), and Vaissièrre (1983), as well as by Fujisaki's model (e.g. Fujisaki 1983).

Interactions between lexical and intonational tones are common in tone languages, where initial or final boundary tones may affect the values of adjacent lexical tones. Processes that refer indiscriminately to lexical and intonational tones strongly support the position that these tones form a single phonological string. For instance, in Mankon, H is upstepped after a floating L preceded by LH. The first L in the LH(L)H sequence can be a lexical tone, as in (10a), or an intonational boundary L_t, as in (10b) (Hyman 1993). The presence of the first L is crucial, since without it, the H *before* (L) is upstepped. Examples of such interactions in Dutch tonal dialects are given in chapter 12.

(10) a. { bi? ɨ sinɔ   b. { bɨ   yiŋɔ }
         | | | | | | |
         L H(L)H L_t H(L)H L
      'termite of bird'   'they have come'

7.2.6 Only two tones

The idea that only two tones, H and L, suffice to describe languages with intonation and some lexical tone was part of Bruce's thesis. Earlier, Liberman (1975) had described the intonation of American English with the help of four tones, raised H, H, raised L, and L, thus staying closer to the older descriptions. At that point, descriptions were still vulnerable to Bolinger's (1951) criticism that four-level transcriptions of English intonation, like (7), were arbitrary, because 2–4 would not be discretely different from, say, 3–4 or 1–4. But perhaps more so than Bruce's (1977) 'pitch rules', which filled in details like the copying of F_0-values through level parts of the contour, Pierrehumbert's implementation rules made it clear that the generation of an infinite number of F_0 values between the highest and lowest pitches allowed the distinction between phonological representations and phonetic contours to become particularly clear. To characterize the contrasts of the language and thus the notion of a possible intonational structure, two tones suffice, for English and for many other languages that have been described since.

7.2.7 The 1986 model

Beckman and Pierrehumbert's (1986) revised model includes six pitch accents, H*, L*, H*+L, L*+H, L+H*, and H+L*. An optional initial boundary %H precedes the ι for high initial pitch, mid and low beginnings being tonally unspecified. The ip and ι are obligatorily closed by boundary tones, as explained above. The grammar can be given as in (11), where parentheses include optional elements, accolades alternative options, and subscripts stand for '*n* or more occurrences', as usual. The part enclosed between the outermost (. . .)₁ indicates the ip, of which there must be one or more, containing one or more pitch accents.

(11) The tonal grammar of Beckman and Pierrehumbert (1986)

$$
\left(
\left(
\left(
\begin{Bmatrix}
H^* \\
L^* \\
H^* + L^* \\
L^* + H^* \\
L + H^* \\
H + L^*
\end{Bmatrix}
\right)_1
\right)
\left\{
\begin{matrix}
H^- \\
L^-
\end{matrix}
\right\}
\right)_1
\left\{
\begin{matrix}
H\% \\
L\%
\end{matrix}
\right\}
\right)
$$

(%H)

The phonetic implementation rules include downstep, which applies to H* and H- after a bitonal pitch accent, expressed in (13). A mid tone at the end of an ι is obtained by the combined working of DOWNSTEP (lowering H- after L+H*) and UPSTEP (14), which raises L% to the level of a preceding H-, and raises H% above the level of a preceding H-. Thus, in (15a), H- is downstepped and L% is upstepped. UPSTEP is also responsible for the extra-high H% in (15b).

(12) PB DOWNSTEP: H →!H / T + T . . . ____ . . . T% (Implementation)

(13)

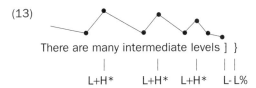

There are many intermediate levels] }

  | | | | |
L+H*   L+H*   L+H*   L- L%

(14) PB UPSTEP: T% → raised T% / H- ____ (Implementation)

(15)

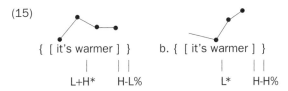

{ [it's warmer] }   b. { [it's warmer] }

  | | | | | |
L+H*   H-L%   L*   H-H%

In addition to the two implementation rules given in (12) and (14), and the abstract downstep-trigger L of H*+L (see section 7.2.3), a final implementation rule was that L* of H+L* was realized as a downstepped H, H+L* therefore being equivalent to H+!H*. This pitch accent is used to describe the contour consisting of high-level pitch followed by a downstepped H* illustrated in (16).

(16)

It's a common type of contour] }

  | | | |
H*   H+L*   L- L%

7.2.8   ToBI

The somewhat abstract tonal grammar (11) was replaced with the practically oriented ToBI ('Tones and Break Indices') transcription system in 1992 (Silverman
et al. 1992). ToBI combines a system for annotating prosodic boundary strength,
essentially a five-point scale running from '0' for the boundary between a word
and a cliticized form to '4' for 'end of sentence', with a user-friendly version
of (11). Its creation was motivated by the need for large prosodically annotated
text corpora and the difficulty that transcribers experienced when applying the
Pierrehumbert–Beckman 1986 grammar. The main difference with Pierrehumbert and Beckman's (1986) analysis is that downstep is explicitly indicated in the
transcription, in the spirit of Ladd (1983). The following specific changes were
made.

(a) A downstepped H* is given as !H*. For instance, {L+H* L+H* L-L%} is
    {L+H* L+!H* L-L%} in ToBI.
(b) A new pitch accent was introduced to describe high-level pitch followed by
    downstep, H+!H*. For instance, {H* H+L* L-L%} (cf. (16)) is {H* H+!H*
    L-L%} in ToBI. Since H+L* is no longer needed to function as H+!H*, it
    was removed from the symbol set.
(c) Because H*+L was in effect a downstep trigger, with no realization of L,
    it was removed from the symbol set. For instance, {H*+L H* L-L%} is
    {H* !H* L-L%} in ToBI.

The pitch accents that ToBI is left with, therefore, are H*, L*, L+H*, L*+H,
and H+!H*, while the downstep symbol is used to create !H* and L+!H*. Since
H- can be downstepped too, H* !H- L% can be used to describe the vocative chant.
The boundary tones, and their phonetic interpretations, were carried over intact.
The only change in convention here is that in *ι*-final position the phrase accent,
T-, is given as part of a complex symbol together with the boundary tone, T%,
as in L-H%. Earlier, the phrase accent was printed where a detectable change
occurred in the F$_0$ track, as in (5) and (6). This follows from the fact that the
phrase accent was reanalysed as a boundary tone of the Intermediate Phrase in
(1986) (cf. ((13), (15), and (16)).

Meanwhile, similar systems have been developed for a number of other languages, like German-ToBI and Korean-ToBI. A good overview is Jun (2003),
who renamed the original system as AE-ToBI to make it explicit that it is an
analysis of American English. To qualify for the label 'ToBI', a system should
include the ToBI software enabling the transcriber to enter annotations on a number of time-aligned tiers. In addition to the tone tier and the Break Index tier,
there is a tier for an orthographic transcription, one for disfluencies, and one for
comments. Entries on all tiers are anchored to timing-points in the waveform, to
be indicated by the transcriber.

Chapter 15 presents an alternative analysis of English intonation; in section 15.8, I will briefly evaluate the analysis represented by Pierrehumbert and Beckman (1986) and AE-ToBI.

7.3 Developments since 1986

This section briefly discusses the developments since 1986, and is structured on the basis of tone types: pitch accents, boundary tones, plus the notion of 'secondary association', and phrase accents.

7.3.1 Pitch accents

By definition, accented syllables are associated with a pitch accent. Functionally, pitch accents may be lexical, as in Japanese or Swedish, or intonational, in which case they are frequently focus-marking, as in English. One of the tones, T*, associates with the TBU, any leading or trailing tone remaining unassociated. A focus-marking pitch accent typically increases the durations of segments in, and to some extent near, the accented syllable, as is the case in English and Dutch (Beckman and Edwards 1990; Cambier-Langeveld and Turk 1999; Cambier-Langeveld 2000), as it is for the functionally equivalent focus-marking tone of Swedish (Heldner and Strangert 2001) (accentual lengthening).

The tone whose target is closer to the rhyme of the accented syllable will typically be designated as the starred tone, but this decision may additionally be based on the more constant timing of its target relative to some segmental point in the accented syllable. Not all pitch accents appear to be timed in this asymmetrical fashion, however. Work on Standard Greek has shown that the low target of the pre-nuclear LH pitch accent occurs just before the stressed syllable and the high target at the CV boundary of the next, causing the rise to vary in duration depending on the number of consonants before and after the stressed vowel (Arvaniti, Ladd, and Mennen 2000). An implication is that it is no longer clear which is the starred tone, L or H. The pitch accent could be interpreted as a branching structure, which as a unit associates with the accented syllable, as the authors suggest. The internal structure of the bitonal pitch accent had earlier been discussed by Grice (1995b), who recognized a 'tone cluster' by the side of a 'tone contour', adopting a tonal root node between the syllable and the tones, as in Yip (1989) (see section 3.3.4). Grice claimed that in English, pitch accents with leading tones like L+H* are clusters (cf. (17a)), but that pitch accents with trailing tones like L*+H are contours (cf. (17b)). One of her arguments is that leading tones tend to be truncated when the accent is ι-initial, while ι-final trailing tones are not. To return to the Greek case, a structure like (17a) could be provided with a star for the whole complex to serve as the pre-nuclear LH (Arvaniti, Ladd, and Mennen 2000).

(17) a.

Timing characteristics have been used by Frota (2002) to decide between an analysis of the European Portuguese focal and non-focal pitch accents as either bitonal H*+L and H+L* or as HL combinations of boundary tone and single-tone pitch accent. The evidence leads her to conclude that both are bitonal pitch accents, but that only the targets of H*+L are characterized by a constant interval.

Detailed phonetic studies of timings of targets have, on the one hand, revealed cross-linguistic and cross-varietal variation, and, on the other, a tendency for targets to be coupled to 'segmental landmarks', like the syllable offset, as in Mandarin lexical tones (Xu 1998), or the CV-boundary (Ladd, Faulkner, Faulkner, and Schepman 1999), while they can be sensitive even to the tenseness of the vowel (Ladd, Mennen, and Schepman 2000). Evidence for the influence of the length of the onset and the sonorant status of consonants is provided in Prieto, van Santen, and Hirschberg (1995), and Rietveld and Gussenhoven (1995), while the role of constraints like the speed of F_0 movements and the time difference between implementation and articulatory effect are discussed in Xu (2002).

The assumption that the targets of bitonal pitch accents are close together is not generally shared. The timing of trailing tones in English was made dependent on the distance to the next accent in Gussenhoven (1983b, 1988, 1999), Féry (1993), and Grabe (1998a). Part of the motivation was functional, as illustrated by (18a), after Gussenhoven (1983b), which has two occurrences of what intuitively appears to be the same neutral pitch accent. The target of the trailing L of the non-final H*L is timed rightmost, and bounded by the following associated tone. The trailing L of the final pitch accent is, however, constrained so as to occur immediately after the target of its T*. Because the timing of the trailing tone is context-dependent, the '+' is avoided, as it suggests that the tones are always realized close together. The representation of contour (18) in Pierrehumbert's 'on-ramp' theory is (18b), which has the pitch accents, H* and L+H*. A second argument for preferring (18a) over (18b) is that, unless the accents are close together, informal observations suggest that both the timing and the scaling of the low target before the second peak are imprecise; the target could be higher and earlier with no appreciable perceptual difference, suggesting that L's rightward drift is variable. This is not what is suggested by the pitch accent L+H*, however, where L's target would be expected to be located at a fixed distance from that of H*. A third argument is that the right-moving trailing tone, or 'displaced' tone, to use Grabe's (1998a) term, also occurs in non-final L*H and H*LH (Gussenhoven 1983b) and that therefore the description generalizes across pitch accents. The rightward displacement was termed a 'partial linking' in Gussenhoven (1983b), where 'linking' referred to the coherence of the two pitch accents, and was seen as a step towards 'complete linking', the deletion of the trailing tone.

(18)

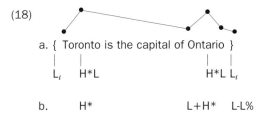

a. { Toronto is the capital of Ontario }
   | | | |
   L$_\iota$ H*L   H*L L$_\iota$

b.   H*   L+H*   L-L%

7.3.2   Boundary tones

The reality of prosodic constituents is apparent from a number of phenomena. The context for segmental processes like assimilation is often defined by the boundaries of specific prosodic constituents (e.g. Nespor and Vogel 1986). Second, their boundaries reveal themselves through lengthening at the end (Wightman, Shattuck-Hufnagel, Ostendorf, and Price 1992; Gussenhoven and Rietveld 1992) and segmental strengthening at the beginning (Fougeron and Keating 1997; Fougeron 2001; Cho and Keating 2001). For instance, in *Tiptoe through the tulips,* the υ-initial [t] in *tip-* will be longer and have a more extensive articulatory contact than the ω-initial [t] in *tu-,* which in its turn will be longer and stronger than the F-initial [t] of *-toe.* Abstracting away from the presence of pitch accents and segmental effects on duration, *-toe,* the last syllable of the φ, will be longer than *tu-,* the first syllable of a ω, due to final lengthening. And third, syntactic movement rules may be sensitive to the size of the constituents they manipulate (Inkelas 1989; Inkelas and Zec 1990).

In intonation, the prosodic structure plays two roles. First, it may codetermine the context of phonological or phonetic rules (e.g. downstep, which is always confined to some prosodic constituent), including those responsible for the distribution of pitch accents (see section 7.4). Second, to return to the topic of this section, prosodic constituents may be marked by boundary tones. One, sometimes two, higher prosodic constituents may come with boundary tones initially and/or finally. These are now reported so frequently that they may well be universal. Some languages have *only* boundary tones, like Unangan, which has L$_\phi$ at the beginning and H$_\phi$ at the end of every φ. The only function of intonational structure in this language is thus to signal phrasing (Taff 1997). Boundary tones may be complex, i.e. consist of a tone sequence. Jun (1993) gives an analysis of Seoul Korean where every α has a string LHLH, which is reduced to just an initial LH if the α has only three syllables (Jun 1998). In the final α, any second occurrence of LH is pre-empted by one of the ι-final boundary tones H$_\iota$, L$_\iota$, L$_\iota$H$_\iota$ or H$_\iota$L$_\iota$, which express different intonational meanings. An example is (19). Formally and functionally, Korean is thus more complex than Unangan but, like Unangan, lacks pitch accents.

(19)

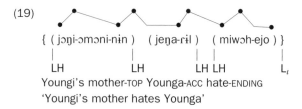

{ (jɔŋi-ɔmɔni-nɨn) (jeŋa-rɨl) (miwɔh-ejo) }
    | | | | |
   LH   LH   LH LH L_ι
Youngi's mother-TOP Younga-ACC hate-ENDING
'Youngi's mother hates Younga'

Bengali combines pitch accents and boundary tones. It closes the ι either by L_ι, or by one of the boundary complexes $L_\iota H_\iota$, for continuation, and $H_\iota L_\iota$, for yes–no questions. This is illustrated in (20), where L^* marks the accented syllables (see also section 4.2.2, figure 4.3). Complex $H_\iota L_\iota$ contrasts with $H_\phi L_\iota$, which contour is used to mark narrow focus with declarative intonation and is realized with an earlier and lower peak, as shown in (21) (Hayes and Lahiri 1991a). The F_0 peak signalling the question is always ι-final and high. Moreover, H_ϕ can move to a non-final ϕ, if the focus ends early, as shown in (22).

(20)

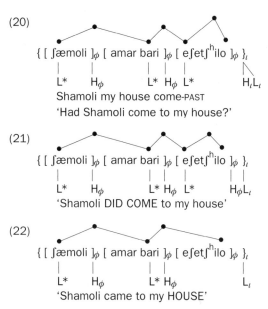

{ [ʃæmoli]$_\phi$ [amar bari]$_\phi$ [eʃetʃʰilo]$_\phi$ }$_\iota$
   | | | | | \
 L^* H_ϕ L^* H_ϕ L^* $H_\iota L_\iota$
Shamoli my house come-PAST
'Had Shamoli come to my house?'

(21)

{ [ʃæmoli]$_\phi$ [amar bari]$_\phi$ [eʃetʃʰilo]$_\phi$ }$_\iota$
   | | | | | | |
 L^* H_ϕ L^* H_ϕ L^* $H_\phi L_\iota$
'Shamoli DID COME to my house'

(22)

{ [ʃæmoli]$_\phi$ [amar bari]$_\phi$ [eʃetʃʰilo]$_\phi$ }$_\iota$
   | | | |
 L^* H_ϕ L^* H_ϕ L_ι
'Shamoli came to my HOUSE'

These examples also illustrate that more than one prosodic constituent may come with boundary tones, since in addition to H_ι, Bengali has H_ϕ. Evidence that H_ϕ is a boundary tone, rather than the leading tone of a possible $H+L^*$ pitch accent, is given by the pronunciation of *amar* 'my' in (20)–(22). The L^* goes to the first syllable of the first lexical word in the ϕ, and thus skips the function word *amar*. Because *amar* is pronounced on a downward slope, H_ϕ cannot be interpreted as the leading tone of the following pitch accent, since this analysis would predict that -*mar* has high pitch. Neither do Bengali sentences begin with high pitch.

Maori equally has a L*H$_\phi$L$_\iota$ interrogative contour, but the middle tone here is a boundary tone for ϕ (de Lacy draft). Since Maori aligns the right edge of the focus constituent with ϕ and disallows pitch accents after the focus, a contour with an early peak is produced which in Bengali serves as the *declarative* early focus contour. For Georgian, Bush (1999) reports a complex boundary L$_\phi$H$_\phi$, as in (23), which is part of a question intonation contour that begins with H$_\iota$. As Bush points out, the L-tone is not a pitch accent, as it spurns the stressed syllable in '*laparakob*. Neither is it a sequence of L$_\phi$H$_\iota$; one of his arguments is that the end of ι may contribute a L$_\iota$ in polite speech which could not be abstracted out of the contour if it was combined with the preceding H-tone.

(23)

{ [rusulat 'laparakob]   }

H$_\iota$ L$_\phi$H$_\phi$ L$_\iota$

Russian you-speak

'Do you speak Russian?'

The Dutch dialect of Venlo has boundary tones of ι and υ (Gussenhoven and van der Vliet 1999): all ιs end in H$_\iota$ or L$_\iota$, while the utterance can have an additional H$_\upsilon$, leading to four utterance-final contours, H$_\iota$, L$_\iota$, L$_\iota$H$_\upsilon$, and H$_\iota$H$_\upsilon$.

Finally, as will be clear from these examples, boundary tones can be optional. Pierrehumbert's decision to have final obligatory boundary tones at two ranks may have led to a tendency to assume obligatory boundary tones in other languages. For English, this assumption is intimately connected with the assumption of two intonationally defined phrases.[1] In chapter 15, an analysis with optional final boundary tones will be presented. To give some examples of this analysis, (24a) gives a half-completed fall, which is contrasted with the fall to low in (24b), while (24c) shows a sequence of high levels, one type of listing intonation. In Pierrehumbert (1980), these three contours are transcribed H*+L H-L%, H* L-L%, and H* H-L%, respectively.

(24)

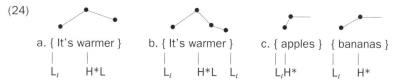

a. { It's warmer }   b. { It's warmer }   c. { apples }   { bananas }

L$_\iota$ H*L   L$_\iota$ H*L   L$_\iota$ L$_\iota$H*   L$_\iota$ H*

Likewise, Grabe (1998a) argues that an analysis of both German and English with an optional, single-rank boundary tone is to be preferred to a system with two constituents and obligatory boundary tones. Both the transcription system developed for Dutch, *Transcription of Dutch Intonation* (ToDI) (Gussenhoven, Terken, and Rietveld 1999) and the partly phonetic transcription system developed for varieties of British English, IViE (Grabe 2001) have optional boundary tones at a single rank only.

7.3.3 Secondary association

Pierrehumbert and Beckman (1988) introduced the concept of a boundary tone associating with a TBU. Their case will be dealt with fully in chapter 10, but the general idea is easily explained. The phrase in (25a) begins with a boundary L-tone and a toneless ('free') initial syllable, the second syllable being associated with H. In this situation, a low target occurs on the first syllable. In (25b), by contrast, the first syllable is associated with H, leaving no time for a low target: the pitch may rise a little towards the target for H at the beginning of the vowel, but nothing like the wide rise of (25a) will occur. Pierrehumbert and Beckman (1988) described this difference phonologically by associating the L-tone in (25a) with the first syllable, as shown, and assumed that the boundary tone with such a 'secondary association' (the 'first' association being with the constituent node) is pronounced fully low, as opposed to the L in (25b), which can only have a mid target.

(25)

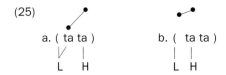

a. (ta ta)   b. (ta ta)
   ⫽ | | |
   L   H   L H

The notion of secondary association was applied by Grice (1995a) to account for the variation between the slight fall on ι-final accented syllables in Palermo Italian question intonation, as in (26a), and the deep fall observed when the accented syllable is non-final, as in (26b).

(26)

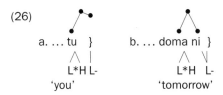

a. ... tu }   b. ... doma ni }
     ∧ | ∧   ∨
     L*H L-   L*H   L-
    'you'   'tomorrow'

There is no necessary implication, however, that a tonal representation like (26a) inevitably leads to a phonetic implementation whereby the final L is not or is barely pronounced. Grønnum (1991) and Ladd (1996: 133) would describe a phonetic contour like (26a) as a case of truncation, and distinguish it from 'compression', i.e. a contour which reaches low pitch. Languages or language varieties may differ in that one is compressing and another truncating, as shown by Grabe (1998b) for RP and northern Standard German, respectively (see section 1.4.4), and by Grabe, Post, Nolan, and Farrar (2000) for Cambridge English and Leeds English, respectively.

While the difference between compression and truncation might arguably be accounted for by language-specific implementation rules, confirmation of the moraic association of boundary tones was provided by data from Venlo Dutch.

This dialect has a privative tone contrast on stressed syllables with two sonorant moras. There are thus three prosodic types of stressed syllable: those with one sonorant mora (27a); those with two but no tone (27b) (also known as Accent 1); and those with two and H on the second mora (27c) (also known as Accent 2). A focus-marking H* associates with the first mora of the stressed syllable of a focused word, and a declarative L_ι closes the ι. As shown in (27b), the fall for Accent 1 is completed inside the Accent-1 syllable, which is explained by the secondary association of L_ι with the sonorant mora in the accented syllable, a TBU which requires tone. Neither in (27a) nor in (27c) is such a 'free' mora available, and as a result the falls in the latter two contours are slower (Gussenhoven and van der Vliet 1999). Measurements for the contrast between (27b,c) were given in Peter van der Vliet's Master's thesis, while Gussenhoven (2000a) gives data for all three conditions in the related dialect of Roermond. When H_ι occurs instead of L_ι in situations like (27b), there are clearly two targets, forming a high level stretch.

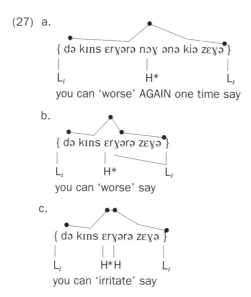

(27) a.
{ də kɪns ɛɣərə nɔɣ ənə kiə zeɣə }
L_ι H* L_ι
you can 'worse' AGAIN one time say

b.
{ də kɪns ɛɣərə zeɣə }
L_ι H* L_ι
you can 'worse' say

c.
{ də kɪns ɛɣərə zeɣə }
L_ι H*H L_ι
you can 'irritate' say

Not only boundary tones acquire secondary associations. Chapter 11, section 11.2.2 will deal with the case of the trailing L of the Swedish pitch accent H*+L, which has been described as associating with a stressed syllable some distance away from its H* in compounds.

7.3.4   Phrase accent

The term 'phrase accent' has a chequered history. Pierrehumbert (1980) applied it to the internal boundary tone T-, equating it with Bruce's (1977) 'sentence accent', the focal H of Stockholm Swedish. What these tones have in common is that they occur between the final boundary tone and the last T*(T), an intonational pitch accent in English and a lexical pitch accent in Swedish. Functionally, the Swedish 'sentence accent' is equivalent to the intonational pitch accents of English. In Beckman and Pierrehumbert (1986), the 'phrase accent' was reanalysed as a boundary tone of the ip, as noted above, allowing for an analysis in which lower ranking ips end in T- and higher-ranking *ι*s end in T-T%. Grice, Ladd, and Arvaniti (2000) narrowed the meaning down to a boundary tone with secondary association. This analysis explains why the English phrase accent (T-) is not in fact pronounced at the boundary, but usually immediately after the last pitch accent, and they therefore claim that T- associates with a stressed syllable inside the ip. They also suggest that the much-discussed issue of the difference between 'fall-rise' and 'fall-plus-rise' in descriptions of British English (cf. Cruttenden 1997) can be explained in terms of 'phrase accents'.

While the dependence of T- on stress may be less obvious in German or English, Grice *et al.*'s comparison between Standard Greek and Cypriot Greek makes the difference between an edge-seeking tone and a stress-seeking 'phrase accent' clear. Both languages have a yes/no question contour, analysed as L* H-L%. In Cypriot Greek, the H- remains close to the *ι*-boundary, with the peak usually falling in the last syllable, while in Standard Greek its target falls in the rightmost stressed syllable. In (28) for instance, H- associates with the unaccented, but main stressed syllable *Le-* in Standard Greek, while L% possibly does too, or else is timed after H-. (In (28), I place the L-target where it would appear to occur in the F$_0$ track.) The Cypriot Greek case is like that of Hungarian (Ladd 1983c; Gósy and Terken 1994; Varga 2002) and Bengali (Hayes and Lahiri 1991a), and shown in (29), where the rightmost stress is [zo], but the F$_0$ peak is on the unstressed final [mu].

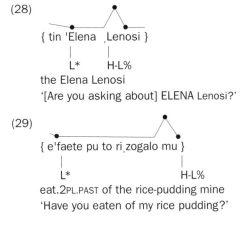

(28)

{ tin 'Elena ˌLenosi }

    L*   H-L%

the Elena Lenosi

'[Are you asking about] ELENA Lenosi?'

(29)

{ e'faete pu to riˌzogalo mu }

    L*   H-L%

eat.2PL.PAST of the rice-pudding mine

'Have you eaten of my rice pudding?'

A third possibility is for the H-tone to have two high targets forming a plateau on post-focal stretches of speech, as occurs in Dutch tonal dialects (Gussenhoven and van der Vliet 1999) and Transylvanian Romanian (Grice, Ladd, and Arvaniti 2000). In Bern Swiss German, a similar plateau is due to H of the L*+H pitch accent, which in broad focus continues until the last stressed syllable of the phrase, where a L_ν seeks a secondary association (Fitzpatrick-Cole 1999). This is shown in (30).

(30)

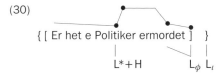

$$\{ [\text{Er het e Politiker ermordet}] \quad \}$$

$$\text{L*+H} \qquad \qquad \text{L}_\phi \; \text{L}_l$$

7.4 Rhythmic adjustments of pitch-accent distribution

In addition to contributing boundary tones, prosodic constituents may determine the rhythmic distribution of pitch accents. Generally, adjacency of prominent syllables is disfavoured (Alternation Principle, Selkirk 1986). This is as true for (accented and unaccented) stressed syllables within words as it is for adjacent pitch accented syllables, whether occurring within the same word or in different words. Many languages manage to live with such 'clashes'. English, for instance, allows adjacency of stressed syllables in underived words, as illustrated by *can'teen, 'syn₍tax*, and, in a rare pattern of (x)(x .), *'cu₍cumber*. Other languages do not. For instance, strong syllables never clash in the simplex word in Dutch (Gussenhoven 1993).

Clashes of accented syllables are, however, avoided in English, as indeed they are in French and Dutch: English *ponTOON*, but *PONtoon BRIDGE*, French *beauCOUP*, but *BEAUcoup PLUS* 'much more' and Dutch *bijGAAND*, but *BIJgaand BRIEFje* 'accompanying letter', but are tolerated in Portuguese, Italian, and Greek (Frota 1998; Farnetani and Kori 1983; Arvaniti 1994). Greek [po'li 'liɣa] 'too small', for instance, will not be pronounced *['poli 'liɣa] (Arvaniti 1994).[2]

There has been some confusion over the phonological nature of clash resolution in English ('stress shift'). Liberman and Prince (1977) proposed an analysis in terms of a metrical grid, following Chomsky and Halle (1986) and others who worked with a 'segmental' feature [*n*stress]. As a result, the insight that English clash resolution concerned the distribution of pitch accents (Bolinger 1965; Bolinger 1986; Vanderslice and Ladefoged 1972) was lost. The renewed claim that English clash resolution amounts to arrangement of pitch accents, typically amounting to a deletion of the leftmost of the two clashing pitch accents (Gussenhoven 1986; Gussenhoven 1991a; Shattuck-Hufnagel 1989; Ladd and Monaghan 1987), was confirmed by acoustic measurements (Horne 1990; Vogel, Bunnell, and Hoskins 1995), and found support in the Boston University Radio News Corpus described in Ostendorf, Price, and Shattuck-Hufnagel (1995), Shattuck-Hufnagel, Ostendorf, and Ross (1979), and Shattuck-Hufnagel (1995). For instance, a word like *Japanese* is typically pronounced as in (31a) when it is the only accented word in the utterance. Depending on its position in the ϕ, either the first or the second accent will be deleted, giving (31a) and (31b), respectively. The latter is said to have undergone 'stress shift' in Liberman and Prince (1977).

Acoustic measurements show that clash resolution in French is likewise a matter of pitch accent distribution (Post 2000a; Post 2000b).

(31) a. It's JAPaNESE
        b. It's GOOD JapaNESE
        c. It's a JAPanese PRINT

Word prosodic structure is involved in the clash resolution of accents in English to the extent that a pitch accent cannot be relocated on an unstressed syllable (Liberman and Prince 1977). Compare (32a), which contains an adjective with two feet, with (32b), which consists of an unstressed syllable and a monosyllabic foot. Similarly, compare (32a) with (32c), from Dutch, which does not allow adjacent footheads, and in which *Chinees* has the word prosodic structure of English *obese*.

(32) a. a CHInese BOOK   b. an oBESE PERson   c. een ChiNEES BOEK
      (cf. CHI-NESE)   'a Chinese book'

The rhythmic redistribution of accents in French and English will be dealt with extensively in chapters 13 and 15.

7.5 Conclusion

On the one hand, this chapter has pulled together information about intonational phonology that already figured in earlier chapters, while on the other it preluded on the language descriptions in chapters 9–15. The next chapter explores the way these intonational structures can be described in Optimality Theory. It is possible to skip that chapter and still profitably study the language descriptions, since the optimality-theoretic element in those descriptions concerns certain selected aspects only.

Notes

1. In my description of standard Dutch, L% and H% were explicitly added in Gussen-hoven (1991a). Earlier they had been understood as part of the phonetic realization of 'basic' H*L and L*H in nuclear position (Gussenhoven 1983a), where they contrasted with 'half-completed' versions of the same contours. Absence of L% and H% in these contours came to stand the half-completed realizations in a synthesis-by-rule programme (Gussenhoven and Rietveld 1992).
2. In Greek, the clash is phonetically resolved by lengthening of the vowel of the first syllable in the clash, and to a lesser extent, of the onset consonant of the second syllable. In Italian, onset consonant lengthening is phonological (RADDOPPIOMENTO SINTATTICO), while first vowels are phonetically lengthened (Farnetani and Kori 1983; Nespor and Vogel 1986).

8

Intonation in Optimality Theory

8.1 Introduction

After the syntactic structures that are needed to express a linguistic message have been assembled, words are selected to 'fill' them. Phonologically, these words come as lexical representations and, depending on the language, may include accents or tones. Prosodic constituents will be constructed on the basis of the morpho-syntactic structure, including the information structure, in simultaneous agreement with phonological conditions on size. After the addition of any postlexical tones, adjustments may be made, and the resulting surface representation is delivered to the phonetic implementation (see also section 4.3.1). Optimality Theory (OT) is a grammatical model that aims to explain the relation between the underlying forms (the input) and the surface representation (the output) by assuming that the latter optimally satisfies a ranked series of constraints (Prince and Smolensky 1993; McCarthy and Prince 1993; McCarthy and Prince 1995; Kager 1999; McCarthy 2002). The constraints are taken to be universal, so that differences between languages are describable as differences in constraint rankings. Different rankings give different results, because constraints may conflict, and in such cases higher ranking constraints are enforced at the expense of lower ranking ones (constraint violation). This chapter contains a brief explanation of the principles of OT and applies this theory to tonal and phrasal structures.

An OT treatment of tone is given in Yip (2002), which also briefly summarizes earlier work. Because intonational structure displays features that are not obviously found in segmental structures or even in lexical tonal structures, it is worth while to bring intonational data to bear on OT.[1] Thus, in this chapter, an important modification to the conception of *tonal alignment* is made, following Gussenhoven (1999c, 2000b, 2000a). As explained in section 8.3.4, an alignment constraint requires that the left or right edge of some constituent, in our case a tone, should coincide with the right or left edge of some other constituent, say the ι. Due to the fact that in tone languages tones are generally *associated* in surface structure, earlier interpretations of tone alignment lumped the notion of association together with that of alignment.[2] In intonation, where many tones, both boundary tones and central tones, exist that do not have an association to a TBU, these concepts must be distinguished.

A second modification concerns the phonological material with which a tone must be aligned if it is to satisfy an alignment constraint. Typically, researchers have assumed that satisfaction of right-edge alignment of T is achieved if T is associated with the last TBU of the constituent in question, even if T shares its TBU with other tones on its right. Chapter 12, section 12.5, presents evidence that satisfaction of alignment must only be granted if no other phonological elements, including other tones, appear closer to the relevant edge. That is, a tone fully satisfies right-alignment only if it is the rightmost tone in the domain *and* is located at its right edge. This point is made in section 8.3.

A third modification concerns the simultaneous satisfaction of alignments with opposite edges. This move is motivated by the widespread existence of tones that receive an early and a late target. A close alternative would be the creation of a copy of the tone, and aligning the original tone with one edge and the copy with the other. The effect cannot always be achieved through spreading, for one thing because such double-target tones need not *associate* in both locations. Indeed, some are not associated at all. For another, the two targets may be scaled noticeably differently due to declination; spreading tones typically retain a single F_0 (Akinlabi and Liberman forthcoming).

More work in OT has perhaps been done on prosodic phrasing, in particular by Selkirk (1995a, 2000) and Truckenbrodt (1995, 1999). In section 8.5, I repeat Selkirk's analysis of ι-phrasing in the English VP, which also involves work by Truckenbrodt, and subject it to a critical discussion. The account aptly illustrates the three types of information that are relevant to prosodic phrasing, morpho-syntactic structure, information structure (focus), and the resulting size of the prosodic constituent. First, however, section 8.2 sketches the broad outlines of OT. The subsequent two sections deal with the tonal representation and with phrasing, respectively.

8.2 Gen, Eval, and Con

OT comprises a component GEN(ERATOR) which freely generates a large set of candidate output forms by improvising on the input form. Constraints that no language violates will keep this generation in check, but otherwise anything goes. Likely universals for GEN to obey are Goldsmith's (1976) NOCROSSING, which bans crossed associations, and LINEARITY, which forbids sequences that contradict any sequencing in the input, like metathesis (McCarthy 2002: 32).[3] Both constraints enforce faithfulness to linear order. NOCROSSING rules out configurations like (1a), while LINEARITY rules out the creation of HL (1b), if the input has the tones in the opposite order, as in a bitonal morpheme.

(1) a. tata   b. tata

    L H   H L

Inviolable constraints in phrasing concern the shape of the prosodic hierarchy. For instance, any representation that features a ϕ encompassing two ιs violates a universal feature of language structure: layeredness (Selkirk 1978, 1995a, and section 8.5.1).

The set of possible output forms generated by GEN is vetted by the constraints in a process known as EVAL(UATOR). The set of universal constraints, referred to as CON(STRAINTS), is ranked for the language in question, and it is this ranking that constitutes the language's grammar. EVAL involves taking the total group of competing output forms produced by GEN to the highest constraint, allowing it to remove forms from the set, and taking the remainder to the next highest, and so on. Any form that violates a constraint where one or more other forms satisfy it, or violates it more where one or more other forms violate it less, is discarded from the set of competing candidates. Whenever more than one form violates the same constraint in equal measure, these all proceed to the next constraint, for as long as is needed for a single, winning candidate to emerge.

8.3 OT and the tonal representation

Broadly, alignment constraints are responsible for creating the underlying tone string, a result that is here taken for granted. (Alignment constraints are considered in section 8.3.4.) Phonological adjustments occur as a result of the interaction of faithfulness constraints, which strive to reproduce the underlying forms in the surface representation, and markedness constraints, which strive to banish phonologically marked forms from the surface representation. Deletion or insertion of a tone or a change in a tone's identity will occur whenever a markedness constraint outranks a conflicting faithfulness constraint. Often, as in the case of Pierrehumbert's account of American English, the tone string arising from the compilation of pitch accent and boundary tones is at the same time the surface representation (Pierrehumbert 1980: 3). Neither does Stockholm Swedish require any phonological adjustments of the underlying tone string. Adjustments of the intonational tone string have been reported for Bengali, which deletes tones that are adjacent to like tones (Hayes and Lahiri 1991a) and the dialect of Venlo, which assimilates a lexical H to intonational L_t in a specific context (see section 12.7.3). However, OT would hold that even in cases like English and Stockholm Swedish it may be argued that adjustments occur, inasmuch as it adheres to *Richness of the Base*. According to this principle, the input to a language's grammar is unrestricted, and any ungrammatical structures are eclipsed by grammatical candidates produced by GEN. In this way, the grammar explains ungrammaticality.

8.3.1 Markedness: OCP and NoContour

Two classes of markedness constraints are OCP and NoContour. The Obligatory Contour Principle (OCP) (Goldsmith 1976, with reference to Leben 1973) militates against the occurrence of adjacent like tones. The strictest interpretation occurs in Bengali, which disallows any L . . . L or H . . . H, however far apart their targets are. The least demanding interpretation is one whereby like tones cannot occur on adjacent TBUs within a morpheme.[4] Since languages like Bengali will necessarily obey the less strict versions, OCP is a scale of inherently ordered constraints, with OCP (T, domain: morpheme), for instance, banning adjacent like tones within a morpheme. While Bengali obeys OCP absolutely, and thus presents not a single instance of adjacent like tones, other languages violate OCP across the board. This is particularly apparent when single occurrences of a multiply associated tone contrast with multiple occurrences of the same tone, as observed in section 6.3.3. In chapter 10, we will see how OCP in Japanese is enforced *in a specific context*, due to the fact that in other contexts, violation of OCP is inevitable because of the need to obey a higher ranking constraint. This type of effect represents a significant argument for assuming violability of constraints, and explains the widespread *non-uniformity of structure*, which arises when a particular form appears in one context, but not in another (McCarthy 2002). OCP is functionally explained by the lack of contrast presented by sequences of similar signals. That is, the hearer is best served by acoustic differences, and repeating phonological elements is therefore not in his interest (cf. Flemming 1995; Boersma 1998).[5]

Articulatory motivations are behind the class of markedness constraints generally referred to as NoContour, which ban complexity in tonal representations. Again, there are more or less lenient enforcements, with LHL being more marked than HL. NoCrowd bans associations of more than one tone with the same TBU. Japanese is a language that I will argue allows only one tone per TBU, the mora. Some languages with moraic associations curb tonal complexity within the syllable, even though no tone is multiply associated. NoRise and NoFall, given in (2a,b), respectively forbid LH and HL contours within the syllable (see section 12.4.3).

(2) a. NoRise: $*(\mu \;\; \mu \;)_\sigma$ b. NoFall: $*(\mu \;\; \mu \;)_\sigma$
                     | | | |
                    L   H   H   L

8.3.2 Faithfulness

Clearly, if NoRise is undominated in a language's grammar, no intrasyllabic LH will survive Eval, but what the surface form will be depends on which input elements the grammar chooses to preserve. Faithfulness is expressed in terms of correspondences between the elements in the input and elements in the output (McCarthy and Prince 1995). By 'element' I mean any phonological substance, like a feature, a segment, a tone, an accent, a constituent like ϕ, but not a relation, like an association or an alignment. There are three constraint 'families', i.e. formulas with variables. One is MAX-IO(Element) ('Maximality': Every element in the input has a correspondent in the output), which disallows deletion. A second is IDENT(Element), which stipulates that any element in the output should be a faithful reproduction of the corresponding element in the input. If the 'Element' is 'T', as in (3) and (4), and MAX-IO(T) $\gg$ ('outranks') IDENT(T), any output form that fails to reproduce all input tones will be removed by MAX-IO(T), as happens to candidates (b) and (c) in tableau (5). As a result, both tones must be preserved, but their value will change. With two tones, H would change to L or L to H. The choice would be determined by whether the identity of H, IDENT(H), is valued more than that of L, IDENT(L). These constraints are left unranked in tableau (5), where HH, candidate (d), and LL, candidate (e), are both optimal. Regardless of the ranking of the IDENT-constraints, candidate (f), where L and H appear in the same order but have each changed their value, always loses to these two, since it violates both identity constraints. (The tableau is to be read in the usual way: constraints are listed from higher to lower as columns, with dashed column separation lines indicating unranked constraints; candidates are listed as rows, with * indicating a violation, *! a fatal violation, and shading exclusion from the candidate set.)

(3) MAX-IO(T): Deletion of tones is prohibited

(4) IDENT(T): * αT_{input}
$|$
$-\alpha T_{output}$

(5)	(L H, $\mu\mu$)	NORISE	MAX-IO(T)	IDENT(H)	IDENT(L)
	a. (μ μ) | | L H	*!			
	b. (μ μ) | L		*!		
	c. (μ μ) | H		*!		
☞	d. (μ μ) | | H H				*
☞	e. (μ μ) | | L L			*	
	f. (μ μ) | | H L			*	*!

By contrast, if IDENT(T) ≫ MAX-IO(T), one of the tones will have to disappear. The choice would be determined by whichever is valued higher given the ranking of the more specific MAX-IO(H) and MAX-IO(L), again left unranked in tableau (6).

(6)

(L H, μμ)	NoRise	Ident(T)	Max-IO(H)	Max-IO(L)
a. (μ μ) | | L H	*!			
☞ b. (μ μ) | L			*	
☞ c. (μ μ) | H				*
d. (μ μ) | | H H		*!		

A third constraint family is DEP(Element), which forbids insertion ('Dependence': Every element in the output has a corresponding element in the input), as in (7). The violation of NoRISE could be avoided in many other ways if we were allowed to add elements. For instance, a third mora in the syllable would allow (8a) to escape the sanctions of NoRISE, but if DEP(μ) were ranked above NoRISE, it would not get anywhere. Similarly, the addition of an M-tone between L and H, as in (8b), would avoid a violation of NoRISE, but the form would be bad if DEP(T) ranks high and weeds out forms with tones that do not appear in the input.

(7) DEP-IO(Element): insertion is prohibited

(8) a. (μ μ μ)σ   b. (μ   μ)σ
        \| \| \| /\
        L   H   L MH

In chapters 10 and 12 we will see three interestingly different effects of a high-ranked NoRISE in Tokyo Japanese and Roermond Dutch. An example of violation of IDENT(T) occurs in the Dutch dialect of Venlo (chapter 12).

8.3.3 Association

As explained in section 7.2.3, tones may or may not associate. Anttila and Bodomo (2000) create associations with the help of a constraint family requiring TBUs to be associated with a tone, TBU←T (9); and another requiring tones to be associated with TBUs, T→TBU (10). In Anttila and Bodomo (2000), these constraints have the combined effect that exactly *one* tone is associated with a TBU and exactly *one* TBU is associated with a tone, respectively. Here, it is assumed there are separate constraints banning contouring and spreading, respectively, NOCROWD (12) (the strictest version of NOCONTOUR) and NOSPREAD (11) (Gussenhoven 2000b).

(9)   TBU←T: TBUs are associated with T

(10) T→TBU: Tones are associated with TBU

(11) NOSPREAD: A tone is associated with at most one TBU

(12) NOCROWD: A TBU is associated with at most one tone

Constraint TBU←T is a family of constraints, ranging from the general (the mora or the syllable) to the specific (the accented mora). Inherently, more specific versions rank above more general versions. If a language associates tones with moras, it will also associate them with accented moras. At some point along this scale, the constraint NOASSOC is located, causing all potential TBUs below it to be devoid of tone. For instance, the ranking $\sigma' \leftarrow$T$\gg$ NOASSOC $\gg \sigma \leftarrow$T would lead to associations with stressed syllables (σ') only.

(13) NOASSOC: TBUs are not associated with tones

In like manner, T in T→TBU splits so as to create as many subconstraints as there are tones. When there are more tones than TBUs, their ranking will determine which tone goes first and which will remain unassociated, if other constraints like NOCROWD are ranked higher. In effect, the star in a H*L pitch accent is a shorthand notation for the ranking H*→TBU ≫ L→TBU. To illustrate, consider (14), where the first [ta] is an accented syllable, which is also the language's TBU, i.e. TBU stands for TBU:σ*. Because the association of H ranks above that of L, and NOCROWD ranks high, H will associate, while L remains unassociated. The other rankings give contouring, in (14b), and association of L, leaving H as a leading tone, in (14c).

(14) a. tá ta ta   b. tá ta ta   c. tá ta ta
        | /\ |
       HL   HL   HL
     NOCROWD, H→TBU   H→TBU, L→TBU   NOCROWD, L→TBU
     ≫ L→TBU   ≫ NOCROWD   ≫ H→TBU

Competition between tones was earlier treated in an OT framework by Lorentz (1995). We will see an example of this kind of competition in Tokyo Japanese (chapter 10), where there is an additional interest in the intervention of OCP and NORISE, which upset the effects of the ranked associations.

8.3.4   Alignment

Alignment constraints determine the location of a phonological or morphological element relative to the phonological or morphological structure of the expression (McCarthy and Prince 1993). They do this by stipulating that the right/left edge of some constituent should coincide with the right/left edge of some other constituent (Selkirk 1986). The English plural suffix [z] is subject to the constraint in (15), according to which the morpheme's right edge coincides with the right edge of the derived word (McCarthy and Prince 1993: 102), characterizing it as a suffix.

(15) ALIGN-Z: Align([z]$_{PLUR}$,Rt,Word,Rt)

Satisfaction of tonal alignment constraints has generally been taken to be determined by the *association* of tones to an edgemost TBU. In this view, right-alignment of H is satisfied not only by (16a), but also by (16b), while violations are incurred by (16c), where H is not associated to the last mora; and (16d), where H is not associated at all.

(16) $\mu\,\mu\,\mu$ $\mu\,\mu\,\mu$ $\mu\,\mu\,\mu$ $\mu\,\mu\,\mu$
            | $\wedge$ |
     a.   H   b.   H L   c.   H   d.   H

There are two reasons why association needs to be distinct from alignment. First, intonational tones are often unassociated, but because unassociated intonational tones are realized, i.e. receive a target, they must be given a location. For instance, the floating (unassociated) trailing L in some language's H*+L is typically realized immediately after the target of H*. I assume that this is because L's left edge is aligned with the right edge of H. In effect, this is like Riad's (1998) CONCATENATE, which I interpret as in (17). Or again, the Swedish focal H does not associate, yet must be characterized as occurring immediately after the last lexical tone as opposed to before it, because that is where it receives its target.[6]

(17) CONCATENATE: Tones in bitonal morphemes are aligned with each other

The second reason for separating OT alignment and association is that tones originating from different morphemic sources may compete for the same edge. In some tonal dialects of Dutch, the lexical tone associating with the last mora of the ι precedes the final boundary tone(s) of the ι, as in (18a), while in other dialects it follows them, as in (18b). Since both configurations would satisfy right-alignment in the traditional interpretation, alignment cannot be used to decide which tonal order is to be generated. Since alignment constraints are generally used as the mechanism to determine the order of morphemes, it would be undesirable to devise a different one just for tones.[7]

(18) $\mu\,\mu\,\mu$ } $\mu\,\mu\,\mu$ }
            $\wedge$ $\wedge$
     a.   L$_\iota$ H   b.   H L$_\iota$

The choice offered in (18) arises because tones are aligned with coinciding, though different, constituent edges. Specifically, H aligns with the right edge of the syllable and L_ι with the right edge of ι. In ι-final position, these edges are identical, prosodic structure being hierarchical. That is, the representation obtaining at the end of an expression is more realistically rendered as (19a) than as the notationally more convenient (19b), which is a left-to-right metaphor of low-to-high constituency. Thus, right-alignment with σ and right-alignment with ι are in conflict if the right edge of σ coincides with the right edge of ι.

(19) $)_\upsilon$
        $)_\iota$
        $)_\phi$
        $)_\omega$
        $)$F
    a. $)_\sigma$ b. $)_\sigma)F)_\omega)_\phi)_\iota)_\upsilon$

Two ways of violating alignment

In order to differentiate between (18a) and (18b), the constituent with which the tone is aligned includes all phonological material in it, *including its tones*. In (18b), the right edge of H does not in fact coincide with the right edge of the ι, which after all ends in L_ι. Observe that in the segmental domain, we would not accept a representation whereby a right-aligned consonant, say, precedes any other segments in its mora. That is, if some suffix [z] is right-aligned with a word that contains [i], satisfaction is achieved by [iz], not *[zi], even if both [z] and [i] are associated with the last mora. For tones, the situation is no different. In the present conception of tonal alignment, therefore, right alignment of H in (16) is satisfied by (16a) and (16d), and not by either (16b) or (16c) (Gussenhoven 2000a, b).

Violation of the alignment of a tone T can thus occur for different reasons. First, a violation is incurred for every tone that separates T from the relevant edge. Second, if T is associated, as many violation marks are incurred as there are TBUs between the T's TBU, or its edgemost TBU in the case of a multiply associated tones, and the constituent edge. There is a potential problem here in that a 'tonal' violation of, say, right-alignment of H by the additional L of (16b), may have to be weighed against a 'TBU' violation, like the association to the penultimate mora in (16b). I have not been able to establish cases where this question is relevant, however.

To illustrate, consider Roermond Dutch (20a), where H_ι associates with the last stressed syllable of the ι. The unaccented word '*eindelik* 'at last' has two unstressed syllables after the first, stressed syllable, and therefore creates an earlier high target than if the last word had been a monosyllabic word like *klaor* 'ready' or *gæt* 'some' (Gussenhoven 2000a). This can be described, first, by ranking TBU$(\sigma')\leftarrow$T $\gg$ NoAssoc, to enforce association to a stressed syllable; and second, by assuming ALIGN(H_ι,Rt) ≫ ALIGN(H_ι,Left). The correct form is (20a): (20b) incurs a fatal violation on ALIGN(H_ι,Rt) for skipping the stressed syllable *ein-*, while (20c) incurs a fatal violation of TBU(σ')←T. In tableau (21), all candidates equally violate right-alignment of H_ι due to the presence of L_ι, a violation which is inevitable, because of LINEARITY, and is not shown.

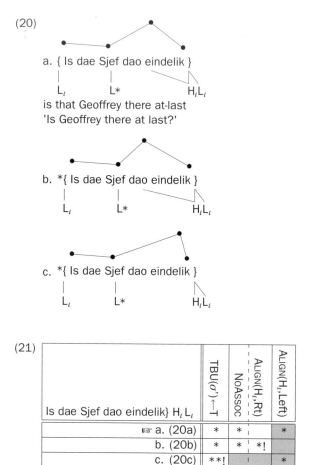

(20)

a. { Is dae Sjef dao eindelik }
L_ι L* $H_\iota L_\iota$
is that Geoffrey there at-last
'Is Geoffrey there at last?'

b. *{ Is dae Sjef dao eindelik }
L_ι L* $H_\iota L_\iota$

c. *{ Is dae Sjef dao eindelik }
L_ι L* $H_\iota L_\iota$

(21)

Is dae Sjef dao eindelik} $H_\iota\,L_\iota$	TBU(σ')←T	NoAssoc	ALIGN(H_ι,Rt)	ALIGN(H_ι,Left)
☞ a. (20a)	*	*		*
b. (20b)	*	*	*!	
c. (20c)	**!			*

8.3.5 Violating CONCATENATE

If a tone is not associated, its realization typically amounts to a target in the syllable at the edge where the tone is aligned, but the timing of the target may vary across tones and languages. For instance, the target of H_ϕ in an *ι*-final Bengali L* $H_\phi L_\iota$ contour occurs in the penultimate syllable if the stress is two syllables away from the edge, but occurs between the last and the penultimate if L* is on the penultimate syllable, while if L* is in the last syllable, the high target would obviously be squarely in the final syllable. By contrast, Bengali H_ι of the interrogative contour L* $H_\iota L_\iota$ occurs in the final syllable, regardless of the distance between the accented syllable and the ι-end. In Hungarian, the equivalent of H_ι would occur further away from the edge if space allows (Ladd 1996; Varga 2002). This kind of detail is to be left to the phonetic implementation, just as would the VOT of an aspirated plosive, which varies cross-linguistically (Shimizu 1996; Ladefoged and Cho 2000). However, a tone's choice of the edge where it is to be realized must be part of the representation, even in the case of unassociated tones. In section 7.3.1, in particular (18), we saw that while the tones of bitonal pitch accents are often pronounced in immediate succession, their targets can also be timed so as to occur as far apart as other tones will let them. For instance, the trailing H of the intonational pitch accent of East Norwegian, L*H, is pronounced as far to the right as the next L* (chapter 11). In this situation, CONCATENATE ranks below a constraint that right-aligns the trailing tone. This is shown in (22a). If CONCATENATE ≫ ALIGN(H,Rt), form (22b) wins, a pattern that is attested for lexical pitch accents in Swedish, Japanese, and many other languages. The assumption that (22a,b) represent different products of the grammar implies that the phonological representation must include the notion 'aligned with', such that HL . . . H is different from H . . . LH. The OT subtheory of alignment in fact nicely predicts that both situations should exist.

(22)

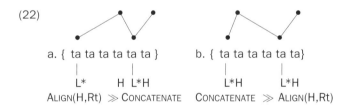

  a. { ta ta ta ta ta ta }   b. { ta ta ta ta ta ta}

     | | | |

     L*   H L*H   L*H   L*H

  ALIGN(H,Rt) ≫ CONCATENATE   CONCATENATE ≫ ALIGN(H,Rt)

In this view, the primary motivation for assuming a bitonal pitch accent is therefore not that the two targets are pronounced close together, as generally assumed (e.g. Frota 1998), but morphological: a pitch accent is bitonal because it represents a single choice in the grammar, and if it is intonational, has non-compositional meaning.

8.3.6 Simultaneous satisfaction of opposite alignments

OT alignment not only predicts that tones can choose an edge, it also provides a mechanism for describing the creation of two targets for one tone, one early and one late, as shown in section 7.3.4. This situation can be explained as the simultaneous satisfaction by a tone of opposite alignment constraints. To give a further example, when in the dialect of Venlo, $H_\iota H_\upsilon$ follow a L*-accented syllable containing two sonorant moras, L* associates with the first and H_ι with the second mora of the accented syllable, as shown in (23). At the same time, H_ι associates with the last stressed syllable of the ι (cf. the Roermond case in (20a)), entitling it to two targets. The other ι-final boundary tone of the Venlo dialect, L_ι, behaves in the same way after H*, and the association with the free TBU in the accented syllable is thus entirely general.

(23)

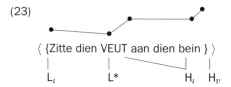

⟨ {Zitte dien VEUT aan dien bein } ⟩

L_ι L* H_ι H_υ

Again, in either location, association will be dependent on other factors, as usual. In the case of Venlo's H_ι, both locations will lead to associations, as in (23). By contrast, in the case of English H*L H_ι, the trailing L does not associate, yet acquires two targets, as in (24). In such cases, we have so far only given the *first* target in graphic representations of the contours, as in the case of the initial boundary L_ι in English, which equally has a target at the beginning of ι and one immediately before the first pitch accent. In (24), both targets are shown, which practice I will follow from now on.

(24)

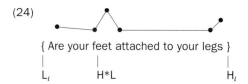

{ Are your feet attached to your legs }

L_ι H*L H_ι

A comment on the semantics of the phonological representation is in order. The claim inherent in (24) is that L, for instance, is immediately adjacent to H* on its left and to H_ι on its right, as well as floating, i.e. not associated. Graphically, this representation might be depicted with the help of a horizontally drawn out L-symbol, if typographical convention and plain esthetics did not militate against this. Also, this notation would incorrectly suggest that phonological objects have size. Really, they only have edges, and the tones's extension in time is governed by the way they are included in prosodic structure through alignment and association. That is, although L in (24) is printed where it is and has no association lines, its alignment is equivalent to that of H_ι in (23). Every alignment entitles the tone to a target, while an alignment that leads to an association may cause that target to be timed more precisely than if there was no association.

Also, our notational conventions need to be more specific. So far, a boundary tone has been shown as having an association with the constituent bracket, following Hayes and Lahiri (1991a), even though the tone is only *aligned* with the edge concerned. As Jörg Peters points out, it is in fact preferable to use association lines only for true (moraic or syllabic) association, and boundary tones will therefore from now on be shown without their 'association line' to the bracket; after all, their printed alignment and their label adequately show their timing and status. Second, if a boundary tone is aligned both left and right, an arrow will be added pointing in the direction of the other edge if there is no association in that location, as in Gussenhoven (1999c).

To illustrate, I deal with (24) in tableau (26). One more constraint is needed. In Gussenhoven (1999c, 2000a), I proposed a constraint SINGLETARGET, according to which a tone may have only one target. Since in OT, markedness constraints typically bar structure, the constraint can be replaced with NOTARGET, as in (25).

(25) NOTARGET: A tone has no target

NOTARGET is high-ranked in the case of unrealized tones, but ranks below the left-edge and right-edge alignment constraints for any tone that creates two targets. In the case of (24), this is true for L_ι and L, but not for H_ι. When opposite alignments of a boundary tone both outrank NOTARGET, their mutual ranking determines whether it is final or initial. The highest ranking edge-alignment represents the usual morphological status of the tone as a right-edge or left-edge tone, while the lower ranking alignment establishes the tone's realization away from the edge. In tableau (26), the ranking ALIGN(L_ι,Left) ≫ ALIGN(L_ι,Rt) makes L_ι a left-edge boundary tone with an early and a late target, as opposed to a right-edge boundary tone with an early and a late target. The trailing tone, too, has two targets, due to ALIGN(L,Left) and ALIGN(L,Rt). (ALIGN(L,Left) is equivalent to CONCATENATE(H^*L).) Right-hand boundary tones never appear to create an early target in English, so that ALIGN(H_ι,Rt) ≫ NOTARGET ≫ ALIGN(H_ι,Left). In tableau (26), I have taken the association of H^* for granted. NOTARGET is violated six times by candidate (a), since both initial L_ι and trailing L satisfy opposite alignments, as is evident from their two targets and the arrows. It is the optimal form, however. Candidate (b) violates ALIGN (L,Rt) in addition to the six violations of NOTARGET, while Candidate (c) does not violate NOTARGET to the same degree, but lacks a late target for L_ι and an early target for trailing L. Candidate (d) fails to align H_ι finally in the ι, incurring a violation of ALIGN(H_ι,Rt). Of course, if this first tone were the initial L_ι of the input, it would not violate any alignment constraint, but the form would instead be rejected by IDENT(T), since, unfaithfully, the surface correspondent of L_ι would be H_ι.

(26)

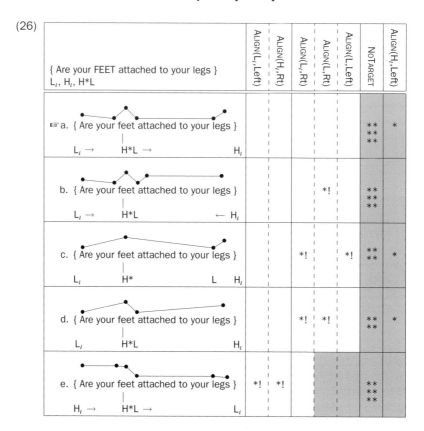

{ Are your FEET attached to your legs } L_t, H_t, H*L	ALIGN(L$_t$,Left)	ALIGN(H$_t$,Rt)	ALIGN(L*,Rt)	ALIGN(L,Rt)	ALIGN(L,Left)	NoTARGET	ALIGN(H$_t$,Left)
☞ a. { Are your feet attached to your legs } $L_t \rightarrow$ H*L → H_t						** ** **	*
b. { Are your feet attached to your legs } $L_t \rightarrow$ H*L ← H_t				*!		** ** **	
c. { Are your feet attached to your legs } L_t H* L H_t			*!		*!	** **	*
d. { Are your feet attached to your legs } L_t H*L H_t			*!	*!		** **	*
e. { Are your feet attached to your legs } $H_t \rightarrow$ H*L → L_t	*!	*!				** ** **	

Crucial ranking of NoTARGET above ALIGN(H_t,Left) would occur is a structure like (27), if only two targets are allowed.

(27)

L* H_t

A note on the behaviour of T* closes this section. To account for the presence of pitch accents in accented syllables, Pierrehumbert extended the notion of 'alignment' to coincidence with prosodic heads, in addition to edges (Pierrehumbert 1993). She thus assumes a constraint like ALIGN(H*,*) which locates H* in the accented syllable. In our framework, this constraint is equivalent to H*→TBU (see section 8.3.3). Since this latter constraint only governs the association of T*, the question arises within our framework whether it is meaningful for T* to be aligned, as distinct from associated. In fact, pitch accents may align, though not associate, and they may also have two targets, just like other tones. In chapter 11, we will see how Norwegian L* only associates with the stressed syllable if that syllable does not already have a lexical H associated to it, a case of *non-uniformity of structure*. In this language, T*→TBU is outranked by H_{Lex}→TBU. The location of L* to the right of the lexical H is governed by its left-alignment with the lexical tone (cf. CONCATENATE). Second, simultaneous satisfaction of ALIGN(H*,*) and ALIGN(H*,Rt), occurs in the English contour in (28), where the left-aligned, but not the right-aligned location results in an association.

(28)

{ Are your feet attached to your legs }

$L_l \rightarrow$ H* $\rightarrow$ H_l

8.4   Positional effects

Phonological contrasts tend to accumulate in particular locations in structure (see section 3.3.2). This means that constraints need to be made sensitive to the phonological context. For instance, it has been noted by Zoll (1997) and Zhang (2000) that the usual alignment constraints cannot deal with one-to-one directional mapping of the sort illustrated for Etung in section 3.3.2. If there are more tones than TBUs, this mapping creates contour tones at the same edge of the word as the edge towards which tones spread if there are more TBUs than tones. Edge-alignment, however, will create contour tones on one edge and spread tones towards the other edge. In tableau (29), high ranking of right-alignment correctly selects right-contouring candidate (a) for HL, but incorrectly selects left-spreading candidate (b) for HLH. If we reverse the ranking, as in tableau (30), the opposite results are obtained. Neither ranking, therefore, can produce the correct candidate forms.

(29)

(L H, $\mu\mu\mu$)	ALIGN(T,Left)	ALIGN(T,Rt)
☞ a. $\mu\ \mu\ \mu$ H L		*
b. $\mu\ \mu\ \mu$ H L	*!	
(H L H, $\mu\mu$)		
a. $\mu\ \mu$ H L H	*!	
☞ ! b. $\mu\ \mu$ H L H		*

(30)

(L H, $\mu\mu\mu$)	ALIGN(T,Rt)	ALIGN(T,Left)
a. $\mu\ \mu\ \mu$ H L	*!	
☞ ! b. $\mu\ \mu\ \mu$ H L		*
(H L H, $\mu\mu$)		
☞ a. $\mu\ \mu$ H L H		*
b. $\mu\ \mu$ H L H	*!	

Zhang (2000) proposes to solve the dilemma by means of positional markedness, which restricts phonological contrasts to specific contexts. By ranking a constraint banning contour tones in non-final syllables above a general NoContour, as in (31), contour tones will be tolerated in final syllables in preference to non-final ones.[8] This solution predicts that words like *tátàtà*, with a contour tone on a non-final syllable, are universally absent. This is most probably incorrect, as historical vowel deletions will readily lead to word-internal contour tones in underlying representations (cf. chapter 6), but such exceptions can be countered by high-ranking faithfulness.

  (31) $*T_1T_2\text{-}\sigma_{\text{nonfinal}} \gg *T_1T_2$ (Zhang 2000)

Positional constraints can account for the neutralization of the lexical tone contrast in the Venlo dialect, which causes minimal pairs like *pǎerd* 'horse' – *páerd* 'horses', which are distinct in (32a,b), to be homophonous in (32c).

  (32) a.

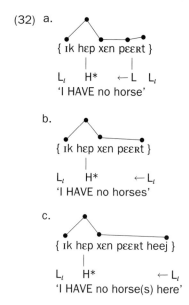

     { ɪk hɛp xɛn pɛɛʀt }

     L$_\iota$ H* ←L L$_\iota$
     'I HAVE no horse'

    b.

     { ɪk hɛp xɛn pɛɛʀt }

     L$_\iota$ H* ←L$_\iota$
     'I HAVE no horses'

    c.

     { ɪk hɛp xɛn pɛɛʀt heej }

     L$_\iota$ H*   ←L$_\iota$
     'I HAVE no horse(s) here'

Unless it occurs in an accented or ι-final syllable, a lexical tone is deleted. Since neither context obtains in (32c), the lexical tone of *paert* 'horse' is lost. The loss of this tone cannot be attributed to NoAssoc, since the syllable from which it disappears standardly serves as a TBU for T_ι. In (20a), for instance, H$_\iota$ associates with the third syllable from the right edge, the rightmost stressed syllable, which must therefore be a valid TBU. Instead of attributing deletion of H to NoAssoc, it can be blamed on its failure to align correctly. If the highest alignment constraint for lexical H is the 'positional' (33), it will not align in locations specified by a lower ranking, more general alignment constraint. In tableau (35), lexical T in the input is preserved in winning candidate (a), while tableau (36) shows how the same ranking leads to the deletion of T in an unaccented, ι-medial syllable.

If the language deletes floating central tones, as indicated by high-ranking * (T) (34), the case for deletion is sealed in (36).[9]

(33) ALIGN($H_{Lexical}$,Rt,$\sigma_{\iota\text{-final}/^*}$,Rt): Align the right edge of H with the right edge of an ι-final or accented syllable

(34) * (T): Delete floating central tones

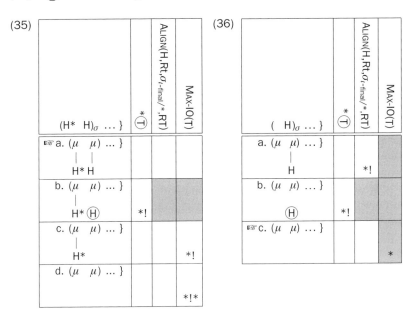

8.5 OT and prosodic phrasing

What determines the division of utterances into prosodic phrases? There are three factors that are likely to figure in any discussion of this topic. First, prosodic constituents tend to have their right or left edges coincide with the corresponding edges of specific morpho-syntactic constituents (Selkirk 1986; Selkirk and Shen 1990). Second, many languages require the left or right edge of the focus constituent, roughly the 'new information', to coincide with some prosodic constituent (Pierrehumbert and Beckman 1988; Kanerva 1989; Hayes and Lahiri 1991a). Third, the length of prosodic constituents tends to be less variable than that of morpho-syntactic constituents, which is due to size constraints on prosodic phrases, like the constraint in Basque requiring the first ip to consist of minimally two αs (see chapter 9), and to constraints which restrict the number of accents, as a result of which languages may require precisely (Bengali, Basque) or maximally (Japanese) one accent per phrase (see chapters 9 and 10). These factors are captured in OT by interacting prosodic structure constraints, as I will illustrate with an account of the intonational phrasing of English by Selkirk (2000). I will also briefly discuss the Strict Layering Hypothesis and the ways in which prosodic structure can deviate from it, following Selkirk (1995a). In section 8.5.2, some observations, mainly from the literature, are presented that expand on this description or suggest a modified approach.

8.5.1   Interacting factors in prosodic phrasing

Morpho-syntactic and focus alignment is used by Selkirk (2000) to describe sentence-internal major phrasing in English. Here data would appear to make this constituent equivalent to our ι-phrasing, even though the alignment of the major phrase is with XP, which in the prosodic hierarchy adopted here makes it equivalent to the ϕ; more about this in the next section. To begin with, there are two conflicting alignment constraints: WRAPXP, which requires that the XP be contained in a single major phrase (henceforth ι), following Truckenbrodt (1995, 1999); and ALIGNXP, which is violated by any right-hand XP-boundary which fails to coincide with an ι-boundary. The ranking WRAPXP $\gg$ ALIGNXP would create a single ι for the VP *(She) loaned her rollerblades to Robin*; the opposite order would create separate ιs for *(She) loaned her rollerblades* and *to Robin*, since the right edge of each PP, NP, or VP will need to coincide with the right edge of an ι. Because both pronunciations are possible, these constraints are not ranked. The interest is in the effect of the higher ranking third constraint, ALIGNFOC, which requires that the focus constituent right-aligns with ι. If the verb *loaned* is a focus, therefore, it will have to end an ι. In this reading, the influence of ALIGNXP can still be observed, in that an ι-boundary is inserted after *her rollerblades*, as shown in tableau (37). Candidates (a) and (b) fail to satisfy ALIGNFOC. Although candidates (c) and (d) both satisfy this constraint, (c) is selected, because (d) fails to satisfy ALIGNXP. Since WRAPXP is violated equally by (c) and (d), it is incapable of deciding between them. The context for (37) is one in which there is a rumour that 'she' has been getting rid of all her stuff. The speaker is checking diary entries for evidence of this, finds the sentence given in (37), and reads it out. While everything is 'new', the verb has a special emphasis.

(37)

She [[lóaned]$_{V,FOC}$ [her róllerblades]$_{NP}$ [to Róbin]$_{PP}$]$_{VP}$	ALIGNFOC	WRAPXP	ALIGNXP
a. (she **lóaned** her róllerblades to Róbin)$_\iota$	*!		*
b. (she **lóaned** her róllerblades)$_\iota$ (to Róbin)$_\iota$	*!	*	
☞ c. (she **lóaned**)$_\iota$ (her róllerblades)$_\iota$ (to Róbin)$_\iota$		*	
d. (she **lóaned**)$_\iota$ (her róllerblades to Róbin)$_\iota$		*	*!

The case parallels Truckenbrodt's (1995) analysis of Chicheŵa, where in a neutral pronunciation a single ϕ is used for the VP in (38), as in (39a), which could

be a reply to 'What happened?' (Kanerva 1989). In this case, Wʀᴀᴘ outranks
AʟɪɢɴXP rather than being unranked with it, but this is not relevant to the point at
issue. Narrow focus again requires a ϕ-boundary after the focus constituent (see
also section 9.4.3), which is apparent from tonal effects as well as penultimate
lengthening. Unless this occurs after [mwalá], the VP-internal boundary will
constitute a violation of Wʀᴀᴘ, and once this constraint is violated, as in (39b,c),
AʟɪɢɴXP will force ι-boundaries after every XP. This is why in (39c) a ϕ-
boundary emerges after the non-focus NP [nyuúmba].

(38) [Anaményá]ᵥ [nyumbá]ɴᴘ [ndí mwalá]ᴘᴘ

(39) a. [Anaményá nyumbá ndí mwáála]_ϕ

he-hit the-house with the-rock

b. [Anaményuá nyuúmba]_ϕ [ndí mwáála]_ϕ

'He hit the HOUSE with the rock'

c. [Anaméenya]_ϕ [nyuúmba]_ϕ [ndí mwáála]_ϕ

'He HIT the house with the rock'

Tableau (37) also makes it clear that if there is no internal focus, the non-ranking
of Wʀᴀᴘ and AʟɪɢɴXP will account for the well-formedness of both (a) and
(b), each of which violates one of these constraints. The phrasing of candidate
(c) is now ungrammatical, however. This is because WʀᴀᴘXP, AʟɪɢɴXP, and
AʟɪɢɴFᴏᴄ interact with phonological constraints that impose size restrictions on
phrases. Prosodic constituents avoid being either too short too or long. Selkirk's
(2000) BɪɴMᴀᴘ, which stipulates that a major phrase consists of exactly two
minor phrases, combines both tendencies. It explains why in a pronunciation
without special focus, the even-balanced candidate (b) in tableau (40) is better
than either candidate (a), which incurs a violation of lower ranked BɪɴMᴀᴘ for
having an ι that is too long; or candidate (c), which incurs two violations of this
constraint for having two ιs which are too short. Since unranked WʀᴀᴘXP and
AʟɪɢɴXP are violated equally by all three candidates, lower ranked BɪɴMᴀᴘ
can decide. Candidate (d) founders on both AʟɪɢɴXP and WʀᴀᴘXP before it
can reach BɪɴMᴀᴘ.

(40)

She [[lóaned] [her róllerblades]ɴᴘ [to Róbin's síster]ᴘᴘ]ᵥᴘ	Aʟɪɢɴ Fᴏᴄ	Wʀᴀᴘ XP	Aʟɪɢɴ XP	Bɪɴ Mᴀᴘ
a. (she lóaned her róllerblades to Róbin's síster)_ι			*	*!
☞ b. (she lóaned her róllerblades)_ι (to Róbin's síster)_ι			*	
c. (she lóaned)_ι (her róllerblades)_ι (to Róbin's síster)_ι			*	*!*
d. (she lóaned)_ι (her róllerblades to Róbin's síster)_ι		*	*!	**

The above description nicely summarizes the ways in which the various factors that determine prosodic phrasing can be made to interact in an OT description. In the remainder of this section I will briefly discuss the possible violations of the Strict Layering Hypothesis, given in (41), after Selkirk (1984).

> (41) Strict Layering Hypothesis: A prosodic constituent of rank n is immediately dominated by a single constituent of rank $n+1$.

For the purposes of OT, Selkirk (1995) broke this principle down into four separate constraints. Two of these are violable: NONRECURSIVITY, which is violated by any constituent that dominates a constituent of the same level; and EXHAUSTIVITY, which militates against skipping levels. The other two belong to GEN, and forbid reversals whereby constituent n is dominated by a constituent $n-1$ (LAYEREDNESS), and incomplete nodes whereby a non-terminal constituent fails to dominate a constituent of a lower rank (HEADEDNESS).

> (42) NONRECURSIVITY A prosodic constituent of level n may not dominate another prosodic constituent of level n.

> (43) EXHAUSTIVITY A prosodic constituent of level n exhaustively dominates constituents of level $n-1$.

Exhaustivity is violated by extraprosodic structures like (44), in which the first (unstressed) syllable is not part of any foot, but is directly dominated by the ω-node (cf. Pierrehumbert and Beckman 1988: 100).

> (44) [tə [mɑːtəʊ]$_F$]$_\omega$

NONRECURSIVITY excludes representations like (45), where ϕ_1 is dominated by a constituent of the same rank, ϕ_2. That is, the ϕ BA in (45a) as well as the ϕ AB in (45b) each dominate a ϕ A. This type of structure has been motivated by Inkelas (1989) for Hausa and by Truckenbrodt (1999) for Kimatuumbi, as well as for Dutch by Lahiri, Jongman, and Sereno (1990) in the case of ω. In chapter 14, we will adopt multiply nested structures like these for the English ϕ and ι. For the ϕ, the procliticized structure in (45a) will be adopted on the basis of the resolution of clashing pitch accents in the NP. For the English ι, an encliticized structure here given for ϕ in (45b) will be motivated on the basis of the pronunciation of reporting clauses and epithets (cf. Bing 1979).

> (45) a. [B [A] ϕ_1]ϕ_2
>   b. [[A]ϕ_1 B]ϕ_2

In section 14.3.3, a solution within OT will be adopted that creates these unbalanced structures by allowing alignment constraints to create prosodic boundaries at one edge without allowing the opposite alignment constraints to create prosodic edges at the other edge. As a result, a morpho-syntactic structure like *[A very interesting [Irish novel]]* can be converted into the prosodic structure *(A very interesting (Irish novel))* (cf. (45a)).

8.5.2   Three issues in the Selkirk–Truckenbrodt account

A number of elements in the above account allow for alternative interpretations. First, non-ranking, which produces multiple correct outputs, may be contrasted with *variable ranking*. Under variable constraint ranking, the grammar actually decides between two possible structures on the basis of a specific ranking of what are unranked constraints in Selkirk's solution. In the case of the French ϕ, variability between coarser and finer phrasing options can be dealt with in this way, as proposed by Anttila (1997) (cf. also Kager 1999: 404). Specifically, constraints demanding alignment with highest and non-highest nodes in the NP may freely rerank, so as to produce ϕs for each lower node or just a single ϕ for the highest node. Depending on the ranking, therefore, a morphosyntactic structure like *[[des garçons] [intelligents]]* can either be converted into the prosodic structure *(des garçons) (intelligents)* or into *(des garçons intelligents)* (see further section 13.2.5). At this point, the difference between non-ranking and variable ranking might seem trivial, but longer expressions may well present a sequence of potential prosodic boundaries which could be decided on independently. If we present the whole expression to EVAL, two constraints may have to appear in one ranking for one boundary and in another for the other in order to produce a required output. There seem to be two possible ways out of this predicament:

1. The constraints are ranked at every point at which a decision must be made, an option we might refer to as ranking 'on the hoof'. Under this option, constraints might be weighted (cf. Boersma 1998) and their weights be influenced by factors like speech style.
2. The evaluation takes place in a cyclic fashion, such that smaller constituents are provided with a prosodic structure which may or may not be copied into the larger constituent.

Truckenbrodt (2002b) has pointed out that non-ranking cannot in fact be maintained by showing that the description in section 8.5.1 fails to account for variable ϕ-phrasing within the Bengali NP. In a left-branching NP like (46), there are four legitimate phrasings. Note that prepositions ('postpositions') come after their NP in Bengali, here 'the king's pictures'. Structures (47a,b,c,d) exhaust the possible pronunciations: no other distribution of the words over ϕs is possible.

(46) NP: [[[[radʒar]ₙₚ tʃʰobir]ₙₚ dʒonno]ₚₚ ṭaka]ₙₚ
      king+GEN pictures+GEN for money
      'money for the king's pictures'

(47) a. [radʒar tʃʰobir dʒonno ̪taka]
     b. [radʒar tʃʰobir dʒonno] [̪taka]
     c. [radʒar tʃʰobir] [dʒonno] [̪taka]
     d. [radʒar] [tʃʰobir] [dʒonno] [̪taka]

However, as will be evident in tableau (48), with WRAP and ALIGN(XP,ϕ), we can get the coarse-grained phrasing of candidate (a) if WRAPXP $\gg$ ALIGN(XP,ϕ), or the fine-grained phrasing of candidate (d) if ALIGN(XP,ϕ) $\gg$ WRAPXP, but it is unclear how the intermediate candidates (b) and (c) are to be obtained. This problem arises whenever there is more than one location in an expression where a phrasing decision must be made.

(48)

[[[radʒar tʃʰobir] dʒonno] ̪taka]	WRAPXP	ALIGN(XP,ϕ)
a. [radʒar tʃʰobir dʒonno ̪taka]$_\phi$		∗∗∗
b. [radʒar tʃʰobir dʒonno]$_\phi$ [̪taka]$_\phi$	∗	∗∗
c. [radʒar tʃʰobir]$_\phi$ [dʒonno]$_\phi$ [̪taka]$_\phi$	∗	∗
d. [radʒar]$_\phi$ [tʃʰobir]$_\phi$ [dʒonno]$_\phi$ [̪taka]$_\phi$	∗	

Of the two above approaches, Truckenbrodt proposes the cyclic type. He adopts Elenbaas's (1999) solution to 'inherited' variable pronunciations of secondary stress in derived Finnish words. Pronunciations (49a) and (49b), where the hyphen indicates a suffix boundary, arise from different rankings of a constraint demanding feet to be leftmost and a constraint demanding that the suffix be included in a binary trochaic foot (see section 2.2). Dominance of leftmost footing gives (49a), and dominance of suffix-footing gives (49b). When a further suffix is added, as in the right-hand column, pronunciation (49b) may persevere in the derived form, as shown in (49d), even though (49c) satisfies both the leftmost footing constraint and the suffix-footing constraint. Elenbaas obtains this effect from Output–Output (OO) faithfulness: form (49d) is faithful to (49b), whereas (49c) is faithful to (49a). In general, OO-faithfulness relates the pronunciation of a form to the pronunciation of a paradigmatically related form, typically a subconstituent (see Kager 1999: ch. 6; McCarthy 2002: 172ff.).

(49) a. (áte)(ría)-na   'meal-1SG
     b. (áte)ri(á-na)   *ditto*
     c. (áte)(ría)(-ná-ni)   'meal-1SG-ESSIVE
     d. (áte)ri(á-na)-ni   *ditto*

To return to the variability in (47), Truckenbrodt proposes that the forms chosen for the subconstituents can be passed on to higher nodes of the NP via OO-faithfulness. Using informal formulations of his constraints, I reproduce his solution here, which pits Max$_{OO}$ (50) against *P (51). EXHAUSTIVITY (43) makes sure that no material remains unparsed at the level concerned.

(50) M$_{AX_{OO}}$: Each ϕ in a subconstituent of a syntactic constituent C corresponds to a ϕ in C

(51) *P: Do not form ϕ

In tableau (52), MAX$_{OO}$ is ranked above *P. If we assume that free-standing [radʒar] is assigned a ϕ, then MAX$_{OO}$ requires this ϕ to be present in [radʒar tʃʰobir]. I have added this output in the tableau for clarity. As will be clear, if MAX$_{OO}$ and *P were to be reranked, coarse-grained candidate (52b) would be selected.

(52)

O: [radʒar]$_\phi$ [[radʒar]$_{NP}$tʃʰobir]$_{NP}$	EXHAUSTIVITY	MAX$_{OO}$	*P
☞ a. [radʒar]$_\phi$ [tʃʰobir]$_\phi$			**
b. [radʒar tʃʰobir]$_\phi$		*!	*
c. [radʒar]$_\phi$ tʃʰobir	*!		*

Moving on to the PP [radʒar tʃʰobir dʒonno], there are now two forms which MAX$_{OO}$ could demand faithfulness to: [radʒar tʃʰobir]$_\phi$ and [radʒar]$_\phi$ [tʃʰobir]$_\phi$. Assuming the latter, as shown in the tableau, and assuming that the ranking MAX$_{OO}$ ≫ *P obtains at the point the PP is evaluated, Truckenbrodt's analysis will select the maximally fine-grained phrasing. This is shown in tableau (53), where candidate (a) faithfully reproduces the ϕs of candidate (a) in (52), while candidate (b) fatally loses the fine-grained phrasing.

(53)

O: [radʒar]$_\phi$ [tʃʰobir]$_\phi$ [[[radʒar]$_{NP}$tʃʰobir]$_{NP}$ dʒonno]$_{PP}$	EXHAUSTIVITY	MAX$_{OO}$	*P
☞ a. [radʒar]$_\phi$ [tʃʰobir]$_\phi$ [dʒonno]$_\phi$			***
b. [radʒar tʃʰobir]$_\phi$ [dʒonno]$_\phi$		*!	**
c. [radʒar tʃʰobir dʒonno]$_\phi$		*!	*
d. [radʒar tʃʰobir]$_\phi$ dʒonno	*!	*	*

To obtain coarse-grained candidate (53c), we need *P ≫ MAX$_{OO}$ to be in force during the evaluation of both the NP and the PP. This will produce a single ϕ for the NP [radʒar tʃʰobir], so that candidate (b) of tableau (52) rather than candidate (a) is to be reproduced. Candidate (53a) now fails, because it fatally splits up that ϕ, and candidate (53b) now violates *P more than does (53c). A continued procedure will thus generate the complete set of pronunciations in (47). On the downside, Truckenbrodt's procedure implies a form of postlexical cyclicity that we have kept at bay in the treatment of pitch-accent distribution (see chapter 14). The issue is here whether the notion of 'free-standing form' can be extended from the lexical to the postlexical domain.

The second issue that arises in connection with the description in section 8.5.1 concerns the prediction of the WRAP-cum-ALIGNXP solution that either *all* or *no* XPs are followed by a phrase boundary in cases like (39). When a further word is added, like *dzulo* 'yesterday', and the focus constituent is 'with a rock', a ϕ-boundary appears after the word for 'rock', as predicted, but, unlike what is predicted, no ϕ-boundary appears after *nyumba* 'house', even though it is an NP (Kanerva 1989).

(54) [Anaményá nyumbá ndí mwáála]$_\phi$ [dzúulo]$_\phi$
     'He hit the house with a ROCK yesterday'

Tableau (55) shows how candidate (55b) is incorrectly selected as the winning candidate, where candidate (55a) (=(54)) is the required form as inferred from Kanerva (1989).

(55)

[[[[Anaményá]$_V$ [nyumbá]$_{NP}$]$_{VP1}$ [ndí mwalá]$_{FOC}$]$_{VP2}$ [dzúulo]$_{AdvP}$]$_{VP3}$	ALIGNFOC	WRAPXP	ALIGNXP
a. [Anaményá nyumbá ndí mwáála]$_\phi$ $_\phi$[dzúulo]$_\phi$		*	*!
☞ !b. [Anaményá nyuúmba]$_\phi$ [ndí mwáála]$_\phi$ $_\phi$[dzúulo]$_\phi$		*	
c. [Anaményá nyumbá ndí mwala dzúulo]$_\phi$	*!		**

This suggests that what governs the appearance of ϕ-boundaries in the data in (39) and (54) is a requirement that the ϕ must correspond to a morpho-syntactic constituent (cf. Hirst 1993; Hayes and Lahiri 1991a). Since [Anaményá nyumbá] is a VP, it can be a single ϕ; and so can [Anaményá nyumbá ndi mwalá]. However, [ndi mwalá dzulo] is not a morpho-syntactic constituent, and could thus never be a ϕ in (54). However, as pointed out by Hubert Truckenbrodt (personal communication 2003), an alternative explanation would be that the adverbial is outside the VP, in which case (55a) satisfies WRAP, making it the winner.

While the above two issues concerned the adequacy of the WRAP-cum-ALIGNXP algorithm, the third, somewhat hairy, issue concerns the identity of the prosodic constituents that align with the various levels of the morpho-syntactic structure. In a recent presentation, Selkirk (2003) proposes a default schema relating prosodic constituents to morpho-syntactic constituents, with reference to a similar proposal by Downing (1970). The ι aligns with the root sentence or matrix sentence, which excludes adverbial clauses and various preposed, postposed, and interposed constituents but includes object clauses as in *They thought he's gone.* The next morpho-syntactic level down, the XP or maximal projection, provides the alignment for the major phrase in Selkirk's scheme, in which there is no ϕ. In the framework adopted here, it is the ϕ that aligns with XP, as indeed in Selkirk (1978), Nespor and Vogel (1986), Hayes (1989), and Gussenhoven (1991a), which constituent has generally been taken to be the domain of 'stress shift', the rhythmically induced distribution of pitch accents. However, in Selkirk (2000), the major phrase appears to be equated with an intonationally defined domain, the Intermediate Phrase in Beckman and Pierrehumbert (1986). As a result, the more recent XP-based prosodic constituent has acquired a larger size than the earlier XP-based prosodic constituent, ϕ, larger in fact than is warranted by the 'stress shift' data. Selkirk additionally assumes a minor phrase between the major phrase and the ω, which aligns with branching constituents like compounds, and is equivalent to the Accentual Phrase (α) in Basque, Korean, and Japanese. However, it is too small to account for the 'stress shift' data. (On the issue of the number of prosodic constituents between the ω and the υ, see also sections 14.5 and 15.8.)

Two levels of phrasing are relevant to the intonational prosody of English and French. First, ϕs account for the distribution of pitch accents, and align with XPs. Second, ιs account for the occurrence of T_ι, and in the default case align with the 'root sentence'.[10] Accordingly, I split 'ALIGNXP' up into ALIGN(XP,ϕ), as in (56), and ALIGN(S,ι), as in (57), where S can be equated with 'root sentence'.

(56) ALIGN(XP,ϕ): ALIGN(XP,Rt,ϕ,Rt), or align the right edge of every XP with the right edge of ϕ

(57) ALIGN(S,ι): ALIGN(S,Rt,ι,Rt), or align the right edge of every S with the right edge of ι

The language descriptions in chapters 9–15 successfully treat the French ϕ and the English ϕ on the basis of the evidence from rhythmic redistributions of pitch accents, remaining within the set of assumptions outlined above. The treatment of the English ι avoids the problem of the potential occurrence of multiple prosodic breaks by considering the occurrence of a single prosodic break only.

8.6 Conclusion

In this chapter, the usual interpretation of tonal alignment, whereby location and association are combined in the same constraint, was rejected in favour of separate families of association constraints and alignment constraints. Various cases of unassociated tones having some edge-aligned target were cited in support of this decision. Also, it was argued that a tonal alignment constraint cannot only be violated by failing to be associated with the last mora (for an associated tone) or for failing to project a target near the edge concerned, but also for being separated from the edge by other tones. This interpretation is motivated by the existence of competing orders for tones that are aligned with the same edge. Third, tones with targets on opposite edges formed the motivation for assuming that NoTARGET can be violated by both left and right alignment, allowing a tone to satisfy opposite alignments. This configuration has generally been described as 'spreading', but since often this type of tone does not associate, no such notion in fact applies.

In the section on phrasing, three factors were identified that influence the higher levels of prosodic structure: the morpho-syntactic structure; the information structure; and phonological length. Selkirk's default mapping of morpho-syntactic constituents on prosodic constituents was adopted, such that the ϕ aligns with the XP and the ι with the S. The difference between finer and coarser phrasings can be approached with the help of OO-faithfulness, as proposed by Truckenbrodt, which obviates the apparent need to rerank constraints during the evaluation of a larger constituent.

In chapters 9–15, I have attempted to steer a middle course between ignoring the evidently beneficial effects of OT on our understanding of prosodic grammars, and burdening the language descriptions with theoretical discussion. As a result, while I have kept an OT model rather than a serial rule-based theory in mind throughout, some chapters are more OT-oriented than others. Tonal alignment and association figure prominently in the descriptions of Japanese, Swedish, and the Dutch Limburg dialects, while phrasing appears in an OT treatment in the case of French and English.

Notes

1. See also Selkirk's (forthcoming) optimality-theoretic analysis of Bengali, which came to my attention as this book was going to press.
2. 'Alignment' has the OT sense of 'location in structure', not that of the phonetic timing of a tone's target. 'Alignment' is also widely used in intonation studies to refer to the timing of tonal targets with respect to the segments in the phonetic implementation of tones (Ladd 1996). See also section 7.3.1.
3. Nothing hinges on the assumption that tones never undergo metathesis. If, like segments, they may, LINEARITY is violable, and part of GEN rather than a universal.
4. The occurrence of identical tones on the same TBU is to be ruled out universally, and thus belongs to GEN. Clements and Keyser (1983) referred to this constraint, applied to features and segments generally, as the TWIN SISTER CONVENTION.
5. Some segmental instances are rather to be explained as the articulatory difficulty of repeating the same gesture within some domain, like the syllable (Boersma 1998: chapter 18).
6. A development from a sequence of associated HL to a bitonal pitch accent H*L, in which H* associates and L left-aligns with H*, would appear to have occurred in Yorùbà (Akinlabi and Liberman forthcoming).
7. In chapter 11, we will see that the dialects really differ in the sequencing of the tones, not in their preference for a particular tone contour.
8. An analogous treatment of edge effects in stress patterns is Kager (2002).

9. Earlier, I adopted Beckman's (1997) positional faithfulness constraints to achieve the same effect (Gussenhoven 2000b). It seems superfluous to make both faithfulness and markedness constraints context-sensitive. Positional markedness in this chapter in a sense began with TBU←T.

10. Frequently, there is an ι-boundary after the subject if this contains more than one word. I avoid the complication by considering only the VP, and by choosing pronominal subjects in the examples.

9

Northern Bizkaian Basque

9.1 Introduction

Northern Bizkaian Basque and Tokyo Japanese are genetically unrelated, but their tonal phonologies are strikingly similar. Both languages have lexical tone, although no tone needs to be included in underlying representations if words can be marked for accent. The vocabulary is divided into accented and unaccented words and roots. Affixes may influence the accentuation of the resulting word, causing accents to be assigned or deleted. Compound formation will similarly impose various accent patterns. In Japanese, further deletions may occur postlexically at the phrasal level. Accents that survive in the surface representation will be provided with a pitch accent, which is H*L in both languages. Intonational tones will complete the surface representation. The Japanese system played a crucial role in the development of the metrical–autosegmental model (Pierrehumbert and Beckman 1988) and greatly influenced the descriptions of Basque on which the account in this chapter is based.

The prosodic constituents of Basque and Japanese do not include the usual phonological word (ω) and phonological phrase (ϕ). Instead, descriptions refer to the Accentual Phrase (α) and the immediately dominating Intermediate Phrase (ip). The α is typically larger than the ω of many European languages. The ip is comparable to ϕ in size. Above the ip, there are the usual intonational phrase (ι) and the utterance (υ), though only one of these will be relevant in the account of each language.

This chapter describes a Basque dialect belonging to a group that is spoken within a band of approximately 10–15 km along the Bizkaian coast, in towns like Gernika, Ondarroa, Lekeitio, and Arteaga, further referred to as Northern Bizkaian Basque. The description is based on Elordieta (1997, 1998) and Hualde, Elordieta, Gaminde, and Smiljanić (2002). Only Gernika and Lekeitio will be dealt with. Elordieta, Gaminde, Hernáez, Salaberria, and Martín de Vidales

(1999) deal with Bermeo, while Elordieta (forthcoming) deals with the dialects of Gipuzkoan and High Navarrese, in addition to Lekeitio.

9.2 Lexical representations

Northern Bizkaian Basque is a tone language (by the definition in section 3.2), because the lexical representation of words may include a phonological feature, accent, which surfaces as tone. The lexicon is divided into 'unaccented' roots, like Lekeitio *sagar* 'apple', *ama* 'mother', *itturri* 'fountain', *etxe* 'house', the majority type; and 'accented' roots, like Lekeitio *arbóla* 'tree', *léku* 'place', *mái* 'table', *béste* 'other'. Accented roots are in the minority, but inflectional and derivational morphological processes will cause many words to be accented. In Gernika, as in most of the other dialects, accented suffixes assign accent to the syllable preceding them, i.e. they are pre-accenting. These include the ablative suffix *-tik* and the comitative/instrumental *-gas* as well as a number of plural suffixes, like *-ak, -ata, -ara*. Sometimes the plural form differs from the singular by accent alone. There are also unaccented suffixes, like allative *-ra*.

Regardless of the number of accents assigned in the morphology, only one occurs in a word's lexical representation made available to the intonational phonology (cf. section 4.3.1). On the basis of the location of the surface accent, two types of dialect are distinguished. In a minority variety, Lekeitio, this is always the penultimate syllable, while in the usual case, represented by Gernika, it is the leftmost of the accents introduced by the stem and the pre-accenting suffixes. In (1), these regularities are illustrated for the expressions 'from the apples', 'to the places', and 'to the place'. Basque orthography is retained, as it is phonologically fairly transparent. *j* is [x], *tx* is [tʃ], *tz* is [ts], while *rr* represents a single consonant in the syllable onset, which as a trill contrasts with the flap, spelled *r*.

(1)	Lekeitio		Gernika	
	sagar-´eta-´tik → sagarretátik		sagar-´ata-´tik → sagárratatik	
	'apple-PLUR-ABLATIVE'			
	léku-´ata-ra → lekuetára		léku-´ata-ra → lékuetara	
	'place-PLUR-ALLATIVE'			
	léku-ra → lekúra		léku-ra → lékura	
	'place-ALLATIVE'			

In addition to suffixes assigning accent, compound formation may be expressed accentually. In Lekeitio compounds, accent occurs on the penultimate syllable, regardless of the accentuation of the input forms, as in *begigórri* 'red-eyed', from *begi* 'eye', *gorri* 'red', both unaccented.

The lexical representations are sent on to the postlexical phonology. In Lekeitio, any such word-sized segmental structure is thus unaccented or accented on the penult. In Gernika, it is unaccented, or accented with the accent occurring on any one syllable except the last, and there are thus as many possible prosodic patterns for any segmental structure as the number of its syllables. In (2), two minimal pairs are shown, in Lekeitio (L) and Gernika (G). The accented words on the right will be provided with H*L on the accented syllable. This is the lexical pitch accent, given in (3).[1]

(2) a. laguneri (G), lagunari (L)   lagúneri (G), lagunári (L)
        'to the friend'   'to the friends'
   b. sagarrena (G,L)   sagarréna (G,L)
        'of the apple'   'of the apples'

(3) Lexical pitch accent: H*L

For the remainder of our discussion, we concentrate on the Lekeitio variety. The postlexical regularities are largely the same in the accentual dialects.

9.3 The Accentual Phrase

The constraint against more than one accent in the word is carried over postlexically to the α (4). Tonally, an α is characterized by an initial pitch rise, due to a sequence of LH-boundary tones (5); and a pitch fall, which in αs with a lexical pitch accent begins on the penultimate syllable, due to H*L. In the next subsection, we will see that a default phrasal pitch accent is assigned to the *final* syllable of the lexically unaccented α. This pitch accent has the same shape as (3) and, apart from its different location, is phonetically indistinguishable from it. What is here called the default pitch accent is referred to as the 'derived pitch accent' in Jun and Elordieta (1997).

(4) An α may contain at most one pitch accent

(5) Accentual Phrase Boundary Tones: $(\underset{L_\alpha H_\alpha}{\quad\quad})_\alpha$

There are in principle two ways in which the constraint in (4) could be met, depending on whether the grammar allows the deletion of lexical accents. In Japanese, accents on words that, for rhythmic or structural reasons, get to occur in the same α are deleted (see chapter 10). However, if no deletions are permitted postlexically, as in Basque, it will be necessary to close off lexically accented words by an α-boundary. Going from left to right, an unaccented word in Lekeitio will share an α with the next word, but an accented word will always align its right edge with the right edge of an α. To illustrate, (6a) contains two unaccented words, and one α. In (6b), an unaccented word in first position is included in the α to its right, but in (6c) and (6d), the accented first word triggers an α break, regardless of whether the next word is accented, leading to two αs. Strings of unaccented words can therefore form quite long αs, and the frequent occurrence of long high-pitched stretches in utterances is a notable feature of the dialect. However, since Basque has no postlexical rules that merge accented αs, there will also be many utterances with sequences of pitch peaks: if all the words in a sentence are accented, there will be as many αs.

(6) a. (lagunen dirua)   friend-GEN+SG money   'The friend's money'
    b. (lagunen umíak)   friend-GEN+SG children   'The friend's children'
    c. (lagúnen) (dirua)   friend-GEN+PL money   'The friends' money'
    d. (lagúnen) (umíak)   friend-GEN+PL children   'The friends' children'

9.3.1   Default H*L

As briefly observed in the previous section, a default pitch accent is inserted on the last syllable of an α if it contains unaccented words only. There are two contexts in which this happens. The first, as may be expected, is the end of the utterance, while the second is the position before the finite verb.

A default H*L on an α-final syllable will therefore either coincide with the end of the sentence (if there is no following finite verb) or with the beginning of the finite verb. Example (7a) is a single NP, and (7b) illustrates the α-boundary before the finite verb. In sentences which consist of lexically unaccented verbs only, the default H*L will go to the first lexical verb, as shown in (7c).

(7) a. { (Lagunen dirua) }   friend-GEN+SG money
                    | 'the friend's money'
       $L_\alpha H_\alpha$ H*L

    b. { (Nire amen dirua) (galdu dot) }
                    |
       $L_\alpha H_\alpha$ H*L
       my mother-GEN money lose have-1SG
       'I have lost my mother's money'

    c. { (emon ein dau) }   give do AUX
             | '(S)he gave it'
       $L_\alpha H_\alpha$H*L

9.3.2   Lexical accent in α

Since no α will contain more than one accent, every accented word will be followed by an α boundary. As said above, in Lekeitio, an α ending in an accented word has the accent on the penultimate syllable, and will not have the default accent. The last H*L occurring before the verb (if present), whether default or lexical in origin, is referred to as the nuclear accent, as in Elordieta (1997,

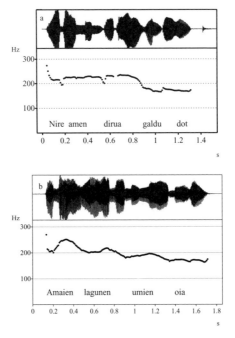

Fig. 9.1 Lexically unaccented α with default H*L on the last syllable of *dirua* in *Nire amen diruá galdu dot* 'I have lost my mother's money' (panel a); and sequence of lexically accented αs in *Amáien lagúnen umíen oiá* 'The bed of the children of Amaia's friends' (panel b).

1998). The NP in (8), which contains three accented αs followed by a lexically unaccented one, is illustrated in panel (b) of figure 9.1.

(8) { (Amaien) (lagunen) (umien) (oia) }
         | | | |
      L$_\alpha$H$_\alpha$ H*L   L$_\alpha$H$_\alpha$ H*L   L$_\alpha$H$_\alpha$ H*L L$_\alpha$H$_\alpha$H*L L$_\iota$
      Amaia-GEN friends-GEN+PL child-GEN+PL bed-ABS
      'The bed of the children of Amaia's friends'

Sequences of accented words, and hence αs, are never subject to rhythmic restructuring.

9.3.3 The pronunciation of L$_\alpha$H$_\alpha$

At the beginning of every α, the boundary sequence L$_\alpha$H$_\alpha$ occurs. Typically, the target of L$_\alpha$ occurs on the first syllable, while that of H$_\alpha$ occurs on the second syllable.[2] However, when the first syllable is occupied by H*, neither L$_\alpha$ nor H$_\alpha$ is realized, and when H* occurs on the second syllable, only L$_\alpha$ is realized. Thus, in (9a), the bitonal L$_\alpha$H$_\alpha$ cannot be realized; in (9b), only L$_\alpha$ is.

(9)

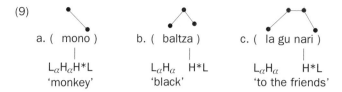

a. (mono)   b. (baltza)   c. (la gu nari)
       | | |
   L$_\alpha$H$_\alpha$H*L   L$_\alpha$H$_\alpha$ H*L   L$_\alpha$H$_\alpha$ H*L
   'monkey'   'black'   'to the friends'

The situation in Basque is parallel to that in Tokyo Japanese, for which Pierre-humbert and Beckman (1988) proposed association as in (10). Without argumentation, I will assume that boundary tones associate in Basque as well, as shown in (10). In section 10.6, an OT treatment is given of the moraic associations in Japanese.

(10) a. (mono)   b. (bal tza)   c. (la gu nari)
         | | | | | |
     L$_\alpha$H$_\alpha$H*L   L$_\alpha$H$_\alpha$ H*L   L$_\alpha$ H$_\alpha$ H*L

9.4 Unaccented α without default H*L

Lexically unaccented words may be closed off by an α boundary which does not coincide with the end of the sentence or the left edge of the finite verb: such αs do not receive a default H*L, and are thus unaccented on the surface.[3] Topicalized constituents may form their own α, like the unaccented NP *Sure erriko alkatia* 'The mayor of your town', which appears in a separate α in (11a) as an alternative to (11b), where it forms a single α with the lexically unaccented *Iruñara*. Possibly a difference in meaning may be felt to exist, with (11a) more so than (11b) suggesting something like 'As for the mayor of our town, he has arrived', but, as Elordieta (1998) points out, the phrasing choice is more likely to depend on the length of constituents. The creation of optional α boundaries appears to be motivated by length, and could fall inside an NP, causing the first α to coincide with a non-constituent NP fragment, as shown in (12).

(11) a.

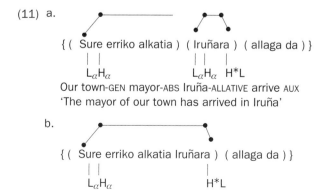

{ (Sure erriko alkatia) (Iruñara) (allaga da) }
        | | | | |
    L$_\alpha$H$_\alpha$ L$_\alpha$H$_\alpha$ H*L
Our town-GEN mayor-ABS Iruña-ALLATIVE arrive AUX
'The mayor of our town has arrived in Iruña'

b.

{ (Sure erriko alkatia Iruñara) (allaga da) }
        | | |
    L$_\alpha$H$_\alpha$ H*L

(12)

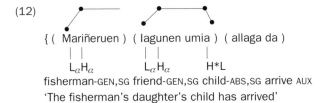

{ (Mariñeruen) (lagunen umia) (allaga da)
    | | | | |
   L$_\alpha$H$_\alpha$ L$_\alpha$H$_\alpha$ H*L
fisherman-GEN,SG friend-GEN,SG child-ABS,SG arrive AUX
'The fisherman's daughter's child has arrived'

At α boundaries in positions other than those in (7), a weak dip occurs, but clearly no H*L. Low pitch occurs on post-accentual syllables and on the first syllables after an accented α, as in the three occurrences of *-en* and the initial syllables *la-, u-,* and *o-* in (8) for instance. Their pitch is clearly lower than the weak dip separating an unaccented α from the next α (Jun and Elordieta 1997).

On H spreading

Elordieta (1998) considers the high-level pitch in a case like (11b) to be due to the rightward spreading of the phrasal H$_\alpha$ to all syllables before H*, rejecting an alternative view whereby the high-level stretch is due to interpolation between two high targets. His motivation for choosing this analysis is that unaccented αs like those in (11a) and (12) have a high-level stretch, too. Spreading, however, represents a position we have learned to suspect since the work of Pierrehumbert and Beckman (1988). A third possible analysis would assume that the initial target of H$_\alpha$ is maintained till the end of the α for lack of further instructions, there being no further tone in the α. Interestingly, as we will see in the next chapter, in Japanese the distance between the equivalents of Basque H$_\alpha$ and L$_\alpha$ *does* in fact show a declining slope, which formed the basis of Pierrehumbert and Beckman's argument that in Japanese there is in fact no spreading of H (see section 11.8). This third option, that of a continued target of a non-associating H$_\alpha$, supports a further position taken by Pierrehumbert and Beckman (1988), who hold that Japanese H$_\alpha$ and L$_\alpha$ occur in the *same* α, as its initial and final boundary tone, respectively. If it is assumed that linear interpolations only take place between tones in the same α, the difference between Basque and Japanese falls out without the need for spreading in either language. I will leave this question open, and treat Japanese H$_\alpha$L$_\alpha$ as a complex initial boundary tone, just as in Basque. Meanwhile, either Eldordieta's spreading analysis, depicted in (13), or an analysis with a continued target could be assumed.

(13) { (Mariñeruen) (lagunen umia) (allaga da)

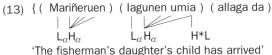

     L$_\alpha$H$_\alpha$ L$_\alpha$H$_\alpha$ H*L
    'The fisherman's daughter's child has arrived'

9.5   The Intermediate Phrase

The relevant constituents above α are the Intermediate Phrase (ip) and the Intonational Phrase (ι). The ι comes with boundary tones that express intonational

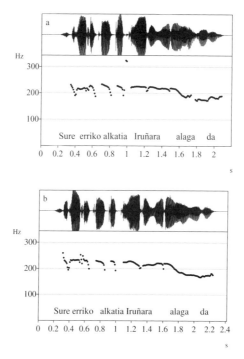

Fig. 9.2 A long unaccented α in *(Sure erriko alkatia Iruñara) (alaga da)* 'The mayor of our town has arrived in Iruña' (panel a, cf. (11b)) and the same sentence with an α-break after *alkatia* (panel b, cf. (11a)).

meanings like declarative, interrogative, listing, etc. Instead of ι, it could also be assumed that it is the υ which provides these boundary tones, rendering the ι superfluous in Basque, as it is in Japanese. (For these intonation contours, see Elordieta 1997, 1998.) A frequently occurring boundary tone is L_ι. There are three aspects of the ip that are discussed in this section. First, the ip is the domain of downstep. Second, the sentence-final finite verb will be argued to be appended to the preceding ip. Third, like ϕ, the ip will be shown to be the prosodic constituent that typically reflects the syntactic phrase.

9.5.1 Downstep

Basque downsteps H*L after H*L. An example was already given in (3.5) and panel (b) of figure 9.1, where there are four instances of H*, causing downstep to apply three times. In (14), downstep will occur on the second α, which has a default H*L. As shown in (14), L_ι is assumed to associate with a final syllable, if it is otherwise unoccupied. This final part of the contour is discussed in the next section.

(14)

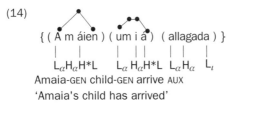

{ (A m áien) (um i á) (allagada) }

L_αH_αH*L   L_α H_αH*L L_αH_α L_ι

Amaia-GEN child-GEN arrive AUX

'Amaia's child has arrived'

(15) BASQUE DOWNSTEP (implementation) H* → !H* / H*L ____ ...]

An ip-boundary will interrupt the downstep, allowing the next H* peak to be reset to fully high pitch. An unaccented α, like the first α of (13), will never be downstepped, since it will never appear after an accented α within the same ip. Nor will it trigger downstep, as it is has no H*L.

9.5.2 Subordinated α

The verbal group following the obligatory α-boundary is pronounced with a drastically reduced pitch range, for which the term 'pitch subordination' could be used, after Crystal (1969: 244). It is clearly to be seen as a phonologization of final lowering (cf. section 6.4).

Elordieta's (1997, 1998, forthcoming) analysis leaves its prosodic phrasal structure undecided, but does observe that, although the phrasal and accentual tones are hard to hear, the tonal structure of the subordinated α remains intact. That is, if the finite verb or the auxiliary is lexically accented, there will be a H*L pitch accent on the pre-final syllable of the α, and if it is not, the L_αH_α will provide a (very low) peak. Although no systematic measurements have been reported, subordinated αs would appear to have a lower pitch range than downstepped αs (Gorka Elordieta, personal communication, June 2001). If a non-initial finite verb following an NP systematically has a lower pitch range than a non-verbal downstepped constituent in sentence-final position, the question arises what the difference in representation is. At the postlexical level, no reference to syntactic categories like 'finite verb' should be possible.

There are at first sight two possibilities for this finite verb group, both of which will have to be rejected. First, if the finite verb is a separate ip, its representation would be indistinguishable from that of a non-verbal ip in sentence-final position. Downstep is bounded by the ip, and representation (16a) would thus incorrectly predict that sentence-final verbs have wide pitch range. Second, if the finite verb were included in the preceding ip, as in (16b), the prediction is that the amount of lowering is the same as that of a downstepped α, which, as said, is untrue. A third possibility is to represent the pitch-subordinated constituent as an enclitic constituent, an α which is not contained in ip-structure, but attached immediately to the ι, as shown in (16c).

(16) a. { [(   )]   [(   )] }

  b. { [(   )   (   )] }

  c. { [(   )]   (   ) }

The cliticized α may or may not have an accent, since there is no default pitch
accent. Because of the subordination, the lexical pitch accent only barely stands
out. A minimal pair is given in (17a,b).

(17) a.

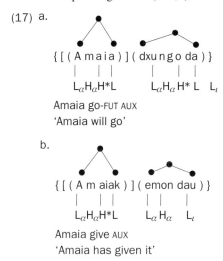

{ [(A m a i a)] (dxu n g o da) }

L$_\alpha$H$_\alpha$H*L   L$_\alpha$H$_\alpha$ H* L L$_l$

Amaia go-FUT AUX
'Amaia will go'

b.

{ [(A m aiak)] (emon dau) }

L$_\alpha$H$_\alpha$H*L   L$_\alpha$ H$_\alpha$ L$_l$

Amaia give AUX
'Amaia has given it'

In addition to accounting for the pitch subordination, the assumption that the
finite verb cliticizes to the preceding ip has an important additional advantage.
Instead of assuming that the domain for the assignment of the default pitch accent
is the (unaccented) α, we can assume it is the ip. First, this explains that in cases
like (11a), where *alkatia* is neither pre-verbal nor sentence-final, no default H*L
is inserted. Second, it explains that in a finite verbal group, no default H*L is
inserted if an ip precedes, precisely the context in which it is not itself included
in an ip, but that in other contexts, the default pitch accent does occur, as in (7c).
It would appear, then, that it is the ip, not αs, that obligatorily right-align with a
pitch accent.

9.6   The construction of ip

In addition to the requirement that H*L should appear on the penultimate or final
syllable of ip, ip-structure obeys the prosodic hierarchy: it cannot be smaller than
α. As we have seen, strings of unaccented words frequently form αs that include
two or more XPs (e.g. (11b)), and since the ip ranks above α, ips, too, may contain
more than one XP. Ranking below these undominated phonological constraints,
there is the morpho-syntactic constraint that the ip should align with the XP (18).

Thus, no ip-boundary will appear inside the NP, and an NP containing four αs will be a single ip. Accented αs representing two NPs may thus occur in separate ips. However, ip-formation is subject to one further phonological constraint which ranks above (18). This is INITIALBRANCHING, which requires that initial ips must not contain a single α, as stated in (19).

(18) ALIGN(XP,ip): Align XP with ip

(19) INITIALBRANCHING: The first ip in the utterance is branching

As a result, there are two ips in (20a), each containing an NP, the first of which branches. However, there is a single ip in (20b), since the first NP cannot form its own ip, due to (19). The ranking that achieves these phrasings is ALIGN(ip,α), INITIALBRANCHING ≫ ALIGN(XP,ip).

(20) a. { [(Amaien) (amumari)] [(liburua)]   (emon dotzo) }
Amaia-GEN grandmother-DAT book-ABS give AUX
'(S)he has given the book to Amaia's grandmother'

b. {   [(Amaiari) (amumen) (liburua   )]   (emon dotzo) }
Amaia-DAT grandmother-GEN book-abs give AUX
'(S)he has given grandmother's book to Amaia'

9.7 Basque focus

The function of the Northern Bizkaian Basque pitch accent is very different from that of phonologically equivalent pitch accents in West Germanic. A word is accented either because it is specified as accented in the lexical representation or, if it is unaccented in the lexical representation, because it ends up before the finite verb or is spoken in isolation. Looking at Basque from a West Germanic perspective, the expression of presentational focus seems seriously compromised by the fact that pitch accents are lexically distinctive. A treatment of Basque focus requires that a distinction is made between presentational focus and corrective focus.

9.7.1 Presentational focus

There is in fact no prosodic marking of presentational focus. A syntactic constraint restricts constituents with presentational focus to the last XP before the final verb phrase or the sentence end. This is the right edge of the rightmost ip, or equivalently the constituent with the nuclear H*L pitch accent (whether lexical or phrasal). It could be expressed as in (21).

(21) ALIGN(Foc, H*,Rt)   Align the right edge of the XP containing the focus
constituent with the nuclear H*L

Thus, a constituent like *dirua* 'the money' can be a focus in (22), because it appears before the finite verb, but *Amáiak* cannot: (22) cannot serve as an answer to 'Who has given you the money?' (Possible answers are *Amáiak* or *Amáiak emon nau.*)

(22) { [(Amáiak) (diruá)] (emon nau) }
Amaia the-money-ABS give AUX
'Amaia has given me the money/MONEY'

Even though subconstituents of the sentence-final or pre-verbal syntactic phrase may have narrow presentational focus, it is not possible to express the focus of such sub-XP focus constituents. In English, different prosodic structures can be used for *I have seen the old woman from our town*, depending on the presentational focus. Different pitch accent locations will be used depending on whether the sentence is an answer to 'Who have you seen?' (*I've seen the OLD WOMan from our TOWN*), 'Which woman from our town have you seen?' (*I've seen the OLD woman from our town*), 'Which old person from our town have you seen?' (*I've seen the old WOMan from our town*), or 'Which old woman have you seen? (*I've seen the old woman from our TOWN*). By contrast, the equivalent Lekeitio expression in (23a) serves as the answer to all of these. Since the entire NP is the phrase aligning with the nuclear pitch accent, (21) is satisfied. Similarly, the structure in (23b), in which the second α is downstepped, is not only a grammatical reply to 'What has she given you?' but also to 'What possession of Amaia's has (s)he given you?' and 'Whose money has (s)he given you?' In the latter interpretation, *Amái-en* is the presentational focus. This contrasts with the impossible focus interpretation of *Amáiak* in (22), where *Amáiak* does not occur in the last NP before the verb.

(23) a. { [(Sure erriko andra sarrá)] (ikusi dot) }
your town-of woman old see AUX
'I have seen the old woman from your town' (see text)

 b. { [(Amáien) (diruá)] (emon nau) }
Amaia-GEN the-money-ABS give AUX
'(S)he has given me AMAIA's MONEY/AMAIA's money/Amaia's MONEY'

9.7.2 Corrective focus

More liberal prosodic means are available for the expression of corrective focus. This is because ALIGN(XP,ip) is dominated by a constraint which allows distinctions to be made within the XP. Corrective focus is signalled by the placement of an ip-boundary before the α containing the focus (cf. Pierrehumbert and Beckman 1988 and below, for a similar situation in Japanese). Because the ip is the domain of downstep, the effect is that the focus constituent will not be downstepped. That is, if the sentence in (23b) were to be an answer to 'I believe that she has given you Amaia's book', its prosodic form would be (24). Here, an ip-boundary occurs before *dirua*. As a result, the peak on the last syllable of *dirua* is not downstepped, and will be higher than that in (23b).

(24) { [(Amáien)] [(diruá)] (emon nau) }
'(S)he has given me Amaia's MONEY' (i.e. not some other
possession of Amaia's)

If the sentence in (23b) were to have corrective focus on *Amáien*, its prosodic
structure would be as in (23b), but its phonetic realization would be different.
This is because the downstepped accent peak on *dirua* would be strongly reduced,
while at the same time the pitch range of the focused α *Amaáien* is expanded.
Thus, constraint (25a) will determine the phonological representation, while
(25b) will assist in the signalling of corrective focus by adjusting the pitch range.
Figure 9.3 gives realizations of 'She has given me Amaia's money' with presentational focus (equivalent to neutral focus) in panel (a), and with corrective focus
on *Amáien* in panel (b). Both of these contours have the structure (23b). Panel
(c) gives the version with corrective focus on *dirua*, with the structure (24).

(25) BASQUE CORRECTIVE FOCUS
      a. ALIGN(CorFoc,ip,Left):   Align the left edge of the corrective
                                  focus constituent with ip
      b. Implementation: Boost the pitch range of the α
                                  containing the constituent with
                                  corrective focus, and reduce the pitch
                                  range of the following α

The opportunities for expressing corrective focus are more limited than in a language like English. First, ALIGN(Foc,H*,Rt) (21) remains in force, regardless of
whether the focus is informational or corrective. Therefore, in (22), no corrective
focus is possible for *Amáiak*, for instance. Second, it is limited by the fact that
the focus constituent must coincide with an α. The extra opportunity afforded by
BASQUE CORRECTIVE FOCUS *vis-à-vis* presentational focus relies on the expansion of the pitch range of αs containing a corrective focus, causing a pre-final H*L
to stand out within the XP. This dependence on α-structure prevents corrective
focus from singling out a word in a multi-word α, because it is either followed
or preceded by another word in the same α, and any pitch range expansion on
the focused word would extend over the other word as well. Thus, in B's reply
in (26), the pitch range of the α *txakur baltza* could be expanded, but not that for
txakur alone (Hualde, Elordieta, Gaminde, and Smiljanić 2002), or indeed that
for *baltza* alone. The reply in (26) is therefore three-way ambiguous. In addition
to *I saw the black DOG*, it could mean *I saw the BLACK dog* or *I saw the BLACK
DOG*. Likewise, it is not possible to single out any of the four words in the α
Sure erriko andra sarra in (23a).

(26) A: { [(Katu baltzá)] (ikusi dozu) }
        cat black see AUX   'Did you see the black cat?
     B: { [(Txakur baltzá)] (ikusi dot) }
        I saw the black DOG!

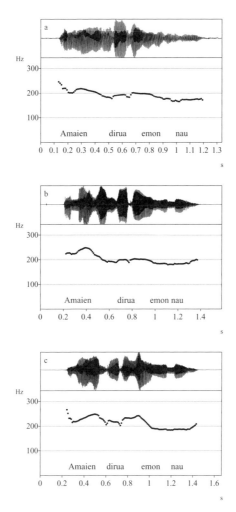

Fig. 9.3 Speech waveforms and F$_0$ tracks of *Amáien diruá emon nau* with neutral focus (panel a) and corrective focus on *Amáien* (panel b), both of which have the structure (23b), and corrective focus on *diruá* (panel c, cf. (24)).

9.8 Conclusion

Lekeitio Basque has accented and unaccented words, roots, and suffixes, producing lexical representations that are either unaccented or accented on the penultimate syllable. An α is generated for every accented word and for a lexically unaccented word in sentence-final position or in a position immediately before the verb, if that context exists. A lexically unaccented α receives a default H*L on its final syllable, while a lexically accented α receives one on its penultimate syllable, the difference in the location of the pitch accent being the only difference between these two types of α. Unaccented αs in *earlier* positions may occur in longer sentences with unaccented words, but these do not receive the default pitch accent. They can be recognized by the shallow pitch dip due to initial $L_\alpha H_\alpha$ with which every α begins.

Downstep affects every post-accentual H* within the ip. A finite verbal group is not included in ip structure if an ip precedes, and is included as a cliticized α in the ι. It is realized with a subordinated pitch range, which amounts to a more extreme lowering than downstep. Since such cliticized αs do not receive a default pitch accent, the assumption could be made that the ip is the domain of default pitch accent assignment.

Additional features of this prosodic system can be listed as follows.

1. The first ip of the sentence must contain two αs if these are available. This constraint, INITIALBRANCHING, a version of Selkirk's (2000) BINMAP, outranks ALIGN(XP,ip). As a result, ips may be produced that contain more than one XP.
2. Presentational focus is not prosodically marked, but expressed solely through the location of the XP containing the focus in syntactic structure.
3. Corrective focus obeys the same constraint, but additionally is marked by means of a left ip-boundary, which overrides INITIAL BRANCHING. There is thus a formal distinction between presentational focus and corrective focus.

A consideration of the behaviour of more Lekeitio speakers has revealed some variation in the way narrow presentational focus is expressed, see Elordieta (forthcoming).

Notes

1. The pitch accent for Bermeo was analysed as H* by Elordieta, Gaminde, Hernáez, Salaberria, and Martín de Vidales (1999), but should be reanalysed as H*+L, according to Gorka Elordieta (personal communication, 2000).
2. Depending on the number of syllables before the syllable with H*, the high target may only be reached in the third syllable. This rightward displacement as a function of the available time is found in many situations, as in that of English H*, whose location depends on the available space before the phrase end (Pierrehumbert and Steele 1989).
3. I use the term 'unaccented α' in the sense of 'α with no surface pitch accent'. An accented α thus either contains a lexically accented word or one or more lexically unaccented words with a default accent on the last.

10

Tokyo Japanese

10.1 Introduction

Japanese is the classic example of what is often called a 'pitch-accent language', and regularly figures in discussions of the typology of tone and accent. Like Northern Bizkaian Basque, Tokyo Japanese has accented and unaccented words, and has an α that can contain at most one accent. Such αs may well contain more than one accented morpheme, but only one of these survives on the surface. In terms of the discussion in chapter 3, Northern Bizkaian Basque and Tokyo Japanese are tone languages, with lexically distinctive accent.

The discussion of Japanese prosodic structure in this chapter follows a path from small to large. We begin in section 10.2 at the level of the word and move on to the α in section 10.3. Section 10.4 deals with the tonal structure of utterances with one α, and section 10.5 with the phonetic implementation of the tones, some of which may fall victim to truncation. The tonal structures in the one-α utterance are summarized in section 10.6 in an OT analysis of tonal associations in short words, when often not all tones can associate. Then, as we move on to utterances with two αs in section 10.7, I present the two classic arguments that Pierrehumbert and Beckman (1988) gave for the phonetic underspecification of tone: the argument in favour of interpolation over spreading and that for the moraic association of boundary tones, respectively. The Intermediate Phrase (ip) is discussed in section 10.8, where Japanese downstep is described and the data are presented that were used by Pierrehumbert and Beckman to show that Japanese downstep is cumulative. In the present description, the largest constituent to be considered, the υ, ends in either L_υ, for declarative intonation, or H_υ, for interrogative intonation. In section 10.9, I will argue that unlike what appears to be the case for the speakers in Pierrehumbert and Beckman (1988), there is no $L_\upsilon H_\upsilon$ boundary sequence in questions. Also in deviation from that description, I will argue that trailing L of the pitch accent H^*L is deleted whenever it cannot associate. Section 10.10 describes the way Japanese expresses focus. It will be seen that Japanese can make finer distinctions that can Basque, but that it does not match the fine-grained focus expression that is possible in English, where subconstituents of the morphological word can be marked for focus, as in *I'm ANTI-Europe*. A final section compares the description with that of Lekeitio Basque in the previous chapter. The description is based on Pierrehumbert and Beckman (1988), the seminal publication that inspired the description of Lekeitio Basque by Elordieta, but is also indebted to Poser (1984), Haraguchi (1991), and Kubozono (1993). The conclusions about the phonology of question intonation and deleted tones are my own.

10.2　Lexical accent

Of the two Basque dialects discussed in the previous chapter, Japanese is more like the Gernika variety: underlyingly, there are accented and unaccented stems (words), and accented words have an accent on one of their syllables. If the accent survives, it will have the pitch accent H*L. The proportion of accented words is just over 50 per cent, but there are large differences between morphological classes. Loanwords are more likely to be accented, while verbs are either unaccented or accented on the final syllable. In addition, there are general preferences for certain locations; for instance, accents before the antepenult are less common. There are many morphological processes assigning or deleting accents. Minimal pairs are common; triplets exist, but are rare. In (1) some illustrations are given.[1]

(1) a. hi   hí
     'sun, day'   'spark, fire'
  b. san   sán
     'three'   'crosspiece'
  c. denki   dénki
     'biography'   'electricity'
  d. hasi   hási   hasí
     'edge'   'chopsticks' 'bridge'
  e. kakera   kokóro   kakeró
     'fragment'   'heart'   'break off+IMP'
  f. garasudama áimitagai   omáwarisan
     'glass beads' 'help each other' 'policeman'

10.3　The α

The Japanese α consists of at least one morphological word, usually with various cliticizing morphemes. Some types of compounds (2a) and Western-style given name–surname combinations (2b) (i.e. not those in the Japanese order surname–given name) also form single αs. An NP consisting of a noun modified by a preceding noun with the genitive/partitive suffix *no* is frequently a single α, but adjectives, which precede the noun, typically form their own α. Thus, (2c,d) are homophonous (Kubozono 1993: 98). All this is true regardless of whether the constituents concerned are lexically accented. In this respect, Japanese differs from Northern Bizkaian Basque, where α-formation is sensitive to the presence of an accented word.

(2) a. (eda-ha)$_\alpha$ branch-leaf   'branches and leaves'
    b. (Kaoru Matumoto)$_\alpha$ cf. (Matumoto)$_\alpha$(Kaoru)$_\alpha$
    c. (siró-i)$_\alpha$ (umá-no kubiwa)$_\alpha$ = [[siró-i umá-no] kubiwa]
      white-INFL horse-GEN collar 'the collar of the white horse'
    d. (siró-i)$_\alpha$ (umá-no kubiwa)$_\alpha$ = [[siró-i] umá-no kubiwa]
      'The white collar of the horse'

Perhaps more so than in Basque, α-structure is dependent on factors like speed of utterance, frequency of use, and style. Moreover, in evident obeyance to Selkirk's BINMAP, there is a preference for structuring combinations of four words into two groups of two, regardless of the morphological structure. Thus, [[[toonan ázia] syókoku] rengoo] (south-east Asia nation union 'The Association of Southeast Asian nations') will typically be pronounced (toonan ázia)$_\alpha$ (syókoku rengooh)$_\alpha$ (Kubozono 1993).

     As said, α has at most one accent: if more than one accented morpheme occurs in the same α, the leftmost survives (cf. the Gernika Basque pattern illustrated in (1) in chapter 9).

10.4 The tonal structure of Utterances with one α

Every α begins with LH, and the expected representation is therefore as in (3a). However, Pierrehumbert, and Beckman (1988) analyse the tonal structure of α as in (3b), where the two tones span the constituent rather than beginning it. In the Pierrehumbert–Beckman analysis, the final L_α is realized in the next α, so that an α-initial rise will result. The first α of the υ will have to have an initial L_υ. This implication is shown in (3c). I will present their argument for this decision in section 10.8, where I will point to a further fact that may support their decision. Nevertheless, in this chapter α-initial rises are analysed as $L_\alpha H_\alpha$, which makes for a more transparent description, and facilitates the optimality-theoretic analysis in section 10.6. This interpretation is given in (4).

(3) a. (   )   b. (   )   c. { (   ) (   ) }
      $L_\alpha H_\alpha$ H_α L_α $L_\upsilon H_\alpha$ $L_\alpha H_\alpha$ L_α

(4) { (   ) (   ) }
     $L_\alpha H_\alpha$ $L_\alpha H_\alpha$ L_υ

The pitch accent is a sharp fall, represented by H*L. The association of tones in the α is in part governed by the sonorant mora. Syllable rhymes are monomoraic if they consist of a short vowel (cf. (5a)). Bimoraic rhymes have a long vowel, a diphthong, or a short vowel plus coda consonant (cf. (5b)). The Japanese coda may contain a nasal or the first half of a geminate. Geminates in native words are voiceless stops, which are non-sonorant (e.g. /hɛtto/ 'fat'), and thus do not count for TBUs. Examples of syllables with two TBUs are given in (5b).

(5) a. Syllables containing one TBU: ítu, kakeró, hasi
    b. Syllables containing two TBUs: sán, sankai, tookyoo

The H* associates with the first mora of the accented syllable, and its target is fairly precisely timed.[2] The trailing L occurs one mora later. For lack of clear evidence for a moraic association, Pierrehumbert and Beckman (1988) assume that the L does not associate with the following mora, but that its target is timed to occur a fixed distance from the target of H*. In the context of the OT account given in section 10.6, it is in fact simpler to assume association of trailing L. An argument vindicating this decision will be presented in section 10.9.

As in Lekeitio Basque, the realization of the $L_\alpha H_\alpha$ sequence depends on the availability of initial TBUs. In unaccented monomoraic utterances, H_α is realized on the only mora, as in (6a); otherwise, H_α associates with the second mora, as in (6b) and (7c). However, in accented αs, H* preempts the association of H_α, as shown in (7a) and (7b). The L_α will associate with the first mora if free: it is not free when the word is monosyllabic (cf. (6a)) or accented (cf. (7a)). So if the first syllable is accented, as in (7a), H* pre-empts the association of either L_α or H_α. When the second syllable is accented and the first is monomoraic, the initial free mora is occupied by L_α. The H_α, squeezed between tones that are associated with adjacent moras, is deleted (or at least has no phonetic effect). In (7b), it has been removed from the representation, as it will from now on in the same circumstances. I will assume a high-ranking constraint * Ⓣ, interpreted as deleting non-peripheral floating tones (see (34) in section 8.4). Association of trailing L will take place whenever there is a mora available after the mora with H*, as in (7b).

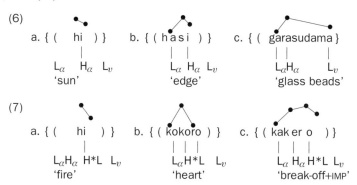

(6)
  a. { (hi) }   b. { (hasi) }   c. { (garasudama }
     L_α H_α L_v L_α H_α L_v $L_\alpha H_\alpha$ L_v
     'sun'   'edge'   'glass beads'

(7)
  a. { (hi) }   b. { (kokoro) }   c. { (kak er o) }
     $L_\alpha H_\alpha$ H*L L_v L_α H*L L_v L_α H_α H*L L_v
     'fire'   'heart'   'break-off+IMP'

While the above tone associations are reminiscent of Basque, although spelled out in more detail, the treatment of α-initial unaccented syllables with two TBUs, as in (8a), is new, since Basque has no long vowels. Most speakers have level pitch or a very slight rise from mid to high, such syllables sounding high-pitched either way (Pierrehumbert and Beckman 1988; Poser 1984). Pierrehumbert and Beckman appear to attribute the absence of a clear pitch rise on the first syllable (which would be expected if L_α associated to the first mora and H_α to the second) to the phonetic implementation, but I will assume it is due to the association of

H$_\alpha$ to the first mora. One argument for a representational account can perhaps be found in the fact that some speakers *do* have a rise from low to high (Vance 1987: 80), a dialectal difference which thus corresponds to a representational difference in the present account. In (8a), from the 'high level' dialect, association of H$_\alpha$ to the first mora prevents L$_\alpha$ from obtaining a secondary association. In (8b), the dialect with monosyllabic rises, both H$_\alpha$ and L$_\alpha$ associate to the first syllable.

(8)

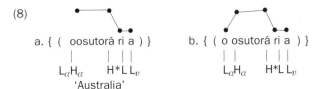

a. { (oosutorá ri a) }   b. { (o osutorá ri a) }

    L$_\alpha$H$_\alpha$ H*L L$_\upsilon$ L$_\alpha$H$_\alpha$ H*L L$_\upsilon$

          'Australia'

10.5 Phonetic implementation of a one-α Utterance

This section looks at the tonal structure of single αs at the level of the Utterance, i.e. one-word Utterances. The initial L$_\alpha$, final L$_\upsilon$, and the fate of υ-final accent are discussed in separate sections.

10.5.1 Initial L$_\alpha$

An initial L$_\alpha$ which can associate with the first mora will be pronounced fully low. However, L$_\alpha$ cannot associate when the first mora has an H-tone, as in (6a), (7a), and (8a). In these cases, a weak rise is sometimes detectable in the onset consonant or the initial part of the vowel. Pierrehumbert and Beckman (1988) assume that L$_\alpha$ is in fact always present, and that the difference between the two allophones of L$_\alpha$ is to be explained by a difference in association. The low-pitched realization of L$_\alpha$ (the 'strong allophone') is due to its association with the free first mora, while the pronunciation as mid pitch (the 'weak allophone') is due to the absence of a moraic association. The idea is that the phonetic implementation will take greater care in producing a low target for a boundary tone with moraic association than for one without. In section 10.7, which deals with sequences of αs, clearer evidence for the two allophones from Pierrehumbert and Beckman (1988) will be presented. The term 'secondary association' for a boundary tone that is associated with a TBU, like L$_\alpha$ in (6b,c), (7b,c), and (8b), implies that the tone's 'primary association' is with the prosodic constituent, shown graphically in chapter 7, (1). Secondary association is here shown as association to a TBU only (cf. section 7.3.3); recall that in section 8.3.4, it was explained that this 'primary association' is (OT) edge-alignment in our terms.

10.5.2 L$_\upsilon$

In an unaccented word like (6c), the distance between H$_\alpha$ and L$_\upsilon$ is interpolated as a weakly falling slope which ends at middish pitch. This contour is clearly

different from that in a word like /omáwarisan/ 'policeman', which has sharply
falling pitch after /ma/, followed by fully low pitch. Depending on the length
of the unaccented word, the auditory impression is that of a middish plateau or
a suspended fall. Earlier descriptions represented this contour by means of the
rightward spreading of H_α (e.g. Poser 1984). While the assumption of an H-tone
late in the unaccented α may seem appropriate because of the contrast with the
fully low pitch that occurs after an accented syllable, it seems inappropriate to
the extent that in longer unaccented αs the pitch continues to fall. In fact, one
of the main results of Pierrehumbert and Beckman (1988) was that the analysis
with a spreading H is incorrect. I return to this point in section 10.7.

   A further question concerns the moraic association of L_υ. The fact that its
phonetic realization tends to be less than fully low could be seen as an argument
that it does not associate to a sonorant mora, and always has a 'weak allophone'.
The fully low pitch after the pitch accent is then due to the target of the trailing L,
after which unassociated L_υ would be low, too. Since in this latter context, L_υ has
low pitch regardless of whether there is a free mora after the accent, there is no
way in which we can make the association of L_υ accountable for its realization.
Again, in the context of the OT description below, it is simplest to assume that
tones associate when they can. The not-fully low realization of L_υ after H_α, then,
is to be attributed to its tonal context, not to a lack of an association.

10.5.3   The α-final accent

Tokyo Japanese is generally described as having high pitch on final accented
syllables with one mora, as in /hí/ 'fire', /hasí/ 'bridge', /kakeró/ 'breakoff+IMP',
without any fall. In this variety, neither trailing L nor L_υ (assuming declarative
intonation) are realized. However, our speaker has a pitch fall to mid in such
utterance-final syllables, as can be seen in figure 10.1, in the second contours
in panels (a), (b), and (c). By contrast, word-internally, a monomoraic accented
syllable is followed by fully low pitch in the next syllable, as in /kokóro/. Both
words of the type /kakeró/ and /kokóro/ differ from unaccented /kakera/, which
has a weak fall stretching across the last two syllables (see figure 10.1, panel (a)).
Final bimoraic accented syllables are pronounced as a complete fall to low within
the syllable, since the L will be realized on the second mora. This realization is
no different from that in other positions in the word.

   It will be clear that, when pronounced in isolation, a word like /hási/, with
its high first syllable and low second syllable, will be audibly different from
both unaccented /hasi/ and accented /hasí/. However, the latter two both have
low pitch in the first syllable and higher pitch in the second. In the analysis
by Pierrehumbert and Beckman (1988), /hasi/ and /hasí/ have different surface
representations, however: the high pitch on the second syllable of /hasí/ is due to
the accent H*, while that in /hasi/ is due to H_α (cf. (6b)). A reasonable prediction
therefore is that they are phonetically different. In fact, H* has higher pitch
than H_α, when measured in equivalent positions, and this difference keeps final

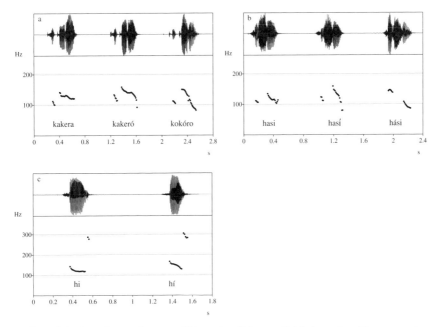

Fig. 10.1 Speech waveforms and F_0 tracks of three-syllabled words with no accent (/kakera/ 'fragment'), final accent (/kakeró/ 'break off-IMP'), and penultimate accent (/kokóro/ 'heart') (panel a); bisyllabic words with no accent (/hasi/ 'edge'), final accent (/hasí/ 'bridge'), and penultimate accent (/hási/ 'chopsticks') (panel b); and monosyllabic words with no accent (/hi/ 'sun') and with accent (/hí/ 'fire') (panel c).

accent auditorily distinct from unaccented syllables with H_α. Figure 10.1 shows pronunciations of these three words in panel (b). By the same reasoning, /hi/ contrasts with /hí/ in having not fully high pitch, as illustrated in panel (c).

10.5.4 Loss of υ-final accent

The above description applies to one variety of Tokyo Japanese. Apparently, in the speech of many speakers, υ-final accent is deleted in monomoraic syllables of monosyllabic αs or bimoraic disyllabic αs, causing /hasi/ 'edge' and /hasí/ 'bridge' as well as /hi/ 'sun' and /hí/ 'fire' to be homophonous in that context (Abe 1980; Poser 1984; Haraguchi 1991). The neutralization does not take place when more than two moras are available in the α. A comparison of (9a,b), given with representations and contours as in the non-neutralizing dialect,[3] with (10a,b) makes it clear that a final third mora will show the lower pitch due to L_α in the unaccented α, as shown in (10a), which is generally distinct from the high pitch of H^*, as in (10b) (Warner 1997). This is also true if the first syllable of a disyllable is bimoraic, since H_α will then also associate in the first syllable, leaving the final syllable for L_υ in the unaccented case.

(9)

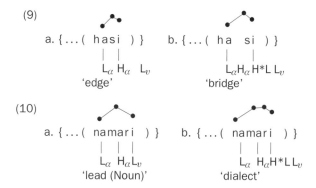

a. {…(ha si) }   b. {…(ha si) }
        | | | |
       L$_\alpha$ H$_\alpha$ L$_\upsilon$ L$_\alpha$H$_\alpha$ H*L L$_\upsilon$
       'edge'   'bridge'

(10)

a. {…(namari) }   b. {…(namari) }
        | | | | | |
       L$_\alpha$ H$_\alpha$L$_\upsilon$ L$_\alpha$ H$_\alpha$H*LL$_\upsilon$
     'lead (Noun)'   'dialect'

The neutralizing dialect can presumably be handled by a deletion of any H*L with an unassociated H$_\alpha$ to its left and unassociated L$_\upsilon$ to its right (cf. Pierrehumbert and Beckman 1988: 134). In turn, this predicts that if the context is not υ-final, no neutralization takes place. In section 10.8, it will be seen that accented, but not unaccented αs cause downstep within the ip, so that α-final monomoraic syllables may reveal their accent in the reducing effect they have on the pitch span of the next α. Across ips, an F$_0$ difference between accented and unaccented words may be maintained, but I am not aware that this question has been investigated.

Of course, in all varieties the difference between words like /hasi/ and /hasí/ will show up when a suffix like /ga/ (expressing subject focus) is added: the L-tone of H*L will readily be revealed in the third syllable of /hasí-ga/, which is distinct from /hasi-ga/, with its not-fully high /si/ and not-fully low /ga/. Before moving on to expressions containing more than one α, an OT analysis is offered of the tonal associations in the α.

10.6 An OT analysis of the tonal structure

This section presents an OT account of the tonal alignments and associations in the one-α Utterance. A number of constraints are undominated. First, the alignment constraints that tell us which edge of which constituent each tone is aligned will trivially rank above constraints that align the same tones in different locations. The effect of satisfying these constraints, given in (11), is that L$_\alpha$H$_\alpha$ are aligned at the beginning of the (first) α, L$_\upsilon$ is aligned at the end, and H* is aligned with the accented syllable. These constraints will only play a role in section 10.6.1, and they will not be included in the earlier tableaux.

(11) a. ALIGN(L$_\alpha$,Left): Align L$_\alpha$ left in the α
     b. ALIGN(L$_\upsilon$,Right): Align L$_\upsilon$ right in the υ
     c. ALIGN(H*,Lex): Align H* with the accented syllable

Four constraints collaborate to create well-formed Japanese associations. First, CONCATENATE left-aligns trailing L with the right edge of H* and H$_\alpha$ with the right edge of L$_\alpha$, and thus requires that there be no other tones or empty TBUs between the tones of the pitch accent H*L and the initial boundary sequence $L_\alpha H_\alpha$ (cf. section 8.3.4). Second, NoContour and NoSpread together ensure that associations are one-to-one. Third, there is TBU←T, which ranks below NoSpread and therefore bans any unassociated tone where an empty TBU is available. These constraints will be summarized as HighRanking.

There are two things to account for. One is the outcome of the competition among the tones when there are fewer TBUs than tones. As could be seen in (6) and (7), tones frequently fail to associate, because other tones occupy a mora they might otherwise have been entitled to. The second aspect is the high-pitched initial syllable of words beginning with unaccented long vowels, shown in (8). Moraic association of boundary tones in Japanese is described as the tone's satisfaction of T→TBU, where the TBU is the sonorant mora. The competition between different tones for the same TBU can be taken care of by making T→TBU sensitive to the morphological or phonological status of the tone. For instance, the association of H_α appears to be preferred over that of L_α if there is only one mora, as shown by (6a). This means that $H_\alpha \to$ TBU $\gg L_\alpha \to$ TBU, causing candidate (a) for /hi/ in tableau (12) to be preferred to candidate (b). Candidate (c) violates NoCrowd, subsumed under HighRanking. Turning to the treatment of /hí/ (7a) in the same tableau, it is clear that H*→TBU $\gg H_\alpha \to$ TBU, making its candidate (a) better than (b). The fact that H* is associated in preference to L, as in candidate (c), means that H*→TBU $\gg$ L→TBU, which is in effect the OT analysis of the star in the tonal notation.

(12)

hi $L_\alpha H_\alpha$ L_υ	HIGHRANKING	H*→TBU	L→TBU	H_α→TBU	L_α→TBU	L_υ→TBU
☞ a. { (hi) } | L_α H_α L_υ					*	*
b. { (hi) } | $L_\alpha H_\alpha L_\upsilon$				*!		*
c. { (hi) } ∧ L_α $H_\alpha L_\upsilon$	*!				*	
hí $L_\alpha H_\alpha$ H*L L_υ						
☞ a. { (hi) } | $L_\alpha H_\alpha$ H*LL_υ			*	*	*	*
b. { (hi) } | L_α H_α H*LL_υ		*!	*		*	*
c. { (hi) } | $L_\alpha H_\alpha$ H*L L_υ		*!	*		*	*

Next, in /hasi/ (7b), L_α and H_α associate to the two available syllables, rather than H_α and L_υ. This means that $L_\alpha \to TBU \gg L_\upsilon \to TBU$, so that candidate (a) for this form can be preferred over (b), as shown in tableau (13). The selection of the correct representation of /hási/ in the same tableau follows from the ranking $L_\alpha \to TBU \gg L_\upsilon \to TBU$, which is why (b) is ill-formed, while (c) is ill-formed due to the ranking $H^* \to TBU \gg H_\alpha \to TBU$, already seen in tableau (12). Tableau (13) also deals with /hasí/, in which H^* associates with the final syllable, and association of L_α is preferred to that of H_α, as in candidate (a). Since we have just concluded on the basis of /hi/ (6a) that H_α is associated in preference to L_α, the failure of H_α to associate in this form must have a different explanation. It is assumed that this is due to OCP (see section 8.3.1), which militates against a sequence of like tones on adjacent moras. This means that OCP outranks $H_\alpha \to TBU$, making candidate (a) better than (b). As said in section 10.4, a non-crucial assumption is that $^*\textcircled{T}$ outranks Max-IO(T) so that H_α is deleted.

(13)

hasi $L_\alpha H_\alpha$ L_υ	HIGHRANKING	H*→TBU	L→TBU	OCP	H$_\alpha$→TBU	L$_\alpha$→TBU	L$_\upsilon$→TBU
☞a. { (ha si) } | | L_α H_α L_υ							*
b. { (ha si) } | | L_α $H_\alpha L_\upsilon$						*!	
hási $L_\alpha H_\alpha$ H*LL_υ							
☞a. { (hasi) } | | $L_\alpha H_\alpha$ H*L L_υ					*	*	*
b. { (ha si) } | | $L_\alpha H_\alpha$ H*LL_υ			*!		*	*	
c. { (ha si) } | | L_α H_αH*L L_υ		*!				*	*
hasí $L_\alpha H_\alpha$ H*L L_υ							
☞a. { (ha si) } | | $L_\alpha \emptyset$ H*LL_υ			*		*		*
b. { (ha si) } | | L_α H_α H*L L_υ			*	*!	*		*

Turning to trisyllables, unaccented /kakera/ 'fragment' in tableau (14) is a perfect candidate, beating any other form. The moraic association of L_υ is not in fact crucially different from candidate (b), which however gratuitously leaves TBUs without tone: candidate (a) fills three TBUs with three tones, and thus fully satisfies TBU←T, subsumed under HIGHRANKING. The treatment of /kokóro/ brings nothing new, and besides the winning candidate, only the OCP-violating candidate (b) is shown, repeating the case of /hasí/ in tableau (13). Observe, however, that the OCP violation in the optimal candidate for /kakeró/ in tableau (14) must be tolerated, since otherwise H_α would be in violation of TBU←T. In Japanese, OCP is obeyed, but not at the expense of well-formed one-to-one associations of all tones.

(14)

kakera $L_\alpha H_\alpha$ L_ν	HIGHRANKING	H*→TBU	L→TBU	OCP	H_α→TBU	L_α→TBU	L_ν→TBU

☞a. { (ka ke ra) }
    | | |
  L_α $H_\alpha L_\nu$							

b. { (ka ke ra) }
    | |
  $L_\alpha H_\alpha$ L_ν
	*!					*	

kokóro $L_\alpha H_\alpha$ H*L L_ν							

☞a. { (ko ko ro) }
    | | |
  $L_\alpha \emptyset$H*L L_ν
					*		*

b. { (ko ko ro) }
    | | |
  $L_\alpha H_\alpha$ H*L L_ν
				*!	*		*

kakeró $L_\alpha H_\alpha$ H*L L_ν							

☞a. { (ka ke ro) }
    | | |
  L_α H_αH*LL_ν
		*	*				*

b. { (ka ke ro) }
    | |
  L_α H_αH*LL_ν
	*!	*		*			*

10.6.1 NoRise

The above account leaves the non-association of L_α in (8a) unexplained. A constraint forbidding the creation of LH within the syllable has in fact been motivated for a number of languages (Cassimjee and Kisseberth 1999; Gussenhoven 1999c). In Hausa, rising tones are categorically excluded (Leben 1978: 206), and in Somali, monosyllabic LH is optionally replaced by H (Banti 1988). Toura has ten distinctive tones on bimoraic syllables, none of which is rising (Bearth 1971, cited from Hermans 1996). In chapter 12 we will see NoRISE play an important role in accounting for the tonal phonology of a Dutch dialect. There is evidence that rises take longer than falls (Ohala 1978; Sundberg 1979); Xu and Sun forth-coming) and thus must be harder to produce. NoRISE (see (2) in section 8.3.1), is a more specific version of NoCONTOUR, and bans associated LH within the syllable.

In tableau (15), only the first two syllables /oosu-/ are relevant: /-toraria/ is held constant and incurs one OCP violation due to the adjacent L-tones on /-ia/ and one TBU←T violation for having no tone on /-to-/. The expected form (b) with $L_\alpha H_\alpha$ associating in the first syllable is thrown out by NoRISE, which may join the constraint complex we have so far indicated by HIGHRANKING. Three other relevant constraints here are CONCATENATE, NoSPREAD, and TBU←T. Candidates (b)–(e) demonstrate that TBU←T must rank below the other three, as this constraint would immediately throw out winning candidate (a), which has three unfilled TBUs. CONCATENATE prevents candidate (c), which ducks NoRISE by moving H_α over to the next syllable, from winning the competition with candidate (a), and NoSPREAD rules out candidates (d) and (e), which avoid the strictures of NoRISE and CONCATENATE by the association of, respectively, L_α and H_α to both moras in the first syllable. The role of TBU←T becomes apparent in a case like /kakero/ in the same tableau, where candidate (a) is preferred to candidate (b), which violates this constraint. It will be clear that the variety of Tokyo Japanese that *does* have a rise on initial long unaccented syllables, shown in (8b), is to be accounted for by a low ranking of NoRISE, causing candidate (b) to win.

(15)

oosutorária $L_\alpha H_\alpha$ H*L L_υ	NoRISE	NoSPREAD	CONCATENATE	TBU←T	H*→TBU	L→TBU	OCP	H_α→TBU	L_α→TBU	L_υ→TBU
☞ a. { (oosutora ri a) } $L_\alpha H_\alpha$ H* L L_υ				***			*		*	
b. { (o osutora ri a) } $L_\alpha H_\alpha$ H* L L_υ	*!			**			*			
c. { (oo sutora ri a) } L_α H_α H* L L_υ			*!	**			*			
d. { (oo sutora ri a) } L_α H_α H* L L_υ		*!		*			*			
e. { (oo sutora ri a) } $L_\alpha H_\alpha$ H* L L_υ		*!		**			*		*	
kakera $L_\alpha H_\alpha$ L_υ										
☞ a. { (ka ke ra) } L_α $H_\alpha L_\upsilon$										
b. { (ka ke ra) } L_α H_α L_υ				*!						

Notice that we cannot allow ALIGN(H_α,Left) to take over the role of CONCATE-
NATE in deciding the choice between candidates (a) and (c) of /oosutorária/.
While it would do this job correctly, as shown in tableau 16, it would incorrectly
select candidate (b) in the case of /kakera/. While CONCATENATE is satisfied if
H_α is adjacent to L_α, and does not therefore decide between these candidates,
ALIGN(H_α,Left) is violated more by the winning candidate (a), where H_α is one
mora removed from the phrase edge, than by candidate (b), where it is associated
with the first mora, as shown in tableau (16).[4]

(16)

oosutorária $L_\alpha H_\alpha$ H*L L_υ	NoRise	NoSpread	Align(H_α,Left)	TBU→T	H*→TBU	L→TBU	OCP	H_α→TBU	L_α→TBU	L_υ→TBU
☞a. { (oosutora ri a) } $L_\alpha H_\alpha$ H*L L_υ				***				*	*	
c. { (oo sutora ri a) } L_α H_α H*L L_υ			*!*	**				*		
kakera $L_\alpha H_\alpha$ L_υ										
a. { (ka ke ra) } L_α $H_\alpha L_\upsilon$			*!							
☞!b. { (ka ke ra) } L_α H_α L_υ				*	*			*		

Since CONCATENATE plays a crucial role in explaining the pronunciation of
[oosutorária], our analysis can only go through if $L_\alpha H_\alpha$ is a morpheme, rather than
single boundaries tones from different αs, as in Pierrehumbert and Beckman's
analysis. On the assumption that CONCATENATE is a well-motivated constraint,
this is an argument in favour of a 'Basque' treatment of the α-initial pitch rise.

10.7 More than one α: secondary association and interpolation

Two issues arise in sequences of αs: the secondary association of L_α and the
resulting difference in pronunciation between 'strong' and 'weak' allophones of
L_α; and the non-spreading of H_α to free TBUs to its right.
    First, a sequence of an unaccented α and an α which has an H-tone on its
first mora provides further evidence that unassociated L_α is not deleted (see also
section 10.5.1). If it were, the implementation of a sequence like H_α. . .)(H^*
(where H^* is associated with the first mora, as in (17a)) or H_α. . .)(H_α (with
initial H_α occurring on a long syllable, as in (17b)), could not be expected to
lead to a rise from low-to-mid pitch before the second α. However, a rise is what

is found. The pitch dips down at the boundary, and L_α is the only tone that can explain this. However, this dip does not reach the low pitch of an associated L_α, as in (18). The contrast between the two inter-α contexts (17a,b), on the one hand, and (18), on the other, therefore provides additional evidence for the difference between the 'strong' and 'weak' allophones of L_α, in other words, of boundary tones with and without secondary association.

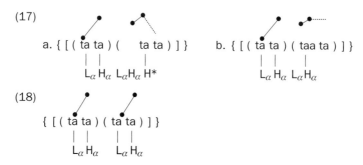

(17)

a. { [(ta ta) (ta ta)] }
          | | |
        L_α H_α $L_\alpha H_\alpha$ H^*

b. { [(ta ta) (taa ta)] }
          | | | |
        L_α H_α $L_\alpha H_\alpha$

(18)

{ [(ta ta) (ta ta)] }
      | | | |
    $L_\alpha H_\alpha$ $L_\alpha H_\alpha$

Second, sequences of αs provided Pierrehumbert and Beckman (1988) with evidence against the rightward spreading of H_α. Consider a representation like (19), a sequence of two unaccented αs, the first of which has three monomoraic syllables so that there is one syllable between H_α (the second syllable of the first α) and L_α (the first mora of the second α).

(19) { [(ta ta ta) (ta ta)] }
          | | | |
        $L_\alpha H_\alpha$ $L_\alpha H_\alpha$

If the words are spoken without a pause, there will be a fall in the last syllable of the first word. It would be hard to argue on the basis of that fact that H_α has failed to spread to the word-final syllable: with or without such spreading, the phonetic record would show a fall somewhere from H_α to L_α, since it takes time to get from one tone to the next. However, lengthening the first α will be diagnostic. A spreading analysis predicts that the slope and timing of this fall is reasonably constant if the length of the first word is increased, since the H_α would be associated with the last syllable in all cases. However, Pierrehumbert, and Beckman (1988: 38) found a different pattern: the fall extends over the entire stretch between the second syllable of the first word and the first syllable of the second. Its slope, therefore, is a function of the distance between these syllables, a pattern that clearly indicates interpolation between H_α and L_α.

Both the lower pitch of L_α with secondary association and the slope varying as a function of distance can be seen in figure 10.2. Every panel shows a sequence of an unaccented α and an accented one in which the slope from H_α to L_α is shown as a dotted line. The contours on the left have second αs with a free first mora (/omáwarisan/); those on the right with H_α on the first mora, due to a long initial syllable (/yoozínboo/). The first words are the same in each row. In every case,

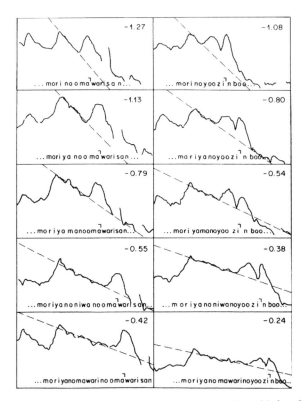

Fig. 10.2 F_0 tracks of ten sequences of unaccented α and α with free first mora (left-hand panels) and H-toned first mora (right-hand panels), with length of first α varying from three (top) to eight (bottom) syllables. Dotted lines indicate the slope between the peak of the first α (due to H_α) and the low point at the beginning of the second α (due to L_α). From Pierrehumbert and Beckman (1988).

the slopes in the contours in the left-hand panels reach a lower pitch than those on the right, demonstrating the effect of moraic association of L_α. Second, the number of syllables in the first word increases from three in the top two panels to eight in the bottom two. As will be clear, slopes are shallower as the number of syllables between H_α and L_α increases, demonstrating interpolation, i.e. no H_α-spreading.

10.8 The Intermediate Phrase

The ip is the prosodic constituent above α, and will consist of one, two, sometimes three αs. In such structures, no rhythmic readjustments are made, and accents may thus be adjacent. For instance, (20), in which a final-accented α precedes an initial-accented one, surfaces with the accents in the lexically specified locations (Kubozono 1993).

(20) [(umái)$_\alpha$ (zyúusu)$_\alpha$]$_{ip}$ *[(úmai)$_\alpha$ (zyúusu)$_\alpha$]$_{ip}$
      'sweet juice'

As in Basque, the ip is the domain of downstep.[5] The trigger is an accented H*, while both H* and H$_\alpha$ undergo it (Poser 1984; Pierrehumbert and Beckman 1988; Kubozono 1992). This means there is no downstep in a sequence of three unaccented αs within the ip, a case shown in (21), while downstep will occur twice if the first and second αs are accented, as in (22). When either the first or the second is accented downstep will occur once, as in (23a,b).

(21) { [(Kono arai)   (ayaori-no)   (obizi-ga)] }
      this rough twill-GEN obicloth-PARTICLE
      'this rough twill obi-cloth'

(22) { (Kono borói)   (orímono-no)   (obizi-ga)] }
      'this ragged woven obi-cloth'

(23) a. { (Kono arai)   (orímono-no)   (obizi-ga)] }
      b. { (Kono borói)   (ayaori-no)   (obizi-ga)] }

To demonstrate that downstep works in this cumulative way, Pierrehumbert and Beckman (1988) measured the peak F$_0$ of the first and the third α in a number of pronunciations of the expressions in (21)–(23). If downstep is cumulative, the differences between first and third peaks ought to be smallest in (21), largest in (22), and intermediate in (23). This is precisely what they found, as shown in figure 10.3. Each data-point represents the two measurements within one utterance, with the value of the first peak plotted along the x-axis and the value of the peak on *obizi* plotted along the y-axis. Data-points for (21), (23), and (22) are labelled '0', '1', and '2', respectively. The speaker deliberately varied his pitch span from utterance to utterance, as a result of which first peaks ranged from around 100 Hz to 210 Hz. Two observations are to be made. First, the value for peak 1 is correlated with that of peak 3, meaning that pitch span was varied for each utterance as a whole. The slopes of the three regression lines show how the F$_0$ of the first peak relates to that of the third for the three sets of data. Second, and more importantly, the different heights of the regression lines indicate that for a given value for the first peak, the value of the third peak is lowest for (22), intermediate for (23), and highest for (21), showing that downstep applied, respectively, twice, once, and not at all.

A more detailed investigation of downstep provided Pierrehumbert and Beckman (1988) with an argument for assuming that L$_\alpha$ is a final boundary tone associating in the next α over, rather than an initial boundary tone, as has been assumed throughout here. They found that at an ip-boundary, where downstep is interrupted, the target of the ip-initial L$_\alpha$ depends on whether the preceding α has undergone downstep. That is, this tone would appear to share the lowering of the pitch span caused by the reduction of the pitch span of the (preceding) α, and therefore, they argue, it belongs to this preceding α. Our discussion of the high plateau of Lekeitio Basque in the previous chapter may provide a second argument

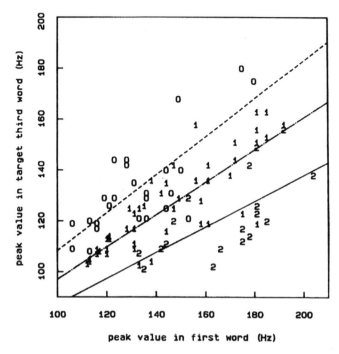

Fig. 10.3 Peak F$_0$ in the first α (horizontal axis) and the third α (vertical axis) in expressions containing three αs with two ('2'), one ('1'), and zero ('0') accented αs. Dashed, dashed-dotted, and solid lines are regression lines fitted to the '0'-plots, '1'-plots, and '2'-plots, respectively. From Pierrehumbert and Beckman (1988).

for this analysis. Recall that Elordieta (1997) assumed that the high plateau was due to spreading of H$_\alpha$. However, since H$_\alpha$ is the last tone in the α, we can simply assume that it provides that last target for it, and so no further changes are to be expected. The fact that Tokyo Japanese *does* have a falling slope may indicate that L$_\alpha$ is part of the same α as preceding H$_\alpha$. The hypothesis would here be that tones interpolate only within their own prosodic constituent. Nevertheless, I have adopted a Basque-style analysis with an initial boundary complex L$_\alpha$H$_\alpha$. One reason is that our OT analysis presupposed a complex boundary tone, rather than a combination of two single boundary tones, when forcing leftmost association of H$_\alpha$ in initial bimoraic syllables, as in /oosutorária/. Also, we might argue that evidence provided by the timing of the target suggests L$_\alpha$ indeed belongs to the righthand α.

10.9   The Utterance: L$_v$ and H$_v$

A declarative pronunciation of an accented α has fully low pitch at the end (except in the situation described in section 10.5.4 above), while unaccented αs end at mid pitch or, for longer αs, not-quite-low pitch. The fully low-pitched endings of

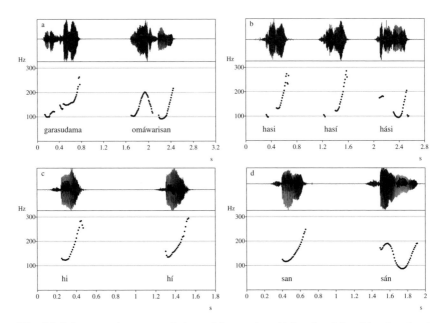

Fig. 10.4 Interrogative pronunciations of /garasudama/ 'glass beads' and /omáwarisan/ 'policeman' (panel a); /hasi/ 'edge', /hasí/ 'bridge', and /hási/ 'chopsticks' (panel b); /hi/ 'sun' and /hí/ 'fire' (panel c); and /san/ 'three' and /sán/ 'crosspiece' (panel d). Speaker KS.

accented αs must be due to the trailing L of the accent, whose target is apparently lower than that of final L_v when not preceded by an accent. Although there is no good basis for deciding whether L_v associates, since the difference in realization of L_v can be accounted for by the left-hand context, the OT analysis went through in the simplest way with maximal association of all tones on a one-to-one basis.

Interrogative sentences end in H_v, which causes a rise on the last syllable (Pierrehumbert and Beckman 1988). In their examples, H_v appears as an additional tone after L_v, since in unaccented αs, F_0 shows a descending trend from the preceding H_α before making the rise for H_v (H% in PB's notation) on the final syllable. In accented αs, like /omáwarisan/, the low target before H_v is fully low, which has the effect that the end-point of the final rise is lower in accented αs. This can be seen in (24b) and panels (a) and (b) in figure 10.4. Pierrehumbert and Beckman (1988: 81) interpret the difference to mean that the pitch accent causes downstep of L_v and H_v. In the present description, we can attribute the F_0 difference between H_v in accented and H_v in unaccented αs to the absence of a L_v in the interrogative. The speaker I recorded clearly did not retain L_v before H_v. This can be seen in panel (b) of figure 10.5, where the unaccented α shows a plateau from H_α to the last syllable, where the pitch rises for H_v. This is shown diagrammatically in (24a). Also, when the unaccented α is quite long, no descending trend could be observed in the interrogative intonation, as can be

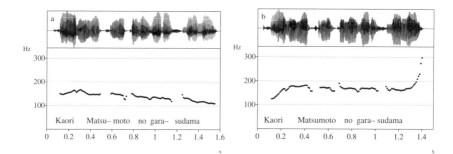

Fig. 10.5 Declarative (panel a) and interrogative (panel b) pronunciations of the unaccented α *Kaori Matumoto no garasudama*. Speaker KS.

seen in panel (b) of figure 10.5, which is to be compared with the declarative version of the same expression in panel (a), where the declination is evident. This suggests that $L_υ$ represents the declarative and $H_υ$ the interrogative, and that in interrogative sentences there just is no $L_υ$ in the representation.

(24)

a. { (garasudama }   b. { (ó mawarisan) }
      $L_α H_α$ $H_υ$ $L_α$ H*L $H_υ$

I have found no discussion of interrogative pronunciations of words with final accented monomoraic syllables, where L cannot associate. A comparison of interrogative /hi/ and /hí/ shows that the accented word ends in higher pitch, and the same is true for /hasi/ and /hasí/. Since this pattern is the reverse of that found in contexts where trailing L can associate, the conclusion must be that unassociated L is deleted. Thus, the contrast in this context is between unaccented $L_α H_α H_υ$ and accented $L_α H_α H^* H_υ$. The deletion might be understood as a constraint against HLH, discussed as PLATEAU by Cassimjee and Kisseberth (1999). However, it also follows from high-ranking $*\text{(T)}$, which was non-crucially active in the deletion of floating $H_α$ between associated $L_α$ and H*. In our OT analysis, the deletion of L is thus due to a violation of L→TBU. In fact, the only tones that in our data appear to survive without moraic association are the peripheral $L_α$, and either $L_υ$ or $H_υ$, depending on whether declarative or interrogative intonation is used. A further implication is that in accented monomoraic declaratives, e.g. /hí/, $H^* L L_α$ is reduced to $H^* L_α$.

(25)

a. { (hi) }   b. { (hi) }
     $L_α$ $H_α H_υ$ $L_α H_α$ H* $H_υ$

(26)

a. { (sa n) }
   | | | |
   L_α H_α H_υ

b. { (sa n) }
      | | | |
   $L_\alpha H_\alpha$ H*L H_υ

The representations of monomoraic words in (25) can be compared with those of bimoraic monosyllables in (26), where L is not deleted. In panel (d) of figure 10.4, the final F_0 of /sán/ 'crosspiece' is indeed lower than that of /san/ 'three', showing the reverse pattern relative to panels (b) and (c).

10.10   Japanese focus

The way focus is expressed in Japanese is reminiscent of the way Northern Bizkaian Basque expresses corrective focus. First, insertion of an ip-boundary before an α containing the focus constituent prevents downstep from lowering the pitch span of the focused α. Second, boosting the pitch span of the focused α causes it to stand out. Again, the first measure is structural, the second is taken in the phonetic implementation, but has a structural context.

10.10.1   The left edge of the focus constituent

Unlike Basque, Japanese can freely focus any word. This is because there is no restriction against unaccented αs, and an ip-boundary will often occur where an α-boundary was created specifically because the word is focused. Thus, while *oranda no hana* 'flowers from Holland' would normally be a single α, the word *hana* can be focused by placing an α-boundary and an ip-boundary before it. This would not be possible in Northern Bizkaian Basque. Neither does Japanese have the restriction that the focus constituent must be contained within some final XP. While the prosodic form of Japanese focus is thus similar to Northern Bizkaian Basque corrective focus, it can be used more liberally. It was given in (25) in chapter 9 and is repeated here for Japanese (information or corrective) focus in (27).

(27) JAPANESE FOCUS
     a. ALIGNFOC,ip: Align the left edge of the focus constituent with the left edge of an ip.
     b. Implementation: Boost the pitch range of the α containing the focus constituent.

In spite of the greater flexibility, however, it is not difficult to reproduce the 'black dog' effect of section 9.7.2. Perhaps barring some forms of metalinguistic focus, the morphological word cannot be divided up into separate αs. Morphological words may be compound, like *mukasi banási* 'folklore' in (28), and the

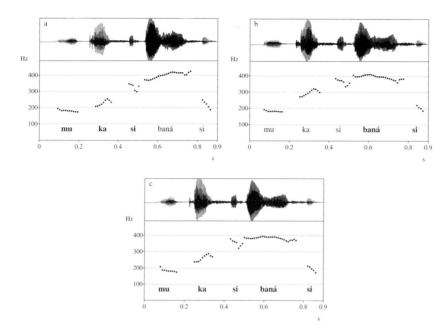

Fig. 10.6 Speech waveforms and F_0 contours of *mukasi banási* with focus for *mukasi* (panel a); for *banási* (panel b); and for *mukasi banási* (panel c).

focus constituent could, of course, meaningfully comprise the first (28a), the second (28b), or both constituents (28c). However, the compound cannot be divided into separate αs to express these differences (Mariko Sugahara, personal communication 2000). Figure 10.6 shows F_0 tracks of the three interpretations of *mukasi banási da yo*: they are all basically the same.

(28) a. [otogi]_FOC banási janakúte, [mukasi]_FOC banási da yo
        fairy tale NEG, folk tale FOC copula-Particle
        'It's not a fairytale, but folklore'
     b. mukasi [monogatári]_FOC janakúte, mukasi [banási]_FOC da yo
        folk story NEG folk tale FOC copula-Particle
        'It's not an old story, but folklore'
     c. watasi ga mitai no wa, [eíga]_FOC janakúte, [mukasi banási]_FOC da yo
        I SUBJ want-see NOM TOP, film NEG, folklore FOC copula-Particle
        'What I want to see is a film, not folklore'

10.10.2   The right edge of the focus constituent

The prosodic structure of Tokyo Japanese is also more malleable after the focus constituent than that of Basque. The presence of an α-boundary after the focus will be sensitive to the kind of prominence profile that results. If a focused accented α were otherwise to precede an accented α (**), it makes sense to avoid an α-boundary after the focus: the post-focal accent will be deleted (cf. section 10.3), causing the post-focal word to be pronounced with post-accentual low pitch (*Ø). This is shown in (29a). Similarly, if a focused accented α were otherwise to precede an unaccented α (*Ø), it makes sense to 'dephrase' the latter, as the post-focal word will now lack a pitch rise due to $L_\alpha H_\alpha$, and will instead be in the low-pitched stretch after H*L. By contrast, if a focused *unaccented* α precedes an accented α (Ø*), it makes sense *not* to 'dephrase' the post-focal α, since keeping it in a separate phrase allows its pitch range to be reduced relative to the preceding focused α, as illustrated in (29b). Deletion of the post-focal α-boundary would transfer the phonetic salience to the post-focal /mamé/, which would bear the accent of the combined α. In the ØØ case, not much is lost or gained by 'dephrasing'. If the second α is included in the preceding α, the highest pitch is in the focused word, due to H_α, and the post-focal word occurs in the slope towards L_υ. If it is kept in a separate phrase, pitch-range reduction will similarly reduce the salience of the second α. These data, from Pierrehumbert and Beckman (1988: 105ff.), show that the choice of prosodic structure can be governed by the biological codes. In this case, the phonological phrasing is chosen so as to exploit the Effort Code. See also Sugahara (2002).

(29) a. { [(u   ma i   mame . . .)] }   b. { [(am   a)   (ma   me . . .)] }
        | | | | | | | | |
        $L_\alpha H_\alpha$ H*L L_υ L_α H_α $L_\alpha H_\alpha$ H*L L_υ
        /umái mamé/   /ama mamé/
        'GOOD-TASTING beans'   'SWEET beans'

10.11 Conclusion

The similarity in the prosodic grammars of Basque and Japanese may lead one to think that the kind of system they have in common, one with lexically unaccented phrases and accented phrases, is a relatively stable stage towards which language change may gravitate (Donohue 1997), a 'prosodic prototype' in the words of Hualde, Elordieta, Gaminde, and Smiljanić (2002), who explicitly make this assumption for these two languages. The similarities and differences in the α are listed in table 10.1. While both languages have maximally one accent per α, in Basque the pre-verbal or utterance-final α *must* have one (the default accent); and while Japanese may have the accent in any location, Lekeitio Basque employs the penult for accent whose presence is lexically determined and the final syllable for the default accent. Since no default insertion of H*L occurs in other locations, Basque forms long αs with strings of unaccented words. In both languages, automatic downstep occurs within the domain above α, ip. Downstep is triggered by H*L in both languages, affecting any phrase in Japanese, but only accented αs in Basque. The latter difference is due to the fact that in Basque unaccented αs

Table 10.1 *Similarities and differences between Japanese and Basque accentual phrases*

	Northern Bizkaian Basque	Japanese
Contrast	* versus $\emptyset$	* versus $\emptyset$
maximum number of *	1 per α	1 per α
location of *	penultimate of α	anywhere
default *	final syllable of pre-verbal or final α	none
pitch accent	H*L	H*L
morphological rules manipulating *	yes	yes
phonetic stress on *	no	no
domain of downstep	ip	ip
context of downstep	after H*L	after H*L
Target of downstep	accented α	any α
ALIGN(FOC, Left, ip, Left)	corrective focus	focus
Allow adjustment of ip-structure for focus	yes	yes
Allow adjustment of α-structure for focus	no	yes
Subordination distinct from downstep	yes	no

cannot occur in the relevant context, since post-accentual unaccented words are included in an α with the next accented word, or receive default accentuation.

The prosodic expression of focus is also similar, the difference being that Japanese uses it for both informational and corrective focus, while Basque uses it for corrective focus only. In both languages, an ip-boundary is inserted before the α containing the focus, which will prevent downstep from lowering the F_0 peak of the α concerned. Japanese is prosodically more versatile than Basque. Unlike Japanese, Basque requires that the focused constituent (whether corrective or informational) is contained in the XP immediately preceding the verb or the sentence end. Moreover, Japanese will readily create an α in order for an ip-boundary to align with the beginning of the focus constituent, if this would otherwise have shared an α with preceding non-focused words. Basque cannot create αs for this purpose. Finally, Basque applies obligatory pitch range subordination to the appended ip which begins at the finite verb.

Notes

1. I use phonemic representations, using IPA /j/ for conventional /y/. /n/ is [ŋ] word-finally and [n] word-internally, with place assimilations creating [m], as in [pompo] /ponpo/ 'pump', [ŋ] as in [déŋki] 'electricity'. Other allophones are [ts] for /t/ before /u/, as in [ítsu] /ítu/ 'when?', and [tɕ,ɕ] for /t,s/ before /i,j/, as in [ɕitɕí] /sití/ 'seven'. [ˊ] marks a syllable with accent.

2. After a monomoraic accented syllable, the F_0 may still be high at the beginning of the next syllable, more so in female than in male speech (Hasegawa and Hata 1994).

3. Haraguchi (1991) observes that the pronunciation in the merging dialect has high pitch, rather than mid pitch, on the final syllable. This could indicate that mid is marked relative to high, and is avoided when it serves no discriminating function.
4. The violation it imposes for not being the leftmost tone is left out of consideration, as it is constant across all forms dealt with.
5. Pierrehumbert and Beckman (1988) use the term 'catathesis' for downstep.

11

Scandinavian

11.1 Introduction

Norwegian and Swedish have intonation systems with pitch accents signalling information status, as has English. However, these languages also have a binary tone contrast on the syllable with primary stress. The two terms in the opposition are referred as Accent 1 and Accent 2 (Bruce 1977).[1] The challenge to separate the intonational tones from the lexical tones was successfully met by Bruce (1977) on the basis of the collection and analysis of a carefully composed corpus of read speech in which lexical tone, intonational focus, and position in the sentence were varied orthogonally. This work played a seminal role in the development of Pierrehumbert's 1980 autosegmental-metrical description of English, as attested by many of the contributions in his Festschrift (Horne 2000).

In section 11.2, I reproduce Bruce's analysis of Stockholm Swedish, including Gussenhoven and Bruce's (1999) modification of the analysis of compounds. Section 11.4 describes East Norwegian on the basis of Kristoffersen's (2000) account of Fretheim (1992), Fretheim and Nilsen (1991). There, I reinterpret their notion of 'Accent Phrase' as the stretch of speech spanned by the left-aligned L* and the right-aligned H-tone of an intonational pitch accent L*H, which implies a 'privative' analysis of the Norwegian tones, as in Lorentz (1995). Finally, section 11.6 tentatively suggests an account of the development of Danish stød from Accent 1.

A number of analyses are possible for the tone contrast, in part depending on the facts of the language variety in question. First, the opposition may be between two tones, a non-privative analysis, or between tone (Accent 2) and absence of tone (Accent 1), a privative analysis. A non-privative analysis, whereby part of the vocabulary is marked with one pitch accent and part with another, will be illustrated for Stockholm Swedish (Bruce 1977; Gårding 1977). The privative option will be illustrated for East Norwegian (Kristoffersen 2000), where words with Accent 2 are marked for tone in the lexicon and other words are toneless.

These toneless words remain toneless in the lexicon, so that sentences without any occurrence of Accent 2 have only intonational tones.

Second, analyses could be accentual or tonal. In an accentual analysis, words are marked for accent, as in the descriptions of Japanese and Basque of the previous chapter; while in a tonal analysis, words come with tones. An accentual analysis is clearly possible if the opposition is privative: words that are marked for accent will receive tone; other words will not. In non-privative descriptions, like Bruce's analysis of Stockholm Swedish, an accentual analysis may seem less desirable, because for every accent a choice from two pitch accents needs to be made, a situation comparable to that in Barasana and Kaure (see section 3.5.2). Alternatively, one pitch accent could be inserted in words marked with accent (say, Accent 2), while the other pitch accent could be regarded as the default, to be inserted in the stressed syllable of unaccented words, a situation comparable to Northern Biskaian Basque. In this chapter, both Swedish and Norwegian will be analysed tonally rather than accentually.

Under a tonal analysis, there is finally a choice to be made between an analysis that includes the associations between the stressed syllable and the tone ('pre-linking') and one that represents them as unassociated. Because the pitch accents are bitonal, non-prelinked representations imply the use of the star to select the tone that is to associate to the stressed syllable, as in the analysis of Bruce (1987) and Pierrehumbert and Beckman (1988: ch. 9). In this chapter, prelinked representations are assumed; a possible argument for choosing this option is given in section 11.5.

11.2 Stockholm Swedish

In the analysis of Stockholm Swedish by Bruce (1977, 1990), both Accent 1 and Accent 2 have a tonal representation, a tone complex HL. Accent 1 associates the L to the stressed syllable, while Accent 2 associates H. Accent 2 cannot occur on final syllables, which is why the unstressed syllable, indicated by the dot in (1b), is obligatory. The two tones in the complex are provided with a '+', mainly to distinguish them typographically from the focal tone, H, which occurs after the lexical tones, and is introduced below.

(1) Accent 1:   (x   Accent 2: (x   .
                      σ   σ
                      | |
                     H+L   H+L

The distribution of the two lexical pitch accents is highly predictable from the phonological and morphological context. Words with initial stress have Accent 2 if the stem ends in [ə] or [a], like ' *ande*, henceforth ²*ande*, but Accent 1 otherwise, like '*polio*, henceforth ¹*polio*. After monosyllabic stems, the suffix determines the tone. For instance, the plural indefinite suffix assigns Accent 2, as in ²*backar* 'girls', cf. definite singular ¹*backen*. A noun with non-initial, penultimate stress has Accent 2, like *kop²pia* 'copy', but otherwise Accent 1 is used if stress is non-initial, as in *be¹tala* 'pay' (Bruce and Hermans 1999). Recently, Lahiri, Wetterlin, and Jönsson-Steiner (ms) have defended the view that the morphological default is Accent 2.

The focal tone is H: it indicates the end of the focus constituent, and is obligatorily present in an utterance. It is sequenced after the lexical tones. Only if the stressed syllable is final in the *ι* will the H actually be pronounced inside the stressed syllable, necessarily after Accent 1. In other contexts, i.e. after non-final Accent 1 and Accent 2, its target occurs after the stressed syllable. A final boundary tone $L_ι$, used in both questions and statements, completes the right edge of the contour. An additional $H_ι$ may be used in continuation intonation (Gösta Bruce, *voce*). Initially, a boundary $L_ι$ occurs. These intonational tones are listed in (2).

(2) a. Focal tone: H
    b. Initial boundary tone: $L_ι$
    c. Finality intonation: $L_ι$
    d. Continuation intonation: $L_ιH_ι$

Example (3a) is an isolated pronunciation of *and* 'duck', suffixed with the definite *en*, while (3b) consists of *²ande* 'ghost', plus the definite suffix. The initial tone sequence $L_ιH$ cannot be pronounced if the first syllable has Accent 1, and $L_ι$ is left unrealized if it has Accent 2. With a preceding syllable, one more tone gets pronounced, as shown in (4a,b). Adding further syllables to (4a) will bring out the $L_ι$ in that expression, too. In (4c), a word with final stress is shown; it can only have Accent 1. Unlike what is found in *ι*-initial position, all tones are pronounced at the end of the *ι*.

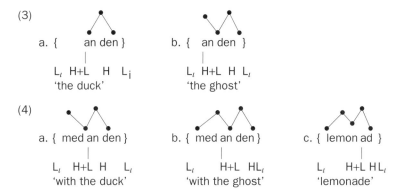

(3)
   a. {   an den }
            |
        $L_ι$ H+L   H L_i
        'the duck'

   b. { an den }
        |
      $L_ι$ H+L H $L_ι$
      'the ghost'

(4)
   a. { med an den }
         |
      $L_ι$ H+L H $L_ι$
      'with the duck'

   b. { med an den }
          |
      $L_ι$ H+L $HL_ι$
      'with the ghost'

   c. { lemon ad }
          |
      $L_ι$ H+L $HL_ι$
      'lemonade'

These representations are well-formed on the assumption that the TBU in Scandinavian is the stressed syllable, as stated in (12.2). In section 11.2.2, it will be argued that the pronunciation of compounds provides evidence that this is correct.

(5) Swedish/Norwegian TBU: 'σ

The term 'pitch accent' has been reserved for the lexical tones, since they are similar to English intonational pitch accents in both timing and in form. The question may arise whether focal H, which is clearly floating (Bruce 1987), is a pitch accent, i.e. a 'central' tone, or a 'boundary tone'. We could see it as a stress-seeking, central tone, H*, which is frustrated in its attempt to associate with the stressed syllable because the association of lexical tones ranks above that of the focal tone. H was tentatively analysed as a final boundary tone of the word by Pierrehumbert and Beckman (1988), which edges into the word as far as the lexical tones would allow this. In this spirit, we could see it as a right-aligned tone that is introduced by the focus constituent (see also Selkirk 2002 and section 11.2.1). The tone has been referred to as the 'sentence accent' (Bruce 1977), the 'phrase accent' (Pierrehumbert 1980), and the 'focal tone' (Gussenhoven and Bruce 1999). A rose by any name will smell as sweet, as William Shakespeare impressed upon us, but I will retain the term 'focal tone', stressing its functional equivalence with the focus-marking pitch accents of English.

11.2.1 Focus

The structures shown in (3) and (4) have either presentational focus or corrective focus, as expressed by the obligatory H, which aligns with the focus constituent. By not aligning it with a prosodic constituent like ω or ϕ, we account for the fact that it does not behave like a typical boundary tone. The timing of the floating focal H is governed by a default concatenation of the tones, to be described below.

(6) ALIGN(FOC,H,Rt): Align the right edge of the focus constituent with H

The focal H can be moved by transferring the focus to a preceding constituent, as shown in (7). Example (7a), for instance, is well-formed as a reply to *What are you doing with the duck?* The lexical tones do not depend on the presence of focal H: *¹anden* retains its lexical pitch accent, even though it occurs after the focus. Parallel observations apply to (7b).

(7)
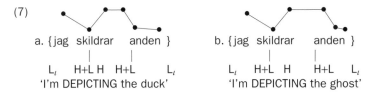

a. {jag skildrar   anden }   b. {jag skildrar   anden }

     L₁   H+L H H+L   L₁   L₁   H+L H   H+L   L₁
     'I'm DEPICTING the duck'   'I'm DEPICTING the ghost'

In fact, retention of pitch accents in content words is the rule: only function words lose the lexical tone, unless they are narrowly focused. In (8a,b), the peaks for Accent-1 words are compared with those for Accent 2 in pre-focal position. Those for Accent 2 occur one syllable later. In (9a,b), the final two words appear after the focus. Again, the peaks in (9b) are later than those in (9a). There is a drastic reduction of the pitch range from the second post-focal H-tone, here the H of the pitch accents on *¹nummer* and *²nunnor* in (9). Phonetically, the prosodic feature that marks the focus is the high plateau after the last focused word, formed between the focal H and the first lexical H on the right. The high plateau includes the stressed syllable of the first post-focal word with Accent 2. Indeed, a post-focal word with Accent 2 may, to speakers of other languages, sound as if it was focused, since its stressed syllable contains that last high pitch (cf *lång-* in (9b)). If the first post-focal word has Accent 1, the high plateau runs as far as the stressed syllable, which is associated with the lexical L. In general, focal H tends to have higher pitch than lexical H-tones.

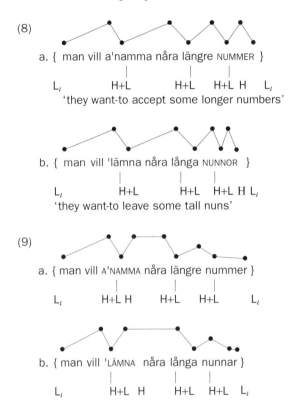

(8)

a. { man vill a'namma nåra längre NUMMER }

L*l*   H+L   H+L   H+L H   L*l*

'they want-to accept some longer numbers'

b. { man vill 'lämna nåra långa NUNNOR }

L*l*   H+L   H+L   H+L H L*l*

'they want-to leave some tall nuns'

(9)

a. { man vill A'NAMMA nåra längre nummer }

L*l*   H+L H   H+L   H+L   L*l*

b. { man vill 'LÄMNA nåra långa nunnar }

L*l*   H+L H   H+L   H+L   L*l*

Timing of targets

The target of the leading H of Accent 1 lies some 120 ms before that of associated L, while the target of the trailing L of Accent 2 lies some 120 ms to the right of the target of the associated H. As shown in Bruce (1987), the duration of the downslope of Accent 2 is particularly stable, and independent of the number of syllables that fit into that time span. Focal H is realized after the word tones; its timing is thus dependent on whether it follows Accent 1 or Accent 2. After Accent 1, it occurs immediately after the stressed syllable, and inside it if the stressed syllable is final. After Accent 2, focal H occurs in the next syllable, or the next unstressed syllable after that, if there is one. Focal H therefore allows its position to be dictated by the lexical tones and the available syllables. The suggestion that focal H floats is further supported by the fact that its timing is also sensitive to the number of syllables that separate it from a final L_i (Bruce 1977; Gussenhoven and Bruce 1999): it tends to be later if there are more syllables between the stress and the i-end.

11.2.2   Compounds

Compounds have Accent 2 on the first constituent and no lexical pitch accent on the second constituent, regardless of the tones the words have in the lexicon. The lexicon therefore includes (10), the functional equivalent of the English Compound Rule (section 14.2.1).

(10) [['σ]$_N$ [   ]$_N$]$_N$
            |
            H+L

The stressed syllable of the second constituent has a low target, with focal H realized after it, just as it would if it had Accent 1. Unlike what would be the case for a 'real' Accent 1 in the second constituent, however, the leading H is absent. In (11a,b), the compound ^{2}*Långa-nummer* 'Långa numbers' (where *Långa* is a geographical name) has a flat contour between the peak of Accent 2 and the focal H on the last syllable. By contrast, the NP ^{2}*långa* ^{1}*NUMMER*, 'long numbers' has an additional peak between these two peripheral peaks, due to the leading H of Accent 1. The effect of the medial peak was demonstrated by Bruce (1977) in a perception experiment with stimuli that could either be interpreted as a compound (^{2}*mellanmålen* 'snack', cf. (11a)) or as a phrase with final focus (^{2}*mellan* ^{1}*målen* 'between meals', cf. (11b)). As shown in panel (a) of figure 11.1, the stimuli varied in the height of the medial peak, which rose from 0 to 40 Hz above the midline. Additional stimuli tested the effect of the height of surrounding peaks. In panel (b), the results are shown: at around 12 Hz, listeners stop hearing the compound and start hearing the phrase. When the first peak is only 20 Hz, and listeners are led to believe that the pitch span of the stimulus is narrower, the medial peak needs only to be around 8 Hz above the baseline to trigger the perception of the phrase. This experiment shows the reality of the leading H-tone in Accent 1, and was particularly significant at the time Gösta Bruce wrote his thesis, since the compound pattern had earlier been described as being the same as a phrase with Accent 2 followed by Accent 1.

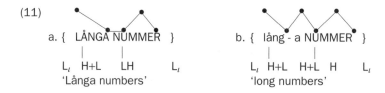

(11)

a. { LÅNGA NUMMER }
         | |
        L$_i$ H+L   LH   L$_i$
   'Långa numbers'

b. { lång - a NUMMER }
          | |
        L$_i$ H+L H+L H   L$_i$
   'long numbers'

The question arises how the L-tone on the second constituent of the compound is to be accounted for. Bruce (1977) assumed a phonetic 'copying rule' which spread targets from specified syllables to following unspecified ones, but it was not clear how this rule could place low targets precisely so as to include the stressed syllable of the second constituent of a compound. This would have required a rule that first positioned the target of the focal H. However, it is clear that the location of the high target depends on that of the low target, since the high target occurs in the same syllable as L if that syllable is final, and after it otherwise. Later, Bruce (1990) assumed an LH pitch accent specifically for compounds, to be inserted on the final constituent, following Accent 2 on a first constituent. This analysis is shown in (12a). In an attempt to avoid the postulation of a special compound pitch accent LH, Gussenhoven and Bruce (1999) proposed that the only pitch accent in compounds is in fact Accent 2, and that the stressed syllable of a non-initial constituent is filled by the trailing L of the pitch accent. Because it is *aligned* via CONCATENATE immediately to the right of associated H, but also *associated* with a stressed syllable later in the compound, it receives two targets, as shown in (12b).

(12)

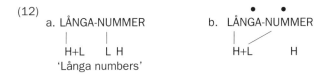

    a. LÅNGA-NUMMER   b. LÅNGA-NUMMER

       H+L   L H   H+L   H

       'Långa numbers'

In addition to avoiding the special LH pitch accent, the solution in (12b) makes the prediction that in compounds containing more than two constituents, like *²Ut˛rikesdeparte˛ments˛råds˛sommar˛byxorna* 'the Foreign Office counsellor summer trousers' (Riad 2000), the stressed syllables of all the non-initial words will associate with L, which thus spreads to all available locations, and that the H appears after the last such stress (here [byk]). This seems correct in that these post-focal stresses have firmly low pitch. In the analysis with LH, the location of H on the last constituent only (instead of all non-initial constituents) needs to be separately stipulated.

We can gain a perspective on the lack of reality of a LH pitch accent by positioning the compound before a focused word. It appears that L is kept in the compound, but that high moves off it. The inter-peak stretch in *Te²ater experiment åti¹ett* is low and flat, *-ment* having a low target, with a high target due to leading H of lexical H+L following on *å-* or *ti*, as shown in (13a). This suggests that there is no compound pitch accent LH, but just a single L-target. As predicted by the present analysis, the late low target disappears but the high target remains when we remove the compound, as can be seen by comparing (13a) with (13b), where *²Britta* and *åtiett* have lexical accents, the intervening words being treated as function words. Here, the pitch rises from the L on *Brit-* to the high target on *åti*, where the leading H of the H+L for *ett* is pronounced.

(13) a.

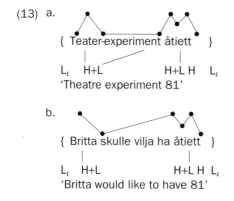

{ Teater-experiment åtiett }

L$_l$ H+L   H+L H   L$_l$

'Theatre experiment 81'

b.

{ Britta skulle vilja ha åtiett }

L$_l$ H+L   H+L H   L$_l$

'Britta would like to have 81'

11.3 An OT analysis of Swedish tone

The solution adopted in (12b) for compounds readily translates into an OT analysis by ranking the association constraint for the focal H below those for the lexical tones. The idea is that all tones try to associate with the TBU, the stressed syllable, but that, as in Japanese, only one tone may associate per TBU. Simplex words are considered first. By ranking a faithfulness constraint protecting lexical associations, FAITH(ASSOC), above T→TBU constraints, we honour the lexical associations that represent the difference between Accent 1 and Accent 2. Other high-ranking constraints that create well-formed associations are TBU←T and NoCROWD, which provide every TBU with one tone, and CONCATENATE, which forbids any tampering with the adjacency of the tones in the lexical pitch accents. TBU←T and NoCROWD are abbreviated as HIGHRANKING in tableau (14). Alignment constraints are ranked so as to create well-ordered strings, with tones in the right locations, and are not included in the tableau. *Anden* 'the duck' has the tone string L$_l$ H+L H L$_l$. Winning candidate (a) retains the lexical association intact. No other associations can take place, as shown by candidates (b,c): there is only one TBU, *an-*. In the same tableau, the compound *Långanummer* is treated. Compounds have minimally two TBUs, here *Lång-* and *num-*. In compounds, the ranking T$_{Lex}$ →TBU ≫ H$_{Foc}$ →TBU is crucial, since it implies trailing tone L of the pitch accent is associated in preference to H$_{Foc}$. Association of L in the winning candidate (a) leads to a target in the second stressed syllable, but at the same time the alignment of its left edge with the right edge of lexical H entitles it to the target after the first stressed syllable, exactly as in (12b). Candidate (b), which fails to produce a low target immediately after the stressed syllable, violates CONCATENATE; while candidate (c) associates H$_{Foc}$ in preference to L$_{Lex}$, thus losing to (a). The correct derivation of compound contours again depends on the distinction between alignment (in the OT sense) and association.

(14)

	Highranking	Concatenate	Faith-(Assoc)	$T_{Lex} \rightarrow$ TBU	$T_{Foc} \rightarrow$ TBU	$T_\iota \rightarrow$ TBU
anden | H+L L_ι H L_ι						
☞ a. { anden } | L_ι H+L H L_ι				*	*	**
b. { anden } | L_ι H+L H L_ι			*!	**		**
c. { anden } | L_ι H+L H L_ι			*!	*	*	**
långanummer L_ι H+L H L_ι						
☞ a. { långa nummer } | / L_ι H+L H L_ι					*	**
b. { långa nummer } | | L_ι H L H L_ι		*!			*	**
c. { långa nummer } | | L_ι H+L H L_ι				*!		**

The two targets of L in compounds do not result from spreading: technically, spreading is the acquisition of multiple associations. Still, NOSPREAD is ranked low in Swedish, since L spreads to all stressed syllables in compounds containing more than two morphological words.

11.4 East Norwegian

In this section, the intonation of East Norwegian is described contrastively with the above description of Stockholm Swedish, based on Fretheim (1992), Fretheim and Nilsen (1991), and the summary of Fretheim's work in Kristoffersen (2000). However, I take the liberty of reinterpreting that analysis somewhat, such that it is privative and no need for an 'Accent Phrase' arises.

11.4.1 Lexical tone

On the basis of a consideration of the surface forms of declarative pronunciations of the lexical tones of East Norwegian, this contrast can be described as

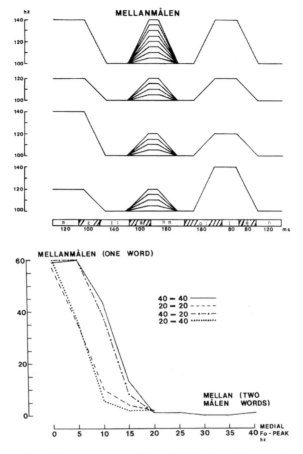

Fig. 11.1 Synthetic F_0 contours on *mellan målen/mellanmålen*, showing variation in initial, medial, and final peaks (panel a); and identification scores for the compound interpretation out of 60 trials as a function of medial peak height (panel b). From Bruce (1977).

privative, whereby Accent 1 is toneless and Accent 2 is a H-tone in underlying representations (Lorentz 1995), as shown in (15). Words with Accent 1 only ever have intonational tones: no default tone is supplied to Accent 1 words.

(15) Accent 1:   (x   Accent 2: (x
                   σ   σ
                                        |
                                        H

A difference with Stockholm Swedish is that Accent 2 may be specified on word-final syllables, and thus also in monosyllabic words. This is not apparent from citation pronunciations of monosyllabic words, since Accent 2 never appears on a word-final syllable in the surface representation. However, when the mono-syllabic word appears as the first constituent in a compound, its true nature is revealed. While Stockholm Swedish has a single prosodic structure for com-pounds, East Norwegian has two, as determined by the lexical accent of the first constituent; as in Swedish, the lexical accent on the second constituent disappears. Thus, combining [¹feːbr] and [¹nɑt] gives [¹feːbr nɑt] 'fever night', and combin-ing [²sɔmmr] and [¹nɑt] gives [²sɔmmr nɑt] 'summer night' (Kristoffersen 2000: 264; Bruce and Hermans 1999). In (16), a minimal pair is given with a monosyl-labic first constituent member, courtesy of Gjert Kristoffersen. He describes these facts by assuming that the underlying representation of Accent 2 monosyllabic roots includes the H lexical tone specifically as a linking tone for compound for-mation, on a par with unpredictable linking phonemes like [ə] or [s], used in e.g. *fiskesuppe* 'fish soup', from *fisk* and *suppe*. This solution makes it unnecessary to delete the lexical H when the morphological word surfaces as a monosyllable, since the root would only acquire a lexical H when occurring in first position in a compound.

(16)   ¹Strandvegen   'Strand Road' (where *Strand* is a proper name)
       ²Strandvegen   'Beach Road'

11.4.2   The intonational tones

The surface declarative pronunciations of Accent 1 and Accent 2 are LH and HLH, respectively. The Fretheim–Nilsen–Kristoffersen analysis factors out the final H, and assigns L to Accent 1 and HL to Accent 2. However, compared to Stockholm Swedish, East Norwegian lacks the leading H-tone of Accent 1 (Kristoffersen 2000: 251), which makes it possible to analyse the L-tone in the stressed syllable as intonational and consider it a pitch accent together with the following H. That is, while from the East Norwegian contrast (LH ~ (HLH a common element LH can be extracted which exhaustively characterizes Accent 1, extraction of H from the Stockholm Swedish contrast H(LH and (HLH leaves a timing difference for HL. (Similarly, extracting LH leaves an H-tone in both cases, which are moreover subject to an awkward timing difference, since the H-tone of Accent 1 must appear before the word that is specified by it; extracting HLH leaves no lexical tone in either case.) Thus, the difference between Accents 1 and 2 in Norwegian lies purely in the presence of the lexical H-tone for Accent 2, as shown in (17), where the pitch accent has been added to the representations of (15). In Swedish dialects that are like the Stockholm dialect, but have lost the initial H of Accent 1, a similar privative analysis would be called for, and is in fact given by Riad (2000) and others. As suggested by Gösta Bruce (personal communication 2003), such dialects may now in fact be used in Stockholm: I recorded two Stockholm Swedish speakers who turned out not to have the leading H in Accent 1.

(17) Accent 1: σ σ Accent 2: σ σ

         | |

       L*H   H   L*H

I give the intonational pitch accent with a starred tone, to indicate the tone that preferentially associates with the TBU, and to distinguish it typographically from the lexical tone. Because FAITH(Assoc) ranks above T*→TBU, the pitch accent only associates if the TBU is lexically empty. While the pitch accent is thus bitonal, it does not obey CONCATENATE. That is, within the ι, an interpolation between L* and H fills up the space between the stressed syllable (plus or minus the H of Accent 2) and the next stressed syllable, which is either occupied by the next intonational pitch accent (L*, for Accent 1) or by the lexical H of Accent 2. In longer ιs, rising movements are thus strung together, with the peaks occurring before the stressed syllables (Accent 1) or both before and on them (Accent 2). Lastly, the ι begins and ends with an L_ι. These intonational tones are listed in (18).

(18) a. Intonational pitch accent: L*H
     b. Initial boundary tone: L_ι
     c. Final boundary tone: L_ι (declarative)
                                H_ι (interrogative)

The space between L* and H can be quite wide, with H often appearing in a different word from L*. The H will always find a tone on its right, either lexical H or the next L_ι, or, if there is no further stressed syllable, L_ι, while L* will creep up to the lexical H on its left, or, if there is no H on that TBU, will itself associate. The pronunciation of non-nuclear pitch accents in Dutch and English is likewise of this 'splayed' type in my analysis (Gussenhoven 1983b; Gussenhoven 1988 and chapter 15). The stretch of speech covered by the rising slope will rarely coincide with a constituent in either Dutch or Norwegian. When the left-hand word has more than one unstressed syllable after the stress and the right-hand word has the stress on a non-initial syllable, the stretch includes word fragments. Nevertheless, Fretheim and Nilsen (1991) and Kristoffersen (2000: 279) consider the stretch a prosodic constituent, the Accent Phrase, in spite of the violation of strict layering implied by this analysis. However, they do not present independent evidence that the stretch encompassed by the tones functions in any sense like a constituent.

    To return to the lexical accents, their representation in one-word declarative utterances is thus as in (19), where [1][moːlə] *målet* 'the measurement' is contrasted with [2][mɑːlə] *male* 'to paint' (Kristoffersen 2000: 242). Stockholm Swedish realizes L_ι at the end of ι, but East Norwegian tends to truncate this boundary tone. In final position, the fall may only be realized at mid pitch or disappear entirely, in part depending on the degree of tonal crowding at the ι-end. In the pronunciations shown in panel (a) of figure 11.2, where L* is realized over the entire stressed syllable, there is a final fall to not-quite-low after penultimate

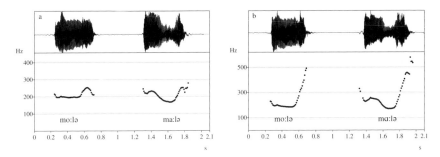

Fig. 11.2 Accent 1 on *måle* and Accent 2 on *male* with declarative intonation (panel a)
and interrogative intonation (panel b).

Accent 1, while after penultimate Accent 2, which has one tone more, it is
truncated entirely. (These utterances are not the same as those whose F_0-tracks are
reproduced in Kristoffersen (2000: 240), in which both falls are fully truncated.)
The interrogative versions are given in panel (b). The H_t is clearly pronounced
both after Accent 1 and Accent 2, as also shown in the schematic representations
in (20).

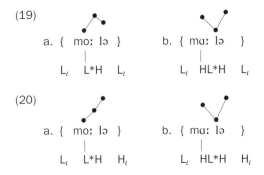

(19)

   a. { mo: lə }   b. { ma: lə }

        | |

    L_t L*H L_t L_t HL*H L_t

(20)

   a. { mo: lə }   b. { ma: lə }

        | |

    L_t L*H H_t L_t HL*H H_t

11.4.3   Norwegian focus

East Norwegian can be interpreted, like Stockholm Swedish, as having a focal
H, which is inserted to the right of L*H on the last word in the focus constituent
(cf. (6)). However, this H_{Foc} is not discernible as a separate target from the
preceding H of L*H; rather, the two tones are realized as an extra-high target,
as shown diagrammatically in (21a,b) for final and non-final focus constituents,
respectively. Arguably, therefore, the two H-tones are reduced to one through
the services of OCP. Alternatively, the focal H might be dispensed with entirely,
and the prosodic signalling of focus in Norwegian be analysed as a matter of
phonetic implementation: the high focal peak would result from a range-expanded
pronunciation of (L*)H. Fretheim and Nilsen's position is that the difference
between narrow focus and neutral focus is discrete, and thus expressed in the
phonology, implying that we need H_{Foc}, the counterpart of Swedish focal H_{Foc}.

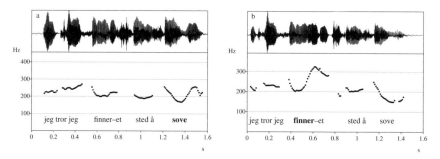

Fig. 11.3 Speech waveforms and F_0 tracks of *Jeg tror jeg finner et sted å sove*, with neutral focus (panel a) and focus on *finner* (panel b). Example sentences from Kristoffersen (2000).

After the focus, both the lexical H and the intonational pitch accent are often retained, although deletion of these tones on the last word is not uncommon. In figure 11.3, the L*H on *sted* and the lexical H and perhaps also L*H on *sove* are retained.

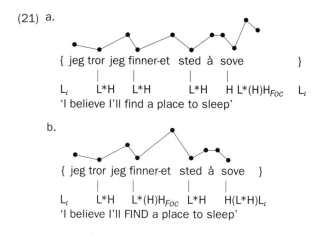

(21) a.

{ jeg tror jeg finner-et   sted å   sove   }

L$_\iota$ L*H   L*H   L*H   H L*(H)H$_{Foc}$ L$_\iota$

'I believe I'll find a place to sleep'

b.

{ jeg tror jeg finner-et   sted å   sove   }

L$_\iota$ L*H   L*(H)H$_{Foc}$ L*H   H(L*H)L$_\iota$

'I believe I'll FIND a place to sleep'

11.5   An argument for prelinking

There may be a motivated way of choosing between a prelinked representation of lexical tone, as adopted here, and an accentual one, as in Pierrehumbert and Beckman (1988) and Bruce (1987). Metalinguistic focus for vowels (cf. English *I didn't say maniFIST*, but *maniFEST*) respects the lexical tone on the main stress syllable, but uses Accent 1 in other locations (Tomas Riad, personal communication 2001). This is shown in (22), which uses Swedish data, but the Norwegian facts are comparable. This suggests that metalinguistic focus is expressed with a default Accent 1, as in (22a), which is overridden by prelinked Accent 2, as in

(22b).[2] Under an accentual analysis whereby the accent is on the main stress, the starred tone of H*L would incorrectly associate in *prin*- in (22a). In compounds, as in the compound for 'beginner' in (22a) (cf. (10)), the stressed syllable of the first constituent has Accent 2 in the metalinguistic use. Since compounds can be freely formed from both Accent-1 and Accent-2 words, the Accent 2 in compounds cannot be prelinked. We can retain our argument, however, by assuming that Accent 2, which is available in the lexicon for compound formation, associates in preference to default Accent 1. In (22), the square brackets mark of the focus constituent.

(22) a.   Jag sa inte [¹PRYN]sessor, utan [¹PRIN]sessor
      b. prin²sessor   Jag sa inte prin[²SOS]sor, utan prin[²SES]sor
      c. ²ny-börjare   Jag sa inte [²NI]-börjare, utan [²NY]-börjare

11.6 Danish

Standard Danish differs from Swedish and Norwegian in lacking a lexical tone contrast (Grønnum 1983a; Basbøll 2003). More particularly, all words receive a L*H pitch accent, causing Danish utterances to have sequences of rising movements from the stressed syllable and to sound somewhat like Norwegian sentences containing only Accent-1 words. However, the language has a register feature called stød, which appears in syllables that etymologically broadly correspond to syllables with Accent 1 in Norwegian and Swedish. Moreover, there are independent reasons for assuming that Danish must have been the innovative dialect *vis-à-vis* the tonal dialects (Riad 2000). Since it is not unreasonable to assume that East Norwegian is innovative with respect to Stockholm Swedish through the loss of the leading H in Accent 1, the question naturally arises of what historical development is responsible for the Danish prosodic system. This question is considered in section 11.6.1, while section 11.6.2 briefly compares Danish intonation contours with East Norwegian contours with Accent-1 words, and concludes that, unlike what previous analyses have assumed, the Danish intonational pitch accent is H*L, not L*H.

11.6.1 Stød

Danish stød amounts to contrastive laryngealization ('creak') of the second mora of stressed syllables (Clements and Keyser 1983; Riad 2000; Basbøll 2003). Minimal pairs include [hun̰] 'dog' – [hun] 'she', [lɛ̰sɔ] 'reads' [lɛɛsɔ] 'reader'. Riad (2000) suggests that the origin of stød may lie in a reinterpretation of a boundary L$_t$. If we assume that the glottalization functioned as an enhancement of low pitch, which is not unreasonable in view of the frequent co-occurrence of creak and L-tones, a question that Riad's suggestion raises is how low pitch at the end of a word helped to distinguish (former) Accent-1 words from (former) Accent-2 words. Also, an additional explanation is required for the occurrence of stød in penultimate stressed syllables. Since the tonal contrast was one of high (Accent-2) pitch versus low pitch (Accent 1) in the stressed syllable, a reinterpretation of L* would appear to provide a more straightforward scenario, as the pitch-lowering gesture would be expected to be made in the stressed syllable, and the glottalization of the end of that syllable would enhance the perceptual quality of low pitch in it. It is therefore plausible that a Norwegian contrast of the type H L*H versus L*H was reinterpreted as L*H versus stød plus L*H. As a first step, the phonetic implementation of Norwegian Accent 2 may have involved a less deep valley between the peaks, as shown in (23), whereby the representation remains intact.

(23)

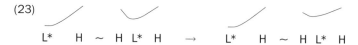

L*   H   ~   H L* H   →   L*   H   ~   H L*   H

At this point, the contrast between Accent 1 and Accent 2 is jeopardized, since the two pitch movements might easily be taken to be simple rises. A likely next step, therefore, is to make firm gesture for the low pitch in Accent 1, which would be a sensible way to maintain the contrast. This behaviour must at some point have led to an interpretation of these syllables as having glottalization, or [+murmur], to use Duanmu's feature for Mandarin L-tones syllables, and the non-interpretation of initial H in Accent 2. This is shown in (24). The innovative phonetics to the right of the arrow in (23) appear to the left of the arrow in (24), but with the new phonological interpretation. Subsequently, speakers will have brought their phonetic implementation in line with their representations, as shown to the right of the arrow in (24). Either immediately or subsequently, stød was restricted to syllables with two sonorant moras.

(24)

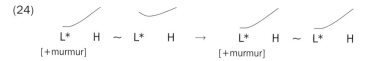

L*   H   ~   L*   H   →   L*   H   ~   L*   H
[+murmur]   [+murmur]

11.6.2 The intonational pitch accent in Danish

While one would thus expect Danish utterances to be like Norwegian utterances that consist exclusively of Accent-1 words, there are two differences worth noting. Unlike Norwegian, which tends to have high pitch for the last H-tone, Danish utterances with neutral focus are pronounced with a declining overall trend. That is, there is no obligatory focal tone to express wide presentational focus (Grønnum 1983b). Second, non-initial pitch-accented words tend to have the lowest pitch *before* the stressed syllable, not in it, while the target of H typically falls one syllable after the stressed syllable if there is one, or sometimes later, but not all the way towards the right, as in East Norwegian. The stressed syllable thus typically lies somewhere halfway up the upward slope. This suggests that the usual autosegmental interpretation of Danish as having a L*H pitch accent (Pierrehumbert 1980: 116) is incorrect, and that it is rather H*L, whereby the H* is aligned late, and downstepped, and L is right-aligned. This is shown graphically in (my interpretation of Grønnum's example) (25), where the targets for H* are considerably delayed. After the interpretation of intonational peaks as H*L, the feature [+murmur] lost its connection with any L-tone.

(25)

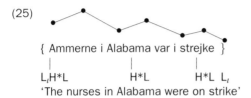

{ Ammerne i Alabama var i strejke }

L$_i$H*L　　H*L　　H*L L$_i$
'The nurses in Alabama were on strike'

A historical development whereby a two-peak contour like L$_i$ L*H L*H L$_i$ was reinterpreted as L$_i$ H*L H*L L$_i$ is supported by three further observations. First, when the focus is narrow, the F$_0$ in the stressed syllable of the focused word, which represents the lower end of a rising movement, is raised. This is what one would expect of a pitch span increase for H*: an L* would be expected to be lowered (cf. Gussenhoven and Rietveld 2000). Second, in declarative sentences, the downward movements in the words before and after the narrow focus tend to begin from the stressed syllables, rather than from a point *after* the stressed syllables. This could be interpreted as a retreat from prominence, as a reduction in the delay of a H* tone (cf. sections 5.7.1 and 5.10), but is hard to interpret as the behaviour of L*. An analysis with L*H would need to decide between an analysis whereby H*L is used in non-focal constituents of narrow-focus sentences, which implies a phonological interpretation of the timing difference, and an analysis whereby the implementation of L*H is speeded up in the syllables flanking the narrow focus, such that the peak occurs early. Neither of these options seems particularly appealing. Third, in questions, focal peaks are even later than in declaratives, as shown in figure 3.1 of Grønnum (1983b). This can easily be interpreted as a case of enhancement of peak height in interrogative intonation, an implementation pattern to be expected for H*, as reported earlier for Dutch (van Heuven and Haan 2002).

The comparison of two Scandinavian tonal dialects showed that the Scandinavian lexical accents may constitute a fully specified (Stockholm Swedish) or a privative contrast (East Norwegian). In addition to the lexical tones, Swedish has a focal H$_{Foc}$ to mark information focus. Norwegian has an intonational pitch accent L*H, which marks focus either by expanding the range of the L*H of the last word in the focus constituent, or – in an alternative analysis – inserts a focal H$_{Foc}$ after the last pitch accent in the focus constituent. The choice between the phonetic and the phonological solutions seems difficult to make without further investigation, although the sheer size of the difference between a focal and non-focal pronunciation would seem to favour a phonological representation of the focus tone. For the South Swedish variety (Malmö), a 'phonetic focus' analysis has been proposed by Bruce (2001). In the case of Danish, too, the assumption has been that focus increases the pitch span of the focal pitch accent. There is consensus that focus in Danish is expressed by means of pitch range expansion, in the present interpretation, by raising H*. As for interrogative intonation, Standard Danish suspends or attenuates declination, leaving the phonological representation intact (Grønnum 1992) (see also chapter 6).

11.7 Conclusion

While following Bruce's analysis of Stockholm Swedish, I modified Fretheim and Nilsen's and Kristoffersen's analysis of East Norwegian in assuming a privative representation of lexical tone: Accent 1 has no representation and Accent 2 has H in the stressed syllable. This implies that the intonational pitch accent is L*H, rather than just H. By allowing trailing H to align right, a conventional prosodic constituent structure could be assumed. The question whether the focal H is a separate tone or represents a wide-span pronunciation of the trailing H could not be solved, and either analysis seems viable. Instead of adding a focal H after the lexical pitch accent, focus is expressed by boosting the distinctively timed peaks of Accent 1 and Accent 2 and, in the case of Malmö, lowering the post-H low pitch.

A speculative account of Danish assumed that stød arose as a reinterpretation of L* in Accent-1 words, with the simultaneous loss of lexical H. Independently of the details of this scenario, it was postulated that after the H vs. L contrast was given up, the Norwegian-style L*H was reinterpreted as a late-aligning H*L intonational pitch accent in Danish.

Swedish and Norwegian have considerably simpler intonation systems than West Germanic. Where English, Dutch, and German have a large number of pitch accents to signal various shades on information status (H*L, H*, L*H, etc.; see chapter 15), Stockholm Swedish has essentially one intonation contour if we disregard the continuation rise, and so has Danish, while East Norwegian has just two, a declarative and an interrogative contour. Of course, the fact that Scandinavian has (had) lexical pitch accents can be related to the sparser inventory of intonational contrasts. However, the next chapter will show that intonation systems can be more elaborate than those of Scandinavian and still have a lexical tone contrast.

Notes

1. These 'lexical accents' or 'word accents' are present in the majority of the dialects. Most Swedish dialects spoken in Finland are toneless; toneless Norwegian dialects are spoken in the countryside around Bergen and north of Tromsø (Kristoffersen 2000).

2. An interesting minimal pair demonstrating the movement of the word stress is ^{2}*NUNnor* spoken with presentational focus and the same word spoken with corrective (metalinguistic) focus on the second (normally unstressed) syllable, as in *Inte nunNER, utan nunNOR*. While the tonal structures are very similar, L$_t$ **H+**.L H L$_t$ versus L$_t$ H+.**L** H L$_t$, where the bold tone is in the stressed syllable, the stressed syllable in each word will be longer than its unstressed counterpart in the other expression, cf. Heldner and Strangert (2001).

12

The Central Franconian Tone

12.1 Introduction

Inevitably, the more intonation contrasts a language has, the harder it is to maintain a system of lexical tone contrasts, and vice versa. West Germanic languages have a large number of intonation contrasts, and so, *a priori*, the introduction of a lexical tone contrast in one of those languages should be problematic. Essentially, this would double the number of required contrasts, since every intonation pattern will have to be usable on words from two tonal word classes. The language is likely to respond to this situation by reducing the number of intonation contours; by enhancing pitch contrasts by means of other phonetic parameters, like duration or vowel quality; or, if all else fails, by banning certain forms that would otherwise be too similar to other forms, or be particularly hard to pronounce. In the last case, forms that are generated by the grammar are simply not used. We may well regret that we cannot artificially introduce a tone contrast in a West Germanic language to see what will happen, but here is the good news: a lexical tone developed quite spontaneously in the Central Franconian dialect of German, probably around 1300. The novel feature spread, probably from Cologne, as far south as Luxembourg and and as far west as Hasselt (Belgium) and Maastricht (the Netherlands). The tonal area must have been larger than it is now, but it still measures some 160 km north-to-south and 125 km east-to-west (Schmidt 1986; de Vaan 1999), covering four countries in the Dutch–German dialect continuum.[1] Enough dialects have meanwhile been investigated to be able to say that there has indeed been a variety of responses to the new situation, and all of the above effects, the non-use of grammatical forms, reduction in the number of contrasts, and enhancement of the contrast are in fact attested.

The dialects will be treated from a historical perspective. Beginning with the tonogenesis, I will give the motivations for a number of phonological changes. Three post-tonogenesis changes will be seen to lead to the remarkable grammar of the dialect of Roermond, but more so than was the case in Gussenhoven

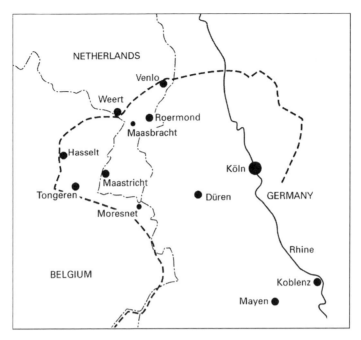

Fig. 12.1 Northern part of the tonal area, showing the locations mentioned in this chapter in Germany, the Netherlands, and Belgium.

(2000c), it will be possible to give data from other dialects that share none (Maastricht) or some of these changes (Mayen, Cologne). They are described in sections 12.4–12.5 and involve the introduction of a rising–falling contour for interrogative intonation, the activation of a ban on intrasyllabic rises, and a reversal of the conventional order $T_{Lex}T_i$ to T_iT_{Lex} in i-final syllables. Moreover, different developments took place in Tongeren and Venlo, which are briefly charted in section 12.7. These places are given in figure 12.1.

This chapter amounts to an exercise in determining the relation between phonetic forms and phonological representations. In addition, because of its historical orientation, it illustrates the different factors that are involved in language change in quite striking ways (Labov 1981; Kiparsky 1982a; Kiparsky 1988). In one type, forms that are ergonomically less successful from the point of their production or perception are improved in the phonetic implementation on an *ad-hoc* basis, causing the next generation to construct a new grammar which incorporates the new behaviour. This kind has become known as 'Neogrammarian change'.[2] In another type, cognitive economy may cause generalizations to be extended, leading to loss of exceptions and paradigm uniformity ('analogy') or the execution of a newly developed grammar so as to produce forms that find no motivation in the phonetics. A third case arises when speakers are confronted with the results of either type of change, and feel a social obligation to incorporate the new forms into their own system, often giving them novel phonological representations. This type may lead to 'lexical diffusion', the word-by-word replacement of old pronunciations by categorically different new ones. I will flesh out these types of change with examples in section 12.8.[3]

12.2 Tonogenesis

The origin of the lexical tone contrast is controversial. I here briefly summarize my own account (Gussenhoven 2000c) and point out the problem noted by Mihm (2002). Other recent work on this issue is de Vaan (1999) and Schmidt (2002). The phonological and morphological configuration which may have led to the lexical tone is given in table 12.1. The chain of events was started by OPEN SYLLABLE LENGTHENING (OSL), which caused short vowels in open syllables to be bimoraic in Middle High German and Middle Dutch (Lahiri and Dresher 1999). The process created a large number of nouns with short vowels in the singular and long vowels in the plural. One reaction to this violation of a one-to-one relation between morpheme and phonological form in the German dialects was to lengthen the vowel in the singular, so as to restore paradigm uniformity. As a result of this ANALOGICAL LENGTHENING (AL), both the plural and the singular of the word for 'road', which had a short vowel before these events took place, has a long vowel in Standard German: [ʋeek-ʋeegə]. If we assume that another phonological change was afoot, APOCOPE, the loss of word-final schwa, we may have an explanation for the introduction of an H-tone. The Central Franconian speakers might have resisted the long vowel in the singular at a point where they had lost the final schwa in the plural, so as to keep singular and plural forms from falling together. In Dutch, AL did not go through, as a result of which it now has some thirty 'irregular' plurals with a long vowel where the singular has a short vowel (e.g. [ʋɛx-ʋeeɣə]) (Lahiri and Dresher 1999). Central Franconian speakers may have phonetically lengthened the short vowel, adopting the phonetics, but not the phonology of the long vowel of their eastern neighbours. As shown graphically in figure 12.2, short vowels may have been somewhat truncated in utterance-final position, creating a higher pitch in the last part of the lengthened vowel than occurred in phonologically long vowels, in which the fall would be complete. The postulation of an H-tone then becomes a plausible interpretation of the phonetic lengthening, in particular an H-tone that occurs late in monosyllabic singular forms that have long-vowelled plurals. The form with the tone became known as *Dehnung* 'lengthening' in German and *sleeptoon* 'drag tone' in Dutch, later, 'Accent 2', while the form without is referred to as *Schärfung* 'sharpening' and *stoottoon* 'push tone' (later Accent 2) (Schmidt 1986; Gussenhoven and van der Vliet 1999).

After the introduction of the tone, the vowel became bimoraic, leading to tonal minimal pairs. The tone spread through the lexicon in phonetically motivated

Table 12.1 *Hypothesized phonological interpretation of* ANALOGICAL
LENGTHENING as a lexical tone in Central Franconian (CF)

	German		CF		Dutch	
Middle Dutch/High German	wex	weɣə	wex	weɣə	wex	weɣə
Open Syllable Lengthening		weeɣə		weeɣə		weeɣə
Apocope		–		weex		weex
Analogical Lengthening	weex		[weːç]		–	
Tonogenesis			wex	weex		
			|			
			H			
			([weːç])			
Present situation	ʋeek	ʋeegə	weex	weex	ʋɛx	ʋeeɣə
			|			
			H			

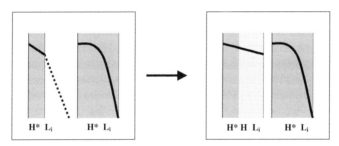

Fig. 12.2 Hypothesized phonetic lengthening of singular forms, leading to a tonal
interpretation of the difference between singular (H*H L$_t$) and plural (H* L$_t$) forms.

ways (see below). Today, monosyllabic nouns with Accent 2 that form their
plural purely by a shift to Accent 1 are in a minority. Dialects typically have
some ten or fifteen of them, with Maastricht still having /weex^2/ – /weex^1/ as the
singular and plural forms of 'road'.

    There are arguments for and against the above scenario. One counter-
argument might be that languages can do without a morphological distinction
for number, and that therefore the pressure to retain it cannot be high. In this
connection, it is relevant to know that an obliteration of morphological contrasts
after APOCOPE was counteracted in the German dialects in a variety of ways.
Generalization of umlaut (/arm/- /ærm/, earlier /armə/) was one strategy; another
was the reinterpretation of the duration difference of vowels before voiced and
voiceless obstruents as a quantity difference, as in /dɛif/ – / dɛiːf/, earlier / dɛivə/).
The latter development led to a three-way quantity contrast before obstruents,
as in /wit – wiːt – wiːːt/ 'white, far, expanse', in the Hamburg area (cf. further
Wiesinger's and Dingeldein's contributions to Besch *et al.* 1983). A more serious

argument against the theory is given by Mihm (2002), who reports a difference in the spelling of certain long vowels in open and closed syllables in a sixteenth-century Cologne manuscript. It is tempting to see these spellings, with Mihm, as reflexes of a tonal contrast. The problem for the theory in table 12.1, however, is that the manuscript regularly has unapocopated words. If the connection between the tonogenesis and APOCOPE is to be maintained, therefore, either the spelling distinctions must not reflect the tone contrast, or APOCOPE must have occurred earlier so as to allow the tonogenesis, its absence in the manuscript being due to the restoration of weak-vowelled suffixes.[4]

An important argument for the theory is that it predicts that the lexical tone was H and that high pitch occurred late in the syllable of singular monosyllabic nouns, all of which are correct. It also predicts that an additional feature of Accent 2 may have been phonetic lengthening. In fact, syllables with Accent 2 are longer than syllables with Accent 1 in the dialects of Maastricht, Cologne, and Venlo, while no dialects have been reported with the opposite pattern. Thirdly, if the creation of phonetic length was at a premium in syllables with Accent 2, other phonetic features that enhance duration may have been used which might still be observable today. There are in fact two such features. One is tongue height. In a number of instances of phonological change, vowels with Accent 2 developed closer reflexes than those with Accent 1. The second is monophthongization. Diphthongal pronunciations are associated with Accent 1, and monophthongal pronunciations with Accent 2. In section 12.3, I will discuss these differences further and explain how they may relate to the need to enhance a duration difference between the two word accents. A fourth argument can be based on the existence of distributional correlations between certain segments and the tone. Although the present-day dialects do not consistently show low pitch at the end of a syllable with Accent 1 and high pitch at the end of a syllable with Accent 2, as presumed in (12.2), the segmental correlations are understandable if this was in fact the original situation. Before voiceless obstruents, Accent 2 appears to be favoured, which must be due to the fact that such obstruents attract high pitch. In addition, high vowels, which have high intrinsic F_0, attract Accent 2. More specifically, according to Wiesinger's (1975) distributional 'Rule A', Accent 2 appears if the vowel is a high monophthong or is a closing diphthong, i.e. if there is a close vowel at the end of the syllable peak, and the following consonant is voiceless. I assume that these correlations arose through contact-tonogenesis or as a result of the propagation of the tone through the lexicon in later developments, as in the case of U described in section 3.6.1, rather than being responsible for any *de novo* tonogenesis (cf. Gussenhoven 2000c).

12.3 The first stage

Let us make the simplifying assumption that speakers were concerned to preserve just two intonation contours for monosyllables, a declarative fall and a rise for questions and non-finality, henceforth the 'interrogative'. Assuming minimal tonal structure, these might have been as in (1) before the introduction of the lexical tone. The rise could have had H* (cf. the open target) or L*, either of which would have given a rising intonation together with the H-boundary tone.

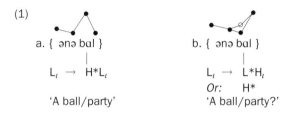

(1)

a. { ənə bɑl }
   |
   $L_\iota \rightarrow H^*L_\iota$

'A ball/party'

b. { ənə bɑl }
   |
   $L_\iota \rightarrow L^*H_\iota$
   Or: H*
'A ball/party?'

The introduction of the lexical H-tone on the second mora would lead to the situation in (2) for Accent 1 in the declarative and interrogative contours, and to (3) for Accent 2 in the same intonation contours. The lexical H in (3a,b) will lengthen the high-pitched section in the phonetics. These examples are from the present-day dialect of Maastricht, whose system would appear to be close to the original situation. Both (3a,b) sound somewhat drawled compared to the clipped pronunciations of (2).

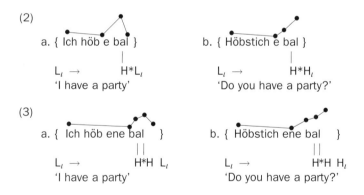

(2)

a. { Ich höb e bal }
   |
   $L_\iota \rightarrow$ H*L_ι
   'I have a party'

b. { Höbstich e bal }
   |
   $L_\iota \rightarrow$ H*H_ι
   'Do you have a party?'

(3)

a. { Ich höb ene bal   }
   ||
   $L_\iota \rightarrow$ H*H L_ι
   'I have a party'

b. { Höbstich ene bal   }
   ||
   $L_\iota \rightarrow$ H*H H_ι
   'Do you have a party?'

The general impression of greater length for Maastricht's Accent 2 has led to the belief that the contrast between the two word accents is durational, rather than tonal. However, across a larger number of contexts the tonal character of Accent 2 is unambiguous. For instance, post-focally, when H* is absent, the lexical H can be observed by itself, as in the word *eike* 'oak' in (4b), which contrasts with *eike* 'little egg' in (4a). In other words, in some contexts, the effect of the lexical H-tone on the F_0 contour amounts to a lengthening of the pitch movement, because its target is similar to one or both adjacent targets, but in those cases where it is not, its existence is also evident from its distinctive F_0 target.

(4)

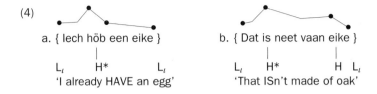

a. { lech höb een eike }   b. { Dat is neet vaan eike }

L_I   H*   L_I   L_I   H*   H L_I
'I already HAVE an egg'   'That ISn't made of oak'

In fact, the way in which the dialect enhances Accent 2 allows us to make a connection with the hypothesized tonogenesis. Not only are syllables with Accent 2 longer, certain developments affecting vowel quality can be interpreted as aiding the perception of greater duration. First, the diphthongization of [iː, yː, uː] to [ɛi, oey, ɔu], which took place in the eighteenth century, failed in words with Accent 2 (de Vaan 2002). Even today, the spread of this diphthongization still occurs at a slower rate in syllables with Accent 2 than in syllables with Accent 1 in a number of villages in Belgium (Peeters and Schouten 1989). Also, in dialects spoken in Belgium that have lost the tone distinction, the reflexes of certain vowels in Accent 1 words are more open than in Accent-2 words (Cajot 2001). This suggests that Accent-2 combines preferably with close vowels. Unpublished research shows that listeners judge close vowels to have longer durations than mid vowels when acoustic durations are equal, which effect must be due to a similar kind of 'compensatory listening' as that found by Silverman (1984) for intrinsic pitch. Since close vowels have higher F_0, listeners hear them as having lower pitch than open vowels with the same physical F_0 (see section 1.4.3). Similarly, because close vowels are shorter than open vowels due to the shorter passage of the tongue body to and from consonantal articulatory positions, they are heard as longer than open vowels when physical durations are equal. The tendency towards closer vowels for Accent 2 may thus be due to the speaker's desire to sound as if the vowel is long.

Independently, diphthongization may aid in the perception of short vowels. It is a striking feature of many Limburgian dialects that the second elements of diphthongs in syllables with Accent 1 are strengthened to [j, w]-glides. There are, for instance, contrasts like /ɛi/ ~/æj/ in the now toneless dialect of Weert whose distribution reflects the tonal distinction of neighbouring tonal dialects. This suggests that a diphthong with Accent 1 was reinterpreted as a short vowel-plus-glide combination and thus kept distinct from the diphthong in former Accent-2 words (Heijmans 1999; Heijmans 2003). By pronouncing [ɛi] as [ɛj], effectively changing a VV-rhyme into a VC-rhyme, the perceived duration of the vowel shifts from 'long' to 'short', since the glide is interpreted as part of the coda. Interestingly, in the Maastricht dialect, quite substantial allophonic differences exist between Accent-1 and Accent-2 pronunciations of the diphthongs /ɛi, oey, ɔu/, where those with Accent 1 are firmly diphthongal and those with Accent 2 are very nearly monophthongal (Gussenhoven and Aarts 1999).

12.4 Improving the interrogative contrast

In declarative contours, the contrast between (2a) and (3a) must have been relatively easy to perceive. Instead of the late-peaking syllable of the Maastricht dialect, the two H-tones in (3a) may have been pronounced as separate peaks, a pronunciation still to be found in Cologne, for instance (Heike 1962). In either case, the drawn-out pronunciation contrasted with the rapid fall to low pitch in Accent 1. In ι-internal declarative contexts, the H*H of focused Accent-2 syllables contrasted with a single H* for Accent 1, which, in combination with final L_ι, plays out as a timing difference for the fall. An illustration from Venlo is given in (5a,b) (see also section 7.3.3).

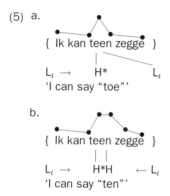

(5) a.

{ Ik kan teen zegge }

$L_\iota \rightarrow$ H* L_ι

'I can say "toe"'

b.

{ Ik kan teen zegge }

$L_\iota \rightarrow$ H*H $\leftarrow L_\iota$

'I can say "ten"'

This contrast between early and late falls is a common feature of the present-day dialects. More usually, contour (5b) has a late peak rather than a late fall, as in the Roermond and other dialects, as shown in (6). This particular difference between Venlo and Roermond is an example of the language-sensitivity of implementation rules. That is, there is no reason to assume that H* changes into a L* in the Roermond dialect. In fact, in section (12.4.3) I will show that this would be an impossible assumption.

(6)

{ Ich kan teen zegge }

$L_\iota \rightarrow$ H*H $\leftarrow L_\iota$

'I can say "ten"'

By contrast, it may have been hard to distinguish rises that differed in speed or excursion size, and the lexical tone contrast must therefore have been vulnerable in interrogative contours (cf. (2b) vs. (3b)). In any event, in a large area, linguistic change affected ι-final and ι-internal focused syllables in interrogative contours. One change amounted to the addition of L_ι after the L*H$_\iota$ contour, and was motivated by a low perceivability of the contrast in focused ι-final syllables. The second introduced a contextually determined adjustment of the lexical H to L, which improved the contrast in focused ι-internal syllables.

12.4.1   Final interrogatives

A drastic measure salvaged the pitch contrast in ι-final interrogatives: so as to suggest that (3a) had Accent 1, a falling movement was added after the rise, as shown in (7a). This must have signalled to the listener that the intonation was that of a question, but that the word was like an Accent-1 word as said with neutral (i.e. declarative) intonation. Example (7) is from Mayen (Schmidt 1986). The final fall in [mɑn] 'basket', shown in (7a), was not commented on in Schmidt's thesis, but attested in F_0 tracks presented there and reproduced in Gussenhoven (2000c). Because of its subtle nature, which may well cause it to be mistaken for a fade-out reversal at the end of sonorant-final utterances, Künzel and Schmidt (2001) refer to it as an 'epitone'. Their data show it is significantly different from the endings of interrogative utterances ending in focused final syllables with Accent 2, like [mɑn] 'man', given in (7b).

(7)

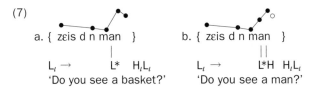

a. { zɛis d n man   }
            |
L$_\iota$ →   L* H$_\iota$L$_\iota$
'Do you see a basket?'

b. { zɛis d n man   }
            ||
L$_\iota$ →   L*H H$_\iota$L$_\iota$
'Do you see a man?'

Contour L* H$_\iota$L$_\iota$ combines with the lexical tone in the case of (7b). In order to explain the non-realization of final L$_\iota$, a phonetic truncation analysis must be assumed, FRANCONIAN TRUNCATION (8), banning the realization of a fourth tone in a syllable, as indicated graphically by the open target in (7b).

(8)   FRANCONIAN TRUNCATION: After T*, pronounce at most
     (Implementation)   two tones in the same syllable

The question might be asked if the grammar could not stipulate that ι-final syllables with Accent 1 have L* H$_\iota$ as the interrogative contour, while those with Accent 2 have L* H$_\iota$L$_\iota$. In the interpretation of Hayes (1990), the theory of Lexical Phonology will allow postlexical contextual information to be included in the lexicon ('precompilation'). Arguably, therefore, we might have an intonational lexicon which includes (9), an allomorphy statement comparable to that required for /ə/ and pre-vocalic /ən/ for the English indefinite article.

(9) Interrogative intonation: $\begin{bmatrix} \text{L*H}_\iota \text{ in the context} & \sigma\}_\iota \\ & | \\ & \text{H} \\ \text{L*H}_\iota\text{L}_\iota \end{bmatrix}$

The problem with (9), however, is that these contours cannot both have lexical status. Unlike /ə/ ∼ /ən/, both of which appear in the same context, as in *villa* ∼ *villain*, L*H$_\iota$ does not occur in other contexts. Therefore, the interpretation of contextually determined phonetic variation is inevitable. In fact, a situation much like (9) does exist in the dialect of Venlo, where the two contours contrast in other contexts. I return to this point in section 12.7.3.

12.4.2 Non-final interrogatives

Even though the motivation for its introduction was found in ι-final syllables with Accent 1, the interrogative contour appears quite generally as L* H$_\iota$L$_\iota$. When L* occurs on an ι-*internal* focused syllable, the fall described by H$_\iota$L$_\iota$ will appear on a final syllable. In the focused syllable, Accent 1 has rising pitch, while Accent 2 has low pitch, as shown in (10), which shows non-final ιs, from Schmidt (1986). The difference in pitch before the final peak shown here in the stylized contours is clear from F$_0$ tracks presented by Schmidt (p. 201, reproduced in Gussenhoven 2000c).

(10)

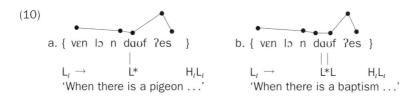

a. { vɛn lɔ n dɑʊf ʔes }   b. { vɛn lɔ n dɑʊf ʔes }
       | | |
   L$_\iota$ →   L*   H$_\iota$L$_\iota$ L$_\iota$ →   L*L   H$_\iota$L$_\iota$
   'When there is a pigeon ...'   'When there is a baptism ...'

The salience of the ι-internal contrast was evidently increased by the creation of a low-level pitch for Accent 2. The resulting contrast between rising (Accent 1) and low-level pitch (Accent 2) represents an improvement over a contrast between two rises, one resulting from L* H$_\iota$ and the other from L*H H$_\iota$, which would have to differ in speed of change. The question arises whether L*L arose from L*H, as assumed in Gussenhoven (2000c), or whether H*H went to L*L at one go. In Gussenhoven (2000c), I assumed that the addition of the 'epitone' changed L* H$_\iota$ to L* H$_\iota$L$_\iota$, but on the basis of the phonology of the Maastricht dialect, which has no L*, we might also assume a development of H*H$_\iota$ to H*H$_\iota$L$_\iota$. In fact, as suggested by John Kingston (personal communication 2003), considerations of contrast enhancement make this move from HHL, where the second H is upstepped, to LHL very probable. Moreover, if L* developed after the addition of the 'epitone', H*H together lowered to L*L at one go. This is a more plausible development, since a change from mid level to low level is a less drastic event than a change from rising to low level pitch. Either way, while the initial motivation for the change of H* to L* may have been to make the accented syllable more different from the following H$_\iota$, a by-product was the creation of the rise vs. low level contrast illustrated in (10).[5]

In terms of OT, NoRISE, given as (2) in chapter 8, must be promoted to ban the expected L*H in the Accent-2 syllable. Of two possible alternatives, deletion of the lexical tone and its change to L, the latter is more highly valued, as MAX-IO(T) outranks IDENT (T_{Lex},). A possible form H*H can be excluded by ranking IDENT(T*) above IDENT(T_{Lex}). This is shown in tableau (11).

(11)

(L * H) ... }	NoRISE	MAX-IO(T)	IDENT(T*)	IDENT(T_{Lex})

☞ a. (μ μ) ... }
  | |
  L* L
				*

b. (μ μ) ... }
  | |
  L*H
	*!			

c. (μ μ) ... }
  |
  L*
		*!		

d. (μ μ) ... }
  |
  H
		*!		

e. (μ μ) ... }
  | |
  H* H
			*!	

12.4.3   The rise of NoRISE

The question arises whether NoRISE became active outside the context which motivated its promotion, (7b). Specifically, we would like to know if the constraint is applicable to L*H sequences in which H represents H_ι instead of the lexical H. We can answer this question on the basis of detailed measurements for the dialect of Roermond. In this dialect, the pitch rise in the equivalent of contour (10a) reaches its end-point *outside* the accented syllable (Gussenhoven 2000a). This suggests that in that dialect, unlike L_ι, H_ι does not associate with the empty mora of focused Accent-1 syllables. While the Accent-1 fall in focused ι-internal syllables with declarative intonation is completed *within* the focused syllable, quite as in the case of the Venlo contour shown in (5a), the Roermond Accent-1 rise does not reach fully high pitch at the end of the focused syllable. Significantly, in the Venlo dialect, in which NoRISE has no role to play, H_ι *does* associate to the empty second mora of accented syllables (see (27), chapter 7).

The Roermond contours are shown in (12a,b). The data in Gussenhoven (2000a) also show that the boundary tones associate in the last stressed syllable, as indicated in (12).

(12) a.

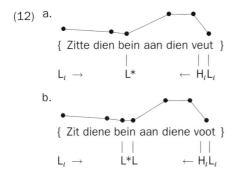

b.

First, tableau 13, which shows evaluations of declarative contours, shows how TBU ← T together with a low ranking of NoTARGET, cause the association of L_t to the second (empty) mora in the focused syllable. Candidates (c) and (d) fail to left-align and right-align, respectively.

(13)

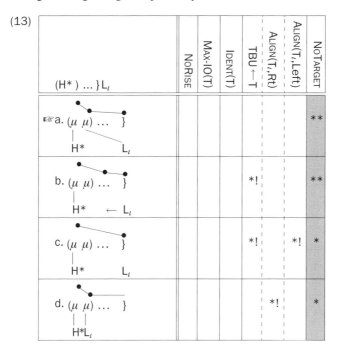

Tableau (14) shows how NoRISE prevents H_t from associating in the interrogative candidate (a). Now, candidate (b), with double alignment of H_t, is optimal, which candidate corresponds to (11a). There is no solace to be had from changing H_t to

L_ι, as in candidate (c), which founders on IDENT(T). Candidate (d) fails because H_ι does not left-align, while candidate (e) fails because it does not right-align. It will now also be clear that the Roermond ι-internal late peak for declarative Accent 2 (see 6) must be described by H*H, and not by L*H, which would be thrown out as illegitimate.

(14)

$(L^*) \dots \} H_\iota L_\iota$	NoRISE	MAX-IO(T)	IDENT(T)	TBU→T	ALIGN(T,Rt)	ALIGN(T,Left)	NoTARGET
a. $(\mu\,\mu) \dots$ } L* $H_\iota L_\iota$	*!						**
☞ b. $(\mu\,\mu) \dots$ } L* ← $H_\iota L_\iota$				*			**
c. $(\mu\,\mu) \dots$ } L* $L_\iota L_\iota$			*!				**
d. $(\mu\,\mu) \dots$ } L* $H_\iota L_\iota$				*		*!	*
e. $(\mu\,\mu) \dots$ } L* H_ι L_ι				*	*!		*

We have thus seen that NoRISE, by targeting any sequence of LH, has two rather different effects. In non-final Accent-2 syllables, it causes H to change to L; but in non-final Accent-1 syllables, it prevents H_ι from associating with the accented syllable. In the next section, we will consider the question whether NoRISE was given any role to play in ι-final syllables.

12.4.4   NoRISE is ι-final syllables

On the basis of the form for the Mayen interrogative ι-final Accent 2, the rise of (7b), it does not seem possible to decide whether NoRISE is active there. The rise could equally well be described by $L^*HH_\iota(L_\iota)$ as by $L^*LH_\iota(L_\iota)$ (where the parentheses indicate phonetic truncation). The dialect of Cologne, however, clearly uses L*L in ɩ-final syllables. This dialect has extended FRANCONIAN TRUNCATION to syllables with Accent 1. In unpublished research with Jörg Peters, we found that the contrast between Accent 1 and Accent 2 relies on a duration difference, with the 'epitone' disappearing in *both* cases, as shown in (15). Crucially, it is the low-pitched part of the syllable which is longer in Accent 2.

(15)

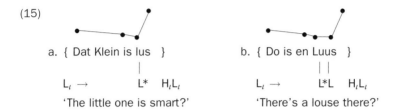

     a. { Dat Klein is lus   }   b. { Do is en Luus   }

                 | | |

      $L_ɩ \rightarrow$ L* $H_ɩ L_ɩ$ $L_ɩ \rightarrow$ L*L $H_ɩ L_ɩ$

    'The little one is smart?'   'There's a louse there?'

NoRISE must be taken to ban associated LH within a syllable, since the sequence of the lexical L and $H_ɩ$ occurring after L* is tolerated.[6] The effects of NoRISE, then, are seen quite generally in the Cologne dialect. In the next section, I will show it is also crucially active in ɩ-final syllables in the Roermond dialect, but there is an interesting twist to the story. For this we must turn to the third and last change for this dialect.

12.5   Improving the contrast in ɩ-final declaratives

The Mayen system represented in (7) and (10) underwent a further change in the west, notably in the dialect of Roermond, but similar dialects are spoken in Düren, a German town roughly equidistant from Cologne and Roermond (Jörg Peters, personal communication 2002), as well as in Maasbracht (Hermans 1994), just west of Roermond. Unlike the surfacing NoRISE and the introduction of the 'epitone', this change had an articulatory rather than a perceptual motivation. Specifically, the two-peak pronunciation that had arisen in ɩ-final syllables in focused declaratives must have developed a dip between the peaks, after which the fall of the second had become truncated. This theoretical stage is shown in (16), illustrated with Roermond sentences.

(16)

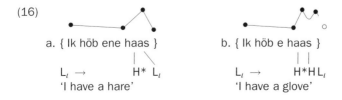

     a. { Ik höb ene haas }   b. { Ik höb e haas }

                  | \\ | |

      $L_ɩ \rightarrow$ H* $L_ɩ$ $L_ɩ \rightarrow$ H*H $L_ɩ$

    'I have a hare'   'I have a glove'

Although the extension of FRANCONIAN TRUNCATION to the declarative context in (16b) may seem quite natural, the relations between HHL and a fall–rise, on the one hand, and LLHL and a rise, on the other, may be too opaque for children to continue to construct the Mayen grammar. A transparent representation for a phonetic fall–rise is HLH and for a rise LH, or perhaps LLH or LHH. The remarkable fact is that these transparent relations can be obtained at one stroke if the lexical H-tone could be sequenced *after* the intonation L_ι and $H_\iota L_\iota$ in ι-final contexts. This is shown in (17a,b), which give the new representations for ι-final declarative Accent 1 and 2, and (18a,b), which does the same for the interrogative intonation. The 'epitone' has acquired a fully low realization in this dialect, as shown in (18a). The representation in (18b) arises from the new ordering of the tones, i.e. $L^*H_\iota L_\iota$ followed by the lexical H. Since the first two moras would now be associated with L^*H_ι in violation of NORISE, the correct representation is $L^*L_\iota L_\iota H$. I show $L_\iota L_\iota$ as L_ι, as it would seem reasonable to assume that it is not meaningful to repeat phonologically *and* morphologically like tones.

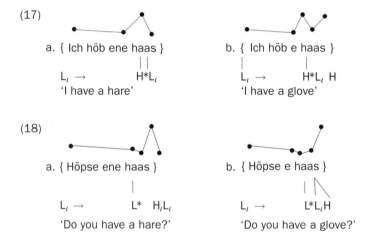

(17)

a. { Ich höb ene haas }
   | |
$L_\iota \rightarrow$ H^*L_ι
'I have a hare'

b. { Ich höb e haas }
   | |
$L_\iota \rightarrow$ H^*L_ι H
'I have a glove'

(18)

a. { Höpse ene haas }
   |
$L_\iota \rightarrow$ L^* $H_\iota L_\iota$
'Do you have a hare?'

b. { Höpse e haas }
   | |
$L_\iota \rightarrow$ L^*L_ιH
'Do you have a glove?'

In terms of OT, this means that the alignment constraint that aligns T_{Lex} rightmost in the syllable (19) is ranked above the alignment constraint that aligns T_ι rightmost in the ι. As explained in section 8.3.4, ALIGN(T_{Lex},RT) is not satisfied if a further tone appears in the syllable, as is doubly the case in candidates (b) and (c) in tableau (20). Candidate (d) fails to satisfy NORISE, while candidate (e) goes overboard by changing both H-tones to L-tones. The correct candidate (a) wins by satisfying both ALIGN(T_{Lex},RT) and NORISE, and remaining otherwise faithful to the input.

(19) ALIGN(T_{LEX},RT): ALIGN-(T_{Lex},Rt,σ,Rt), or T_{Lex} is
         aligned right in its syllable

(20)

(L*H) }H_ι L_ι	ALIGN(T_Lex,Rt)	NoRISE	Max-(IO)	IDENT(T)	TBU→T	ALIGN(T,Rt)	ALIGN(T, Left)
☞ a. (μ μ) } L* L_ι L_ι H				*		*	
b. (μ μ) } L* H H_ι L_ι	*!*	*!	*!				
c. (μ μ) } L* L H_ι L_ι	*!*	*				*	
d. (μ μ) } L* H_ι L_ι H		*!				*	
e. (μ μ) } L* L_ι L_ι L					**!	*	

By adopting ALIGN(T_Lex,Rt) ≫ ALIGN(T_ι,Rt), the Roermond-type dialect ended up with a grammar that produces transparent relations between representations and phonetic contours. In addition, the lexical tone distinction is reasonably clear in final position, as shown in (17) for the declarative and (18) for the interrogative, as well as in non-final position, where the contrasts are equivalent to those given for Venlo in (5) and Mayen in (7). Significantly, Roermond has no enhancement of the lexical pitch contrast, either by means of duration or vowel quality.

12.6 Outside the focus

The three changes in the grammar that followed the introduction of the tone were motivated on the basis of the perceptual and articulatory ergonomics in the processing of intonationally accented syllables. Interestingly, the realization of Accent 1 and Accent 2 in syllables without an intonational pitch accent confirms the grammar we have derived for the Roermond dialect. While the contrast is lost in unaccented, non-final syllables in Roermond and Venlo (Gussenhoven and van der Vliet 1999; Gussenhoven 2000b; see also section 8.4), it is maintained in unaccented ι-final syllables. The forms that the word tones take in this position, shown in (21) and (22), must be innovative pronunciations that were created purely as the result of the grammar having taken the shape it had. To begin with the interrogative, Accent 1 is realized by a wide pitch fall, the result of (non-truncated) H_ι L_ι, shown in (21a). Spectacularly, (21b) has H_ι L_ι H on the last syllable, describing a fall–rise which listeners with a Standard Dutch or German background are almost certain to misinterpret as a focusing pitch accent. To be sure, if the syllable *knien* were to be spliced out from this example, it would be an impeccable pronunciation of a focused, declarative *ι*-final realization, just as a spliced-out *knien* from (21a) will sound like a declarative Accent 1. For the Roermond listener, however, the perception of lack of focus is induced by the low pitch on the preceding word, representing L*.

(21) a.

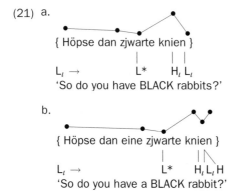

'So do you have BLACK rabbits?'

b.

'So do you have a BLACK rabbit?'

Similarly, the contrast in the declarative contours is predictable from the grammar, in that the H comes after the lone Lι in non-focused *ι*-final syllables with Accent 2. This is shown in (22b), which contrasts with Accent 1 in (22a).

(22) a.

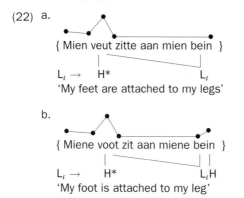

'My feet are attached to my legs'

b.

'My foot is attached to my leg'

From a historical perspective, the interest in (21b) and (22b) lies in their cognitive motivation. Their phonetics was *created by the specification of the grammar*; it did not arise from articulatory or perceptual ergonomics, and did not have a role in shaping that grammar, which is the usual direction in the chain of cause and effect.

12.7 Other reinterpretations

In this section, data from two further dialects are presented that illustrate other developments, Tongeren and Venlo. As for the Tongeren dialect, the interest is in the reversal of tone values that has taken place as a result of a reinterpretation of delayed contours. For the Venlo dialect the case will be made that it acquired the tone contrast relatively recently, and that it created a compromise form for *ι*-final Accent 2 between that of the Roermond-type dialects on its south and its non-tonal equivalent on its north. Also, the dialect's grammar produces a form that is not used.

12.7.1 Tongeren delay

Delayed peaks must have lain at the basis of a strikingly different system in the dialect of Tongeren (Belgium), where the contrast is between a lexical L (Accent 2) and no tone (Accent 1), a development that can be explained as the reinterpretation of strongly delayed pronunciations. In (23), the *ι*-internal declarative contrast is shown. Like the contrast between (5a), which contour is used both in Venlo and Roermond, and Roermond's (6), the contrast amounts to timing difference of the peak, but, relative to the Roermond contrast, the peaks occur further to the right, with the one for Accent 2 appearing in the next word. As a result, the accented syllable has a fall in both cases, but in (23a), a subsequent rise begins just inside the syllable, which in (23b) occurs after it. The phonological interpretation[7] is that Accent 1 is toneless, but Accent 2 has an L-tone, which is sequenced *before* the intonational pitch accent, quite as in Scandinavian. Before the pitch accent, the pitch is high, so that instead of a default initial L_ι, Tongeren has initial H_ι. As in Maastricht, the lexical tone is maintained in post-focal position, which here causes the pitch to fall to low at the end of the stressed syllable of the word for 'listen'. In a number of ways, then, the tonal system of the dialect of Tongeren is the reverse of the systems of the more northerly dialects spoken in the Netherlands. First, it has reversed values of the lexical tone, the declarative pitch accent, and the initial boundary tone; and second, the order of T_{Lex} and the pitch accent is the reverse of that in other dialects.

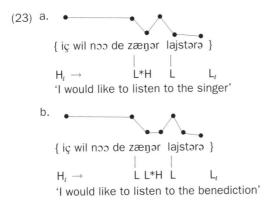

(23) a.

{ iç wil nɔɔ de zæŋər lajstərə }

$H_\iota \rightarrow$ L*H   L L_ι

'I would like to listen to the singer'

b.

{ iç wil nɔɔ de zæŋər lajstərə }

$H_\iota \rightarrow$ L L*H L L_ι

'I would like to listen to the benediction'

The assumption that, historically, (23a,b) are delayed peaks is supported by a second striking feature of the dialect, its excessive truncation. Monosyllabic utterances exemplifying the singular and plural forms of the word for 'rabbit' are given in (24). In the Accent-1 form (24a), the rise begins in the last part of the vowel. By contrast, that in the Accent-2 form (24b) does not start until the [n]. The rest of the contour is truncated in both forms. By adding further unstressed syllables, the complete contours would gradually appear, roughly one syllable earlier for Accent 1 than for Accent 2. While more work on Tongeren is needed, it is clear that this dialect is structurally very close to the Stockholm Swedish system described in chapter 11. Panel (a) of figure 12.3 shows pronunciations of (24a,b).

(24)

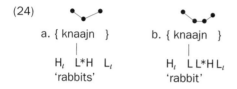

a. { knaajn }   b. { knaajn }
       | |
H_l L*H L_l H_l L L*HL_l
'rabbits'   'rabbit'

In (23) and (24), the assumption is that the stressed syllable is the TBU, and that there are no contouring associations. However, this assumption is not strongly motivated. Phonetically, the lexical L appears late in the syllable, and so does the L* in Accent 1. The CV transition of the accented syllable has a high target, causing the first part of the syllable to have falling pitch. The question arises, therefore, whether lexical L and L* might not associate with the second sonorant mora, leaving the first sonorant mora for H_l (in the case of the first accented syllable) or trailing H (in the case of following accented syllables) to associate with. I give this alternative analysis of (23b) in (25).

(25)

{ iç wil nɔɔ de zæŋər lajstərə }
———————— | / |
H_l L L*H L L_l

While (25) would appear to be an adequate representation for the phonetic form concerned, it is not clear that the dialect actually uses the sonorant mora as its TBU. The account in (25) predicts that in syllables with one sonorant mora, like [kas] 'candle', the pitch is low from the CV-boundary onwards, since the only mora will be occupied by L*, preventing preceding H-tones from associating. While this prediction appears correct on the basis of some of the data, there are also instances of such syllables with a falling or falling–rising contour. At this point, we will conservatively assume that the representations in (23a,b) are correct.

12.7.2   Venlo's non-salient tones

The most northerly tonal dialect in the Netherlands is that of Venlo. Some data
were already given in (5), as well as in (27) in chapter 7. To the ear of speakers
of non-tonal varieties of Dutch, nothing would seem to make it distinct from the
intonation of the standard language, all its contours falling within the range of
phonetic variation of Standard Dutch contours. The dialect has in fact retained
a Dutch-type intonation system, using four nuclear contours, as observed in
section 8.3. By and large, it maintains the lexical tone contrast within the phonetic
space that is available for a single phonological category in the standard language.
Understandably, these contrasts can be quite subtle. An example is (26). While,
like the Roermond dialect, the dialect has a lexical H on the second sonorant
mora of stressed syllables, this tone assimilates to L before L_ι if it occurs on the
last TBU of ι. Thus, the final declarative Accent-1 syllable is (26a), which is the
same as the corresponding form in Roermond, while (26b) is Accent 2. The L_ι
will have a fully low target when it can associate, but tends to have the same
or a somewhat higher target than the (assimilated) lexical L when it cannot, as
in (26b).

(26)

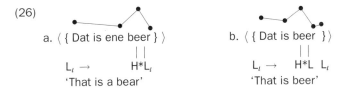

a. ⟨ { Dat is ene beer } ⟩   b. ⟨ { Dat is beer } ⟩

         | | | |

    $L_\iota \rightarrow$ H^*L_ι $L_\iota \rightarrow$ H^*L L_ι

   'That is a bear'   'That is beer'

In many of the toneless dialects to the immediate west and north of Venlo, the
equivalents of the members of tonal minimal pairs are homophones. Form (26b)
may therefore be seen as a compromise between the fall–rise of the more southerly
Roermond form shown earlier in (17b) and the plain fall of the non-tonal dialects.
In general, by making the lexical tone identical to the immediately following
T_ι, it only ever has LL_ι or HH_ι in ι-final syllables with Accent 2, which in part
explains the lack of salience of the tonal contrasts. Panel (b) in figure 12.3 shows
pronunciations of the Venlo forms in (26).

12.7.3   Venlo's ι-final interrogatives

In the interrogative intonation, the dialect contrasts two contours to express the
difference between Accent 1 and Accent 2 that in the standard language represent
different intonation contours. Before $H_\iota H_\upsilon$, the contrast between Accent 2 and
syllables without lexical tone (regardless of the number of sonorant moras) is
expressed by H^*H (Accent 2) versus L^*. This is shown for ι-final syllables in
(27). Gussenhoven and van der Vliet (1999) treated this distinction as a case of
allomorphy. That is, L^* occurs on syllables that do not have a lexical tone in ιs
ending in $H_\iota H_\upsilon$. As pointed out by Rachel Fournier, the distinction can equally
be treated as resulting from a phonological adjustment. If the intonation contour

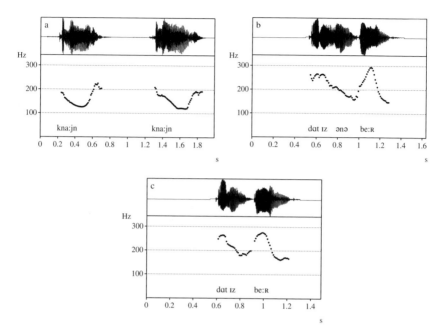

Fig. 12.3 Accent 1 on [kna:jn] 'rabbits' and Accent 2 on [kna:jn] 'rabbit' in the Tongeren dialects with declarative intonation (panel a); and the Venlo declarative utterances 'That is a bear' (Accent 1, panel b) and 'That is beer' (Accent 2, panel c).

is L^* $H_{\iota}H_{\upsilon}$ underlyingly, we can change L^* to H^* before H in the same syllable to create the correct distribution. The contrast is shown in ι-final position in (27). As said above, it exists in the standard language as an intonational contrast, that between the 'low rise', or L^*H H_{ι}, and the 'high rise', or H^* H_{ι} (see also section 15.2.1).

(27)

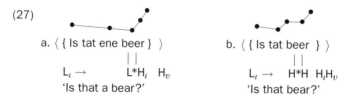

   a. ⟨ { Is tat ene beer } ⟩   b. ⟨ { Is tat beer } ⟩
                      | | | |
      $L_{\iota} \rightarrow$ L^*H_{ι} H_{υ} $L_{\iota} \rightarrow$ H^*H $H_{\iota}H_{\upsilon}$
      'Is that a bear?'   'Is that bear?'

The Venlo dialect in fact has two interrogative contours. By the side of L^* $H_{\iota}H_{\upsilon}$, it has H^* $L_{\iota}H_{\upsilon}$. The latter contour can be used on all ι-internal syllables, but in ι-final syllables it only combines with Accent 2. That is, monosyllabic H^* $L_{\iota}H_{\upsilon}$ does not occur (28a), and a monosyllabic fall–rise is thus always analysed as H^*H $L_{\iota}H_{\upsilon}$ (28b). The explanation lies in the contradictory meanings of lengthening cues. A falling–rising pitch movement on a single syllable requires a long time compared to syllables with simpler pitch movements. Since in the Venlo dialect, lengthening may be used to enhance the perceptibility of Accent 2, a monosyllabic falling–rising contour combines best with Accent 2. Comments by native speakers that the syllable would have to be spoken 'too quickly' for it to signal Accent 1 appear to confirm this.

(28)

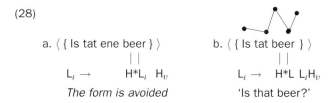

    a. ⟨ { Is tat ene beer } ⟩   b. ⟨ { Is tat beer } ⟩
               | | | |
       $L_\iota \rightarrow$ $H*L_\iota \; H_\upsilon$ $L_\iota \rightarrow$ $H*L \; L_\iota H_\upsilon$
     The form is avoided   'Is that beer?'

12.8 Conclusion

This chapter has presented a speculative account of a number of tonal changes that may have occurred in a dialect area around Cologne. It is perhaps inevitable that aspects of this account are simply wrong. However, I feel that the exercise has succeeded in yielding a number of instructive instances of interaction between phonetics and phonological representations. These can be categorized on the basis of the kind of motivation that lay behind the change. The first cut is between changes that are motivated by efficiency, types (a) and (b) in (29), and those for which such motivation is demonstrably absent and which can therefore only be understood as socially motivated changes. These second-hand changes are listed as type (c). The first group divides into changes that are motivated by cognitive economy, type (a), and those that have a phonetic motivation, type (b). Changes of type (a) are traditionally grouped under the heading of 'analogy', suggesting that there is always some form that serves as a model for the new form, but they also include the creation of new forms that a newly evolved grammar produces (section 12.6). A straightforward example of analogical change is ANALOGICAL LENGTHENING, which amounted to the restoration of paradigm uniformity after OPEN SYLLABLE LENGTHENING had lengthened vowels in some forms but not in others sharing the same word stem (/wex/ ∼ /weeɣə/). Another well-known type of analogy occurs when a phonetically motivated process is extended to a wider context, such as when the OCP-relieving s-insertion between stems ending in [k] and the diminutive [kə] was extended to stems ending in any dorsal consonant in many dialects of Dutch. As a result, not only do these dialects have [ʀœkskə] for underlying /ʀɔk-kə/ 'skirt-DIM', but also [ʀɪŋskə] for /ʀɪŋ-kə/ 'ring-DIM' and [kʀæːçskə] for [kʀaːx-kə] 'collar-DIM' (cf. [kœpkə], from /kɔp-kə/ 'cup-DIM'). Significantly, however, a new form may also be generated by a newly changed grammar and no specific form can be identified that can have served as the direct model for the new form. This is the case for declarative and interrogative post-focal contours in the dialect of Roermond. The clearest example is the fall–rise on ι-final non-focused syllables with Accent 2, given as (21b). It is clearly type (a), however, since it is phonetically very different from the equivalent contours in dialects that did not share the de-sequencing of lexical tone and the T_ι, to use Frota's (2002) term, and thus cannot be seen as an ergonomic improvement of any precursor.

(29) Types of phonological change
  a. Cognitive economy
      (i) Paradigm uniformity: MHG Analogical Lengthening
      (ii) Extended generalization: Roermond post-focal contours
  b. Improving speech ergonomics
      (i) Articulation: Roermond truncation and DE-SEQUENCING
                MHG/Middle Dutch OPEN SYLLABLE LENGTHENING
      (ii) Perception: Mayen's 'epitone'
                Mayen's H-ASSIMILATION
  c. Second-hand changes, i.e. the adoption of the results of types
      (a) and (b) without the motivation:
                Central Franconian tonogenesis
                Venlo fall-to-not-quite-low

Type (b) is motivated by the phonetics, i.e. by the ergonomics of speaking and listening. This type of change is known as 'Neogrammarian change', in particular if its progress to the new representation is fully regular (Labov 1981; Kiparsky 1988). A case was presented where a poorly discriminable contrast was repaired with the help of a new phonetic behaviour which was subsequently interpreted phonologically. This is the addition of a subtle fall at the end of ι-final interrogative rises with Accent 1, which led interrogative $L^* H_\iota L_\iota$ through the addition of what Künzel and Schmidt (2001) have called the 'epitone'. The change of L^*H, or more probably H^*H, to L^*L is another such case. In addition, I presented a case of a phonetic form which was hard to produce, the ι-final two-peak declarative contour of proto-Roermond, phonologically H^*HL_ι. This was truncated so as to produce a fall–rise, which was subsequently interpreted as $H^*L_\iota H$, the tone de-sequencing that led to a drastic restructuring of the grammar.

   Third, changes may be 'second hand', in the sense that they are motivated by the desirable behaviour of speakers of a different variety. Three phonological changes passed in review that resulted from a different phonological interpretation of a phonetic form than existed in the grammar of the speakers from whom the form was adopted. In one case, a long vowel was interpreted as a short vowel plus H-tone, the tonogenesis described in section 12.2. In a second case, diphthongs with Accent 1, which were phonetically shorter than diphthongs with Accent 2, were interpreted as short vowel-plus-glide combinations in Weert, with /stɛin²/~/stɛin¹/ going to /stɛin/ ~/stæjn/. Phonetically, short vowel-plus-glide combinations are shorter than diphthongs in the dialect of Weert, spoken on the periphery of the tonal area. In a third case, a fall–rise (HLH) was interpreted as a fall–plus-level (HLL), when Venlo speakers adopted the ι-final Accent 2 declarative (H*L$_\iota$H) as H*LL$_\iota$. Given that a dialect continuum is typically characterized by phonetically gradual differences, once every so often phonetically similar forms will inevitably have different phonological representations in speakers of neighbouring communities, while the same must be true for consecutive generations in the temporal continuum. In two cases, an interpretation identical to that which exists in the source dialect could be shown to be problematic. In the case of the Central Franconian tonogenesis, an interpretation of the long vowel as a bimoraic vowel was ruled out because of the existence of bimoraic vowels in otherwise identical plural forms. And in the Venlo case, a fall–rise (H*L$_\iota$H$_\upsilon$) was in use as a question intonation.

Two final remarks are made. First, there may be a lingering belief that phonological changes are gradual in the sense that representations are only minimally changed by any innovating generation of speakers. This view ignores the fact that the construction of grammars is a function of surface phonetics and our grammar-building faculty. Language learners cannot inspect their parents' phonological representations; they can only create phonological interpretations of their parents' phonetic forms. Cases of 'drastic' phonological change are therefore not inherently implausible. A second observation concerns the chain of events leading from the lengthening of singular monosyllabic nouns that have long-vowelled plurals to the emergence of the fall–rise of ι-final non-focused syllables with Accent 2, which represents a laborious series of *ad-hoc* repairs of undesirable aspects of the phonology and the phonetics. While each of the phonological changes discussed in this chapter may illustrate that speakers' behaviour during phonological change is somehow motivated, it is striking to see that they reveal a blatant disregard for the possible wider consequences.

Notes

1. The contrast has very probably disappeared completely from Lëtzebuergesch (Goudailler 1987; Gilles 1999).
2. The term 'Neogrammarian' is a mistranslation of German *Junggrammatiker* ('Young grammarians'), which was a 'calque or the expressions "Jungdeutschen", "Junghellenen", or "Jungtürken", denoting a series of impetuous nationalistic literary and political movements in Germany, Greece and the Ottoman Empire, respectively' (Seuren 1998). The change is known as 'Neogrammarian' because this group of nineteenth-century linguists had a working hypothesis that phonological change is exceptionless.
3. These scenarios leave out of account the case of phonetically unmotivated ('arbitrary') change arising within a speech community. This type may well exist.
4. Mihm's contribution represents an argument against any theory that seeks to relate the tonogenesis to the loss of word-final schwa. However, some connection between the Central Franconian tonogenesis and apocope is pervasive in the literature on this topic.

5. So far, no dialects have been found that contrast L* H$_\iota$L$_\iota$ with L*H H$_\iota$L$_\iota$, which contrast would be predicted by the original theory, in which the 'epitone' is added to L*H$_\iota$.
6. In Gussenhoven (2000b), I interpreted NoRise generally, and protected the final rise by means of position faithfulness. These descriptions would appear to be equivalent, but the present one saves a column in the tableaux.
7. The Tongeren examples and their tonal analyses are from unpublished work by Linda Heijmans, who is not, however, responsible for the historical speculations.

13

French

13.1 Introduction

This chapter presents a phonological description of ω, ϕ, and ι in French, an intonation-only language. Also, a tonal grammar will be presented that accounts for the language's intonation contours: it predicts what the contrasts are and explains why contours that are well formed in other languages are not possible in French. The ϕ and to a lesser extent the ω determine the distribution of pitch accents, which arise from the interplay between clash resolution and the desire to mark boundaries of ϕs and ωs with pitch accents. Pitch accents are relatively frequent, and there is usually more than one in a ϕ, often in the same word. Since ϕs also tend to be shorter than in English, there are more pitch accents in French than in English. Delais (1995) estimates that 40 per cent of all syllables are accented in read speech, while for the same speech style Post (2000b) reports a mean distance between accented syllables of 1.74 syllables, which puts the percentage of accented syllables at 36 per cent. My own estimate for English is 27 per cent. When there is more than one pitch accent in a ϕ, their distribution is in part governed by rhythmical considerations. Occurrences of adjacent pitch accents within the same ϕ are rare (cf. Verluyten 1982).

One of the exciting challenges of French intonational phonology is to account for this distribution of pitch accents. There is considerable variation in this distribution, in part depending on the variety and in part on the speech style. For instance, an expression like *enfant adoptif* 'adoptive child' may be pronounced *enFANT ADopTIF*, *enFANT adopTIF*, or *ENfant adopTIF*, though not *??ENfant ADopTIF* or *??enfant ADopTIF*, assuming an unemotional, full-focus pronunciation. We will see that this variation can in part be laid at the door of optionality in the ϕ-structure, which leads to alternative placements of accents, and in part to optionality in ϕ-internal accent distributions. As explained in section 8.5.1, optionality can be accounted for by constraint reranking (Anttila 1997). Among other things, we will see that left-alignment in the phrase competes with right-alignment in the word, so as to cause alternative accentuations in some structures. Also, these alignment constraints may or may not be dominated by a constraint that bans the occurrence of 'remote clashes', i.e. accents that have only a single unaccented syllable between them. The present analysis is a revised version of the analysis of Post (2000b). The main differences concern the introduction of the constraint NOREMOTECLASH referred to above, a revision of her constraint HAMMOCK, which is here interpreted as banning ϕs with fewer than two accents (as opposed to banning ϕs with fewer or more than two), and in regarding initial accents as being due to the left-alignment of accents with the ϕ, not with the ω. Section 13.2 is devoted to this topic.

It is only the ι that is attended by boundary tones. Since French ϕs have no boundary tones, they are not as clearly demarcated by the intonation as Bengali ϕs, which typically end in H_ϕ, as illustrated in section 7.3.2. The ϕ-structure in French thus reveals itself through the patterns of pitch accent distribution, as well as by final lengthening on the ϕ's last syllable (Post 2000a). The final boundary tones of ι are optional. The prosodic break at the end of an ι is nevertheless fairly clearly audible even without T_ι because of the mid pitch at the end, whose salience is comparable to that created by the realization of a boundary tone.

Section 13.3 presents an analysis of the melodic structure of French intonation, which is essentially that of Post (2000b). In this analysis, the only accented tone of French is H*. In pre-nuclear position, it varies with H*L, where L *blocks* downstep, which generally occurs on H* after an H-tone within ι. Interestingly, the analysis allows us to identify a number of illegitimate contours that are in fact unattested, like a series of downstepping peaks, a 'flat hat' with equal accentual peaks, or monosyllabic rise–falls and fall–rises. Moreover, by assuming that central tones associate, we can account for the absence of L in final position, as well as for a melodic restriction on utterances with adjacent accents.

Although it is possible to deaccent after the focus in French, the language is biased towards the retention of pitch accents throughout the utterance, and towards the expression of information structure by means of word order (Jun and Fougeron 2000; Di Cristo and Jankowsky 1999). This topic is not discussed here.

13.2 Prosodic phrasing

In this first section, the OT analysis of ϕ-phrasing and of its effects on the distribution of pitch accents is presented in a number of separate subsections (13.2.1–13.2.4). It will be seen that different constraint rankings produce the required range of variation in accent distribution for a given ϕ-phrasing. In section 13.2.5, the variability in ϕ-phrasing itself is described, including its effects on the pitch-accent distribution, which again can be accounted for by constraint reranking. Accentuation of function words is briefly discussed in section 13.2.6, while a summary appears in section 13.2.7.

13.2.1 Basic patterns

As observed in the introduction, pitch-accent distribution in French is determined by the ω and ϕ. As for ϕ, we will for the time being equate ϕ with XP, and introduce the constraints that are responsible for the pitch accents at their beginning and end, ALIGN(ϕ,H*,Rt) (1) and ALIGN(ϕ,H*,Left) (2), as well as the constraint that may seek their deletion, NOCLASH.

(1) ALIGN(ϕ,H*,Rt): Align the right edge of every ϕ with a pitch accent.

(2) ALIGN(ϕ,H*,Left): Align the left edge of every ϕ with a pitch accent.

(3) NOCLASH: Pitch accents are not adjacent.

The constraints ALIGN(ϕ,H*,Rt) and NOCLASH outrank ALIGN(ϕ, H*,Left), as can be seen by considering a disyllabic ϕ like *Marie*, shown in tableau (4). Because of NOCLASH, it can have only one accent, and the ranking of the alignment constraints determines it will be on the second syllable. Thus, a two-ϕ structure like *MaRIE PLEURE* 'Mary is crying' will contrast with the single ϕ *MArie CLAIRE*. As shown for the isolated word *Marie* in tableau (4), a single disyllabic ϕ loses its initial accent.[1] By contrast, in the ϕ *MArie CLAIRE*, violation of NOCLASH can be avoided and accents on first and last syllables will result.

(4)

	ALIGN(ϕ,H*,Rt)	NOCLASH	ALIGN(ϕ,H*,Left)
$_\phi$(Marie)$_\phi$			
☞ a. maRIE			*
b. MArie	*!		
c. MARIE		*!	
$_\phi$(Marie Claire)$_\phi$			
☞ a. MArie CLAIRE			
b. maRIE CLAIRE		*!	*
c. marie CLAIRE			*!

The relevance of ω can be seen in ϕs that begin with function words. I assume that ω corresponds to a lexical item. This excludes articles, prepositions, and pronouns, like *le* 'DEF+SG+MASC', *au* 'to+DEF+SG+MASC', *je* 'I'. (Pronouns are proclitic to the verb. In non-clitic positions, there are accentable, strong forms of pronouns, as in the one-word utterance *Moi!* 'Me!/I!', for instance.) Example (5a) gives *garçon* with an accent on the final syllable. The first syllable (*le*) is unaccented, even though the syllable count is identical to that of (5c), which does have an initial accent. Similarly, in (5b) there is an initial accent, but it appears on the first syllable of the ω *nécessité*, not on the first syllable of the ϕ. The reason for the avoidance of the first syllable of *l'impossibilité* will be given below.

(5) a. { [le (garÇON)] }   b. { [la (NÉcessiTÉ)] }
       'the boy'   'the necessity'
    c. { [l'INduSTRIE)] }   d. { [(l'imPOSSibiliTÉ)] }
       'the industry'   'the impossibility'

To account for the avoidance of accent on *le* in (5a), I assume a high-ranking constraint that disallows accents outside ω. In effect, therefore, the first syllable of *garçon* counts as the first syllable of the ϕ for the purposes of ALIGN(ϕ,H*,Left). Moreover, the ω indirectly influences the location of the first accent through an interaction between the onset of its first syllable and the number of syllables it has. To account for the unaccented first syllable of *l'impossibilité*, Post makes use of a constraint PEAKPROMINENCE, which requires that a syllable with a pitch accent must correspond with a syllable that has an onset in the lexical representation. Thus, in (5d), ALIGN(ϕ,H*,Left) is non-optimally satisfied by the pitch accent on the second syllable. However, *l'INduSTRIE does* have an accent on its initial syllable. In order to avoid that, in an attempt to satisfy both PEAKPROM and NOCLASH, *l'industrie* ends up with accent on its final syllable only, Post (2000) assumes a constraint HAMMOCK, which requires that there are exactly two accents in the phonological phrase. Because this formulation makes problems for the description of ϕ with more than two accents, HAMMOCK is here taken to require that there be *minimally* two accents in a ϕ.

(6) PEAKPROM: An accented syllable corresponds with a syllable with an onset in the input.

(7) HAMMOCK: A phonological phrase has at least two accents.

Tableau (8) shows how these patterns are derived. NOCLASH outranks HAMMOCK, to ensure that we do not end up with *le GARÇON*; with HAMMOCK ≫ PEAKPROM, we select *l'INduSTRIE* over single-accented **l'induSTRIE*, while PEAKPROM ≫ ALIGN(ϕ,H*,Left) ensures that *l'IMpossibiliTÉ* does not take over from *l'imPOSsibiliTÉ*.[2]

(8)

le garçon	ALIGN(φ,H*,Rt)	NOCLASH	HAMMOCK	PEAKPROM	ALIGN(φ,H*,Left)
☞a. le garÇON			*		*
b. le GARÇON		*!			
c. le GARÇon	*!		*		
la nécessité					
☞a. la NÉcessiTÉ					
b. la néCEssiTÉ					*!
c. la néCESsité	*!		*		*
l'industrie					
☞a. l'INduSTRIE				*	
b. l'inDUSTRIE		*!			*
c. l'indusTRIE			*!		*
l'impossibilité					
☞a. l'imPOssibiliTÉ					*
b. l'IMpossibiliTÉ				*!	

To prevent accents from proliferating, *T ranks above the alignment of accent with a syllable. For instance, *l'imPOssiBIliTÉ* would so far be equally good by (8) as the correct version *l'imPOssibiliTÉ*, because, like the latter form, it does not violate any of the constraints in tableau (8). *T is ranked below the constraints discussed so far, allowing accents where we have transcribed them, and disallowing them elsewhere.

While the above account does what it is meant to do, there are two concerns. First, PEAKPROM attributes the reluctance of onsetless syllables to bear pitch accents to lack of prominence (cf. Prince and Smolensky 1993). However, phonetic research into the perception of durational differences suggests that the effect of onsets on prosodic structure is not due to syllable weight or syllable sonority (Goedemans 1998: 122). Word beginnings are universally selected for carrying the phonologically most sensitive contrasts, while also playing a special role in lexical encoding and word recognition (Nooteboom 1996; Beckman 1997). From this point of view, one would expect word beginnings to be exploited phonologically, rather than avoided. The paradoxical avoidance of accent and stress on onsetless word-initial syllables may be explained as a policy of abandoning an imperfect word beginning altogether. See Downing (1998) for a phonological treatment of this issue.

Another problem concerns the fact that, on the surface, the first syllable of a vowel-initial word typically does have an onset, as provided by the preceding word (cf. (5c,d)). For the purposes of PEAKPROM, the presence of an onset is therefore established on the basis of the phonological structure in the lexicon, not the postlexical ω. The way in which this discrepancy is to be accounted for depends in part on the model of OT that one adopts. In a widely espoused view, there are no intermediate levels of representation between the underlying representation, where words like *impossibilité* have an open syllable, and the surface representation. Since the initial syllable may be provided with an onset on the surface, a constraint that bans pitch accents from onsetless syllables would be ineffective in *l'impossibilité*. Under this view, PEAKPROM might be formulated as an OO-faithfulness constraint, such that a pitch-accented surface syllable corresponds to a syllable with an onset in an isolated pronunciation of the word, when the definite article is not there (see section 8.5.2). In an alternative view, there are intermediate levels of representation, and every pair of adjacent levels can be served by its own OT grammar (Kiparsky forthcoming). Thus, lexical items could be provided with an initial accent and a final accent in the lexicon, with the exclusion of any initial open syllable. Postlexically, such syllables would be closed, and the ultimate surface pattern derived. In chapter 14, there are in fact compelling considerations for English accentuation patterns for adopting this 'level-ordered' solution.

13.2.2 ω-final accents

The data discussed in the previous section could be accounted for either by assuming that ϕs attract pitch accents, as we have done, or by assuming that ωs do. It has fairly generally been assumed that the French accent is essentially a phrase-level phenomenon (Pulgram 1965; Fox 2000). However, the need for ϕ-internal ω-final accents is not hard to establish. First, in formal pronunciations of multi-word ϕs like *TRÈS joLIS garÇONS* 'very nice boys', the location of the medial accent cannot be determined by phrasal alignment. Second, cases like *JoLIS garÇONS* 'nice boys' show that the first accent of ϕ may go to an ω-final syllable in preference to a ϕ-initial syllable. (Although *JOlis garÇONS* is a possible pronunciation, it is not part of the formal speech style assumed here; see further below.) If only ALIGN(ϕ,H*,Rt) is active, neither of these cases is accounted for by the analysis so far. Constraint (9) ALIGN(ω,H*,Rt) must therefore be active.

(9) ALIGN(ω,H*,Rt): The right edge of every ω coincides with an accent.

To obtain *JoLIS garÇONS*, left-alignment must not only rank below ALIGN(ϕ,H*,Rt), as shown earlier in tableau (8), but also below ALIGN(ω,H*,Rt). Tableau (10) makes it clear that if left-alignment were to rank above ALIGN(ω,H*,Rt), *un JOli garÇON*, candidate (b), in which the first accent is on the ϕ-initial syllable, would be optimal. However, pronunciation (a) is the form we want. Similarly, in *une asSEZ jolie JUPE* 'a rather nice skirt', the first accent is on the final syllable of *assez*, since *jolie* is now unavailable for accentuation on account of the violation of NoCLASH by candidate (d). Only if there is no lexical word to the left of *jolies* in *des jolies jupes* 'Nice skirts' will an accent go to the initial syllable of *jolies*, in order to avoid running foul of HAMMOCK, as does candidate (b), or NoCLASH, as does candidate (c).

(10)

un joli garçon	ALIGN(ϕ,H*,Rt)	NoCLASH	HAMMOCK	ALIGN(ω,H*,Rt)	Align(ϕ,H*,Left)
☞ a. un joLI garÇON					*
b. un JOli garÇON				*!	
une assez jolie jupe					
☞ a. une asSEZ jolie JUPE				*	*
b. une ASsez JOlie JUPE				**!	
c. une ASsez jolie JUPE				**!	
d. une asSEZ joLIE JUPE	*!				*
des jolies jupes					
☞ a. des JOlies JUPES				*	
b. des jolies JUPES		*!		*	*
c. des joLIES JUPES	*!				*

ALIGN(ω,H*,Rt) must rank below both NoCLASH and ALIGN(ϕ,H*,Rt). This can be demonstrated with the two-word ϕ *très VITE* 'very quickly', as shown in tableau (11). If ALIGN(ω,H*,Rt) had its way, candidate (a) would be worse that either candidate (b) or (c). This also shows that ALIGN(ω,H*,Rt) is active *in combination* with ALIGN(ϕ,H*,Rt).

(11)

très vite	ALIGN(ϕ,H*,Rt)	NoCLASH	HAMMOCK	ALIGN(ω,H*,Rt)	Align(ϕ,H*,Left)
☞ a. très VITE			*	*	*
b. TRÈS vite	*!		*	*	
c. TRÈS VITE		*!			

The ranking ALIGN(ω,H*,Rt) $\gg$ ALIGN(ϕ,H*,Left) thus accounts for Di Cristo's (1999) minimal pair *PERsonaliTÉ* 'personality' and the single ϕ *perSONNES* *aliTÉES* 'bed-ridden persons', the latter being equivalent to *un joLI garÇON* in (10). However, as indicated above, frequently used phrases may be pronounced as if they were single words in recent varieties of French, according to the 'accentual bi-polarization principle' (Di Cristo 2000). If, for the sake of the argument, this tendency were to apply to 'bed-ridden persons', the pronunciation would be *PERsonnes aliTÉES*. To account for this pronunciation, we do not have to assume that ωs merge into ϕs; this assumption may be unwarranted, since the syllable durations of phrasal *-sonnes a-* are likely to be longer that of *-sonna-* in the word, despite the identical accentuation patterns. Instead, we need only rerank ALIGN(ω,H*,Rt) and ALIGN(ϕ,H*,Left), something that will be clear without an additional tableau. This variable ranking of ALIGN(ω,H*,Rt) and ALIGN(ϕ,H*,Left) accounts for the first case of variation in French accent placement. In section 13.2.4, ϕ-medial variation is discussed.

13.2.3   No ω-initial accents

Post (2000b: 96) assumes that left-alignment of accents is word-based, rather than ϕ-based, on the basis of the argument that in pronunciations like *la NÉcessiTÉ* the accent is on the first syllable of the ω, not on the first syllable of the ϕ. However, as said in section 13.2.1, a high-ranking constraint that only allows accentuation of lexical words would be an adequate theoretical response to this fact. Moreover, an active constraint Align(H*,ω,Left) would predict the occurrence of a medial accent on *vê-* in the ϕ **un TRÈS vieux VÊteMENT* 'very old garment'. If this is an acceptable pronunciation at all, it would only be so in very formal speech, and the constraint is therefore best kept invisible, i.e., ranked below T*. Similarly, in neither the conservative nor the more modern variety does the pronunciation *?PERsonnes AliTÉES* occur, even in speech styles that do allow pronunciations like *TRÈS joLIS garÇONS*. I conclude that initial accents are due to left-alignment with ϕ, not with ω.

13.2.4   Variation in medial accents

In the previous section, it was seen that ϕ may have more than two accents, in which case the medial accents are word-final, which was accounted for by allowing ALIGN(ω,H*,Rt) to be effective. Medial accents will disappear in less-formal speech, however. As a result, the medial accent in expressions like *un asSEZ joLI garÇON* 'a rather nice boy', *TRÈS joLIS garÇONS* 'very nice boys', *EXcelLENT traVAIL* 'excellent work' is variably present. Post (2000b) does not discuss this type of variation. I interpret the disappearance of the medial accent as a case of clash avoidance, and accordingly propose NoREMOTECLASH (12), which forbids the occurrence of accents maintaining only one unaccented syllable between them. That is, while NoCLASH bans [* *], NoREMOTECLASH bans [* . *].

(12) NoRemoteClash: Accents are more than one unaccented syllable apart.

In our tableaux so far, NoRemoteClash has been invisible, i.e. ranked below all constraints that were shown to be active. Promotion of this constraint will first cause it to be reranked with Align(ϕ,H*,Left), the lowest constraint we have considered. Moving it up further will place it above Align(ω,H*,Rt). I begin by showing the effect of NoRemoteClash in this latter ranking for the phrase *très jolis garçons* 'very nice boys'. To begin with, tableau (13) shows the situation with NoRemoteClash ranked out of sight. As seen above, this ranking gives us the multi-accented form, due to satisfaction of Align(ω,H*,Rt) and lower ranking Align(ϕ,H*,Left).

(13)

TRÈS jolis garçons	Align(H*,ϕ,Rt)	NoClash	Hammock	Align(ω,H*,Rt)	Align(H*,ϕ,Left)	NoRemoteClash
☞a. TRÈS joLIS garÇONS						**
b. TRÈS jolis garÇONS				*!		

If NoRemoteClash outranks Align(ω,H*,Rt), the middle accent disappears, since it now fatally violates NoRemoteClash. This is shown in tableau (14).

(14)

TRÈS jolis garçons	Align(ϕ,H*,Rt)	NoClash	Hammock	NoRemoteClash	Align(ω,H*,Rt)	Align(ϕ,H*Left)
a. TRÈS joLIS garÇONS				*!	*	
☞b. TRÈS jolis garÇONS						*

NoRemoteClash interacts with Align(ϕ,H*,Left) in situations where the effect of Align(ω,H*,Rt) is cancelled out, which happens when two forms violate the constraint in equal measure. The decision is then left to NoRemoteClash or Align(ϕ,H*,Left), depending on which dominates which. This occurs in structures of the type (15), instantiated by expressions like *toujours près de vous* 'always near you', *beaucoup plus civil* 'much more polite', *jamais bien construit* 'never well built'.

(15) [(* *)   (*)   (* *)]
       1 2   3   4 5

If we assume that NoClash will have its way, two forms result that each violate Align(ω,H*,Rt) once, 1 Ø 3 Ø 5 and Ø 2 Ø Ø 5. The competition between these forms is to be decided by lower ranking constraints: the first form violates NoRemoteClash; the second Align(ϕ,H*,Left). It is in structures like (15), therefore, that the ranking of Align(ϕ,H*,Left) and NoRemoteClash is critical. Tableaux (16) and (17) illustrate the situation for *beaucoup plus civil*. Notice that avoiding all violations for the latter two constraints, as achieved by candidate (c), is pointless, as it incurs two violations of Align(ω,H*,Rt). (Of course, the ranking NoRemoteClash $\gg$ Align(ϕ,H*,Left) $\gg$ Align(ω,H*,Rt) *would* select candidate (c) as the optimal form, in conformity with Di Cristo's (1999) 'accentual bi-polarization principle'.)

(16)

beaucoup plus civil	Align(H*,ϕ,Rt)	NoClash	Hammock	Align(ω,H*,Rt)	Align(ϕ,H*,Left)	NoRemoteClash
☞ a. BEAUcoup PLUS ciVIL				*		**
b. beauCOUP plus ciVIL				*	*!	
c. BEAUcoup plus ciVIL				**!		

(17)

beaucoup plus civil	Align(H*,ϕ,Rt)	NoClash	Hammock	Align(ω,H*,Rt)	NoRemoteClash	Align(ϕ,H*,Left)
a. BEAUcoup PLUS ciVIL				*	*!*	
☞ b. beauCOUP plus ciVIL				*		*
c. BEAUcoup plus ciVIL				**!		

It is not hard to see that further promotion of NoRemoteClash would cause initial accents to disappear in structures like *des jolies jupes*. If ranked above Hammock, the latter constraint is incapable of forcing an accent on the first syllable, since the remote clash with the accent on *jupes* must be avoided. Interestingly, therefore, this analysis with gradual promotion of NoRemoteClash makes predictions as to which accent 'deletions' are most likely. The first to be affected are structures like (15), with *plus* being unaccented in *beaucoup plus civil*. Next, *excellent travail*, *très jolis garçons*, etc. will lose the medial accent from the antepenultimate syllable. The least likely to be affected are initial accents in trisyllabic ϕs like *jolies jupes*, *bien construit* 'well built', *pas toujours* 'not always'.

13.2.5   Variation in ϕ-structure

In the previous sections, it was shown among other things that variable ranking of ALIGN(ϕ,H*,Left) and ALIGN(ω,H*,Rt) will produce variation between *perSONNES aliTÉES* and *PERsonnes aliTÉES*, and also that variable ranking of NoREMOTECLASH and ALIGN(ω,H*,Rt) will produce variation between *DEUX garÇONS joYEUX* and *DEUX garçons joYEUX* 'two happy boys'. To compound matters further, French ϕ-structure is variable. In fact, these very examples may be single ϕs, as assumed so far, or consist of two ϕs. It will be clear that the presence of a ϕ-boundary between the noun and the adjective in these NPs will affect the accent distribution. With a ϕ-boundary between *personnes* and *alitées*, the ranking of ALIGN(ϕ,H*,Left) and ALIGN(ω,H*,Rt) becomes immaterial. Either way, the pronunciation would be *perSONNES AliTÉES*, where the accent on *A-* is due to ALIGN(ϕ,H*,Left). And a ϕ-boundary after *-çons* in *DEUX garÇONS joYEUX* would put a stop to the variation in the accentuation of this syllable, as it would be ϕ-final and thus accented regardless of the ranking of NoREMOTE-CLASH and ALIGN(ω,H*,Rt).

In this section, it is shown that the syntactic constituent that right-aligns with ϕ is either an XP-internal XP or the highest XP, a choice which causes variation in complex NPs. Let us first establish that XP right-aligns with ϕ. For instance, sentence (18a), which consists of two clauses, has three ϕs, as indicated. Since there is no ϕ boundary before *rejoigne*, the right edge of ϕ must be aligned with the right edge of each XP, and the stray, non-lexical *nous* must be included in a ϕ with *rejoigne*. Now, an instruction to align the right edge of XP with the right edge of ϕ would produce the right results in (18b) if XP is taken to be the internal NP *de petits garçons*. However, if by XP is meant the higher NP-node, NP', the resulting ϕ-structure is as in (18c). The point is that both phrasings occur. Selkirk (1986) refers to these two constituents as the 'small phonological phrase' and the 'maximal phonological phrase'. I assume, therefore, that right-alignment of ϕ with the NP is responsible for the medial ϕ-boundary in (18b), while those in (18c,d) are due to right-alignment with a superordinate NP' (not necessarily the highest NP). It has widely been assumed that adjective phrases before the noun deserve some characterization to distinguish them from post-modifying adjective phrases, to the extent that pre-nominal ones do not create their own ϕ-boundary (Verluyten 1982; Nespor and Vogel 1986; Selkirk 1986; Post 1999). There is, however, no need for this, since the ϕ-boundary after the post-modifying adjective is there because it is right-aligned with the XP', not the AdjP. Thus, no AdjP is entitled to a ϕ-boundary, regardless of its position. In a pile-up of adjectives as in (18d), where they are obligatorily separated by ϕ-boundaries, they are each dominated by an NP' node.

(18) a. [Vous permettez] [que Marianne] [nous rejoigne]
     'Will you allow Marianne to join us?'
   b. [de petits garçons] [intelligents]
     'intelligent little boys'
   c. [de petits garçons intelligents]
   d. [de petits garçons intelligents] [français]
     (*[de petits garçons intelligents français])

In has been assumed in the literature that the variation between right-alignment
with XP and right-alignment with XP' depends on the presence of only a *single*
ω in the post-modifying constituent (Selkirk 1984; Nespor and Vogel 1986).
However, experimental research has shown that restructuring is also possible
with more than one ω in the post-modifying constituent. The two ωs in *autres*
and *(qu'en) Afrique* in (18e) can therefore be included in a ϕ with *des hivers*
(Post 1999).[3] In other words, ALIGN(XP,ϕ) (20a) and ALIGN(ϕ, XP') (20b) are
variably ranked in French.

(19) [des hivers autres qu'en Afrique]
    'different winters from those in Africa'

Tableau (21) illustrates the effect of the two options for the medial boundaries in
de petits garçons intelligents hollandais. When ALIGN(XP,ϕ) $\gg$ ALIGN(ϕ, XP'),
a ϕ-boundary is required at every morpho-syntactic boundary of the rank XP and
every morpho-syntactic boundary dominating NP. Candidate (a) is the only form
that satisfies the higher ranked constraint, and so wins. Candidate (b) fails to
have the required boundary at the first location, an XP-boundary, and candidate
(c) incurs violations at both boundaries, since both are of rank XP or over. In
tableau (22), where the opposite ranking is assumed, it is candidate (b) that wins.
It alone satisfies the first constraint. Candidate (a) has an illegitimate boundary
at a lower rank, while candidate (c) fails to place one at the second location, an
XP'-boundary.

(20) a. ALIGN(XP,ϕ): Align the right edge of every XP with the right edge of ϕ.
   b. ALIGN(ϕ, XP'): Align ϕ with the right edge of every XP'.

(21)

de petits garçons intelligents hollandais	ALIGN(XPϕ)	ALIGN(ϕ,XP')	Align(H*,ϕ,Rt)	NoClash	Align(ω,H*,Rt)	Align(ϕ,H*,Left)
☞ a. [de peTITS garÇONS] [inTELliGENTS] [HOLlanDAIS]		*				**
b. [de peTITS garÇONS intelliGENTS] [HOLlanDAIS]	*!					*
c. [de peTITS garÇONS intelliGENTS hollanDAIS]	*!*	*				*

(22)

de petits garçons intelligents hollandais	ALIGN(φ,XP')	ALIGN(XP,φ)	Align(φ,H*,Rt)	NoClash	Align(ω,H*,Rt)	Align(φ,H*,Left)
a. [de peTITS garÇONS] [inTELliGENTS] [HOLlanDAIS]	*!					**
☞ b. [de peTITS garÇONS intelliGENTS] [HOLlanDAIS]			*			*
c. [de peTITS garÇONS intelliGENTS hollanDAIS]	*!	**				*

In this analysis, candidate (c) in the above two tableaux is unobtainable. The nearest we can get is a form where a high ranking of NoRemoteClash removes the accents on both -çons and ho-.

13.2.6   Accented function words

Function words like *le* '3RD+SG+MASC' and *en* 'PARTITIVE' are accented when they appear in ι-final position, which they only do in the imperative construction, as in *Prends-LE!* 'Take it!', *Va-t'EN!* 'Go away!' This is unexpected under the assumption of word-based accentuation, since words like *le* are non-lexical. Indeed, they do not have an accent when appearing in non-final position, as in *le garÇON* (??*LE garÇON*). A solution would be to include in the lexicon under the lemma *le* the forms [lə]_{Accentable Function Word} /——}_ι, by the side of the general form [lə]_{Function Word}, to be used elsewhere. This is the way this would be done in Hayes's 'precompiled phonology' (Hayes 1990): some words have specific allomorphs in specific (morpho-syntactic or phonological) contexts. The fact that ι-final *je* does not attract an accent, as in *Que SAIS-je?*, is compatible with this lexical solution.

13.2.7   Phrasing: Summary

Behind the seeming simplicity of French accentuation lies a complex interaction of constraints that locate pitch accents at constituent boundaries and constraints that match up prosodic constituents with morpho-syntactic constituents. The unmarked, conservative situation is represented in (23).

(23) a. ALIGN(XP,φ) $\gg$ ALIGN(φ, XP')

    b. ALIGN(φ,H*,Rt), NoClash $\gg$ Hammock $\gg$ PeakProm $\gg$ ALIGN(ω,H*,Rt) $\gg$ ALIGN(φ,H*,Left) $\gg$ NoRemoteClash

The ranking ALIGN(XP,φ) $\gg$ ALIGN(φ, XP') is variably reversed; reversal will have the effect of increasing the size of the φ with a post-modifier. Similarly, ALIGN(ω,H*,Rt) and ALIGN(φ,H*,Left) may be reranked, to favour accentuation in the φ-initial syllable instead of on the post-initial syllable in φs that begin with a disyllabic word followed by a polysyllabic word (e.g. *de joyeux garçons*). ALIGN(φ,H*,Left) and NoRemoteClash may be reversed, to cause the opposite effect in φs that begin with a disyllabic word followed by a non-final monosyllabic (e.g. *beaucoup plus civil*). And once the latter pair is reversed, a further reranking of ALIGN(ω,H*,Rt) ≫ NOREMOTECLASH will cause deletion of medial accents.

There is one form that remains to be accounted for. NOCLASH may be violated in disyllabic φs, provided a particular intonation contour is used. Because of the involvement of the melodic structure, I postpone discussion till section 13.3.3.

13.3 The tonal analysis

The crux in Post's (2000) analysis of the intonation contours of French is, first, that there is no L*, and second, that downstep affects H* after H. There have been other analyses recently, in part in the Pierrehumbert framework (Mertens 1987; Di Cristo and Hirst 1993a; Di Cristo 1998; Jun and Fougeron 2000). In the interest of conciseness, however, I will not explicitly argue against those proposals; for arguments against other analyses, see Post (2000b, 115ff.).

In (24), an example is given of a complex intonated sentence. It consists of four phonological phrases divided one-three over two intonational phrases.

(24) { [Jean-Pierre] }   { [vous permettez] [que Marianne] [nous rejoigne] }
          | | | | |
      L$_\iota$ H*   L$_\iota$ H*L   H*L   H*L   H*   L$_\iota$
      'Jean Pierre, is it all right if Marianne joins us?'

The example illustrates, first, that only the ι is bounded by boundary tones, and that final boundary tones are optional, as shown in the first ι, which has no final T$_\iota$. Second, the only accented tone is H*. In nuclear (ι-final) position, H* occurs before the optional T$_\iota$, giving the three contours listed in (25). (Post does not give the meanings.)

(25) a. H* L$_\iota$ fall   'Declarative'
      b. H* H$_\iota$ high rise   'Interrogative'
      c. H* }$_\iota$ (plain) rise   'Continuative'

The other option for the nuclear pitch accent is H+H*, the less common *cliché mélodique*, to which a separate section is devoted. There are two pre-nuclear accents, H*L, illustrated in (25), and H*, both of them common. If there are two or more pre-nuclear accents, as in (26), only one of these will occur. Thus, ignoring the *cliché mélodique*, the analysis so far predicts that an intonational phrase with two or more accents can be pronounced in six ways. These are illustrated in figure 13.1, on the phrase (27). In figure 13.1, the contours on the left have pre-nuclear H*L; those on the right have pre-nuclear H*. The three boundary conditions are arranged top-to-bottom. In the next section, the phonetic realization of these contours is explained.

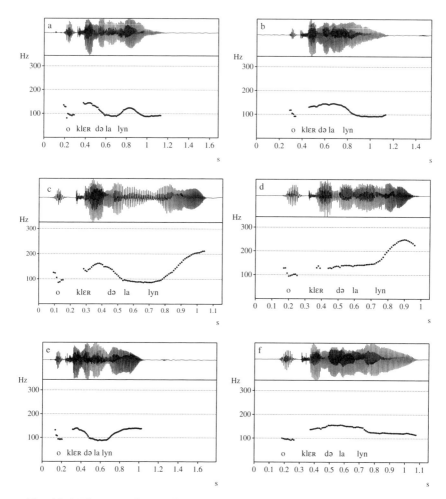

Fig. 13.1 The expression *au clair de la lune* said with H*L on *clair* and H* on *lune* (panels a, c and e), with H* on both *clair* and *lune* (panels b, d, f); with final L_t (panels a, b), final H_t (panels c, d) and no final boundary tone (panels e, f).

(26) a. nuclear pitch accents: H*, H+H*
      b. pre-nuclear pitch accents: H*, H*L

(27) { [Au (CLAIR)] [de la (LUNE)] }
      'By the light of the moon'

13.3.1   Downstep

The realization of pre-nuclear H*L in the contours in the left-hand panels of figure 13.1 covers the stretch between the accented syllables: a gradual slope ends just before the next H*. French thus right-aligns the trailing tone, as is visible in the contour in panel (a), for instance. The contours on the right undergo DOWNSTEP of the nuclear H*. In chapter 6, it was seen in some languages that H is downstepped after H, a pattern that was explained as a way of phonetically cushioning the impact of the phonological OCP violation. In Post's analysis, French is such a language. In effect, therefore, the intervening L-tone in the corresponding contour on the left actually *blocks* DOWNSTEP. The effect of this implementation rule can be seen in panels (b) and (f). In panel (f), the downstepped H*, phonetically a mid tone, remains level, due to the absence of a boundary tone. The contour in panel (d), in which the second H* is followed by H_ι, is not downstepped, however. If anything, it has higher pitch than *clair de la*. Downstep is blocked by following H_ι, which is not uncommon for downstep rules generally. Rule (28) therefore stipulates that either L_ι or no tone must close the ι. Lastly, the dots in the right-hand context imply that the downstepped H* may be followed by further H*s. This 'terracing' is described below.

(28) FRENCH DOWNSTEP (implementation) H* → $^!$H* / H __ . . . (L_ι)

The above analysis involves two decisions which require some clarification. First, the question arises why the valley in the contours in the left-hand panels is attributed to a trailing L which strays off, instead of to a leading L of a following L+H*. Since the language already has leading H, such a choice would not be out of character: we would have pre-nuclear H*, L+H* and nuclear H*, L+H* and H+H*. Post (2000b: 167) points out, however, that the leading-L analysis predicts that there is a categorical difference between L_ι L+H* and L_ι H* in single-accent ϕs. However, (29a) is equivalent to (29b).

(29)

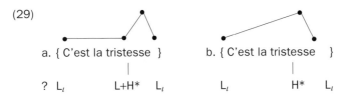

  a. { C'est la tristesse }   b. { C'est la tristesse   }
            | |
  ? L_ι L+H* L_ι L_ι H* L_ι

A second incorrect prediction is that after initial H_ι, the pitch can fall before H* in a representation like H_ι L+H*, as in (30). There is no such contour, however. A third incorrect prediction of an analysis with L+H* is that it rules out an attested contour with an unaccented two-syllable low–high sequence before a mid-pitched accented syllable. A leading tone analysis would require a tritonal L+H+H* pitch accent to account for this contour. By contrast, an analysis with H*L readily predicts its existence. I return to this issue in section 13.3.2.

(30) *

    { la tristesse   }
            |
  ? H_ι L+H* L_ι

A second decision that calls for comment concerns the absence of L*. It might be thought that what is here described as downstepped H* should in fact be analysed as L*. There are three arguments for not doing this. One is that the distribution of L* would be contextually predictable, i.e. be allophonic: after H*, but not when the intonational phrase is closed by H$_ι$ (the context of the phonetic implementation rule postulated in (28)). Second, FRENCH DOWNSTEP is needed independently of the low final pitch accent. For instance, $ι$s may have more than one pitch accent, and sequences of H*s display the well-known pattern of chaining downsteps (Di Cristo and Hirst 1993a). It would be odd to have a downstep rule which fails to apply to final H*, precisely in the position where L* appears. Interpreting downstepped series of H*s as L*s is typologically unattractive, as downstep of L would seem to presuppose downstep of H. Third, the downstepped H* is not really low-pitched. Typically, in languages where it can be motivated, a L* can be pronounced at a generously low pitch, but that would not be generally possible in the French contours.

The analysis with downstepped H* after H, moreover, makes two interesting predictions, both of which are correct. First, it correctly predicts there are no contours with downstepping peaks, of the type that commonly occur in West Germanic and many African languages (see (31a)). Di Cristo and Hirst (1993b) indeed discuss downstep only in connection with terraced sequences of level tones, not of peaks. Second, it predicts there can be no contours like the 'flat hat' with two high pitch accents: a rise and a fall separated by a level stretch whose corners mark accented syllables. The absence of this contour is immediately explained by the analysis in (28), but would be an arbitrary stipulation under the assumption of a L*: why should a sequence of H* H*L$_ι$ be ungrammatical (see (31b))?

(31) *

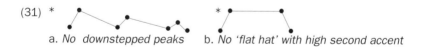

  a. *No downstepped peaks*   b. *No 'flat hat' with high second accent*

The downstepping analysis is further supported by the fact that downstep takes place after H generally, not just H*. There are two types of H-tone in addition to H* which could provide the left-hand context. First, French opposes L$_ι$ to H$_ι$ initially in the IP. The latter is rare, but interestingly, it too triggers downstep on following H*. Figure 13.2 illustrates this for single-accented *la lune* (panel a) and two-accent *au clair de la lune* (panel b). The prediction that *la lune* cannot be pronounced with an unaccented, high-pitched first syllable and a high-to-low fall on the second, a quite common contour in English, is correct. The contour in panel (a), therefore, has the representation (32a), while the phonological representation of the terraced contour in panel (b) is (32b). (From here on, only $ι$-boundaries are specified.)

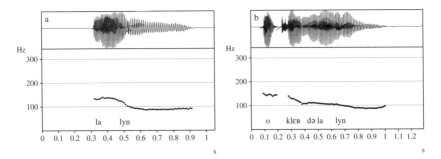

Fig. 13.2 The expression *la lune* (panel a) and *au clair de la lune* (panel b) said with initial H$_\iota$, which causes downstep on following H*-tones.

(32)

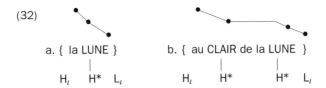

a. { la LUNE }   b. { au CLAIR de la LUNE }

H$_\iota$ H*   L$_\iota$ H$_\iota$ H*   H*   L$_\iota$

The third downstep context is that of H+H*, as shown in the next section.

13.3.2 Cliché mélodique

The pronunciation of the nuclear pitch accent H+H* involves a high-pitched syllable before the accent and a mid-pitched accented syllable. Internally, the pitch accent therefore has downstep, as expected on the basis of FRENCH DOWNSTEP (28). The adequacy of this solution is underlined by the fact that the three boundary conditions interact with its realization precisely as predicted. The mid level may continue till the end of the ι, in which case there is no final T$_\iota$. This pitch accent has been discussed as the *cliché mélodique* in the literature, and is illustrated on one-accent *Elle est arrivée* in panel (a) of figure 13.3. The contour in panel (b) has final L$_\iota$, and falls to low pitch. The third, in panel (c), has final H$_\iota$. As predicted, FRENCH DOWNSTEP is prevented from applying to H* because the ιs end with H$_\iota$. However, the representation H+H* H$_\iota$ will nevertheless lead to a different contour than the representation L$_\iota$H*H$_\iota$, whose contour is shown in panel (d), because the leading H will cause high pitch to begin on the syllable *before* the accented syllable with H*.

FRENCH DOWNSTEP also predicts that H+H* and H* are neutralized by an immediately preceding H-tone, like H* or H$_\iota$, because the leading H, which is not a target of downstep, will not be distinct from the preceding H. I can now return to the contour that forms the basis of the third argument against analysing the valley between accents as due to a leading L-tone. In (33), the fall described by prenuclear H*L occurs before H+H*. Here, *de* is low-pitched and *la* high-pitched, while accented *lune* has mid pitch. (With final L$_\iota$, the pitch would fall further to

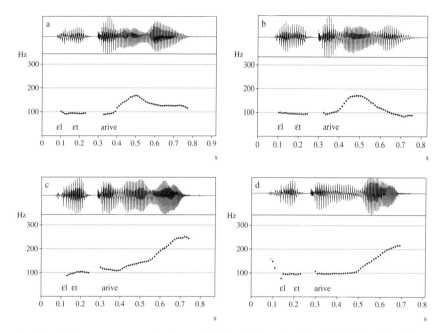

Fig. 13.3 Four contours on *Elle est arrivée* 'She has arrived' with L_ι H+H* (panel a), L_ι H+H* H_ι (panel b), L_ι H+H* H_ι (panel c), and L_ι H* H_ι (panel d).

low.) As said in section 13.3.1, the leading L-analysis would incongruously have to come up with a L+H+H* pitch accent on *lune*.[4] An analysis with a trailing L in a 'splayed' pitch accent therefore appears to be correct.

(33)

{ Au CLAIR de la LUNE }

L_ι H*L   H+H*

13.3.3 Violating NoClash

According to Mertens (1992), adjacent accents may occur in a single ϕ, but only if the intonation pattern is one that is here analysed as H*H*, i.e. high pitch for the first syllable and low pitch (i.e. downstepped H*) for the second. In addition, the syllables concerned must be the only accentable syllables in the ϕ. The pattern might thus occur in expressions like *un mouchoir* 'a handkerchief', *très vite* 'very quickly', and so on. This form can be obtained, first, by reranking NoClash with Hammock, which will cause adjacent accents to be allowed only if they are, respectively, ϕ-final and ϕ-initial; and second, by ranking L→TBU high. This constraint was seen to be active in Japanese, where it was responsible for the deletion of the floating L of the lexical H*L in expressions with final monomoraic accented syllables (see chapter 10, section 10.9). If L cannot associate with a syllable, as in (34b), it either deletes or else remains floating but fails to block downstep. The fact that the problem of the existence of adjacent H* accents in disyllabic φs can be solved so simply provides interesting support for the analysis presented here. Tableau (34) demonstrates the effect of the reranking.

(34)

trés vite	L→TBU	ALIGN(φ,H*,Rt)	HAMMOCK	NOCLASH	ALIGN(ω,H*,Rt)	ALIGN(φ,H*,Left)
☞a. TRÈS VITE │ │ H* H*					*	
b. TRÈS VITE │ │ H*L H*	*!				*	
c. très VITE │ H*				*!	*	*

These facts suggest that the absence of a *nuclear* H*L pitch accent is in fact due to L→TBU. Since a φ-final accent always occurs on the last accentable syllable, there never is an opportunity for L to show up. If more clarity were to exist about deaccentuation, the further hypothesis could be tested that nuclear H*L *can* occur if the φ-final word is deaccented. Lastly, these facts suggest that, in general, central tones associate in French, but boundary tones do not. The other central tones are H*, which will always have a syllable available to it, and leading H. In initial position, on the monosyllable *Bon!*, for instance, H+H* neutralizes with H$_i$ H*. In either case, a fall from high pitch, beginning right at the initial consonant, will occur (see figure 13.2, panel (a)). (Disambiguation of these contours can be achieved on the structure *C'est la lune*, which point I leave for the reader to establish.) The most general assumption then is that floating tones delete. This solution further presupposes that NOCONTOUR is ranked high in French so as to prevent L or H from showing up on the same syllable as H*.

13.3.4 Summary of the tonal grammar

The intonational phonology of French thus represents a quite elegant grammar. Formula (35), from Post (2000b: 154), sums it up. The deletion of floating tones potentially simplifies the grammar still further. The only phonetic implementation rule that was identified is DOWNSTEP (28).[5]

(35) French tonal grammar: $\left\{\begin{array}{c}H_\iota\\L_\iota\end{array}\right\}$ $(H^*(L))_0$ $(H+)H^*\left\{\begin{array}{c}H_\iota\\L_\iota\\\emptyset\end{array}\right\}$

I close the tonal section by drawing attention to the lack of overt tritonal contours. The grammar in fact does explain why there can be no rise–fall or fall–rise contours on single syllables. While a monosyllable like *Bon!* has three tones in $L_\iota\ H^*\ L_\iota$, the first of these precedes the accent, and as is often the case, is not realized. Even when three tones *are* realized on a monosyllable, as in the case of $H_\iota\ H^*\ L_\iota$, the resulting falling movement constitutes neither a rise–fall nor a fall–rise.

Notes

1. A possible pronunciation of disyllables with high pitch for the first and low pitch for the second syllable is treated in section 13.3.3.
2. The pronunciation *l'IMpossibiliTÉ* does in fact occur, and can be obtained by ALIGN(ϕ,H*,Left) $\gg$ PEAKPROM. Under that ranking, PEAKPROM is invisible.
3. Additionally, Post found that the ϕ-structure as determined on the basis of the distribution of pitch accents is independently confirmed by the distribution of final lengthening. Post also presents evidence that LIAISON, the process that prevents deletion of word-final consonants in pre-vocalic position (cf. *peti*[t] *ami*) is not governed by the ϕ, but is lexically conditioned, cf. Post (2000a) and references therein.
4. For discussion see also Ladd (1996: 140ff.).
5. In Post (2000: ch. 5,6), more information is given about phonetic variation in French intonation.

14

English I: Phrasing and Accent Distribution

14.1 Introduction

One way of thinking about the structure of English intonation is as a complicated form of the intonational structure of French. The features in table 14.1 have been arranged such that the first six are common to French and English, while the next three show English to be more complex than French. To put this comparison in some perspective, the data for Bengali, from Hayes and Lahiri (1991a), have been added in the third column.

As shown by the first two features, the role of the ϕ in English and French is to create rhythmic distributions of pitch accents. There is no principled limit to the number of pitch accents in a ϕ, although there will commonly be one or two, and rarely more than three. Feature 2 shows that both French and English readjust the locations of these pitch accents within the ϕ. In English, the transparency of these rhythmic adjustments is reduced by the fact that accentuation is in part governed by lexical rules, such as the Compound Rule.

Features 3–6 show that French and English both have optional right-hand T_ι-tones, which always come as singletons. The two languages differ from Bengali, which has H_ϕ, and in which T_ι is obligatory and may be bitonal ($T_\iota T_\iota$). The more complex nature of English *vis-à-vis* French lies in its richer pitch accent paradigms, as shown in rows 7 and 8, and most dramatically in the number of different nuclear contours, i.e. combinations of nuclear pitch accents and boundary tones.[1] In one salient aspect, Bengali is similar to English. Unlike French, both English and Bengali employ tritonal contours on a single syllable, as indicated in rows 10 and 11. Bengali has HLH, for instance, on a monosyllable said with with continuation intonation, i.e. $H^*L_\iota H_\iota$, while LHL occurs either as the contrastive declarative intonation, $L^*H_\phi L_\iota$, or as the Yes–No interrogative $L^*H_\iota L_\iota$ (cf. chapter 7). Lastly, the liberal deaccentuation after the focus of Bengali is repeated in English; French deaccentuation patterns are still in need of research, but are clearly less liberal.

Table 14.1 *Intonational features compared across French, English, and Bengali. Five of the first six features are not shared by Bengali, while features 10 and 11 show that by disallowing tritonal contours French is melodically less complex than English and Bengali. Features 7, 8, and 9 show that English is melodically the most complex.*

		French	English	Bengali
1	nr of * per ϕ	n	n	1
2	ϕ-based readjustment of *	Yes	Yes	No
3	Boundary tones on ϕ	No	No	Yes
4	Boundary tones on ι	Yes	Yes	Yes
5	Final T_ι obligatory	No	No	Yes
6	Bitonal $T_\iota T_\iota$	No	No	Yes
7	Number of prenuclear PAs	2	5	1
8	Number of nuclear PAs	3	8	3
9	Number of nuclear contours	8	24	7
10	Contour HLH	No	Yes	Yes
11	Contour LHL	No	Yes	Yes
12	Frequent deaccentuation	No	Yes	Yes

In this chapter, we will deal with ϕ-phrasing and ι-phrasing. The former is relevant to the rhythmic distribution of pitch accents, the latter to the melodic organization, in particular the placement of boundary tones. Since the presence of pitch accents in English is determined by lexical rules, section 14.2 gives an account of the accent distribution in lexical representations. Section 14.3 deals with the ϕ-structure needed to explain the postlexical adjustments of these accentuation patterns, and argues that this structure includes procliticized ϕs on the basis of data that have earlier been explained as due to cyclicity.

Moving on the ι in section 14.4, an account of the location of VP-internal ι-breaks using Truckenbrodt's output–output faithfulness solution is presented in section 14.4.1. In addition, section 14.4.3 deals with the ι-phrasing of various right-hand extra-clausal constructions and will argue that, depending on their morpho-syntax, these are either incorporated in the preceding ι, are encliticized as separate unaccented ιs or constitute regular, accented ιs by themselves.

14.2 The distribution of pitch accents

In French, accent assignment is entirely postlexical, and as a result the morpho-syntax can only make itself felt indirectly, through the derivative boundaries of ω and ϕ. By contrast, rhythmic readjustments of accents in English interact with morphological constraints on accent locations. As far as I know, this was first noted by Prince (1983). Consider the difference between (1a) and (1b). Both NPs contain four words, but differ in the location of the first accent. It might at first sight be thought that this is due to a difference in bracketing, since

(1a) has the structure [[A B][C D]], while (1b) is [[[A B] C] D]. (Note: the assumed pronunciation for the phrase *Big Band* in isolation is *BIG BAND*, like *HUDson BRIDGE*, not *BIG band*, like *HUDson Street*.) However, this cannot be the whole answer, since (1c), my example, is also [[[A B] C] D], yet patterns like (1a).

(1) a. TOM Paine Big BAND (i.e. a Big Band led by Tom Paine)
    b. Tom PAINE Street BLUES (i.e. blues induced by Tom Paine Street)
    c. TOMcat-free ROOF (i.e. a roof free of tomcats)

A second difference with French is that English ϕs are procliticized, causing the presence of left-hand boundaries without corresponding right-hand boundaries. This structure will arise in premodified NPs of the type (2a), which are distinct from (2b) (Gussenhoven 1991a).

(2) a. with GROWing CHINese supPORT
       'with Chinese support which is growing'
    b. with ETHnic ChiNESE supPORT
       'with support from the ethnic Chinese population'

These two problems are very different in character, and are dealt with in separate subsections.

14.2.1 Deaccentuation in the lexicon

The expressions in (1) differ because they present themselves to the postlexical grammar of English in different guises: they leave the lexicon with different accent distributions. In the model of Lexical Phonology proposed by Kiparsky (1982b), there are two modules in which morphological operations and the accompanying phonological adjustments take place, Level 1 and Level 2. Level 3 is reserved for affixations which leave the prosodic structure of the base intact, among which are inflections like plural [z], past [d], and numeral and comparative suffixes. At Level 1, underived words like *cellar*, *elephant*, and *tapioca* receive their lexical stress patterns. At this level, certain suffixation processes take place, which reveal themselves through affecting the position of the lexical stress. For instance, the Level-1 suffixes *-ity* and *-ic* cause shifts in the main stress from *SEnile* to *seNILity*, and from *STRATegy* to *straTEgic*. A recent treatment is Zonneveld *et al.* (1999). I make the assumption that the structure which is output by Level 1 includes feet, a marker for main stress, and accents on all feet except those after the main stress (Gussenhoven 1994).

   This section presents an OT treatment of the accent deletions at Level 2. In this module, compounds are formed, like those in (3a), and suffixations which do not affect the position of the main stress in the base, like those in (3b), as is evident from such examples as *STRATegy – STRATegist; GENtleman – GENtlemanly – GENtlemanliness*. To these, we should add similarly 'stress-neutral' suffixes like those in (3c). These are semantically and prosodically weightier, but are unaccented, like the suffixes in (3b). Examples are *COLourfast, STRIKE-prone, MONey-wise, ROADworthy*, etc. Finally, there is the lone suffix *-esque*, which is itself accented, as in *RembrandTESQUE*, something which needs to be recorded in its lexical entry.

(3) Morphological operations at Level 2
    a. language conference, book exhibition, highchair
    b. -ish, -ist, -ly, -less, -ness
    c. -fast, -free, -proof, -prone, -style, -tight, -type, -wise, -worthy
    d. -esque

One type of lexical accent deletion is due to the COMPOUND RULE (CR), which deletes accents in right-hand constituents of compound words, here given as constraint (4). Every accent in the right-hand constituent is to be counted as a violation. As a result of the high ranking of CR, any compound formation can survive with accents in the left-hand constituent only. Thus, the compounds in (3) are pronounced *LANGuage conference, BOOK exhibition, HIGHchair*. The non-accentuation of the suffixes in (3c) could be explained either by their status as suffixes, so that they are treated like (3b), or by assuming they are treated as right-hand constituents of compounds, i.e. as falling under (3a).[2]

The second constraint operative at Level 2 is INITIAL ACCENT DELETION (IAD) (5) (Gussenhoven 1991a). It causes all accents except the rightmost to be deleted in any formation listed in (3). In OT, IAD is an alignment constraint, requiring accent to align with the right edge of a Level-2 formation. Thus, every non-final accent violates IAD by as many accentable positions (= stressed syllables) as it is removed from the right edge. A separate constraint is required to prevent a completely unaccented output of the lexicon, LEXACC (6). The high ranking of LEXACC, CR, and IAD is specific to Level-2 morphology: they do not have anything to say about other structures. Kiparsky (2000, forthcoming) argues for just such a level-ordered OT grammar, where sequentially ordered subgrammars, each containing their own constraint ranking, produce intermediate representations of the kind envisaged here.

(4) COMPOUND RULE (CR)(Level 2): The right-hand constituent of compound words is unaccented.

(5) INITIAL ACCENT DELETION (IAD) (Level 2): Align accent with the right edge of a Level-2 formation.

(6) LEXACC: A lexical expression is accented.

The treatment of *Tom Paine Street* and *tomcat free* is shown in tableau (7). Winning candidate *Tom PAINE Street* maximally satisfies IAD without violating CR. In the case of *tomcat free*, we are dealing with a phrasal formation, in which two lexical representations are joined in an Adjective Phrase, like *Swedish-Chinese*. Both constituents are therefore treated separately at Level 2. Candidate (a) is better than candidate (b), due to CR. A fully unaccented *tomcat* is ruled out, since at the end of the lexicon, LEXACC requires an accented expression. This constraint rules out candidate (c), which violates LEXACC in its first constituent, and candidate (d), which violates it in both *tomcat* and *free*. Finally, *Rembrandtesque* has an accent in final position only, due to IAD. (I suppress high-ranking DEP-IO(Acc), which forbids gratuitous addition of accents, so that *-wise*, etc. will not be accented (cf. (3).) Without a tableau, it should be clear that the phrases *Tom Paine* and *Big Band* in *Tom Paine Big Band* cannot violate CR or IAD, and that since *Tom Paine Big Band* is also a phrase, this expression enters the postlexical phonology as a fully accented *TOM PAINE BIG BAND*.

(7)

[[TOM PAINE] STREET]$_{Level2}$	LEXACC	CR	IAD
☞a. tom PAINE street			*
b. TOM paine street			**!
c. TOM PAINE street			**!*
d. TOM paine STREET		*!	**
e. tom paine STREET		*!	
[TOM CAT]$_{Level2}$ FREE			
☞a. TOM cat FREE			*
b. tom CAT FREE		*!	
c. tom cat FREE	*!/-		
d. tom cat free	*!/*		
[REMbrandTESQUE]$_{Level2}$			
☞a. rembrandTESQUE			
b. REMbrandTESQUE			*!*

As a result of IAD, pre-nuclear pitch accents are contrastive in a phrase like *SECond LANGuage conference* 'second of a series of language conferences', where both *second* and *language conference* are accented. It contrasts with the compound *second LANGuage conference* 'conference on the topic of second language acquisition'. Similarly, a phrasal adjective like *UN-KIND* is formed in the same way as *ANGlo-aMERican*, *PROto-GerMANic*, and thus pronounced with two pitch accents. By contrast, the word *unKINDness*, which is a Level 2-formation, has a pitch accent on *kind* only when spoken in isolation (Gussenhoven 1991a), just as *Proto-GerMANic teacher* 'teacher of Proto-Germanic' only has one on *-MAN-*.

14.3 Postlexical rhythm: ϕ-structure

While English differs from French in having accents in the input to the postlexical rhythmic grammar, these grammars themselves are similar. Constraints ALIGN(ϕ,T*,Rt) and ALIGN(ϕ,T*,Left) require accents at both edges, while NOCLASH and the less fastidious NOREMOTECLASH weed out intermediate accents. (See section 13.2.1; I use T* in the case of English, which unlike French has both L* and H*.) The clash-relieving constraints rank below the alignment constraints. Without a tableau, it will be clear that in a disyllabic expression like *THREE BOOKS*, the clashing accents are tolerated, so as to satisfy alignment: an incorrect ranking of NoClash ≫ Align(ϕ,T*,Left), Align(ϕ,T*,Rt) will lead to *THREE books* or *three BOOKS*, depending on whether right or left alignment ranks highest. These constraints were given in chapter 13, in (1), (2), (3), and (12), respectively.

English relies on faithfulness to preserve lexical accent distributions. In particular, we need Max-IO(Accent) (8) to keep the deletion of accents at bay, and Dep-IO(Accent) (9) to prevent the addition of accents where we removed them in the lexicon. To begin with, the characterization of the correct candidate for *Tom Paine Big Band* is shown in tableau (10): only the version with accents on the first and last words satisfies the alignment constraints and NoClash. Clearly, Max-IO(Acc) ranks below these.

(8)   Max-IO(Accent): Do not delete accents.

(9)   Dep-IO(Accent): Do not insert accents.

(10)

TOM PAINE BIG BAND	Align(ϕ,T*,Rt)	Align(ϕ,T*,Left)	NoClash	Max-IO(Acc)
☞a. TOM paine big BAND				**
b. TOM paine BIG BAND			*!	*
c. tom PAINE big band		*!		**
d. tom paine big BAND		*!**		***
e. TOM paine BIG band	*!			**

Because any medial accent leads to a violation of NoClash, we cannot see the effect of NoRemoteClash, which is universally ranked below NoClash. If *Tom* were replaced with disyllabic *Thomas*, however, the deletion of the medial accent on *Paine* would depend on the ranking of Max-IO(Accent). If Max-IO(Accent) ≫ NoRemoteClash, the pronunciation would be *THOMas PAINE Big BAND*, while the opposite ranking would give *THOMas Paine Big BAND*. We might assume a further constraint NoVeryRemoteClash, penalizing [* .. *]. If it were ranked above Max-IO(Accent), medial deaccentuation would occur even in *JEREmy Paine's Big BAND*.

Next, to obtain *TOMcat-free ROOF*, we need to expose the input *TOMcat-FREE ROOF* to the strictures of NoClash for the accent of *free* to disappear. In addition to NoClash ≫ Max-IO(Accent), which allows deletion of clashing accents, we must prevent accents being added where they were removed in the lexicon, to avoid *tomCAT-free ROOF*. Accordingly, we rank Dep-IO(Accent) at the top of the hierarchy. To show that its role can be crucial, tableau (11) also shows the case of *Tom PAINE Street BLUES*, where DEP-IO(Accent) prevents the re-accentuation of *Tom*, as in candidate (b).

(11)

TOM-cat FREE ROOF	DEP-IO(Accent)	ALIGN(ϕ,T*,Rt)	ALIGN(ϕ,T*,Left)	NOCLASH	MAX-IO(Accent)
☞a. TOM-cat free ROOF					*
b. TOM-cat FREE ROOF				*!	
c. tom-cat FREE ROOF			*!*	*	*
d. tom-CAT free ROOF	*!		*		**
Tom PAINE Street BLUES					
☞a. tom PAINE street BLUES			*		
b. TOM paine street BLUES	*!				

14.3.1 Bracketing effects

As argued in Prince (1983), Selkirk (1984), and Gussenhoven (1987a) on the basis of examples like (2), rhythmic adjustments in complex NPs unmistakably reveal the effects of the constituent structure. However, the Lexical Phonology version of OT does not allow for postlexical cyclicity: the assumption is that there is a single postlexical module. In this section, I will argue that this assumption is correct, and that a cyclic treatment is in fact inadequate. Instead, the prosodic structure in NPs must include procliticization. The difference between these approaches for a structure like *ethnic Chinese support* is illustrated in (12). A cyclic treatment would deal with the subconstituents *ethnic Chinese* and *support* separately (cycle 1), pass the output on to cycle 2, where the complete structure is dealt with. This is shown in (12a). By contrast, a treatment with a procliticized structure deals with the entire structure at once, which however lacks an internal left-hand ϕ boundary, as in (12b).

(12)
a. $_\phi$[ethnic-Chinese]$_\phi$, $_\phi$[support]$_\phi$ cycle 1   b. $_\phi$[ethnic Chinese $_\phi$[support]$_\phi$]$_\phi$
$_\phi$[ethnic Chinese support]$_\phi$ cycle 2
Cyclic treatment   *Procliticized structure*

At first sight, postlexical cyclicity might appear to work. Tableau (13) deals with *with ETHnic ChiNESE supPORT*. The first cycle correctly gets rid of the medial accent in *Chi-* through the services of NOCLASH. The adjusted form then combines with *supPORT* to form a phrase, where no further adjustments are needed. Removal of the medial accent on *-nese* is uncalled for, as shown by candidate (e), while incorrect accentuation of *Chi-* is prevented by DEP-IO(Accent), since this syllable was unaccented in the input to the second cycle.

(13)

[ETHnic CHINESE] [with ETHnic CHINESE supPORT]	DEP-IO(Accent)	ALIGN(ϕ,T*,Rt)	ALIGN(ϕ,T*,Left)	NoCLASH	MAX-IO(Accent)	NoREMOTECLASH
☞a. ETHnic chiNESE					*	
b. ETHnic CHINESE				*!		*
c. ETHnic CHInese		*!			*	*
[with ETHnic ChiNESE supPORT]						
☞d. with ETHnic chiNESE supPORT						*
e. with ETHnic chinese supPORT					*!	
f. with ETHnic CHInese supPORT	*!				*	

Turning to *with GROWing CHInese supPORT*, we see in tableau (14) that on the first cycle NoCLASH correctly removes the medial accent on *-nese* in *CHInese supPORT*, as in candidate (a). Candidate (b) fails to satisfy NoCLASH and candidate (c) is ruled out by ALIGN(ϕ,T*,Left). On the second cycle, there is no problem deriving the end product, candidate (d). In particular, we cannot reaccent *-nese*, as in candidate (f), due to DEP-IO(Accent), and cannot gratuitously delete the accent on *Chi-*, as in candidate (e). As explained before, candidate (e), a possible form, can be derived by reranking MAX-IO(Accent) and NoREMOTECLASH. This ranking would also cause the medial accent on *Chi-* in (2a) to disappear, annihilating the intonational difference between (2a) and (2b), as may indeed happen in less formal speech.

(14)

[CHINESE supPORT] [with GROWing CHINESE supPORT]	DEP-IO(Accent)	ALIGN(ϕ,T*,Rt)	ALIGN(ϕ,T*,Left)	NoCLASH	MAX-IO(Accent)	NoREMOTECLASH
☞a. CHInese supPORT					*	
b. CHINESE supPORT				*!		
c. chiNESE supPORT			*!		*	*
[with GROWing CHInese supPORT]						
☞d. with GROWing CHInese supPORT						*
e. with GROWing chinese supPORT					*!	
f. with GROWing chiNESE supPORT	*!					

We may even derive the complex (15), originally due to Janet Pierrehumbert (Prince 1983; Selkirk 1984: 194). Observe that if the expression is a single ϕ, there is no way to obtain the correct output. When the phrasal structure (15a) is combined into a higher phrasal structure together with compound (15b), the resulting pronunciation is (15c) or (15d), never (15e). However, in terms of the severity of the clashes, (15c) equals impossible (15e). If the expression is a single ϕ, we cannot distinguish among these alternatives. The correct result can, however, be obtained by dealing with (15a) first so as to delete the accent on *Brooke* through NoClash (and with (15b), but there is no action here, since *station* has already lost its accent in the lexicon through CR), and consider the whole phrase on the second cycle. The accent on *Park* can again disappear, if NoRemoteClash ≫ Max-IO(Accent), to give (15d). However, impossible candidate (15e) is now unobtainable.

(15) a. ALEwife Brooke PARKway (*from* ALEwife BROOKE PARKway)
     b. SUBway station
     c. ALEwife Brooke PARKway SUBway station
     d. ALEwife Brooke Parkway SUBway station
     e. ??ALEwife BROOKE Parkway SUBway station

As explained in section 8.5.2, OT can deal with cyclicity by the inclusion of Output–Output faithfulness constraints in the (monocyclic) grammar (see also Kager 1999: 6). Output–output faithfulness relates the pronunciation of a form to the pronunciation of a paradigmatically related form.[3] In our case, we would need a constraint Faith-OO(Accent) (16), which requires that, say, *Alewife Brooke Parkway* in *Alewife Brooke Parkway Subway Station* is pronounced as (15a): *ALEwife Brooke PARKway*. A cyclic effect is created, because of the selection of the candidate that most closely corresponds with the citation pronunciation of the internal constituent. Being identical to it, candidate (a) is closer to (15a) than is candidate (b), which violates Faith-OO(Accent) twice for having lost an accent on *Parkway* and gained one on *Brooke*. While also violating Faith-OO(Accent) more than does candidate (a), candidate (c) is ruled out by the extra violation of higher ranking Max-IO(Accent).

(16) Faith-OO(Accent): The accentuation of a subconstituent in XP' is identical to that of a citation pronunciation of that subconstituent.

(17)

ALEwife BROOKE PARKway SUBway station	DEP-IO(Accent)	ALIGN(ϕ,T*,Rt)	ALIGN(ϕ,T*,Left)	NoClash	Max-IO(Accent)	NoRemoteClash	Faith-OO(Accent)
☞a. ALEwife brooke PARKway SUBway station		**				*	*
b. ALEwife BROOKE parkway SUBway station		**				*	*	*!*
c. ALEwife brooke parkway SUBway station		**				**!		*

14.3.2 Why postlexical cyclicity does not work

Correct as these result may seem, this postlexical cyclic treatment cannot be maintained. This becomes clear once we replace *PARKway* with *PARK*. Observe that Faith-OO(Accent) ranks below NoClash, because we need to be able to remove clashing accents even in embedded constituents. Thus, if the name of the subway station in question had been *ALEwife Brook PARK*, the clash between *PARK* and *SUB-* would have to be relieved. However, only the accent on *PARK* can be deleted, not that on *SUB-*. We might think that we can protect the accent on *SUB-* on the ground that it is closer to the end of the ϕ. However, the problem does not specifically concern final accents in the ϕ, and ALIGN(ϕ,T*,Rt) therefore cannot be used to generate the correct form, even though it is true that ι-final . . . *PARK subway station* violates this constraint three times and ι-final . . . *Park SUBway station* only twice. To show this, ϕ-final *East* has been added to the example to provide the rightmost accent in tableau (18).

(18)

ALEwife BROOKE PARK SUBway station EAST	DEP-IO(Accent)	ALIGN(φ,T*,Rt)	ALIGN(φ,T*,Left)	NoCLASH	MAX-IO(Accent)	NoREMOTECLASH	IDENT-OO(Accent)
☞! a. ALEwife brooke PARK subway station EAST					**		**
☞ b. ALEwife brooke Park SUBway station EAST					**		**
c. ALEwife brooke PARK SUBway station EAST				*!	*		

The problem, then, is that a cyclic treatment, however it is effected, cannot tell which of the clashing accents *PARK* and *SUB-* is to be deleted. But the cyclic solution does not merely suffer from indecision, as in (18); it may also make the wrong choice, as in the case of (19). Pronunciation (19a) represents a formal speech style, one that preserves accents that are flanked by at least one unaccented syllable on each side. However, a cyclic treatment would produce (19b), as shown in the cyclic tableau (20). On the first cycle, candidate (a) is selected, since both (c) and (d) violate ALIGN(T*,ϕ,Left), while candidate (b) unnecessarily violates MAX-IO(Acc). On the second cycle, a clash arises on *Ten Jap-*, causing candidate (e), i.e. (19b), to be incorrectly selected as the winner.[4]

(19)   a.   TEN JAPaNESE conSTRUCtions

      b.   ??TEN JapaNESE conSTRUCtions

(20)

[JAPaNESE conSTRUCtions] [TEN [JAPaNESE conSTRUCtions]]	DEP-IO(Accent)	ALIGN(φ,T*,Rt)	ALIGN(φ,T*,Left)	NoCLASH	MAX-IO(Accent)	NoREMOTECLASH
☞ a. JAPaNESE conSTRUCtions						**
b. JAPanese conSTRUCtions					*!	
c. japaNESE conSTRUCtions			*!		*	*
d. japanese conSTRUCtions			*!*		**	
TEN JAPaNESE conSTRUCtions						
☞! e. TEN japaNESE conSTRUCtions					*	*
f. TEN JAPaNESE conSTRUCtions				*!		**

Neither is (21a) available under a cyclic treatment. If we rerank NoREMOTE-CLASH and MAX-IO(Accent), as shown in tableau (22), *JAPanese conSTRUCtions* will be the input to the second cycle, and NoCLASH will select candidate (a), i.e. (21b): on the second cycle, the accent on *Jap-* will again disappear.

(21) a. TEN JAPanese conSTRUCtions
     b. TEN Japanese conSTRUCtions

(22)

TEN JAPanese conSTRUCtions	DEP-IO(Accent)	ALIGN(φ,T*,Rt)	ALIGN(φ,T*,Left)	NoCLASH	NoREMOTECLASH	MAX-IO(Accent)
☞ a. TEN japanese conSTRUCtions						*
b. TEN JAPanese conSTRUCtions				*!		

Likewise, the result for *Fifteen Japanese constructions* would be the unlikely (23b) under this ranking, again, to the exclusion of the entirely natural (23a). On the first cycle, *-nese* loses its accent, and on the second *Jap.* If we reverse the ranking of NoREMOTECLASH and MAX-(Acc), both syllables will remain accented, as in (23c), since neither violates NoCLASH. However, the point is that if an accent is maintained on *Japanese* at all, it will be the one on *Jap-*: the cyclic treatment is incapable of explaining this.

(23) a. FIFteen JAPanese conSTRUCtions
     b. ?FIFteen Japanese conSTRUCtions
     c. FIFteen JAPaNESE conSTRUCtions

Example (23a) also demonstrates that we cannot adopt a solution as for French in the previous chapter, where the NP-internal ϕ-boundary accounted for the presence of the medial accent in *perSONNES ALiTÉES* (section 13.2.5). This was achieved by making ϕ-formation sensitive to the occurrence of a post-modifier like *alités*, allowing it to form its own ϕ. If we made a similar assumption for English pre-modifications, we would end up with $_\phi$[FIFTEEN]$_\phi$ $_\phi$[JAPanese conSTRUCtions]$_\phi$. Clearly, under this phrasing, the final accent in the first ϕ would always be preserved, contrary to fact. While a ϕ-boundary after *Fifteen* would correctly preserve the accent on *Jap-*, it would incorrectly preserve the accent on *-teen*. The failure is not restricted to numerals, but is quite general, as illustrated by *HIGH-tech JAPanese conSTRUCtions*, where deletion of the accent on *tech* is the norm.

    The next section argues that the bias towards the retention of the constituent-initial accents and deletion of the constituent-final accents is to be found in a procliticized ϕ-structure.

14.3.3 Procliticized ϕs

The asymmetry of NP-internal clash resolutions would be reproduced in a structure that can have a left-hand ϕ-edge without at the same time creating a right-
hand ϕ-edge, so that the working of ALIGN (ϕ,T*,Rt) can be suspended internally in the ϕ. This can be done by adopting a proclitic prosodic structure (see
also section 8.5.1). Specifically, I assume that ϕs can be multiply nested as
in (24a) and (24b). Thanks to this minimal deviation from NONRECURSIVITY
(see section 8.5.1), accents at the locations of the arrows can be preserved by
ALIGN(ϕ,T*,Left), without at the same requiring ALIGN(ϕ,T*,Rt) to preserve
accents in immediately preceding syllables.

(24) a. $_\phi$[Ten $_\phi$[Japanese constructions]$_\phi$]$_\phi$
          ↑   ↑

     b. $_\phi$[Twenty-six $_\phi$[very nice $_\phi$[Japanese constructions]$_\phi$]$_\phi$]$_\phi$
          ↑   ↑   ↑

The morpho-syntactic constituent label of internal constituents in multiply pre-
modified structures like (24) is usually taken to be a super-Noun (N'), rather than
an NP, because they do not allow determiners (Radford 1981: 95). Such NP-
internal constituents, like *Ten* or *Japanese constructions* in (24), can be provided
with ϕs if we assume that ALIGN(XP,ϕ) refers to these internal constituents
(regardless of whether we are dealing with an Adjective Phrase, a Numeral, or a
high N'), leaving ALIGN(XP',ϕ,Rt) to require an ϕ-edge on the right of the larger
constituent (see also section 13.2.5). Second, in addition to ALIGN(XP,ϕ), which
is a shorthand for the right-alignment constraint introduced as (56) in chapter 8
and here repeated in (27), we need its left-hand counterpart ALIGN(XP, Left,
ϕ,Left), given in (26). Finally, we need to rank ALIGN(XP',ϕ,Rt) above, but
ALIGN(XP,ϕ,Rt) below a constraint forbidding right-hand ϕ-boundaries, given
as *ϕ,Rt in (28). This latter constraint is one half of Truckenbrodt's *P, given as
(51) in chapter 8.

(25) ALIGN(XP',ϕ,Rt): Align the right edge of XP' with the right edge of ϕ.

(26) ALIGN(XP,ϕ,Left): Align the left edge of every XP with the left edge of ϕ.

(27) ALIGN(XP,ϕ,Rt): Align the right edge of every XP with the right edge of ϕ.

(28) *ϕ,Rt: Do not have a right edge of ϕ.

Tableau (29) shows the intended effect. Notice that *ϕ,Rt can only be violated
once at any edge (cf. also section 8.3.4, as shown in candidate (a)). Candidate (b)
fails to have a final right-hand boundary at all, candidate (c) has one too many,
while candidate (d) lacks the required internal left-hand boundary.

(29)

FIFTEEN JAPaNESE conSTRUCtions	ALIGN(XP',φ,Rt)	*φ.Rt	ALIGN(XP,φ,Left)	ALIGN(XP,φ,Rt)
☞ a. φ[FIFTEEN φ[JAPaNESE conSTRUCtions]φ]φ		*		*
b. φ[FIFTEEN JAPaNESE conSTRUCtions...	*!		*	**
c. φ[FIFTEEN]φ φ[JAPaNESE conSTRUCtions]φ		**!		
d. φ[FIFTEEN JAPaNESE conSTRUCtions]φ		*	*!	*

Given that the proclitic φ-structure (29a) wins, the accent distribution of (23a), or candidate (a), will be taken care of as in tableau (30). As will be clear, reranking of MAX-IO(Accent) and NoREMOTECLASH will identify candidate (b) as the winner, (23c). Candidate (c) is unobtainable. I believe this is the correct result, also for adjacent accents. An expression such as *SIX GREEK MEN*, with left-hand φ-boundaries before *six* and *Greek* is not pronounced like *SIXteen MEN*. And if it is, its φ-structure has been restructured to a single φ, and a description as for French (see section 13.2.5) would be required.

(30)

[FIFTEEN [JAPaNESE conSTRUCtions]φ]φ	DEP-IO(Accent)	ALIGN(φ,T*,Rt)	ALIGN(φ,T*,Left)	NoClash	NoRemoteClash	Max-IO(Accent)
☞ a. [FIFteen [JAPanese conSTRUCtions]φ]φ					*	**
b. [FIFteen [JAPaNESE conSTRUCtions]φ]φ				**!	*	*
c. [FIFteen [japanese conSTRUCtions]φ]φ			*!			***
d. [FIFteen [japaNESE conSTRUCtions]φ]φ			*!		*	**

To account for the fact that pre-modified NPs in English retain leftmost accents, a proclitic φ-structure needs to be assumed. This assumption allows a final accent in the pre-modifiers to be deleted, while the initial accent is preserved.

14.3.4   Focus and φ

Phrasing is sensitive to focus, as in many other languages (Selkirk 1984; (Kanerva 1989; Truckenbrodt 1999; see also section 8.5). In English, phrasing is likely to have an effect on the distribution of pitch accents. For instance, if *light-blue* is a focus constituent, the accent on *blue* is preserved, even if an accented word follows in the same NP (Vogel and Kenesei 1990). The pattern in (32) may be characteristic of corrective focus (section 5.7.1), since *She was wearing a*

LIGHT-blue SWEATer also seems possible in the informational focus context given here.

(31) ALIGN(FOC,Rt, ϕ): Align the right edge of a focus constituent with ϕ.

(32) (A: She never wore anything but WHITE clothes)
B: She was wearing a LIGHT-BLUE]$_{FOC}$ SWEATer]$_{FOC}$

It would at first sight seem correct to assume right-alignment of ϕ with the focus constituent. It is not clear, however, that in a case like *She didn't wear a WHITE sweater, but a LIGHT-BLUE sweater*, there is an ϕ-boundary after *LIGHT-BLUE* rather than after *LIGHT-BLUE sweater*. Because *sweater* in unaccented, the absence of 'stress shift' could either be due to the presence of a ϕ-boundary after *LIGHT-BLUE* or to the lack of accent on *sweater*. Since other than clash resolving accent deletions ('stress shift'), no reliable diagnostics for English ϕs appear to be available, so it is not clear how this question is to be answered. An alternative assumption for the ϕ-boundary in (32) is that different focus constituents must occur in different ϕs, where each ϕ may also contain unfocused constituents. In section 14.4, the English ι is discussed; one issue that is briefly considered in section 14.5.1 is the relation between ιs and the focus constituent.

14.4 Intonational phrases

The English ι, which is marked by boundary tones in a way that will be explained in chapter 15, in some unmarked sense lines up with the clause (Halliday 1970; Selkirk 1978, 1984), more recently specified as the 'matrix sentence' (Selkirk 2003) (cf. also section 8.5.2). A sentence at most containing a nominal clause will typically consist of a single ι, as illustrated in (33a). A topicalized element, or a parenthetical, will not be included in the same ι, however, as shown in (33b). In addition, ι-phrasing is sensitive to length, as shown in (33c), where the long subject is likely to be phrased as a separate ι (Selkirk 1978).

(33) a. {Tuesday is a holiday in Pakistan}
b. {In Pakistan} {Tuesday} {which is a weekday} {is a holiday}
c. {The second Tuesday of every month} {is a holiday}

The unmarked coincidence of ι and S was captured by the alignment constraint the requires every S to 'co-end' with ι given in section 8.5.2 as (57).

14.4.1 VP-Internal ι-boundaries

Clearly, performance will affect the placement of ι-boundaries below the level of S. The subject of the sentence is a likely candidate for separate phrasing, but ι-breaks within the VP are not uncommon. There has been considerable discussion of these VP-internal prosodic breaks, often in connection with 'low' and 'high' attachment of PPs. The minimally different structures in (35) represent one such pair illustrating this difference. In (35a), we have a case of 'high' attachment of the PP, while that in (35b) illustrates 'low' attachment, i.e. attachment within the NP. Pronunciation (34) is ambiguous between these interpretations.

(34) {We welcome every guest with champagne}

(35) a. [V [N[PP]]$_{NP}$]$_{VP}$: We appreciate every guest who brings champagne
    b. [[V NP]PP]$_{VP}$: We treat every guest to a glass of champagne

The location of a VP-internal break is sensitive to the difference in morpho-syntactic structure. A break after *welcome*, as in (36), is only compatible with the interpretation (35a).

(36) {We welcome} {every guest with champagne}

To rule out pronunciation (36) for the meaning in (35b), Hirst (1993) proposed that the right-hand ι should be a morpho-syntactic constituent: since *guests with champagne* is not a constituent, it cannot be an ι. This view is compatible with the fact that pronunciation (37) is appropriate for *both* interpretations (35a) and (35b), since *with champagne* is a constituent in both structures.

(37) {We welcome every guest} {with champagne}

In order to account for these data, we need to break up the ι at a location that respects the morpho-syntactic constituency of the right-hand ι. Truckenbrodt's MAX$_{OO}$ could create both effects if we assume that the right-hand constituent was subjected to an OT analysis on the grounds of being a free-standing form and be assigned an ι. MAX$_{OO}$ could then demand faithfulness to this ι if it outranked $*\iota$, the relevant equivalent of $*$P. Candidate (a) in tableau (38) is obtained by ranking MAX$_{OO} \gg *\iota$. Candidate (b) founders because it fails to reproduce the ι of *with champagne*, and so does candidate (c). It will be clear that reranking MAX$_{OO}$ and $*\iota$ will select candidate (c), as it has the fewest violations of $*\iota$.

(38)

'treat every guest to champagne' O: {with champagne}$_\iota$ [[welcome [every guest]$_{NP}$]$_{VP1}$ [with champagne]$_{PP}$]$_{VP2}$	Max$_{OO}$	$*\iota$
☞ a. {welcome every guest} {with champagne}		**
b. {welcome} {every guest with champagne}	*!	**
c. {welcome every guest with champagne}	*!	*

Interpretation (35a) is available in both pronunciations (36) and (37). Since the final ι of (37) corresponds to an NP-internal ('low') PP in the case of (35a) and to a VP-internal ('high') PP in the case of (35b), we can obtain either pronunciation, depending on whether MAX$_{OO}$ refers to free-standing *every guest with champagne* or *with champagne*. In tableau (39), the former case is assumed. Three breaks would be obtained if at the point where *every guest with champagne* was evaluated, prior evaluation of *with champagne* had assigned this constituent an ι, which would be preserved at the points that the NP and the VP are evaluated.

(39)	'appreciate every guest who brings champagne' O: {every guest to champagne}$_\iota$ [welcome [every guest [with champagne]$_{PP}$]$_{NP}$]$_{VP}$	Max$_{OO}$	$_{\sim}$*
☞ a. {welcome} {every guest with champagne}			**
b. {welcome every guest} {with champagne}		*!	**
c. {welcome every guest with champagne}		*!	*

While this analysis produces the desired outputs in these cases, it is not straight-fowardly combined with constraints on size, to which we turn in the next section.

14.4.2 Introducing size constraints

Constraints Max$_{OO}$ and *ι cannot explain all the data. Consider again (37) as a pronunciation for the morpho-syntactic structure in (35a), where we have an ι-boundary within an NP. The preference for this ι-boundary increases if we replace *with champagne* with a longer constituent, as has been done in (40). (Henceforth, I will use non-ambiguous *appreciate* and *treat* for the two meanings of *welcome*.) The more balanced phrasing can be obtained by a constraint like Selkirk's (2000) BinMap (41), which I here interpret as requiring binary branching of ι, i.e. {[ϕ] [ϕ]}$_\iota$. It has been included in tableau (42) in third position (cf. also section 8.5.1).

(40) {We appreciate guests} {with champagne from France}
     (i.e. who bring French champagne)

(41) BinMap: An ι consists of just two ϕs.

In order for a phonological constraint like BinMap to interact with Max$_{OO}$, we must allow it to influence Max$_{OO}$'s choice of the subconstituent whose phrasing is to be reproduced in the higher level constituent. If Max$_{OO}$ were to demand faithfulness to {*with champagne from France*}$_\iota$, the result is better by BinMap than if it were to demand faithfulness to {*guests with champagne from France*}$_\iota$. Let us assume for now that the output candidates that result from both choices of Max$_{OO}$ can be evaluated in the same tableau (42). The choice between candidate (a) and candidate (b) now falls to BinMap, and even-balanced candidate (a) thus wins. As always, candidate (c) would be chosen if *i ≫ Max$_{OO}$. For candidate (c), I have entered two violations, one for each of the possible outputs to which faithfulness is required. Likewise, *ι is violated under either choice of Max$_{OO}$.

(42)	O$_1$: {guests with champagne from France}$_\iota$ O$_2$: {with champagne from France}$_\iota$ [appreciate [guests [with champagne from France]$_{PP}$]$_{NP}$]$_{VP}$	Max$_{OO}$	$_{\sim}$*	BinMap
☞ a. {appreciate guests} {with champagne from France}			**/**	
b. {appreciate} {guests with champagne from France}			**/**	*!*
c. {appreciate guests with champagne from France}		*!/*!	*/*	*

Finally, to demonstrate that BINMAP ranks below MAX$_{OO}$, consider (43), where an ι-break after *invariably treat* is ungrammatical. This is because we would end up with an ι encompassing the non-constituent *every guest to champagne*, which word group could never have been evaluated by MAX$_{OO}$, and so cannot be an ι. Tableau (44) assumes that MAX$_{OO}$ demands faithfulness to the ι *champagne*. As a result, even-balanced candidate (b) is not selected in this case.

(43) *{We invariably treat} {guests to champagne}

(44)

[invariably treat [guests]$_{NP}$] [to champagne]$_{PP}$]$_{VP}$	Max$_{OO}$	_*	BinMap
☞ a. {invariably treat guests} {to champagne}		**	**
b. {invariably treat} {guests to champagne}	*!	**	
c. {invariably treat guests to champagne}	*!	*	*

The treatment of the VP-internal break in this section raises the issue of the extent to which performance factors should be taken into account. First, there is the conceptual problem of how to combine phonological size constraints with the quasi-cyclic treatment of MAX$_{OO}$. In tableaux (42) and (44), we assumed that BINMAP can decide between outputs from two interpretations of MAX$_{OO}$, much as if we were evaluating outputs from different grammars. One way of avoiding this would be to split MAX$_{OO}$ into a constraint requiring postlexical prosodic constituents to correspond to a morpho-syntactic constituent and a constraint requiring ιs to split up, a free instruction that would be kept in check by LAYEREDNESS, which forbids ι to be dominated by ϕ (cf. section 8.5.1). Second, just as prosodic constituents may be smaller than the morpho-syntactic constituent given by their default alignment, so they may be larger, a phenomenon known as 'restructuring' (Selkirk 1978; Nespor and Vogel 1986). For instance, the two-clause structure *He loves skiing and so he went* may well be a single ι. As in the case of fine-grained phrasing, phonological length as well as performance factors are likely to play a role in the decision to restructure. At this point, research has not progressed to a point where decisions can be made as to which of these factors belong in the grammar, and how performance factors are to be brought to bear on the construction of phonological representations.

A further question concerns the right-hand orientation of MAX$_{OO}$: why should only right-hand ιs correspond to a morpho-syntactic constituent? This observation of Hirst's (1993) is reminiscent of Elordieta's (1997) for Basque that the first ip of the sentence must be branching, *regardless* of morpho-syntactic structure (cf. INITIALBRANCHING in (19) in chapter 9).

14.4.3   Incorporated and encliticized ιs

Procliticized ϕs were needed to explain the asymmetric deletion of accents in premodified NPs in section 14.3.3. The ι may be expanded on the right beyond the matrix sentence in certain limited ways (Bing 1979; Firbas 1980; Pierrehumbert 1980: 51; Gussenhoven 1985). Bing termed these extra-sentential elements 'Class O expressions', where O stands for 'outside'. They come in two types, both of which are unaccented. Extra-sentential (ES) inclusions into the ι are 'incorporations', as in (45a), and with Selkirk (1995a) I distinguish these from encliticized ιs, as in (45b). They differ from an accented, separate ι, shown in (45c).

(45) a. { X   Y   ES }
      b. {{ X   Y } ES }
      c. { X   Y } { ES }

In (46), some examples are given of incorporations. Contrary to orthographic practice, I leave out the comma between the main clause and the incorporated item. Example (46a) is an 'approximative' marker; (46b) a 'cohesion' marker; (46c,d) are 'hearer-appeal' markers, which type includes vocatives and positive polarity tags; while (46e) represents a reporting clause, which belongs to a class of textual markers that also includes comment clauses, like *I should imagine*. Next, (46f) is an 'epithet', and (46g) an 'expletive' (Bing 1979).[5] All of the examples in (46) can be pronounced in exactly the ways that a single brief clause can, and there is therefore no intonational motivation for a prosodic break before the extra-sentential item.

(46) a. {They'll break the PLATES and that sort of thing}
      b. {Must have been a bit of a SHOCK though}
      c. {Stop MOANing John}
      d. {It's SANta Claus is it?}
      e. {NO she said}
      f. {John wouldn't give me his CAR the stupid bastard}
      g. {It's TRUE damn it!}

Encliticized ιs also occur utterance-finally, are unaccented, but are set off from the ι on the left by a boundary tone (Trim 1959; Gussenhoven 1990). Brief reformulations of the sort illustrated in (47) typically have this structure. Although the question of how cliticized ιs are pronounced is properly dealt with in section 15.7 in the next chapter, at this point the generalization can be made that a cliticized ι typically receives a copy of the tones after the last T*. For instance, if the contour used on *-scuss this* is H*L H$_\iota$, the cliticized *the two of us* is pronounced with L H$_\iota$, as shown. In effect, the first copied tone serves as an initial boundary tone.

(47)

{ Shouldn't we discuss this }   the two of us? }

L$_\iota$ →   H*L → H$_\iota$ L →   H$_\iota$

Reporting clauses are either incorporating or cliticizing, both of (48a,b) being grammatical (Gussenhoven 1992a). If they are pronounced with H*L H$_\iota$, cliticized (48a) will have two instances of L H$_\iota$, and incorporating (48b) one. There are restrictions on incorporation. For instance, while items that obligatorily incorporate, such as vocatives and positive polarity tags, may appear together in the same ι, as suggested by (49a,b), complex reporting clauses cannot be incorporated. While structures (50a,b) are fine, (50c) is ungrammatical.

(48) a. {{Is it TRUE?} she asked}
     b. {Is it TRUE she asked?}

(49) a. {That's NICE Mary is it}
     b. {Could you pass me the SALT please John}

(50) a. {{{Is it TRUE?}H$_\iota$ asked Mary}H$_\iota$ a frown appearing on her forehead}H$_\iota$
     b. {{Is it TRUE asked Mary?}H$_\iota$ a frown appearing on her forehead}H$_\iota$
     c. *{Is it TRUE asked Mary a frown appearing on her forehead?}H$_\iota$

Finally, incorporation and encliticization should be distinguished from right-hand extra-sentential elements that are accented and require an ι to themselves, as in (45c). Notably, this is the case for negative polarity tags, which consist of an accented auxiliary and a pronominal subject, with the opposite polarity of the host clause. They can have a fall or a rise independently of the nuclear contour on the preceding ι, though cannot take H*L H$_\iota$ (Quirk *et al.* 1985: 810; Bing 1979). Two examples are given in (51).

(51) a. {It's TRUE} {ISn't it}
     b. {You're NOT a GIRL anymore} {ARE you}

14.5 Between the ϕ and the ι

Most phonologists recognize a prosodic hierarchy for English in which there are only two constituents between the phonological utterance (υ) and the phonological word (ω). In this chapter, we have taken these to be ϕ (motivated on the basis of postlexical pitch-accent distributions) and ι (to be motivated on the basis of the tonal structure in chapter 15). The question arises if a third constituent is needed to explain the data, as in Selkirk (2003), who has an intonational phrase, a major phrase, and a minor phrase covering the same distance in the prosodic hierarchy; and other researchers, who assume the presence of an intermediate phrase by the side of, rather than instead of (Beckman and Pierrehumbert 1986), a ϕ. I have used examples like (52) and (53) to argue that two levels are in fact insufficient (Gussenhoven 1990; Gussenhoven and Rietveld 1992). Example (52) contains an indirect and a direct object, and might be a suggestion to someone who is eager to sell their honour to someone, while (53) contains a direct object and a vocative, where *Janet* might be a filly and the addressee a judge who breeds horses for a hobby.

(52) {[Sell JANet] [your honour]}

(53) {[Sell JANet] [Your Honour]}

My case was based on the belief that in (52), the [t] will coalesce with the following [j] into [tʃ], while in (53) the normal realization of the final consonant of *Janet* is that of an unexploded, glottalized plosive, a phonological difference which neither the φ-structure nor the ι-structure can account for. The solution was to divorce the ι from its intonational properties, but to grant it its segmental properties (like allowing palatalization of [t] before [j]). There would thus be an ι-boundary between *Janet* and *Your Honour* in (53), but not in the equivalent position in (52). The more rigid mapping of morpho-syntactic and phonological structure would be counter-balanced by the fact that the intonational boundary tones would be freed from any specific prosodic constituent, and would in principle be able to align with φ, ι, or, as in (52) and (53), the υ, among other things depending on speech rate. There is some suggestive experimental evidence for this view (Gussenhoven and Rietveld 1992), but the facts of (52) and (53) have also been called into question (Lodge 2000), and I will not pursue the issue here. As for other languages, only in the case of Basque would there appear to be a need for three constituents between ω and υ; to account for Japanese, no reference to an ι was needed.

14.5.1 Focus and ι

In section 14.3.4, we have seen that the focus constituent is contained within a φ, which may lead to differences in accent distribution between broad and narrow focus. It has been suggested that English also requires ι-boundary to occur on the right of the focus constituent (Vogel and Kenesei 1990; Selkirk 2000). This claim is unexpected, since there is no final $T_ι$ at the end of the focus constituent: the boundary tone occurs at the end of what would have been the ι in the broad focus condition, as in Schmerling's (1974) *Even [a TWO-year-old]$_{FOC}$ could do that}$T_ι$.[6] In the context of (54), a red and a black jacket had mysteriously disappeared from the rack in a menswear shop. The owner has discovered that the new shop assistant had given away the red jacket to a friend earlier that day, while the fate of the black jacket is still unclear. Not knowing any of this, the manager, in an attempt to reassure the owner, suggests that the reason why the jackets have disappeared is simply that they have been sold, upon which the owner responds with (54). Even with two corrective foci, no ι boundary is required after the first focus, as in (54a), and if there is a boundary, it is not after the focus constituent *red*, but at the morpho-syntactic boundary, as in (54b). While focus would thus appear to have an effect on φ-structure in English, either in requiring a right-edge alignment with φ or in requiring a WRAP-style containment of a focus constituent in a φ, its effect in ι-structure is not evident.

(54) a. (The BLACK jacket may have been SOLD)$T_ι$ {but the [RED]$_{FOC}$ jacket was given aWAY}$T_ι$

b. ... {the [RED]$_{FOC}$ jacket}$T_ι$ {was given aWAY}$T_ι$

14.6 Conclusion

The distribution of pitch accents in English is determined by the interaction of lexical accent rules, such as the Compound Rule and Initial Accent Deletion, and postlexical rhythmic readjustments. The latter are due to clash avoidance within the ϕ, just as in French, which lacks any lexical accent rules. In order to account for these readjustments, we needed to assume a ϕ-structure with procliticization. I considered and rejected analyses making use of cyclicity, a single, restructured ϕ, and separate ϕs, but proclitic structure turned out to be the only way in which we could systematically delete the final accent in pre-modifying adjectives or numerals, and preserve the initial accent in the pre-modified NP, as in *TWENty- six CHInese conSTRUCtions* (**TWENty-SIX ChiNESE conSTRUCtions*).

The criterion for ι-structure was taken to be intonational. While the ι tends to coincide with the clause, clause-internal ι-boundaries frequently occur. The restriction on their locations appears to be that the remainder should be a constituent (Hirst 1993). I adopted an output–output faithfulness approach proposed by Truckenbrodt to create such boundaries in legitimate locations. Some issues for further research were identified, such as the interaction between size constraints and morpho-syntactic constraints in long expressions.

Extra-sentential additions to the sentence, like vocatives, tag questions, and comment clauses, are of three kinds. First, the addition may be incorporated into the preceding ι, as is the case with vocatives and positive polarity tags; second, the ι can be encliticized, as may occur with reporting clauses and reformulations; and third, the addition may receive its own ι, as in the case of negative polarity tags. In the next chapter, we turn to the tonal structure of English, which will be dealt with in a traditional, descriptive fashion.

Notes

1. Some caution may be called for when comparing the twenty-four English contours with the seven or eight of the other two languages. The description of the intonation of West Germanic languages has a long tradition, and it may be that a wider coverage has been achieved. However, even when we make allowance for the possibility that not all French or Bengali contours have been described, there is still a comfortable lead by English in the number of possible contours.
2. In older words, *free* is a suffix of type (3c), as in *'carefree*, but in new formations it behaves like a phrasal element, as in *'lead-'free* (Wells 1990).
3. OO-faithfulness could, without further principles, relate the expression under consideration to pronunciations of any of its subconstituents in any other context (Kiparsky forthcoming). For instance, in *OLD Alewife Brooke PARKway*, the accent on *ALEwife* will disappear, but we would not wish OO-faithfulness to be able to relate this form to the pronunciation of the expression in tableau (17). A different solution, one featuring faithfulness to selected 'sympathetic' forms, is proposed by McCarthy (1999).
4. It is important to see that (19b) is a non-neutral pronunciation of the phrase. This form *is* appropriate if all three words are pronounced as separate ϕs, a pronunciation that

would be used contrastively with *Eleven Australian demolitions*, when all elements have corrective focus, but this is not the intended reading.

5. In Gussenhoven (1984: ch. 3), I incorrectly excluded expletives and epithets from Bing's class of 'O expressions', arguing that they are accented in English. It is true that they are frequently pronounced with a rising intonation, but this is to be interpreted as a boundary H%, as held by Bing (1979).

6. Selkirk (2000) attributes the absence of a boundary tone immediately after the focus constituent to a constraint that bans unaccented ιs: if T_ι appeared after *old*, the words *could do that* would have to form an unaccented ι. Since this constraint outranks ALIGN(Foc,ι,Rt), the requirement for a boundary after *old* is overridden, which means that there can be no empirical effect of ALIGN(Foc,ι,Rt), rendering its status in the grammar vacuous. More recently, Selkirk (2002) has pursued the Focus Prominence Theory, originally due to Truckenbrodt (1995), which claims that the focus constituent is always attended by some prominence tone, from which other effects, like phrasing, are derived. Under this view, the unwanted prosodic break might be prevented by other constraints.

15

English II: Tonal Structure

15.1 Introduction

This chapter continues the discussion of English with a treatment of its tonal structure. It is easily the most widely discussed topic in studies of intonational melody, and has been treated both by phonologists (Pike 1945; Bolinger 1958; Crystal 1969; Gibbon 1975; Liberman 1975; Ladd 1980; Pierrehumbert 1980; Brazil 1985; Gussenhoven 1983b; Cruttenden 1997), among others, and by pedagogically oriented linguists (Palmer 1922; Jassem 1952; Halliday 1970; O'Connor and Arnold 1973), again among others. The variety of English described here is middle-class southern British English (BrE). Its intonational grammar is very similar to that of Standard Dutch, American English, and North German, and is complex, in the sense that it generates a large number of discretely different contours. To keep the discussion manageable, I will present the grammar in stages. First, a mini-grammar is presented, itself in two steps. Section 15.2 deals with the nuclear pitch accents plus the final boundary tones, together referred to as the 'nuclear contours'; section 15.3 with the pre-nuclear pitch accents; and section 15.4 with the initial boundary tones, or 'onsets'. These three sections define the mini-grammar, whose further elaboration is the topic of section 15.5. In section 15.6, 'chanting' contours are dealt with as an additional contour type, while section 15.7 discusses the pronunciation of unaccented ɩs. Section 15.8, finally, points out a number of cases where the description in Beckman and Pierrehumbert (1986) and ToBI would appear to fall short of the description offered in this chapter.

15.2 Nuclear contours

15.2.1 The fall, the fall–rise, the high rise, and the low rise

The nuclear contours in (1) are among the most frequently used intonation patterns in BrE. The fall in (1a) is a declarative intonation. The fall is fairly steep, also when the accented syllable is followed by unaccented syllables in the ι. The pitch before the target of H* is attributed to preceding tones. The illustration in panel (a) of figure 15.1 shows the fall after a low unaccented *I don't*, but equally there might have been a H* pitch accent in *don't*, or the unaccented part might have been high pitched, as in panels (b) and (c), respectively. These structural possibilities are discussed in section 15.3 and 15.4. This is the neutral intonation contour, and is used in citation pronunciations, for instance. Its meaning was described by Brazil (1975) as 'proclaiming': the speaker intends to establish his message as forming part of the common knowledge shared by speaker and hearer, a meaning I adopted as 'Addition' in Gussenhoven (1983b).

   The fall–rise is identical to the fall, except for the rise on the ι-final sylla-ble due to $H_ι$. More so than in (2a), the contour in (2b) shows that the trailing tone is doubly-aligned, keeping the phonetic effect $T_ι$ in the last part of the ι. It has been claimed that the early or late targets of (what I analyse as) the trailing tone result from tonal associations with stressed, though unaccented, syl-lables (Grice, Ladd, and Arvaniti 2000 and section 2.2.4), which claim is still in need of empirical support. The fall–rise contour readily occurs on a single sylla-ble. Brazil's meaning for the fall–rise was 'referring', adopted as 'Selection' in Gussenhoven (1983b). Steedman's (1991) meaning 'theme' for the complex of ToDI's L+H* plus the boundary sequence L-H%, our $H*LH_ι$, also corresponds to this meaning, his H*L-L% being the 'rheme', corresponding to 'Addition'. The speaker refers to knowledge, or wishes to be understood as referring to knowl-edge, already shared by him and his listener. Indeed, the contour often creates the impression of a reminder. This meaning is not very evident in other uses, such as Yes–no questions, yet can perhaps be appreciated when comparing the communicative effect of a 'Selection' question with that of a 'Testing' question (see below).

(1)   a. H*L $L_ι$ fall   'Addition'
       b. H*L $H_ι$ fall-rise   'Selection'

(2)

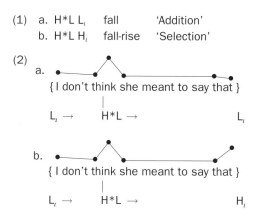

   The high rise in (4a) is another interrogative intonation, which appears to be rare in BrE, but is common in American English (Cruttenden 1997; Bolinger

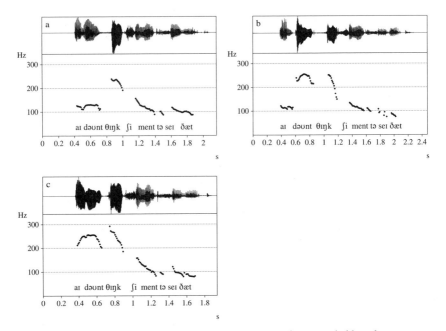

Fig. 15.1 H*L L$_\iota$ on *I don't THINK she meant to say that* preceded by a low onset
(panel a), by an accent on *don't* (panel b), and a high onset (panel c).

1998). It has a target at mid pitch in the accented syllable, followed by a rise due
to H$_\iota$, which is upstepped after H, as in Pierrehumbert (1980). Unlike her upstep
rule, implementation rule (3) does not apply to L-tones.

(3) ENGLISH UPSTEP: H$_\iota$ → extra high / H ---
     (Implementation)

The pitch before the target of H* will again depend on the tonal specification
for the preceding part of the expression; if it is low-pitched, a low target right at
the start of the accented syllable will occur, giving a rising movement from low
to mid pitch across the first half of the syllable. This movement contrasts with
the more sustained low pitch of the low rise. This contour, given in (4b), has a
low accented syllable, followed by a rise in the next syllable, and a further rise
due to H$_\iota$ on the last. The difference between the high rise and the low rise in
ι-internal position is illustrated schematically in (5a,b). It can be subtle, as in the
equivalent Dutch contrast illustrated in figure 4.7 (section 4.4.2). A monosyllabic
pronunciation of the high rise is a rise from mid to high pitch. By contrast, if the
three tones of the low rise L*H H$_\iota$ appear on a single syllable, the first part of
the accented syllable is low, a single rising movement being carried out in the
second part.

(4) a. H*   H$_\iota$ high rise   'Testing'
     b. L*H H$_\iota$ low rise   'Testing'

(5)

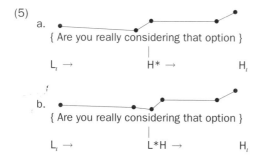

a.
{ Are you really considering that option }

L$_l$ → H* → H$_l$

b.
{ Are you really considering that option }

L$_l$ → L*H → H$_l$

Brazil (1975) gave 'intensified referring' as the meaning of L*H H$_l$, analysing contours (4a) and (4b) as variants of the fall–rise with 'intensified' meaning.[1] In Gussenhoven (1983b), I claimed the meaning 'Testing' for (4b). While 'Addition' refers to the commitment of the message to the discourse model and 'Selection' to activation of elements already in it, 'Testing' leaves it up to the listener to decide whether the message is to be understood as belonging to the background. The meaning explains the contour's ready interpretation as an interrogative: the speaker invites the listener to resolve the issue. Also, it can be used as threat, as well as to indicate that the message is not yet to be committed to the discourse model, although it is not typically used for the expression of non-finality in BrE. I find it hard to discern any meaning difference between the high rise and the low rise.

15.2.2 The high level, the half-completed rise, and the half-completed fall

Contours (6a), the high level, and (6b), the half-completed rise, can be used as 'listing intonations'. The contours, illustrated in (7), are phonetically identical to the high rise and low rise, respectively, but lack the final rise. The meaning of the high-level contour was described by Ladd (1978) as 'Routine'. That is, the speaker considers that his message ought to come as no surprise, because it is, in some sense, an everyday occurrence. The term 'half-completed' suggests a contour type that does not run its full course, due to the absence of a T$_l$. Its meaning represents a milder form of Ladd's 'Routine' (Gussenhoven 1983b).

(6) a. H*   } High level   'Routine, testing'
     b. L*H } Half-completed rise   'Moderate routine, testing'

(7) a.

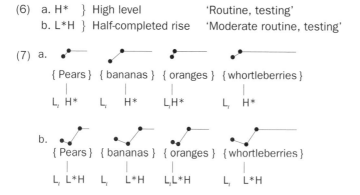

{ Pears } { bananas } { oranges } { whortleberries }

L$_l$ H*   L$_l$ H*   L$_l$H*   L$_l$ H*

b.

{ Pears } { bananas } { oranges } { whortleberries }

L$_l$ L*H   L$_l$ L*H   L$_l$L*H   L$_l$ L*H

Contour (8) is the half-completed fall, described as a 'suspended fall' by Crystal (1969). Instead of the steep fall of H*L L$_\iota$, the pitch falls gradually after the accented syllable to a final mid target for the trailing L. If it is given an early target, so as to create a mid level, the contour sounds like the vocative chant, dealt with in section 15.6. I assume that (9) is to be described as right-alignment for trailing L, but it is not clear how this exceptional alignment is to be accounted for. Like the half-completed rise, the half-completed fall expresses moderate routineness. Example (9) could be used to convey that the clean cup is not to be taken as particularly unexpected.

(8)   H*L   }   half-completed fall   'Moderate routine, addition'

(9)

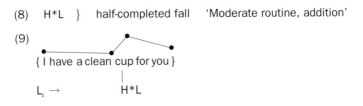

{ I have a clean cup for you }

L$_\iota$ →   H*L

15.2.3   The low low rise, scathing intonation, and the low level

As its name suggests, the low low rise in (10) is like the low rise (4), but dispenses with the first rising movement. Regardless of how long the post-nuclear stretch is, it is fully low until the last syllable, where a rise takes place. The contour is not always included in the descriptions, and it is probably infrequent. Pierrehumbert (1980) described it for American English, as (H+)L* L-H%. Cruttenden (1997) characterizes it as a dullish type of rising intonation. The effect here may, however, depend on how briskly the final rise is made.

(10)   L* H$_\iota$ low low rise

(11)

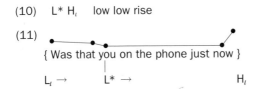

{ Was that you on the phone just now }

L$_\iota$ →   L* →   H$_\iota$

Two further contours that are rarely discussed are given in (12a,b).

(12) a. L*   L$_\iota$ scathing intonation 'Scathing'
      b. L*   } Low level   'Routine, scathing'

Contour (12a) is the 'scathing intonation'. In an email message on the Linguist List, Alex Monaghan gave the example (13) (my analysis), and described its meaning as conveying 'something like "Work it out for yourself" or "That's a stupid question" or even "who breaks everything around here?"' (Monaghan 2000). Scathing intonation would appear impossible as a conversation opener, and typically occurs as a repetition of the listener's last utterance. It has low pitch throughout, phonologically interpretable as the replacement of all pitch accents in the original utterance by L*; the last syllable is lowered further, the effect of L_i.

(13)

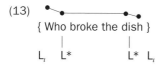

{ Who broke the dish }

    | |

  L_i L*   L* L_i

The corresponding contour without the boundary tone is the 'low level', in (12b), the phonological counterpart of the high level. While the contour for B's utterance in (13) has final lowering, a somewhat different effect is obtained if the pitch remains more nearly constant. It is still disparaging, but with an additional element of routineness, a note of *Here we go again!* By using (14) as a repetition of an utterance by the listener, the speaker is suggesting the listener is routinely but inappropriately putting the blame on his or her mother.

(14)

{ It's your mother's fault again }

               |

  L_i L*

15.2.4 NoSlump

Taking stock, we have seen that BrE employs H*, H*L, L*, and L*H in nuclear position, and three boundary conditions, H_i, L_i, and Ø. Combining them should produce twelve nuclear contours, but we have only discussed ten. The two missing combinations are L*H L_i and H* L_i. Both of these describe a fall on the ι-final syllable, the counterpart of the final rise, while the accented syllable is low and followed by a rise (L*H), or has a rise early in the accented syllable (H*). The contours are not part of standard BrE. In a discussion of non-standard BrE intonation, Cruttenden (1997: 139) labels the pattern as 'rise–plateau–slump', a contour-type that commonly occurs in northern urban varieties, like Manchester (also Cruttenden 2001), Liverpool, Birmingham, and Tyneside, as well as in Belfast. An example spoken by a male speaker of Liverpool English, from the IViE corpus (Grabe 2001), is given in (15). The contour is truncated and only barely ends in a fall: there is even some (phonetic) H-raising just before the end. However, a reporting clause after this utterance would no doubt show a falling pattern.

(15)

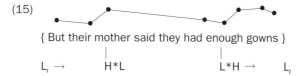

{ But their mother said they had enough gowns }

              | |

  L_i →   H*L   L*H → L_i

The exclusion of combination HL$_i$ is given as NoSlump (17) in the mini-grammar (16).

(16) Nuclear contours: $\begin{Bmatrix} H^*(L) \\ L^*(H) \end{Bmatrix} \begin{Bmatrix} H_\iota \\ L_\iota \\ \emptyset \end{Bmatrix}$

(17) NoSlump: *H L$_\iota$

To conclude these initial sections, English initial L$_\iota$, T*, and trailing T align left as well as right, in the sense of chapter 8, section 8.3.6. Final T$_\iota$ thus always defines a single target at the end of the ι. T* and its trailing T fill up the space between them with trailing T, and ALIGN(T,Left) therefore outranks ALIGN(T*,Rt). This effect can be seen in (2), for instance, as well as in (5b). Only if there is no trailing T will T* have a chance to right-align, as in (5a). Unlike the starred tones of Pierrehumbert (1980) and subsequent work, our T* therefore 'spreads' rightwards (in the sense of satisfying opposite alignments) if there is no trailing tone. Second, if there is no final T$_\iota$, the target of the preceding tone continues until the ι-end, again as explained in section 8.3.6. The one exceptional pattern is the half-completed fall, H*L}, whose L right-aligns, creating a slowly descending interpolation to mid pitch in the post-nuclear stretch. This exceptional nuclear pattern is the normal behaviour of pre-nuclear pitch accents, quite like the Norwegian pattern of section 11.4.2. To this we turn next.

15.3 Pre-nuclear pitch accents

Although there are just four nuclear pitch accents, the pre-nuclear paradigm consists of five pitch accents. I discuss the interloper in section 15.5.1 and devote the present section to the pre-nuclear fall (H*L), the pre-nuclear rise (L*H), the pre-nuclear high level (H*), and the pre-nuclear low level (L*). (The low level already made an appearance in the scathing intonation.) They correspond, respectively, to the falling, rising, high, and low heads of O'Connor and Arnold (1973).

Pre-nuclear H*L, probably the commonest pre-nuclear contour, is just like the nuclear fall, except that it will tend to slope down more gradually, and take up the space between it and the next T*, a pattern earlier described as a result of 'partial linking' (Gussenhoven 1983b). Here, it is a case of right-alignment (see also chapter 7). In (18a), H*L occurs before H*L, while in (18b), it occurs before L*H. Similarly, pre-nuclear L*H is illustrated (18a,b) in the same contexts. Again, pre-nuclear L*H is like the nuclear pitch accent, except that the rise may take up the space available before the next accent. In (19a), the rise connects up with the target of H*, although an extra, faster rise may occur just before the target of H*. In (19b), the rise may end before the syllable preceding the next accent. In general, if the intervening stretch is long, the rise may end earlier, slowly rising patterns apparently being somewhat hard to produce.

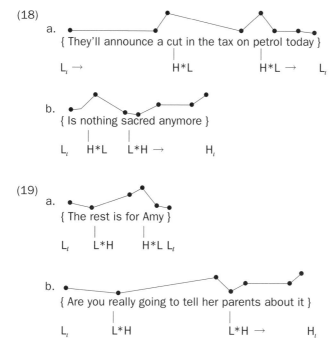

(18)

a.
{ They'll announce a cut in the tax on petrol today }

L$_I$ →   H*L   H*L →   L$_I$

b.
{ Is nothing sacred anymore }

L$_I$ H*L   L*H →   H$_I$

(19)

a.
{ The rest is for Amy }

L$_I$ L*H   H*L L$_I$

b.
{ Are you really going to tell her parents about it }

L$_I$ L*H   L*H →   H$_I$

Pre-nuclear H* occurs before H* H$_I$ in (20a). The second H* may be a little higher than the first, to increase perceptibility. Without final H$_I$, the pitch of the second H* may be a little lower, for the same reason. These are effects to be described in the phonetic implementation. The weak lowering will be different from DOWNSTEP (see section 15.5.3), which tends to be a larger step down. In (20b), H* occurs before L*H. If the interaccentual stretch is longer, some slumping down in the syllables before the second L* may occur without affecting the identity of the contour.

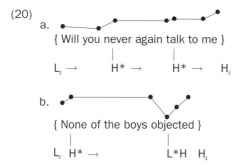

(20)

a.
{ Will you never again talk to me }

L$_I$ →   H* →   H* →   H$_I$

b.
{ None of the boys objected }

L$_I$ H* →   L*H   H$_I$

Pre-nuclear L* similarly describes a low level pre-nuclear stretch. In (21a) it is illustrated before H*L, while in (21b) it occurs before L*H. When L* precedes L* the pitch of each accented syllable and that of the intervening syllables may be very close, but the auditory impression of accentuation may nevertheless be very clear. Presumably, other phonetic features, like syllable duration and spectral tilt, may play a greater role in perception in this case. A similar comment applies to contours with sequences of three H*s, where the F_0 of the middle one may not stand out, but the accentuation is nevertheless clearly audible.

(21)

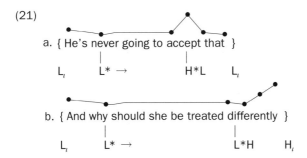

a. { He's never going to accept that }

    L_ι $L^* \rightarrow$ H^*L L_ι

b. { And why should she be treated differently }

    L_ι $L^* \rightarrow$ L^*H H_ι

To achieve the 'splayed' pronunciations of pre-nuclear bitonal pitch accents, ALIGN(T, Rt) could be made sensitive to the presence of a following T*.

15.4 Onsets

The unaccented syllables in the ι preceding the first accent, known as the 'prehead' (O'Connor and Arnold 1973) or 'onset' (Gussenhoven 1983b), have so far been given with low or mid pitch. This 'neutral' pronunciation is generally taken to result from the absence of a boundary tone (Liberman 1975; Pierrehumbert 1980; Beckman and Pierrehumbert 1986), which could be seen to explain the fact that the pitch tends to be mid, but might be low without changing the identity of the contour. I have assumed an initial L_ι for no other reason than that an L-boundary tone was used in the case of Swedish and French, but nothing hinges on this decision. It contrasts with a high beginning, described as H_ι, as in (22). Where the low onset is several syllables long, it typically falls somewhat from mid, while a longer high onset may fall slightly from high pitch. The frequency of the high onset may be biased towards occurrences before L*, except in the case of the low scathing contour, $L^* L_\iota$, where L_ι seems appropriate.

(22)

{ The man servant }

    H_ι $H^*L \rightarrow$ L_ι

Grammar (16) can thus be completed as (23), the mini-grammar announced in section 15.1. In the next section, it will be expanded so as to account for a range of further contours, which can largely be interpreted as variants of the contours described by this mini-grammar.

(23)

$$
\left\{ \begin{matrix} H_\iota \\ L_\iota \end{matrix} \right\}
\left\{ \begin{matrix} H^*(L) \\ L^*(H) \end{matrix} \right\}_0^n
\left\{ \begin{matrix} H^*(L) \\ L^*(H) \end{matrix} \right\}
\left\{ \begin{matrix} H_\iota \\ L_\iota \\ \emptyset \end{matrix} \right\}
$$

NoSlump

15.5 Expanding the tonal grammar

In this section, we discuss the pre-nuclear H*LH, the L-prefix (DELAY), DOWN-STEP, and Leading H, all of which elements will be incorporated in the grammar of (23), whose expanded version will appear in (43).

15.5.1 Pre-nuclear fall-rise

An unexpected feature of West Germanic intonation is the occurrence in pre-nuclear position of what in nuclear position amounts to a pitch accent plus a boundary tone. Nuclear contour H*L H_ι may appear as a rise-plus-steep fall on a pre-nuclear accented syllable, followed by a gradual rise. In (24a), the pre-nuclear fall–rise appears before nuclear H*L L_ι. It should be compared with H*LH$_\iota$ H*L L_ι in (24b), which is phonologically identical except for the intervening ι-boundary.

(24)

a. { But the finance committee }   { needn't be involved in this }

$L_\iota \rightarrow$ H*L $\rightarrow$ H_ι L_ι $\rightarrow$ H*L L_ι

b. { But the finance committee needn't be involved in this }

$L_\iota \rightarrow$ H*LH   H*L L_ι

It seems reasonable to think that non-final ιs that ended in H*L H_ι were at some point merged with a following ι occurring in the same υ. The stranded υ-internal H_ι could no longer be a boundary tone, and was treated in the same manner as the final tones of pre-nuclear H*L and L*H: its target drifted rightwards,

so as to end up before the next pitch accent. This analysis, given in Gussenhoven (1983b: 62ff.) as 'partial tone linking', has a number of advantages. It
first of all meshes with the rightward drift of trailing L and H of H*L and L*H,
and thus shows that right-alignment of a tone before T* is a general feature
of English. Second, pre-nuclear H*LH combines with other pitch accents, like
L*H, as in the surprised (25), which suggests it is freely usable in pre-nuclear
position.

(25)

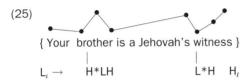

{ Your brother is a Jehovah's witness }
       | |
  L$_\iota$ →   H*LH   L*H   H$_\iota$

Third, it explains the similarity in meaning between the contours in (24a) and
(24b) (Gussenhoven 1983b, Cruttenden 1997: 67). This can be illustrated with
the minimal pair in (26a,b). The intonational phrase *HOPEfully he LOOKED
at her* is ambiguous between 'He looked at her hopefully', where the adverb
modifies the verb, and 'It is to be hoped that he looked at her', where the adverb
is a sentence modifier. When pronounced with a sharp fall on *Hope-* and a gradual rise across *-fully he*, as in (26a), the second meaning is preferred. Sentence
adverbials like *fortunately, hopefully, usually* typically take H*L H$_\iota$ when pronounced sentence-initially as a separate ι (Allerton and Cruttenden 1974, 1978),
and the interpretation of (26a) reflects this. By contrast, verb-modifying adverbs
typically take H*L in the same position, and (26b) therefore easily invokes the
latter meaning.

(26)

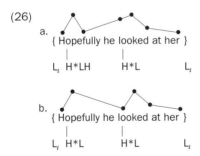

a.
{ Hopefully he looked at her }
       | |
  L$_\iota$ H*LH   H*L   L$_\iota$

b.
{ Hopefully he looked at her }
       | |
  L$_\iota$ H*L   H*L   L$_\iota$

15.5.2 Delay

As we have seen in chapters 3 and 4, phonetic implementation will allow speakers to have more or less rightward displacement of accent peaks. However, the
results of the experiment by Pierrehumbert and Steele (1989), summarized in
chapter 5, section 5.4, suggest that the 'scooped' contours of Vanderslice and
Ladefoged (1972) and Ladd (1980) are discretely different from the 'unscooped'
H*L L$_\iota$ and H*L H$_\iota$. In the scooped versions, low pitch appears in the accented

syllable, while the peak is shifted towards the right. Rise–fall(–rise) nuclear tones have in fact generally been recognized as distinct categories from the fall(–rise) tones (Crystal 1969; Halliday 1970; O'Connor and Arnold 1973; Pierrehumbert 1980). In Gussenhoven (1983b), I proposed a morpheme [DELAY] with the meaning 'significant' which could apply to H*L(H) and L*H, causing the starred tone to be realized late, in the next syllable over if there is one (cf. chapter 6, section 6.3.6). That is, if H*L$_i$ means 'Addition', its delayed version means 'significant addition' (cf. Brazil's 'intensified' falls Brazil (1975)).[2] Ladd (1983c) independently proposed a phonological feature [+delayed peak] for H*, replacing his earlier [+scooped].[3] Morpheme (27) was implemented by Gussenhoven and Rietveld (1992) as L-prefixation, whereby the L takes over the association with the accented syllable, and the H* is timed after L. To ensure the correct association, the star is transferred to the prefix-L: scooped H*L L$_i$ thus shows up as L*HL L$_i$.

(27) DELAY: [L* [T . . .]$_{PitchAccent}$]$_{PitchAccent}$ 'Significant'

In (28), both falls are delayed. As usual, the interaccentual slope is gradual. The monosyllabic use of L*HL H$_i$ is BrE; it is ruled out for AmE by Leben (1975). Because of their L-prefix, delayed pitch accents are morphologically complex. Implications of this view are discussed in sections 15.5.3 and 15.7.

(28)

{ But your auntie could change her mind   }

L$_i$ →   L*HL   L*HL H$_i$

15.5.3 Downstep

While the phenomenon had been described earlier (e.g. O'Connor and Arnold's (1973) 'terraced contour') Pierrehumbert (1980) was the first to incorporate downstep, which up to then had been applied to lexical tone, in the analysis of an intonation-only language. In Beckman and Pierrehumbert (1986), downstep applies to H* and their phrase accent H-, when occurring after a bitonal pitch accent. Ladd (1983c), with reference to Pierrehumbert (1980), pointed out that this analysis fails to capture the impressionistic similarity of different types of downstepped contours in English. The four panels in figure 15.2, from Ladd (1983c), reproduce four downstepping contours from her thesis. In contour (a), the first bitonal pitch accent causes downstep of the following H*, and because this pitch accent, too, is bitonal, the next H* is also downstepped. As explained in chapter 7, L* of H+L* is realized as ¹H* (i.e. the pitch accent amounts to H+¹H*). In contour (c) the second and third peaks are downstepped because they are preceded by a bitonal pitch accent, while the same is true in contour (d), except that the peaks are formed by the second tone of the bitonal pitch accent L*+H instead of the H* of L+H*. Ladd's point was that the representations of

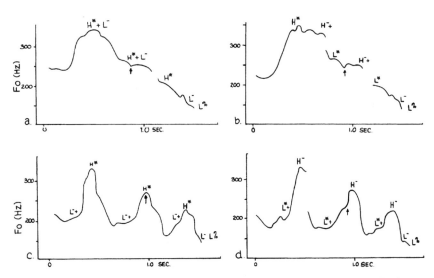

Fig. 15.2 Four downstepping contours in English, with transcriptions as per Beckman
and Pierrehumbert (1986). From Ladd (1983).

these four contours do not have more in common than each of them with, say,
L* L*+H L* L-H%, a contour without downstep. To remedy this, he introduced
a phonological feature [±downstep] for H-tones, turning $^{!}$H into a phonological
tone, rather than the result of an implementation rule (cf. section 6.3.4).

In addition to a rejection of the view that downstepped H is phonemically
H, not $^{!}$H, Ladd's proposal implies that downstepping contours should resemble
each other beyond the fact that they share the context for downstep. Strictly
speaking, this is comparable to requiring vowels before voiceless coda obstruents
in English to have a feature [+clipped], to reflect the fact that the context 'before
tautosyllabic fortis obstruent' will create a shortened vowel in words like *beat,
rice*, as compared to *bee, bead, rise*. What this suggests is that downstep is
a *morpheme*, adding a common element of meaning to contours that have it.[4]
Downstep was analysed as a morpheme for Dutch (Gussenhoven 1991b; van den
Berg, Gussenhoven, and Rietveld 1992), affixed to the ι, which is implemented
by downstepping H* after H (see also section 6.3.6 in chapter 6). The morpheme
is given as a feature on the ι, in (29), its implementation in (30).

(29) ENGLISH MORPHOLOGICAL DOWNSTEP: [DOWNSTEP]$\{ \ldots \}$

(30) ENGLISH DOWNSTEP: H* $\rightarrow$ $^{!}$H* / [DOWNSTEP] $\{ \ldots H \ldots \underline{\quad} \ldots \}$
(Implementation)

The representations of the four contours in figure 15.2 in my analysis are given
in (31). The contours in panels (a) and (b) are phonetic variants in our analysis,
and only differ in when the high pitch of *many inter-* is abandoned, allowing it to

slump down to the downstepped target of the H* on -*med*-.[5] Their representation is (31a). The contour in panel (c) is (31b) and consists of a series of H*L accents. The contour in panel (d), finally, is given in (31c). Even though I write the star on prefix-L of [DELAY] to express its timing, the H* that (29) applies to includes delayed H*.

(31) a. [DOWNSTEP]{L$_i$ H* H* H*L L$_i$}   (=contours a, b, fig. 15.2)
    b. [DOWNSTEP]{L$_i$ H*L H*L H*L L$_i$}   (=contour c)
    c. [DOWNSTEP]{L$_i$ L*HL L*HL L*HL L$_i$}   (=contour d)

An objection that could be raised against the analysis of downstep as a phrasal affix is that *nuclear* H* may escape downstep. As is clear from O'Connor and Arnold's (1973) 'High Drop' and 'Switchback' contours, downstep may leave the nuclear H* unaffected, which can be pronounced at high pitch, just as if there had been no downstep in ι (Gussenhoven 1983c; Ladd 1983c) (see also note 3). An example from Beckman and Pierrehumbert (1986) was given in figure 7.1 in chapter 7. The nuclear H* is alone in being able to escape downstep: an interruption at earlier points will create an ι-break. To account for this fact, Ladd (1993a) has suggested that ι is a branching constituent, whose right-hand head is the nucleus. A problem with this analysis is that the boundary between the pre-nuclear and nuclear constituents would have to occur in improbable locations, such as between *fall* and *through* in *The WHOLE BUSIness will FALL THROUGH* (Gussenhoven 1983c), or even in the middle of a word, as in (32).

(32)
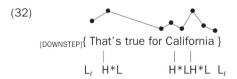

[DOWNSTEP]{ That's true for California }
              | | | |
            L$_i$ H*L   H*LH*L L$_i$

Recently, Truckenbrodt (2002a) has suggested that the difference between a consistently downstepped series of H*s and one whereby the last H* returns to the original pitch height, termed 'upstep' by Truckenbrodt, is to be accounted for by an association of the final, non-downstepped pitch accent to the ι-node, as opposed to an association to the node of a lower ranking accentual phrase.[6] In our OT model, where association with a constituent amounts to alignment with that constituent's right or left edge, Truckenbrodt's analysis amounts to a right-edge alignment of the last pitch accent, whose T* will associate with the last accented syllable. (Recall that 'accent' is independently present as a marker in representations, chapter 3.)

A downstepped nuclear H* is sometimes mistaken for lack of accent by inexperienced transcribers. The problem may be greater in German, where instead of a fall from mid to low pitch, there may be low pitch throughout the nuclear accented syllable in the equivalent contour, by the side of falls from mid to low (Grabe 1998a: 196). Since the low pitch resembles post-focal low pitch after H*L, confusion may arise when judging contours by themselves. A direct comparison of narrow-focus (33a) and downstepping (33b) shows that the difference lies mainly in the steeper fall for 'contrastive' H*L in (33a), which differs from the more sustained high pitch of H* in (33b).

(33)

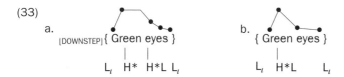

The phonological context of English downstep

While only H*, whether or not delayed, can undergo downstep, the H on its left in (cf. (30)) can come from different sources:

- H*, as in the examples presented so far;
- Initial H_i, as in (34). This intonation might be used when reading the title of a story which is subsequently read in full. The realization of H*L is the same as that of the last H*L in contours like (17a) (see also (22)).

(34)

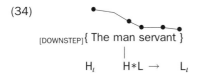

- Trailing H of L*H. This is shown in (35), where the highest pitch, coinciding approximately with *in the*, is due to trailing H.

(35)

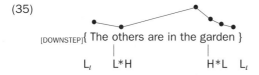

In addition to this morphologically triggered downstep, English has phonologically triggered downstep within the pitch accent. We turn to cases of this type in sections 15.5.4 and 15.6.

15.5.4   Leading H

Grice (1995b) drew attention to the contour in (37), where the high pitch on *the* cannot be explained as resulting from an initial H_i, owing to the low pitch on *To*.

Indeed, if we replace *To* with unaccented *And then we decided to go to*, it would still be the case that only *the* is high-pitched. That is, we are dealing with a contour like the French *cliché mélodique*, where the leading H is responsible for the high-pitched pre-accentual syllable and the downstepped H* on the accented syllable. Unlike other cases of downstep, downstep is independent of the [DOWNSTEP] morpheme, and purely phonologically triggered internally in the pitch accent (PA) (Grice 1995b). This is expressed in (36).

(36) English PA-Internal Downstep: H → !H / [H . . . __]$_{PitchAccent}$

Grice characterizes the contour as expressing predictable information: (37) could follow a rhetorical question by the same speaker.

(37)

{ To the market }

L$_I$ H+H*L L$_I$

Because downstepped nuclear H* has fairly low pitch, the question might arise why it is not analysed as L*. Recall that for French there were three arguments why that analysis is undesirable: defective distribution of L*, the independent need for a downstep rule for pre-nuclear H*, and the phonetic realization as a fall from mid to low (section 13.3.2). Since English has L* in many other locations, the first argument does not apply, but the other two do. Moreover, in the case of English, downstepped H* contrasts with L*. This was noted by Bruce Hayes (personal communication 1991), as shown in (38) (his examples, my transcription). Example (38a) uses a downstepped fall–rise as a listing intonation, while (38b) is a surprised question.

(38)

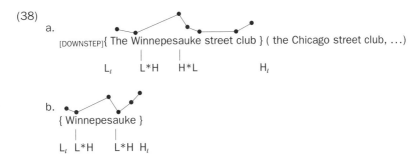

a.

[DOWNSTEP]{ The Winnepesauke street club } (the Chicago street club, ...)

L$_I$ L*H   H*L   H$_I$

b.

{ Winnepesauke }

L$_I$ L*H   L*H H$_I$

Grice pointed out that this contrast also exists after leading H. The difference may be subtle, as in the minimal pair in (39). This means that English has a morpheme meaning something like 'superfluous information', which takes the shape of (40). Leading H must be a rare feature of English intonation, and is possible on nuclear pitch accents only.

(39) a. [A: What are we still waiting for?]

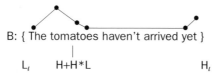

B: { The tomatoes haven't arrived yet }

L₁   H+H*L   H₁

b. [A: We've got all the salad stuff now, haven't we?]

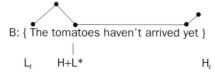

B: { The tomatoes haven't arrived yet }

L₁   H+L*   H₁

(40) ENGLISH LEADING H: [H+[T* . . .]ₚₐ]ₚₐ} 'Self evidence'

Analytically, Grice collapses (39a,b) with a right-shifted trailing H of a pre-nuclear L*H, as in (38a,b), respectively. This equation leaves unexplained why a leading H-tone is realized precisely in the preceding syllable, while a right-shifting trailing H will cause a gradual rising slope to the next accent. For instance, *In the direction of the MARket* pronounced with L₁ H+H*L₁ has low-pitched *In the direction of* and high-pitched *the*, but *In the diRECtion of the MARket* pronounced with L₁ L*H !H*L L₁ has rising pitch over *-ion of the*. This clear phonetic difference by itself already motivates a separation of leading H and right-shifting H, as in the analysis defended here. In addition, the present analysis correctly predicts that right-shifting H implies a preceding accent, while leading H does not.

Finally, I need to explain the dots in the context of PA-internal downstep (36), which imply that the H-tones within the pitch accent need not be adjacent. This configuration arises if H*L is provided *both* with leading H *and* with prefix-L. The prediction is that downstep on the second PA-internal H is obligatory. I believe the combination is grammatical, and also that the prediction of downstep is correct, as illustrated in (41).

(41)

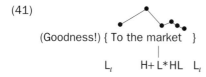

(Goodness!) { To the market   }

L₁   H+ L*HL L₁

The obligatory downstep is also evident in (42), where the high level is significantly lower than the target for the leading H. The example expresses exasperation at someone's habitual absence by listing the places (s)he appears to be going to. By contrast, downstep would not be obligatory in H₁ H*, the high level contour after a high onset.

(42)

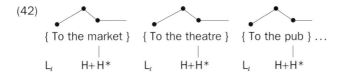

{ To the market }   { To the theatre }   { To the pub } ...

L_ι   H+H*   L_ι   H+H*   L_ι   H+H*

The discovery of two downstep 'rules' in English, a morphological one that attaches to the ι and a phonological one that applies within the pitch accent, may provide evidence for the morphological structure of English intonation. In particular, for the trailing H in (41) to undergo downstep, it must occur inside the same pitch accent as leading H, an analysis that is excluded if trailing H is taken to be a boundary tone of the Intermediate Phrase (see further section 15.8).

15.5.5 An extended tonal grammar

If the pre-nuclear fall–rise, downstep, L-prefixations, and leading-H are added to the mini-grammar of section 15.2.3, we arrive at (43). Clearly, although we still do not have a sizeable collection of exhaustive descriptions of intonation systems to measure this by, the intonation of English must be fairly complex. A coarse impression of the difference between English and French can be obtained by just comparing (43) as a typographical object with (35) in chapter 13. And we are not done yet, as English also has a vocative chant, to be discussed in the next section.

(43)

$$
([\text{DOWNSTEP}]) \begin{Bmatrix} H_\iota \\ L_\iota \end{Bmatrix} (L) \begin{Bmatrix} H^*(L(H)) \\ L^*(H) \end{Bmatrix}_0^n (H+)(L) \begin{Bmatrix} H^*(L) \\ L^*(H) \end{Bmatrix} \begin{Bmatrix} H_\iota \\ L_\iota \\ \emptyset \end{Bmatrix}
$$

N_oS_lump

15.6 The vocative chant

The vocative chant, briefly discussed in chapter 4, section 4.2.2, is a pitch accent consisting of a sequence of a high- and a mid-level pitch. The high pitch begins on the accented syllable, the mid pitch on a stressed syllable after the accented syllable, i.e. on the next foot, or if there is no stressed syllable, on the ι-final syllable (Liberman 1975; Ladd 1978; Hayes and Lahiri 1991b). The first syllable of each level, and optionally at most one unstressed syllable thereafter, is lengthened. This lengthening is phonological, in that it neutralizes the difference between short and long vowels, causing e.g. *Jen* and *Jane* to have the same duration when chanted (Hayes and Lahiri 1991b).

The two levels are obligatory, as shown in (45a), repeated from chapter 4, where they occur on an ι-final syllable, each of them lengthening one half of the syllable. In (45b), the second level starts on an ι-internal syllable, the beginning of a foot. In (45c), finally, the second level defaults to the ι-final syllable. The representation H*H (44) implies that ENGLISH PA-INTERNAL DOWNSTEP treats H after H* as a downstepped tone, i.e. the pitch accent appears as H*[!]H in the phonetics.

(44) H* H}   Vocative chant

(45)

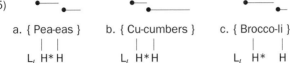

a. { Pea-eas }   b. { Cu-cumbers }   c. { Brocco-li }

L_l H* H L_l H* H L_l H*   H

The vocative chant is less felicitous if more than one foot follows the accented syllable (Bob Ladd, *voce*). While the words in (46a) readily lend themselves to the chant, this does not go for those in (46b). In this respect, the English vocative chant differs from its Dutch counterpart, which may have an indefinite number of post-nuclear feet, each of which may begin one of a series of descending levels (Gussenhoven 1993; Grice, Ladd, and Arvaniti 2000).

(46)   a.   'syn‚tax, 'cu‚cumber, 'coffee ma‚chine, 'air con‚ditioner
       b.   'sentence ‚syn‚tax, 'cu‚cumber ‚flavour

This pitch accent provides a diagnostic for secondary stress (Liberman 1975; Hayes 1995; Gussenhoven and Bruce 1999). For instance, the fact that the second syllable of *cucumber* starts the second pitch level implies that it is the head of a foot -*cumber*; in *cubicle*, a single foot, the second level occurs on the third syllable. As a result, the pitch accent can be used to diagnose the status of word-final syllables like -*ke* in *Nike*. If it is a foot, /kiː/, it ought to be hard to chant a compound containing the word: *NIke flavour!* should be less good than *COFFee flavour!*, independently of the peculiar semantics, and *INstant Nike!* should be hard compared to *INstant coffee!* By contrast, if the pronunciation is /ˈnaiki/, *Nike* should behave just like *coffee* (for English feet, see chapter 2, section 2.2.2).

According to Hayes and Lahiri (1991b), the representation of the English vocative chant includes a metrical component to account for the sustainment of the pitch as well as for the association of the H to an unaccented foot, for which see their paper or its summary in Gussenhoven (1993). This section considers the tonal representation. In addition to the vocative chant of (44), there is a version which has the second level fully low pitched, the 'low vocative chant' (47), illustrated in (49a). Its meaning differs from that of (44) in that it expresses impatience, in addition to routineness (*I've told you a thousand times!*). In addition, in Gussenhoven (1983b), I reported a wheedling version of the contour, in which the second level is followed by a rise in the last section of the last syllable, given in (48) and illustrated in (49b). The chants in (45), (49a), and (49b) reflect the three ways in which an *ι* can end in our analysis. The implementation module must be held responsible for the low-level realization of HL$_l$ in (49a).

(47) H* H L, Low vocative chant

(48) H* H H, Vocative fall-rise

While it appears to be ungrammatical to have leading H in any of these contours, prefix-L would seem possible. When combined with (44), the pitch for the vowel begins low, and the two levels are carried out as usual. The meaning of this contour results from the two morphemic meanings: there is routine, due to the vocative chant, but at the same time the contour signals there is some special significance. It is shown in (49c).

(49)

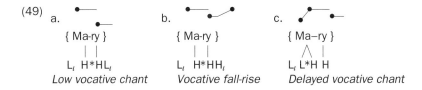

a. { Ma-ry }   b. { Ma-ry }   c. { Ma–ry }

L, H*HL,   L, H*HH,   L, L*H H

Low vocative chant   *Vocative fall-rise*   *Delayed vocative chant*

15.7 Tone Copy

Finally, there is the question that arose in section 14.4.3. How are encliticized ιs pronounced? The pitch contour of such an unaccented ι depends on that of the preceding ι. With reference to Dutch, Gussenhoven (1987b) formulated a rule of TONE COPY (see also Pierrehumbert 1980: 51, Gussenhoven 1987a, 1990 for English; and Ladd 1996: 141 for French). In a frequent pattern, the last two tones after T* of the preceding ι are copied to the encliticized ι. In (50a,b,c), this is illustrated for H*L L,, H*L H, and L*H H,, respectively. Notice how the enclitized ι of (50b) begins low-pitched, but that in (50c) mid-pitched, which difference is to be attributed to the value of the trailing tone, L in (50b), but H in (50c).

(50)

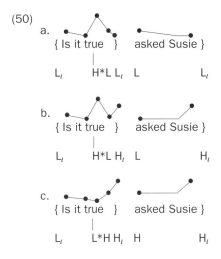

a. { Is it true } asked Susie }

L,   H*L L,   L   L,

b. { Is it true } asked Susie }

L,   H*L H,   L   H,

c. { Is it true } asked Susie }

L,   L*H H,   H   H,

Prefix L of L*HL (section 15.5.2) is ignored by the rule. That is, reporting clauses after delayed pitch accents and their non-delayed counterparts are indistinguishable. The rule may serve to distinguish truncated half-completed falls that look like rising movements from real rises. In (51), for instance, the H*L on *it*, with its short vowel before [t], may look and sound like a rising movement, but the pitch of the reporting clause treats it as a half-completed fall.[7]

(51)

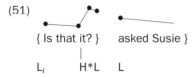

{ Is that it? }   asked Susie }

L*ɩ*   H*L   L

An alternative pronunciation of the enclitic *ɩ* has low pitch regardless of the preceding tones, which may represent a phonologically toneless expression. Recall, too, that the reporting clause may be incorporated in the preceding *ɩ*, causing the entire expression to be pronounced as a single *ɩ*, as explained in section 14.4.3.

15.8 Some comparisons with Pierrehumbert and Beckman's analysis

An important feature of the description in this chapter is that it assumes a single tonally defined domain, the *ɩ*, rather than two, *ɩ* and a lower ranking intermediate phrase (ip). It is evident that intonational breaks in English vary in salience. For instance, when an actor rehearsing Shakespeare's *As You Like It* produces the *υ*-medial H*ɩ* of (52a), he will more clearly interrupt his line than if he were to produce the toneless *ɩ*-boundary of (52b). The latter pronunciation may be phonetically close to the single *ɩ*-version (52c) (which might well in fact be more to the liking of his director).

(52)

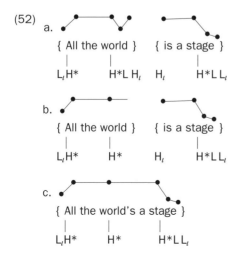

a.

{ All the world }   { is a stage }

L*ɩ*H*   H*L H*ɩ*   H*ɩ*   H*L L*ɩ*

b.

{ All the world }   { is a stage }

L*ɩ*H*   H*   H*ɩ*   H*L L*ɩ*

c.

{ All the world's a stage }

L*ɩ*H*   H*   H*L L*ɩ*

In Beckman and Pierrehumbert (1986) as well as in ToBI (Beckman and Ayers 1994) (see also sections 7.2.7 and 7.3), (52a) would have an ι-break, (52b) an ip-break, and (52c) would have no break. In our analysis, the phrasing difference is between (52a,b), on the one hand, and (52c), on the other. It determines, for instance, whether *is* can have a reduced form [z] (Selkirk 1984). The difference between (52a) and (52b) in the salience of the break after *world* is due to the tonal structure.[8] In fact, other tonal treatments of the internal ι-boundary are likely to lead to finer distinctions. Contours L*H} and H*L}, for instance, will create intermediate impressions. Yet, this will not motivate the existence of a further intonational constituent.

The ip has never been shown to fulfil a role that cannot be catered for by φ and ι. It has been claimed to be the domain of rhythmic adjustments, as if it were the φ (Beckman and Pierrehumbert 1986; Nespor 1999; Shattuck-Hufnagel, Ostendorf, and Ross 1979), but rhythmic clash-based readjustments in pitch-accent distribution do not necessarily occur in domains that are closed off by an intonational break. While (53) can be pronounced with or without an intonational break between *ChiNESE* and *STRIKE*, clash resolution is ungrammatical (*CHInese will STRIKE), in any style in British English, while in (53b), clash resolution is obligatory. It is the φ-structure that explains these facts, and so any role for the ip must be sought elsewhere. Earlier, it was argued that two examples of ip-boundaries were readily reanalysed (see sections 7.2.1 and 15.5.3).

(53) a. The ChiNESE will STRIKE when they have a SERious GRIEvance
     b. CHInese LANterns are FUN

In addition, the Pierrehumbert–Beckman analysis predicts ip-boundaries in suspect locations. For instance, their prediction that a steep fall implies an intonational boundary runs foul of example (24a), repeated here as (54), which can only be described in their system by assuming a phrase accent L- after the first accent. The problem is threefold. First, there is no perceivable intonational break in the stretch between the accented syllables *fi-* and *-volved* to begin with. Second, if there *were* a phrase break, it would come after *committee*, not after *fi-*, but the low pitch occurs after *fi-*. Third, if we replaced *needn't* with *has been*, a pronunciation of *has* as [z] is entirely grammatical, which confirms that there is no break after *committee*.

(54)

There is a similar problem in contours with pre-nuclear H*L, as pointed out by Ladd (1996: 96). If the fall of the pre-nuclear peak is rapid and to low pitch, the impression of an ι-boundary is unmistakable and unproblematic in either

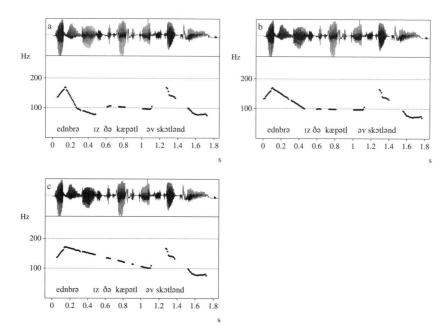

Fig. 15.3 Three F_0 manipulations of the same source utterance *Edinburgh is the capital of Scotland*. The contour in panel (a) has an internal *ι*-boundary; those in panel (b) and (c) do not.

analysis. If the fall is slower or less deep, the impression of a boundary disappears. However, it is not evident that an intermediate kind of boundary is to be perceived between this slacker fall and a slowly descending slope between the first peak and the beginning of the next. I give the F_0 tracks of three manipulated versions of the same source utterance in figure 15.3. Contour (a) has an internal *ι*-boundary. Contours (b) and (c) are predicted to be identical by our analysis, both being instances of L_ι H*L H*L L_ι which vary in the amount of rightward shifting of the first trailing L-tone. Indeed, although phonetically these contours are different, they sound similar. By contrast, ToBI must find employment for both H* L-L+H* L-L% and H* L+H* L-L%, in addition to H* L-L% L+H* L-L%, but no evidently contrasting contour triplet seems available for these representations.

In addition, there are a number of contrasts that ToBI cannot express. Earlier, Nolan and Grabe (1997) deplored the inability of ToBI to describe late post-focal falls. Since H-L% is used to represent mid pitch, there is no representation available for the level-slump of urban varieties spoken in the north of England and in Northern Ireland (see section 15.2.4). Some contrasts are not accommodated in ToBI, like that between 'scathing intonation' (12a) and the low-level contour (12b), or the three varieties of the vocative chant.

While these latter problems could be solved by expanding the ToBI system, the decision to have two tonally defined domains seems a more fundamental problem.

Finally, there is the problem of Pierrehumbert and Beckman's superfluous L+H*. If we ignore non-downstepped H$_2$ H*L L$_\iota$ and H$_2$ L*HL L$_\iota$ and down-stepped H$_2$ L*HL L$_\iota$, a monosyllabic utterance like *Fine!* can have three types of fall, a downstepped fall, a plain fall, and a delayed fall, as shown respectively in (55). This description, including the characterization of (55b) alone as morphologically simplex, seems entirely satisfactory. In ToBI, pronunciation (55a) is %H ¹H* L-L%, (55b) is H* L-L%, and (55c) is L*+H L-L%. However, ToBI predicts the existence of a fourth contour, L+H* L-L%, which must be like (55d), but have an earlier peak than (55c). This prediction seems wrong. If downstep is included, English has three contrastively aligned accentual falls (cf. Kohler 1990 for German), not four.

(55)

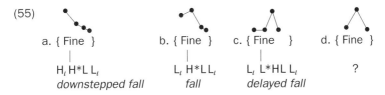

a. { Fine }

|

H$_\iota$ H*L L$_\iota$

downstepped fall

b. { Fine }

|

L$_\iota$ H*L L$_\iota$

fall

c. { Fine }

|

L$_\iota$ L*HL L$_\iota$

delayed fall

d. { Fine }

?

15.9 Conclusion

Perhaps even more so than previous analyses of English, the above application of the Autosegmental–Metrical model to the intonation of British English has revealed a highly complex system, which nevertheless yields to a grammar taking just a few lines of print. Among the features of Gussenhoven (1983b), I have been able to maintain (a) an 'off-ramp' analysis, i.e. one employing bitonal pitch accents with trailing tones only; (b) a single intonational phrase; (c) right-aligning trailing tones in pre-nuclear pitch accents; and (d) the pre-nuclear occurrence of H*L H. Features (a) and (b) were adopted from the 'British' tradition, as represented for instance in O'Connor and Arnold (1973), while (c) and (d) followed from an interpretation of their 'heads' as pre-nuclear nuclear pitch accents. In addition, the three right-edge conditions (L$_\iota$, H$_\iota$, and no boundary tone), introduced in the computer implementation of that description (Gussenhoven and Rietveld 1992) (see also section 7.3.2 and Grabe 1998a) were consistently found to produce the correct contours, as in the case of the vocative chant. While 'delayed rises', i.e. L*LH, could not be shown to be a distinct contour from L* H$_\iota$, the implementation of delay as L-prefixation in Gussenhoven and Rietveld (1992) was maintained, which analysis characterizes L*HL as a kind of fall, H*L, not a kind of rise, L*H. *Tone Copy* and the notion of unaccented ιs, here encliticized ιs, was carried over from Gussenhoven (1987a). I have included two less-common contour types, scathing intonation and leading H, reported by Monaghan (2000) and Grice (1995b), respectively, as well as the high rise (H* H$_\iota$), whose existence as a separate contour from L*H H$_\iota$ had escaped me until the mid-nineties. Downstep of H* was shown to represent two phenomena. First, there is a phonologically triggered (i.e. obligatory) PA-INTERNAL

DOWNSTEP of H* after any H within the pitch accent; and second, a morphologically triggered rule downstepping H* after any H-tone within the ι, ENGLISH DOWNSTEP. Moreover, I included examples of (morphological) downstep after initial H$_\iota$, a phenomenon first pointed out to me by Peter van der Vliet (personal communication around 1992). The rule of ENGLISH UPSTEP applies to H$_\iota$ after H. As always, many issues remain.

Notes

1. Brazil, like others writing in the British English tradition, uses 'high rise' for L*H H$_\iota$, taking the adjective to refer to the contour end-point, rather than the beginning-point, as in the American usage. In British English usage, 'low rise' refers to a contour which does not rise a great deal, due to a reduced pitch span; or to a contour to be described later as the 'low low rise'. In the literature on British English, no distinction is usually made between what are here called the low rise and the high rise, and both would presumably count as 'high rises' (but see Crystal 1969). Brazil's meaning of his 'low rise', i.e. a low rise with reduced pitch range, was that of 'neutrality', of a withdrawal from the informational interaction.
2. My delayed L*H has not been recognized as a contour by other researchers (Cruttenden 1997: 123); indeed, the hypothesis that delayed rises are morphologically akin to delayed falls requires more evidence if it is to be upheld.
3. Bob Ladd and I had frequent and lively discussions on the structure of the intonation of English in 1981, and, as he notes in his book, the correct attribution of some of the similar elements in our analyses may be unclear.
4. In a different context, Ladd (1993a) observed that downstep is in fact meaningful.
5. I find that native speakers cannot readily hear (a) and (b) as distinct, and need guidance to hear the difference in resynthesized utterances, while each of (a) and (b) is easily distinguished from both (c) and (d).
6. For this solution to work, the assumption of an Accentual Phrase is not really needed, since the pre-nuclear accents could be distinguished from the nuclear one in not having any association with a prosodic constituent.
7. A case like (51), in which only the trailing tone appears to be copied, suggests that there should be minimally one tone. Perhaps the generalization is that the copy contains minimally one and maximally two tones, one of which must be left-aligned, to exclude the occurrence of a solitary T$_\iota$ in the enclitic ι.
8. It is striking that examples of υ-internal ι-breaks in work that uses the ip are virtually always marked by H*L H$_\iota$.

References

Abe, I. (1980). How vocal pitch works. See Waugh and Van Schooneveld (1980), pp. 1–24.

Abrahamson, A. S. (1999). Fundamental frequency as a cue to word-initial consonant length: Pattani Malay. In *Proceedings of the 14th International Congress of Phonetic Sciences*, Volume 1, pp. 591–594.

Ahoua, F. (1996). *Prosodic Aspects of Baule.* Cologne: Køppe.

Akinlabi, A. and M. Liberman (forthcoming). Tonal complexes and tonal alignment. *Proceedings of the North East Linguistic Society (NELS)* 31.

Allerton, D. and A. Cruttenden (1974). English sentence adverbials: their syntax and their intonation in British English. *Lingua* 34, 1–29.

Allerton, D. and A. Cruttenden (1978). Syntactic, illocutionary, thematic and attitudinal factors in the intonation of adverbials. *Journal of Pragmatics* 2, 155–188.

Andersen, T. (1987). The phonemic system of Agar Dinka. *Journal of African Languages and Linguistics* 9, 1–27.

Anderson, A. H., M. Bader, E. G. Bard, E. Boyle, G. Doherty, S. Garrod, S. Isard, J. Kowtko, J. McAllister, J. Miller, C. Sotillo, H. Thompson, and R. Weinert (1991). The HCRC Map Task Corpus. *Language and Speech* 34, 351–366.

Anttila, A. (1997). Variation, change and phonological theory. In F. Hinskens, R. van Hout, and W. L. Wetzels (eds.), *Deriving Variation from Grammar*, pp. 35–68. Amsterdam: Benjamins.

Anttila, A. and A. B. Bodomo (2000). Tonal polarity in Dagaare. In V. Carstens and F. Parkinsons (eds.), *Trends in African Linguistics 4: Advances in African linguistics*, pp. 119–134. Trenton, NJ: African World Press.

Appels, R. (1985). Een productiemodel voor declinatie en onderzoek naar declinatie-resets binnen spraakuitingen. Internal Report no. 498, Institute for Perception Research, Eindhoven.

Arvaniti, A. (1994). Acoustic features of Greek rhythmic structure. *Journal of Phonetics* 22, 239–268.

Arvaniti, A. and M. Baltazani (2003). Intonational analysis and prosodic annotation of Greek spoken corpora. In S.-A. Jun (ed.), *Prosodic Typology and Transcription: A Unified Approach*, Oxford: Oxford University Press.

Arvaniti, A., D. Ladd, and I. Mennen (2000). What is a starred tone? Evidence from Greek. See Broe and Pierrehumbert (2000), pp. 119–131.

Bakkes, P. (1996). *Variatie en verandering in het Montforts.* Amsterdam: J. P. Meertens-Instituut.

Banti, G. (1988). Two Cushitic systems: Somali and Oromo nouns. See Hulst and Smith (1988), pp. 10–49.

Bao, Z. (1999). *The Structure of Tone.* Oxford: Oxford University Press.

Bartels, C. (1997). *Towards a compositional interpretation of English statement and question intonation.* Ph.D. thesis, University of Massachusetts at Amherst.

Basbøll, H. (2003). Prosody, productivity and word structure: the stød pattern of Modern Danish. *Nordic Journal of Linguistics* 26, 5–44.

Bateman, J. (1990). Iau segmental and tone phonology. In B. K. Purwo (ed.), *Miscellaneous Studies of Indonesian and Other Languages in Indonesia*, Jakarta, pp. 29–42. Badan Penyelenggara Seri NUSA, Universitas Atma Jaya.

Bearth, T. (1971). *l'Enoncé Toura.* Ph.D. thesis, University of Geneva.

Beattie, G. W., A. Cutler, and M. Pearson (1982). Why is Mrs Thatcher interrupted so often? *Nature* 300, 744–747.

Beck, J. M. (1997). Organic variation of the vocal apparatus. In *The Handbook of Phonetic Sciences*, pp. 256–297. Oxford: Blackwell.

Beckman, J. N. (1997). Positional faithfulness, positional neutralisation and Shona height harmony. *Phonology* 14, 1–46.

Beckman, M. E. (1986). *Stress, and Non-stress Accent.* Dordrecht: Foris.

Beckman, M. E. (1996). The parsing of prosody. *Language and Cognitive Processes* 11, 17–67.

Beckman, M. E. and G. M. Ayers (1994). ToBI annotation conventions. <http://ling.ohio-state.edu/~tobi/ame_tobi/>

Beckman, M. E. and J. Edwards (1990). Lengthenings and shortenings and the nature of prosodic constituency. See Kingston and Beckman (1990), pp. 152–178.

Beckman, M. E. and J. B. Pierrehumbert (1986). Intonational structure in English and Japanese. *Phonology Yearbook* 3, 255–309.

Bel, B. and I. Marlien (eds.) (2002). *Speech Prosody 2002. An International Conference*, Aix-en-Provence. Laboratoire Parole et Langage, CNRS and Université de Provence.

Berinstein, A. (1979). A cross-linguistic study: the perception and production of stress. *UCLA Working Papers in Phonetics* 47. Los Angeles: UCLA Phonetic Laboratory.

Besch, W., U. Knoop, W. Putschke, and H. E. Wiegand (eds.) (1983). *Dialektologie. Ein Handbuch zur deutschen und algemeinen Dialektforschung.* Berlin: de Gruyter.

Bezooijen, R. v. (1984). *Characteristics and recognizability of vocal expressions of emotion.* Dordrecht: Foris.

Bezooijen, R. v. (1993). Verschillen in toonhoogte: Natuur of cultuur? *Gramma/TTT* 2, 165–179.

Bezooijen, R. v. (1995). Sociocultural aspects of pitch differences between Japanese and Dutch women. *Language and Speech* 38, 253–265.

Biemans, M. (2000). *Gender Variation in Voice Quality.* Utrecht: Landelijke Onderzoekschool Taalwetenschap LOT, Utrecht University.

Bing, J. M. (1979). Aspects of English prosody. Distributed by Indiana University Linguistics Club (IULC). Bloomington, Indiana.

Bird, C. S. (1966). *Aspects of Bambara syntax.* Ph.D. thesis, UCLA.

Boersma, P. (1998). *Functional Phonology: Formalizing the Interactions Between Articulatory and Perceptual Drives.* The Hague: Holland Academic Graphics.

Bolinger, D. (1951). Intonation – levels versus configurations. *Word* 7, 199–200.

Bolinger, D. (1958). A theory of pitch accent in English. *Word* 14, 109–149. Reprinted in Bolinger (1965), pp. 101–117.

Bolinger, D. (1961). *Generality, Gradience and the All-or-None.* The Hague: Mouton.

Bolinger, D. (1964). Around the edge of language: Intonation. *Harvard Educational Review* 34, 282–293. Reprinted in Bolinger (1972), pp. 19–29.

Bolinger, D. (1965). Pitch accent and sentence rhythm. In Isamu Abe and Tetsuya Kanekiyo (eds.), *Forms of English: Accent, Morpheme, Order*, pp. 139–180. Tokyo: Hokuou.

Bolinger, D. (1972). *Intonation: Selected Readings.* Harmondsworth: Penguin.

Bolinger, D. (1978). Intonation across languages. In J. Greenberg (ed.), *Universals of Human Language*, Volume 2 (*Phonology*), pp. 471–524. Stanford: Stanford University Press.

Bolinger, D. (1981). Two kinds of vowels, two kinds of rhythm. Included as Appendix A in Bolinger (1986).

Bolinger, D. (1986). *Intonation and its Parts: The Melody of Language.* Stanford, CA: Stanford University Press.

Bolinger, D. (1998). American English. See Hirst and Di Cristo (1998), pp. 45–55.

Botinis, A. (ed.) (2000). *Intonation: Analysis, Modeling and Technology*, Dordrecht: Kluwer.

Botinis, A., G. Kouroupetroglou, and G. Carayannis (eds.) (1997). *Intonation: Theory, Models and Applications. Proceedings of an ESCA Workshop*, Athens (Greece). ESCA and University of Athens, Department of Informatics.

Braunschweiler, N. (2003). *Automatic Detection of Prosodic Cues.* Ph.D. thesis, University of Constance.

Brazil, D. (1975). *Discourse Intonation I.* Birmingham: English Language Research, Birmingham University.

Brazil, D. (1985). *The Communicative Value of English.* Birmingham: Bleak House Books. Published jointly with English Language Research, University of Birmingham.

Brazil, D., M. Coulthard, and C. Johns (1980). *Discourse Intonation and Language Teaching.* London: Longman.

Broe, M. and J. B. Pierrehumbert (eds.) (2000). *Papers in Laboratory Phonology V: Acquisition and the Lexicon.* Cambridge: Cambridge University Press.

Brown, P. and S. C. Levinson (1987). *Politeness: Some Universals in Language Usage.* Cambridge: Cambridge University Press.

Bruce, G. (1977). *Swedish Word Accents in Sentence Perspective.* Lund: Gleerup.

Bruce, G. (1987). How floating is focal accent. In K. Gregersen and H. Basbøll (eds.), *Nordic Prosody* IV, pp. 41–49. Odense: Odense University Press.

Bruce, G. (1990). Alignment and composition of tonal accents: Comments on Silverman and Pierrehumbert's paper. See Kingston and Beckman (1990), pp. 107–114.

Bruce, G. (2001). Secondary stress and pitch accent synchronization in Swedish. In W. A. van Dommelen and T. Fretheim (eds.), *Nordic Prosody. Proceedings of the VIIIth Conference*, pp. 33–44. Frankfurt am Main: Peter Lang.

Bruce, G. and B. Hermans (1999). Word tone in Germanic languages. See van der Hulst (1999), pp. 605–658.

Büring, D., M. Gordon, and C. L. Lee (eds.) (forthcoming). *Topic and Focus: Papers from a Workshop on Intonation and Meaning*, Dordrecht. Kluwer.

Burzio, L. (1994). *Principles of English Stress*. Cambridge: Cambridge University Press.

Bush, R. (1999). Georgian yes–no question intonation. In *Phonology at Santa Cruz*, Volume 6, pp. 1–11. Santa Cruz, CA: UC Santa Cruz, Department of Linguistics.

Cahill, M. (2000). Tonal diversity in languages of Papua New Guinea. Paper presented at the Tromsø Tone Symposium, University of Tromsø, 5–7 June 2000.

Cajot, J. (2001). Een toonloze enclave in polytoon gewaand gebied. Een les in structurele fonologie? *Jaarboek van de Vereniging voor Limburgse Dialect-en Naamkunde* 3, 71–88.

Cambier-Langeveld, T. (2000). *Temporal Marking of Accent and Boundaries*. The Hague: Thesus (Subsidiary of Holland Academic Graphics).

Cambier-Langeveld, T. and A. E. Turk (1999). A cross-linguistic study of accentual lengthening: Dutch vs. English. *Journal of Phonetics* 27, 255–280.

Campbell, W. N. (1995). Loudness, spectral tilt, and perceived prominence in dialogues. In *Proceedings of the 13th International Congress of Phonetic Sciences*, Volume 3, pp. 676–679.

Caspers, J. (2003). Local speech melody as a limiting factor in the turn-taking system of Dutch. *Journal of Phonetics* 31, 251–276.

Cassimjee, F. and C. J. Kisseberth (1999). Tonal variation across Emakhuwa dialects. See Kaji (1999), pp. 261–287.

Chao, Y.-R. (1930). A system of tone letters. *Le Maître Phonétique* 45, 24–27.

Chen, A., C. Gussenhoven, and T. Rietveld (2002). Language-specific uses of the Effort Code. See Bel and Marlien (2002), pp. 211–214.

Chen, A., T. Rietveld, and C. Gussenhoven (1999). Language-specific effects of pitch range on the perception of universal intonational meaning. In *Proceedings of the 9th Eurospeech Conference*, Volume II, pp. 1403–1406.

Chen, Matthew, Y. (2000). *Tone Shandhi: Patterns across Chinese Dialects*. Cambridge: Cambridge University Press.

Cho, T. and P. A. Keating (2001). Articulatory and acoustic studies of domain-initial strengthening in Korean. *Journal of Phonetics* 29, 155–190.

Chomsky, N. and M. Halle (1986). *The Sound Pattern of English*. New York: Harper and Row.

Clements, G. (1979). The description of terraced-level tone languages. *Language* 55, 536–558.

Clements, G. (1996). Review of van der Hulst and Snider (1993). *Language* 72, 847–852.

Clements, G. N. (1983). The hierarchical representation of tone features. In *Current Approaches to African Linguistics*, Volume I, pp. 145–176. Dordrecht: Foris.

Clements, G. N. (1990). The status of register in intonation theory. See Kingston and Beckman (1990), pp. 58–71.

Clements, G. N. and K. C. Ford (1980). On the phonological status of downstep in Kikuyu. See Goyvaerts (1980), pp. 309–357.

Clements, G. N. and J. Goldsmith (1984a). Autosegmental studies in Bantu tone: Introduction. See Clements and Goldsmith (1984b), pp. 1–18.

Clements, G. N. and J. Goldsmith (eds.) (1984b). *Autosegmental Studies in Bantu Tone*, Dordrecht: Foris.

Clements, G. N. and S. J. Keyser (1983). *CV-phonology*. Cambridge, MA: MIT Press.

Cohen, A. and J. t. Hart (1967). On the anatomy of intonation. *Lingua* 19, 177–192.

Cohn, A. (1990). *Phonetic and phonological rules of nasalization.* Ph.D. thesis, UCLA.

Collier, R. (1975a). Perceptual and linguistic tolerance in intonation. *International Review of Applied Linguistics* 13, 293–308.

Collier, R. (1975b). Physiological correlates of intonation patterns. *Journal of the Acoustic Society of America* 58, 249–255.

Connell, B. (2000). The perception of lexical tone in Mambila. *Language and Speech* 43, 163–182.

Connell, B. (2002). Tone languages and the universality of intrinsic f_0: Evidence from Africa. *Journal of Phonetics* 30, 101–129.

Connell, B. and D. R. Ladd (1990). Aspects of pitch realisation in Yoruba. *Phonology* 7, 1–29.

Couper-Kuhlen, E. (1986). *An Introduction to English Prosody.* Tübingen: Niemeyer.

Cruttenden, A. (1997). *Intonation* (2nd edn.). Cambridge: Cambridge University Press.

Cruttenden, A. (2001). Mancunian intonation and intonational representation. *Phonetica* 58, 53–80.

Crystal, D. (1969). *Prosodic Systems and Intonation in English.* Cambridge: Cambridge University Press.

Crystal, D. (1987). *The Cambridge Encyclopedia of Language.* Cambridge: Cambridge University Press.

Cutler, A. and D. R. Ladd (eds.) (1983). *Prosody – Models and Measurements.* Berlin: Springer.

Cutting, J. E., B. Rosner, and C. Foard (1976). Categories and boundaries in speech and music. *Quarterly Journal of Experimental Psychology* 28, 361–378.

Dainora, A. (2001). *An empirically based probabilistic model of intonation of American English.* Ph.D. thesis, University of Chicago.

Dainora, A. (2002). Does intonational meaning come from tones or tunes? Evidence against a compositional approach. See Bel and Marlien (2002), pp. 235–338.

de Jong, K. J. (1995). The supraglottal articulation of prominence in English: Linguistic stress as localized hyperarticulation. *Journal of the Acoustic Society of America* 97, 491–504.

de Lacy, P. (draft). Intonation in Maori. University of Massachusetts at Amherst.

de Pijper, J. W. (1983). *Modelling British English Intonation.* Dordrecht: Foris.

de Vaan, M. (1999). Towards an explanation of the Franconian tone accents. *Amsterdamer Beiträge zur Älteren Germanistik* 51, 23–44.

de Vaan, M. (2002). Wgm *ī en *ū vóór *r* in Zuid-Limburg. *Taal en Tongval* 54, 171–182.

Delais, E. (1995). *Pour une approche parallèle de la structure prosodique.* Ph.D. thesis, Université de Toulouse-Le Mirail.

Di Cristo, A. (1998). Intonation in French. See Hirst and Di Cristo (1998), pp. 195–218.

Di Cristo, A. (1999). Vers une modélisation de l'accentuation de français. première partie: la problématique. *Journal of French Language Studies* 9, 143–179.

Di Cristo, A. (2000). Vers une modélisation de l'accentuation du français. *Journal of French Language Studies* 10, 27–44.

Di Cristo, A. and D. Hirst (1993a). Prosodic regularities in the surface structure of French questions. See House and Touati (1993), pp. 268–271. Working papers 41.

Di Cristo, A. and D. Hirst (1993b). Prosodic regularities in the surface structure of French questions. See House and Touati (1993), pp. 268–271. Working papers 41.

Di Cristo, A. and L. Jankowsky (1999). Prosodic organization and phrasing after focus in French. In *Proceedings of the 14th International Congress of Phonetic Sciences*, Volume 2, pp. 1565–1568.

Diehl, R. L. (1991). The role of phonetics within the study of language. *Phonetica* 48, 120–134.

D'Imperio, M. (1997). Narrow focus and focal accent in the Neapolitan variety of Italian. See Botinis, Kouroupetroglou, and Carayannis (1997), pp. 87–90.

D'Imperio, M. and D. House (1997). Perception of questions and statements in Neapolitan Italian. In *Proceedings of EUROSPEECH '97*, Volume 1, pp. 251–254.

Dobrovolsky, M. (1997). Animal communication. In W. O'Grady, M. Dobrovolsky, and F. Katamba (eds.), *Contemporary Linguistics. An Introduction*, pp. 625–663. London and New York: Longman.

Docherty, G. and D. R. Ladd (eds.) (1992). *Papers in Laboratory Phonology II: Gesture, Segment, Prosody*. Cambridge: Cambridge University Press.

Donohue, M. (1997). Tone systems in New Guinea. *Linguistic Typology* 1, 347–386.

Downing, L. (1970). *Syntactic structure and phonological phrasing in English*. Ph.D. thesis, University of Texas, Austin, Texas.

Downing, L. (forthcoming). Accent in African languages. In R. Goedemans and H. Van der Hulst (eds.), *Stress Patterns of the World: Data*. Amsterdam: Benjamins.

Downing, L. J. (1996). *The Tonal Phonology of Jita*. Munich: LINCOM Europa.

Downing, L. J. (1998). On the prosodic misalignment of onsetless syllables. *Natural Language and Linguistic Theory* 16, 1–52.

Duanmu, S. (2000). *The Phonology of Standard Chinese*. Oxford: Oxford University Press.

Dwyer, D. (1978). What sort of tone language is Mende? *Studies in African Linguisics* 9, 167–208.

Edmondson, T. and J. T. Bendor-Samuel (1966). Tone patterns of Etung. *Journal of African Languages* 5, 1–6.

Elenbaas, N. (1999). *A Unified Account of Binary and Ternary Stress: Considerations from Sentani and Finnish*. The Hague: Holland Academic Graphics.

Elordieta, G. (1997). Accent, tone and intonation in Lekeitio Basque. In F. Martínez-Gil and A. Morales-Front (eds.), *Issues in the Phonology and Morphology of the Major Iberian Languages*, pp. 4–78. Washington, DC: Georgetown University Press.

Elordieta, G. (1998). Intonation in a pitch-accent variety of Basque. *Anuario del Seminario de Filología Vasca Julio de Urquijo (International Journal of Basque Linguistics and Philology)* 32, pp. 511–569.

Elordieta, G. (forthcoming). Constraints on intonational prominence of focalized constituents. See Büring, Gordon, and Lee (forthcoming).

Elordieta, G. (forthcoming). Intonation. In J. I. Hualde and J. O. de Urbina (eds.), *A Grammar of Basque*. Berlin: Mouton de Gruyter.

Elordieta, G., I. Gaminde, I. Hernáez, J. Salaberria, and I. Martín de Vidales (1999). Another step in the modeling of Basque intonation: Bermeo. In V. Matoušek, P. Mautner, J. Ocelíková, and P. Sojka (eds.), *Text, Speech and Dialogue*, pp. 361–364. Berlin: Springer.

Farnetani, E. and S. Kori (1983). Rhythmic structure in Italian noun phrases: A study on vowel durations. *Phonetica* 47, 50–65.

Faure, X., D. J. Hirst, and M. Chafcouloff (1980). Rhythm in English. Isochronism, pitch, and perceived stress. In L. R. Waugh and C. H. van Schooneveld (eds.), *The Melody of Language*, pp. 71–79. Baltimore: University Park Press.

Feng, S. (1999). A tone sandhi in Chinese Northern dialects. See Kaji (1999), pp. 109–119.

Féry, C. (1993). *German Intonational Patterns*. Tübingen: Niemeyer.

Fikkert, P. and H. Jacobs (eds.) (2003). *Development in Prosodic Systems*, New York and Berlin: Mouton de Gruyter.

Firbas, J. (1980). Post-intonation centre prosodic shade in the modern English clause. In S. Greenbaum, G. Leech, and J. Svartvik (eds.), *Studies in English Linguistics for Randolph Quirk*, pp. 125–133. London: Longman.

Fitzpatrick-Cole, J. (1999). The Alpine intonation of Bern Swiss German. In *Proceedings of the 14th International Congress of Phonetic Sciences*, Volume 1, pp. 941–944.

Flemming, E. (1995). *Auditory representations in phonology*. Ph.D. thesis, Stanford University, Stanford, CA.

Fougeron, C. (2001). Articulatory properties of initial segments in several prosodic constituents in French. *Journal of Phonetics* 29, 109–136.

Fougeron, C. and P. A. Keating (1997). Articulatory strengthening at edges of prosodic domains. *Journal of the Acoustic Society of America* 101, 3728–3740.

Foulkes, P. and G. Docherty (1999). Standard English in Edinburgh and Glasgow: The Scottish Vowel Length Rule revisited. In *Urban Voices*, pp. 230–244. London: Arnold.

Fourcin, A. and E. Abberton (1971). First applications of a new laryngograph. *Medical and Biological Illustrations* 21, 172–182.

Fox, A. (2000). *Prosodic Features and Prosodic Structure: The Phonology of Suprasegmentals*. Oxford: Oxford University Press.

Fretheim, T. (1992). Themehood, rhemehood and Norwegian focus structure. *Folia Linguistica* XXVI, 111–150.

Fretheim, T. and R. A. Nilsen (1991). In defense of [±foc]. In *ESCOL 90. Proceedings of the Seventh Eastern Conference on Linguistics*, pp. 102–111. Ohio State University.

Fromkin, V. A. (ed.) (1978). *Tone: A Linguistic Survey*. New York: Academic Press.

Frota, S. (1998). *Prosody and focus in European Portuguese*. Ph.D. thesis, University of Lisbon. Published by Garland, New York (2000).

Frota, S. (2002). Tonal association and target alignment in European Portuguese nuclear falls. See Gussenhoven and Warner (2002), pp. 387–418.

Fry, D. (1958). Experiments in the perception of stress. *Language and Speech* 1, 205–213.

Fry, D. B. (1955). Duration and intensity as physical correlates of linguistic stress. *Journal of the Acoustic Society of America* 27, 765–769.

Fry, D. (1964). The dependence of stress judgments on vowel formant structure. In *Proceedings of the 5th International Congress of Phonetic Sciences*, pp. 306–311.

Fujisaki, H. (1983). Characteristics of voice fundamental frequency in speech and singing. In P. F. MacNeilage (ed.), *The Production of Speech*, pp. 37–47. New York and Berlin: Springer.

Gårding, E. (1977). *The Scandinavian Word Accents*. Lund: Gleerup.

Gårding, E. (1983). A generative model of intonation. See Cutler and Ladd (1983), pp. 11–25.

Geluykens, R. and M. G. Swerts (1994). Prosodic cues to discourse boundaries. *Speech Communication* 15, 69–77.

Gibbon, D. (1975). *Perspectives of Intonation Analysis*. Bern: Lang.

Giegerich, H. J. (1997). *English Phonology: An Introduction.* Cambridge: Cambridge University Press.

Gilles, P. (1999). *Dialektausgleich im Lëtzebuergeschen. Zur phonetisch-phonologischen Fokussierung einer Nationalsprache.* Tübingen: Niemeyer.

Goedemans, R. (1998). *Weightless Segments: A Phonetic Study concerning the Metrical Irrelevance of Syllable Onsets.* The Hague: Thesus (Subsidiary of Holland Academic Graphics).

Goldsmith, J. (1984). Tone and accent in Tonga. See Clements and Goldsmith (1984b), pp. 19–51.

Goldsmith, J. A. (1976). *Autosegmental phonology.* Ph.D. thesis, MIT. Distributed by IULC (1976), published by Garland Press, New York (1979).

Goldsmith, J. A. (1980). English as a tone language. See Goyvaerts (1980), pp. 287–308.

Gomez-Imbert, E. (2001). More on the tone versus pitch accent typology: Evidence from Barasana and other Eastern Tukanoan languages. See Kaji (2001), pp. 369–412.

Gomez-Imbert, E. and M. Kenstowicz (2000). Barasana tone and accent. *International Journal of American Linguistics* 66, 419–463.

Gordon, M. K. (1999). The intonational structure of Chickasaw. In *Proceedings of the 14th International Congress of Phonetic Sciences*, Volume 3, pp. 1993–1996.

Gósy, M. and J. Terken (1994). Question marking in Hungarian: timing and height of pitch peaks. *Journal of Phonetics* 22, 269–281.

Goudailler, J.-P. (1987). Einige Spracheigentümlichkeiten der lëtzebuergeschen Mundarten im Licht der instrumentellen Phonetik. In J.-P. Goudailler (ed.), *Aspekte des Lëtzebuergeschen*, pp. 207–230. Hamburg: Buske.

Goyvaerts, D. (ed.) (1980). *Phonology in the 80s*, Ghent: Story Scientia.

Grabe, E. (1998a). *Comparative intonational phonology: English and German.* Ph.D. thesis, University of Nijmegen. Published in Max Planck Institute Series in Psycholinguistics.

Grabe, E. (1998b). Pitch realization in English and German. *Journal of Phonetics* 26, 129–143.

Grabe, E. (2001). The IViE labelling guide. Version 3. <http://www.phon.ox.ac.uk/ ⁻esther/ivyweb/guide.html>

Grabe, E., C. Gussenhoven, J. Haan, E. Marsi, and B. Post (1997), Preaccentual pitch and speaker attitude in Dutch. *Language and Speech* 41, 63–85.

Grabe, E., B. Post, F. Nolan, and K. Farrar (2000). Pitch accent realization in four varieties of British English. *Journal of Phonetics* 28, 161–185.

Grice, M. (1995a). *The Intonation of Interrogation in Palermo Italian: Implications for Intonational Theory.* Tübingen: Niemeyer.

Grice, M. (1995b). Leading tones and downstep in English. *Journal of Linguistics* 12, 183–233.

Grice, M., D. R. Ladd, and A. Arvaniti (2000). On the place of phrase accents in intonational phonology. *Phonology* 17, 143–185.

Grimes, B. F. (ed.) (2000). *Ethnologue: Languages of the World*, Dallas, Texas. SIL International. 14th edn. (CD-ROM Version).

Grønnum, N. (1983a). Standard Danish sentence intonation. Phonetic data and their representation. *Folia Linguistica* 17, 187–220.

Grønnum, N. (1983b). Two issues in the prosody of Standard Danish. See Cutler and Ladd (1983), pp. 27–38.

Grønnum, N. (1991). Prosodic parameters in a variety of regional Danish standard languages. *Phonetica* 47, 188–214.

Grønnum, N. (1992). *The Groundworks of Danish Intonation*. Copenhagen: Museum Tusculanum Press.

Grønnum, N. (1998). A critical remark on intonational phonology. *Journal of Phonetics* 26, 109–112.

Gussenhoven, C. (1983a). A semantic analysis of the nuclear tones of English. Distributed by Indiana University Linguistics Club (IULC). Bloomington, Ind. Published as ch. 6 in Gussenhoven (1984).

Gussenhoven, C. (1983b). Stress shift and the nucleus. *Linguistics* 21, 303–339. Reprinted in Gussenhoven (1984).

Gussenhoven, C. (1984). *On the Grammar and Semantics of Sentence Accents*. Dordrecht: Foris.

Gussenhoven, C. (1985). The intonation of 'George and Mildred': Post-nuclear generalisations. In C. Johns-Lewis (ed.), *Intonation in Discourse*, pp. 77–121. London: Croom Helm. Also published as ch. 6 in Gussenhoven (1984).

Gussenhoven, C. (1986). Review of Selkirk (1984). *Journal of Linguistics* 22, 455–474.

Gussenhoven, C. (1987a). Lexical accent rules in English. In W. Bahner, J. Schildt, and D. Viehweger (eds.), *Proceedings of the XIVth International Congress of Linguists. Berlin/GDR, 10–15 August 1987*, pp. 432–436. Berlin: Akademie-Verlag. 3 vols.

Gussenhoven, C. (1987b). Toonsegmenten in de intonatie van het Nederlands. *GLOT* 10, 313–322.

Gussenhoven, C. (1988). Adequacy in intonation analysis: The case of Dutch. See Hulst and Smith (1988), pp. 95–121.

Gussenhoven, C. (1990). Tonal association domains and the prosodic hierarchy in English. In S. M. Ramsaran (ed.), *Studies in the Pronunciation of English. A Commemorative Volume in Honour of A. C. Gimson*, pp. 27–37. London: Routledge.

Gussenhoven, C. (1991a). The English Rhythm Rule as an accent deletion rule. *Phonology* 8, 1–35.

Gussenhoven, C. (1991b). Tone segments in the intonation of Dutch. In T. F. Shannon and J. P. Snapper (eds.), *The Berkeley Conference on Dutch Linguistics 1989*, pp. 139–155. Lanham, MA: University Press of America.

Gussenhoven, C. (1992). Intonational phrasing and the prosodic hierarchy. In W. U. Dressler, H. C. Luschützky, O. E. Pfeiffer, and J. R. Rennison (eds.), *Phonologica 1988. Proceedings of the 6th International Phonology Meeting*, pp. 89–99. Cambridge: Cambridge University Press.

Gussenhoven, C. (1993). The Dutch foot and the chanted call. *Journal of Linguistics* 29, 37–63.

Gussenhoven, C. (1994). English stress in lexical phonology. In W. U. Dressler, M. Prinzhorn, and J. J. Rennison (eds.), *Phonologica 1992*, pp. 87–96. Turin: Rosenberg & Sellier.

Gussenhoven, C. (1999a). Discreteness and gradience in intonational contrasts. *Language and Speech* 42, 281–305.

Gussenhoven, C. (1999b). Tone systems in Dutch Limburgian dialects. See Kaji (1999), pp. 127–143.

Gussenhoven, C. (1999c). Why question intonations rise and why they sometimes don't. Paper presented at the Second International Conference of the North-West Centre for Linguistics, 'Questions', University of Liverpool, 12–14 November.

Gussenhoven, C. (2000a). The boundary tones are coming: On the non-peripheral nature of boundary tones. See Broe and Pierrehumbert (2000), pp. 132–151.

Gussenhoven, C. (2000b). The lexical tone contrast of Roermond Dutch in Optimality Theory. See Horne (2000), pp. 129–167. Also Rutgers Optimality Archive 382.

Gussenhoven, C. (2000c). On the origin and development of the Central Franconian tone contrast. See Lahiri (2000), pp. 213–260.

Gussenhoven, C. (2002). Intonation and interpretation: Phonetics and phonology. See Bel and Marlien (2002), pp. 47–57.

Gussenhoven, C. (2003). Vowel duration, syllable quantity and stress in Dutch. In K. Hanson and S. Inkelas (eds.), *The Nature of the Word: Essays in Honor of Paul Kiparsky*. Cambridge, MA: MIT Press. Also Rutgers Optimality Archive 381.

Gussenhoven, C. (forthcoming). Types of focus in English. See Büring, Gordon, and Lee (forthcoming).

Gussenhoven, C. and F. Aarts (1999). The dialect of Maastricht. *Journal of the International Phonetic Association* 29, 155–165.

Gussenhoven, C. and G. Bruce (1999). Word prosody and intonation. See van der Hulst (1999), pp. 233–271.

Gussenhoven, C. and A. Chen (2000). Universal and language-specific effects in the perception of question intonation. *Proceedings of the 6th International Conference on the Processing of Spoken Language* 1, pp. 91–94.

Gussenhoven, C. and H. Jacobs (1998). *Understanding Phonology*. London: Arnold.

Gussenhoven, C., B. Repp, T. Rietveld, W. Rump, and J. Terken (1997). The perceptual prominence of fundamental frequency peaks. *Journal of the Acoustic Society of America* 102, 3009–3022.

Gussenhoven, C. and A. Rietveld (1988). Fundamental frequency declination in Dutch: Testing three hypotheses. *Journal of Phonetics* 16, 355–369.

Gussenhoven, C. and A. Rietveld (1992). Intonation contours, prosodic structure and preboundary lengthening. *Journal of Phonetics* 20, 283–303.

Gussenhoven, C. and T. Rietveld (1998). On the speaker-dependence of the perceived prominence of f_0 peaks. *Journal of Phonetics* 26, 371–380.

Gussenhoven, C. and T. Rietveld (2000). The behavior of H* and L* under variations in pitch range in Dutch rising contours. *Language and Speech* 43, 183–203.

Gussenhoven, C., J. Terken, and T. Rietveld (1999). Transcription of Dutch intonation – courseware. < http://lands.let.kun.nl/todi >

Gussenhoven, C. and P. van der Vliet (1999). The phonology of tone and intonation in the Dutch dialect of Venlo. *Journal of Linguistics* 35, 99–135.

Gussenhoven, C. and N. Warner (eds.) (2002). *Laboratory Phonology* 7, Berlin and New York: Mouton de Gruyter.

Haan, J. (2002). *Speaking of Questions: An exploration of Dutch Question Intonation.* Utrecht: Netherlands Graduate School of Linguistics.

Haan, J., L. Heijmans, T. Rietveld, and C. Gussenhoven (2002). Explaining attitudinal ratings of Dutch rising contours: Morphological structure vs. the Frequency Code. *Phonetica* 59, 180–194.

Haan, J., V. J. van Heuven, J. J. A. Pacilly, and R. van Bezooijen (1997). An anatomy of Dutch question intonation. In J. Coerts and H. de Hoop (eds.), *Linguistics in the Netherlands 1997*, pp. 97–108. Amsterdam: John Benjamins.

Hadding-Koch, Kerstin and M. Studdert-Kennedy (1964). An experimental study of some intonation contours. *Phonetica* 11, 175–185. Reprinted in Bolinger (1972), pp. 348–358.

Halle, M. and J.-R. Vergnaud (1987). *An Essay on Stress*. Cambridge: Cambridge University Press.

Halliday, M. A. (1970). *A Course in Spoken English: Intonation*. London: Oxford University Press.

Hammond, M. (1999). *The Phonology of English: A Prosodic Optimality-theoretic Approach*. Oxford: Oxford University Press.

Haraguchi, S. (1991). *A Theory of Stress and Accent*. Dordrecht: Foris.

Hasegawa, Y. and K. Hata (1994). Non-physiological differences between male and female speech: Evidence from the delayed f_0 fall phenomenon in Japanese. *Proceedings of the 3rd International Conference on the Processing of Spoken Language* 2, 1179–1182.

Haudricourt, A.-G. (1954). De l'origine des tons en viêtnamien. *Journal Asiatique* 242, 69–82.

Hayes, B. (1980). *A Metrical Theory of Stress Rules*. Ph.D. thesis, MIT. Published by Garland Press, New York (1985).

Hayes, B. (1989). The prosodic hierarchy in meter. In P. Kiparsky and G. Youmans (eds.), *Phonetics and Phonology. Rhythm and Meter*, pp. 201–260. New York: Academic Press.

Hayes, B. (1990). Precompiled phrasal phonology. See Inkelas and Zec (1990), pp. 85–108.

Hayes, B. (1994). 'Gesture' in prosody: comments on the paper by Ladd. In P. A. Keating (ed.), *Phonological Structure and Phonetic Form: Papers in Laboratory Phonology III*, pp. 64–75. Cambridge: Cambridge University Press.

Hayes, B. (1995). *Metrical Theory*. Chicago: Chicago University Press.

Hayes, B. and A. Lahiri (1991a). Bengali intonational phonology. *Natural Language and Linguistic Theory* 9, 47–96.

Hayes, B. and A. Lahiri (1991b). Durationally specified intonation in English and Bengali. In J. Sundberg, L. Nord, and R. Carlson (eds.), *Music, Language, Speech, and Brain*, pp. 78–91. Basingstoke: Macmillan.

Heijmans, L. (1999). Lexical tone in the Dutch dialect of Weert? *Proceedings of the 14th International Congress of Phonetic Sciences* 3, 2383–2386.

Heijmans, L. (2003). The relationship between tone and vowel length in two neighbouring Dutch Limburgian dialects. See Fikkert and Jacobs (2003), pp. 7–45.

Heike, G. (1962). Suprasegmentale Merkmale der stadtköhlner Mundart: Ein Beitrag zur 'Rheinische Schärfung'. *Phonetica* 8, 147–165.

Heldner, M. and E. Strangert (2001). Temporal effects of focus in Swedish. *Journal of Phonetics* 29, 329–361.

Helsloot, C. J. (1995). *Metrical Prosody: A Template-and-constraint Approach to Phonological Phrasing in Italian. Based on the Poetry of Giuseppe Ungaretti and Eugenio Montale*. The Hague: Holland Academic Graphics.

Henton, C. (1995). Cross-language variation in the vowels of female and male speakers. In *Proceedings of the 13th International Congress of Phonetic Sciences* 4, pp. 420–423.

Henton, C. (1999). Where is female synthetic speech? *Journal of the International Phonetic Association* 29, 49–60.

Henton, C. and A. Bladon (1988). Creak as a socio-phonetic marker. In L. M. Hyman and C. N. Li (eds.), *Language, Speech and Mind: Studies in Honor of Victoria A. Fromkin*, pp. 3–29. London.

Hermann, E. (1942). *Probleme der Frage.* Göttingen: VandenHoeck & Ruprecht. 2 vols.

Hermans, B. (1985). Het Limburgs en het Litouws als metrisch gebonden toontalen. *Spektator* 14, 48–70.

Hermans, B. (1994). *The composite nature of accent: with case studies of the Limburgian and Serbo-Croatian pitch accent.* Ph.D. thesis, Katholieke Universiteit Brabant, Tilburg.

Hermans, B. (1996). Paper presented at the Linguistics in the Netherlands Meeting, Utrecht, 20 January 1996.

Hermes, D. (1993). Pitch analysis. In M. Cooke, S. Beet, and M. Crawford (eds.), *Visual Representation of Speech Signals,* pp. 3–25. Chichester: Wiley.

Hermes, D. and J. van Gestel (1991). The frequency scale of speech intonation. *Journal of the Acoustic Society of America* 90, 97–102.

Hess, W. J. (1983). *Pitch Determination of Speech Signals Algorithms and Devices.* Berlin: Springer.

Hirst, D. (1993). Detaching intonational phrases from syntactic structure. *Linguistic Inquiry* 24, 781–788.

Hirst, D, and A. Di Cristo (eds.) (1998). *Intonation Systems: Survey of Twenty languages,* Cambridge: Cambridge University Press.

Hockett, C. F. (1958). *A Course in Modern Linguistics.* New York: Macmillan.

Hockettt, C. F. (1960). The origin of speech. *Scientific American* 203 (3), 88–96.

Holmberg, J., R. Hillman, and J. Perkell (1988). Glottal airflow and transglottal air pressure measurements for male and female speakers in low, normal, and high pitch. *Journal of the Acoustic Society of America* 84(2), 294–305.

Hombert, J.-M. (1978). Consonant types, vowel quality and tone. See Fromkin (1978), pp. 77–111.

Hombert, J.-M., J. J. Ohala, and W. G. Ewan (1979). Phonetic explanations for the development of tone. *Language* 55, 37–58.

Horne, M. (1990). Empirical evidence for a deletion analysis of the rhythm rule in English. *Linguistics* 28, 959–981.

Horne, M. (ed.) (2000). *Prosody: Theory and Experiment. Studies presented to Gösta Bruce,* Dordrecht, Boston, and London: Kluwer.

House, D. and P. Touati (eds.) (1993). *Proceedings of the ESCA Workshop on Prosody.* Lund: Lund University Department of Linguistics. Working papers 41.

Hualde, J., G. Elordieta, I. Gaminde, and R. Smiljanić (2002). From pitch-accent to stress-accent in Basque. See Gussenhoven and Warner (2002), pp. 547, 584.

Hulst, H. v. d. and N. Smith (eds.) (1988). *Autosegmental studies on pitch accent.* Dordrecht: Foris.

Huss, V. (1975). Neutralisierung englischer Akzentunterschiede in der Nachkontur. *Phonetica* 32, 278–291.

Huss, V. (1978). English word-stress in post-nuclear position. *Phonetica* 35, 86–105.

Hyman, L. M. (1978). Tone and/or accent. In D. J. Napoli (ed.), *Elements of Tone, Stress, and Intonation,* pp. 1–20. Washington, DC: Georgetown University Press.

Hyman, L. M. (1979). A reanalysis of tonal downstep. *Journal of African Languages and Linguistics* 1, 9–29.

Hyman, L. M. (1981). Tonal accent in Somali. *Studies in African Linguistics* 12, 169–203.

Hyman, L. M. (1985). *A Theory of Phonological Weight.* Dordrecht: Foris.

Hyman, L. M. (1986). The representation of multiple tone heights. In *The Phonological Representation of Suprasegmentals,* pp. 109–152. Dordrecht: Foris.

Hyman, L. M. (1987). Prosodic domains in Kukuya. *Natural Language and Linguistic Theory* 5, 311–333.

Hyman, L. M. (1993). Register tones and tonal geometry. See van der Hulst and Snider (1993), pp. 75–108.

Hyman, L. M. (2001a). Privative tone in Bantu. See Kaji (2001), pp. 237–257.

Hyman, L. M. (2001b). Tone systems. In M. Haspelmath, E. König, W. Oesterreicher, and W. Raible (eds.), *Language Typology and Language Universals: An International Handbook*, Volume 2, pp. 1367–1380. Berlin and New York: Mouton de Gruyter.

Hyman, L. M. and A. Ngunga (1994). On the non-universality of tonal association 'conventions': Evidence from Ciyao. *Phonology* 11, 25–68.

Inkelas, S. (1989). *Prosodic constituency in the lexicon*. Ph.D. thesis, Stanford University.

Inkelas, S. and W. R. Leben (1990). Where phonology and phonetics intersect: The case of Hausa intonation. See Kingston and Beckman (1990), pp. 17–34.

Inkelas, S. and D. Zec (Eds.) (1990). *The Phonology–Syntax Connection,* Chicago: Chicago University Press.

Iwata, R. (2001). Tone and accent in Chinese dialects. See Kaji (2001), pp. 267–291.

James, D. J. (1994). Word tone in a Papuan language: An autosegmental solution. *Language and Linguistics in Melanesia* 25, 125–148.

Jassem, W. (1952). *The Intonation of Conversational English.* Warsaw: La Société des Sciences et des Lettres.

Johnson, K. (1997). *Acoustic and Auditory Phonetics.* Cambridge, MA: Blackwell.

Jun, S.-A. (1993). *The phonetics and phonology of Korean.* Ph.D. thesis, Ohio State University.

Jun, S.-A. (1998). The accentual phrase in the Korean prosodic hierarchy. *Phonology* 15, 189–226.

Jun, S.-A. (2004). *Prosodic Typology: The Phonology of Intonation and Phrasing.* Oxford: Oxford University Press.

Jun, S.-A. and G. Elordieta (1997). Intonational structure of the Western Basque tonal accent. See Botinis, Kouroupetroglou, and Carayannis (1997), pp. 193–196.

Jun, S.-A. and C. Fougeron (2000). A phonological model of French intonation. See Botinis (2000), pp. 209–242.

Kager, R. (1999). *Optimality Theory.* Cambridge: Cambridge University Press.

Kager, R. (Ms). Rhythmic directionality by positional licencing.

Kaji, S. (ed.) (1999). *Proceedings of the Symposium Cross-Linguistic Studies of Tonal Phenomena: Tonogenesis, Typology, and Related Topics*, Tokyo. Tokyo University of Foreign Studies. Institute for Languages and Cultures of Asia and Africa.

Kaji, S. (ed.) (2001). *Proceedings of the Symposium Cross-Linguistic Studies, of Tonal Phenomena: Tonogenesis, Japanese Accentology, and Other Topics*, Tokyo. Tokyo University of Foreign Studies. Institute for Languages and Cultures of Asia and Africa.

Kaji, S. (ed.) (2003). *Proceedings of the Symposium Crosslinguistic Studies of Tonal Phenomena: Historical Development, Phonetics of Tone, and Descriptive Studies.* Tokyo, Tokyo University of Foreign Studies, Institute for Languages and Cultures of Asia and Africa.

Kanerva, J. M. (1989). *Focus and phrasing in Chicheŵa phonology.* Ph.D. thesis, Stanford University, Palo Alto.

Keating, P. A. (1985). Universal phonetics and the organization of grammars. In V. A. Fromkin (ed.), *Phonetic Linguistics*, pp. 115–132. New York: Academic Press.

Kingston, J. (2003). Mechanisms of tone reversal. See Kaji (2003), pp. 57–120.

Kingston, J. and M. E. Beckman (eds.) (1990). *Papers in Laboratory Phonology I: Between the Grammar and Physics of Speech*, Cambridge: Cambridge University Press.

Kingston, John and Diehl, R. L. (1994). Phonetic knowledge. *Language* 70, 419–454.

Kiparsky, P. (1982a). *Explanation in Phonology.* Dordrecht: Foris.

Kiparsky, P. (1982b). From cyclic phonology to lexical phonology. In H. van der Hulst and N. Smith (eds.), *The Structure of Phonological Representations. Part II*, pp. 131–175. Dordrecht: Foris.

Kiparsky, P. (1988). Phonological change. In F. J. Newmeyer (ed.), *Linguistics: The Cambridge Survey*, pp. 363–415. Cambridge: Cambridge University Press.

Kiparsky, P. (2000). Opacity and cyclicity. *The Linguistic Review* 17, 351–3657.

Kiparsky, P. (forthcoming). *Paradigms and Opacity.* Stanford, CA: CSLI.

Kirsner, R. S. and V. J. van Heuven (1996). Boundary tones and the semantics of the Dutch final particles *hè, hoor, zeg* and *joh.* In C. Cremers and M. den Dikken (eds.), *Linguistics in the Netherlands 1996*, pp. 133–145. Amsterdam: John Benjamins.

Kiss, K. E. (1998). Identificational focus and information focus. *Language* 74, 245–273.

Kluender, K. R., R. L. Diehl, and B. A. Wright (1988). Vowel-length differences before voiced and voiceless consonants: an auditory explanation. *Journal of Phonetics* 16, 153–170.

Kohler, K. J. (1987). Categorical pitch perception. In *Proceedings of the 11th International Congress of Phonetic Sciences*, pp. 331–333.

Kohler, K. J. (1990). Macro and micro f_0 in the synthesis of intonation. See Kingston and Beckman (1990), pp. 115–138.

Kraehenmann, A. (2001). Swiss geminate stops: geminates all over the word. *Phonology* 18, 109–145.

Kristoffersen, G. (2000). *The Phonology of Norwegian.* Oxford: Oxford University Press.

Kubozono, H. (1992). Modeling syntactic effects on downstep in Japanese. See Docherty and Ladd (1992), pp. 368–387.

Kubozono, H. (1993). *The Organization of Japanese Prosody.* Tokyo: Kurosio.

Künzel, H. J. and J. E. Schmidt (2001). Phonetische Probleme bei Tonakzent I: Eine Pilotstudie. In A. Braun (ed.), *Beiträge zu Linguistik und Phonetik. Festschrift für Joachim Göschel zum 70. Geburstag*, pp. 421–439. Stuttgart: Steiner. ZDL-Beihefte 118.

Kutsch Lojenga, C. (1994). *Ngiti: A Central-Sudanic Language of Zaire.* Cologne: Rüdiger Köppe.

Labov, W. (1963). The social motivation of a sound change. *Word* 19, 273–309.

Labov, W. (1981). Resolving the Neogrammarian controversy. *Language* 57, 267–309.

Ladd, D. R. (1978). Stylized intonation. *Language* 54, 517–540.

Ladd, D. R. (1980). *The Structure of Intonational Meaning: Evidence from English*, Bloomington: Indiana University Press.

Ladd, D. R. (1981). Intonational universals. In T. Myers, J. Laver, and J. Anderson (eds.), *The Cognitive Representation of Speech*, pp. 389–397. Amsterdam: North Holland Publishing.

Ladd, D. R. (1983a). Peak features and overall slope. See Cutler and Ladd (1983), pp. 39–52.

Ladd, D. R. (1983b). Phonological features of intonational peaks. *Language* 59, 721–759.

Ladd, D. R. (1984). Declination: A review and some hypotheses. *Phonology Yearbook* 1, pp. 53–74.

Ladd, D. R. (1988). Declination 'Reset' and the hierarchical organization of utterances. *Journal of the Acoustic Society of America* 84(5), 538–544.

Ladd, D. R. (1990a). Intonation: Emotion vs. grammar. *Language* 66, 806–816.

Ladd, D. R. (1990b). Metrical representation of pitch register. See Kingston and Beckman (1990), pp. 35–57.

Ladd, D. R. (1993a). In defense of a metrical theory of intonational downstep. See van der Hulst and Snider (1993), pp. 109–132.

Ladd, D. R. (1993b). On the theoretical status of the 'Baseline' in modelling intonation. *Language and Speech* 36, 435–451.

Ladd, D. R. (1996). *Intonational Phonology*. Cambridge: Cambridge University Press.

Ladd, D. R. (2000). Bruce, Pierrehumbert and the elements of intonational phonology. See Horne (2000), pp. 37–50.

Ladd, D. R., D. Faulkner, H. Faulkner, and A. Schepman (1999). Constant 'segmental anchoring' of f_0 movements under changes in speech rate. *Journal of the Acoustic Society of America* 106(3), 1543–1554.

Ladd, D. R., I. Mennen, and A. Schepman (2000). Phonological conditioning of peak alignment in rising pitch accents in Dutch. *Journal of the Acoustic Society of America* 107(5), 2685–2696.

Ladd, D. R. and A. Monaghan (1987). Modelling rhythmic and syntactic effects on accent in long noun phrases. In J. Laver and M. Jack (eds.), *Proceedings of the European Conference on Speech Technology*, 2, pp. 29–32. Edinburgh: CEP.

Ladd, D. R. and R. Morton (1997). The perception of intonational emphasis: Continuous or categorical? *Journal of Phonetics* 25, 313–342.

Ladd, D. R. and J. Terken (1995). Modelling intra- and inter-speaker pitch range variation. In *Proceedings of the 13th International Congress of Phonetic Sciences*, 2, pp. 386–389.

Ladefoged, P. (1996). *Elements of Acoustic Phonetics*. Chicago: University of Chicago Press. 2nd edn.

Ladefoged, P. (1999). American English. In *Handbook of the International Phonetic Association*, pp. 41–44. Cambridge: Cambridge University Press.

Ladefoged, P. and T. Cho (2000). Linking linguistic contrasts to reality: The case of VOT. *UCLA Working Papers in Phonetics* 98, 1–9.

Lahiri, A. (ed.) (2000). *Analogy, Levelling, Markedness: Principles of Change in Phonology and Morphology*. Berlin: Mouton de Gruyter.

Lahiri, A. and E. Dresher (1999). Open Syllable Lengthening in West-Germanic. *Language* 75, 678–719.

Lahiri, A. and J. Fitzpatrick-Cole (1999). Emphatic clitics and focus intonation in Bengali. In W. Zonneveld and R. Kager (eds.), *Phrasal Phonology*, pp. 119–144. Nijmegen: Nijmegen University Press.

Lahiri, A., A. Jongman, and J. A. Sereno (1990). The pronominal clitic [dər] in Dutch: A theoretical and experimental approach. *Morphology Yearbook* 3, 115–127.

Lahiri, A., A. Wetterlin, and E. Jönsson-Steiner (Ms.). Unmarked tone in Scandinavian. Sektion Sprachwissenschaft, University of Constance.

Laniran, Y. and G. Clements (2003). Downstep and high raising: Interacting factors in Yoruba tone production. *Journal of Phonetics* 31, 203–250.

Laniran, Y. d. (1990). *Intonation in tone languages: The Yoruba example*. Ph.D. thesis, Cornell University.

Laver, J. (1980). *The Phonetic Description of Voice Quality.* Cambridge: Cambridge University Press.

Laver, J. (1990). *Phonetics.* Cambridge: Cambridge University Press.

Leben, William, R. (1978). The representation of tone. See Fromkin (1978), pp. 177–219.

Leben, W. R. (1973). *Suprasegmental phonology.* Ph.D. thesis, MIT.

Leben, W. R. (1975). The tones in English intonation. *Linguistic Inquiry* 2, 69–107.

Leer, J. (1999). Tonogenesis in Athabaskan. See Kaji (1999), pp. 37–66.

Liberman, A. M., F. Cooper, D. Shankweiler, and M. Studdert-Kennedy (1967). Perception of the speech code. *Psychological Review* 74, 431–461.

Liberman, A. M., K. Harris, H. S. Hoffman, and B. Griffith (1957). The discrimination of speech sounds within and across phoneme boundaries. *Journal of Experimental Psychology* 61, 379–388.

Liberman, M. and J. Pierrehumbert (1984). Intonational invariance under changes in pitch range and length. In M. Aronoff and R. T. Oehrle (eds.), *Language and Sound Structure*, pp. 157–233. Cambridge, MA and London: MIT Press.

Liberman, M. and I. Sag (1974). Prosodic form and discourse function. In *Proceedings of the Chicago Linguistics Society*, 10, pp. 416–427.

Liberman, M. Y. (1975). *The intonational system of English.* Ph.D. thesis, MIT. Distributed by IULC (1978). Published by Garland Press, New York (1985).

Liberman, M. Y. and A. Prince (1977). On stress and linguistic rhythm. *Linguistic Inquiry* 8, 249–336.

Lieberman, P. (1967). *Intonation, Perception, and Language.* Cambridge, MA: MIT Press.

Lieberman, P. (1980). The innate, central aspect of intonation. See Waugh and Van Schooneveld (1980), pp. 187–199.

Lieberman, P., W. Katz, A. Jongman, R. Zimmerman, and M. Miller (1985). Measures of the sentence intonation of read and spontaneous speech in American English. *Journal of the Acoustic Society of America* 77, 649–665.

Lindblom, B. (1990). Explaining phonetic variation: A sketch of the H & H theory. In W. J. Hardcastle and A. Marchal (eds.), *Speech Production and Speech Modeling*, pp. 403–440. Dordrecht: Kluwer.

Lindsey, G. (1985). *Intonation and interrogation: Tonal structure and the expression of a pragmatic function in English and other languages.* Ph.D. thesis, UCLA.

Lodge, K. (2000) [No title]. *Journal of Linguistics* 36, 593–598. Review of four phonology textbooks, among which Gussenhoven and Jacobs (1998).

Löfqvist, A., T. Baer, N. S. McGarr, and R. S. Story (1989). The crycothyroid muscle in voicing control. *Journal of the Acoustic Society of America* 85, 1314–1321.

Longacre, R. E. (1952). Five phonemic pitch levels in Trique. *Acta Linguistica* 7, 62–82,

Lorentz, O. (1995). Tonal prominence and alignment. *Phonology at Santa Cruz* 4, 39–56.

Maddieson, I. (1977). *Universals of tone: Six studies.* Ph.D. thesis, UCLA.

Maddieson, I. (1978). Universals of tone, In J. Greenberg (ed.), *Universals of Human Language*, 2, pp. 337–465. Stanford: Stanford University Press.

Maddieson, I. (1984). The effects on f_0 of a voicing distinction in sonorants and their implications for a theory of tonogenesis. *Journal of Phonetics* 12, 9–15.

Maddieson, I. and K.-F. Pang (1993). Tone in Utsat. In J. A. Edmondson and K. J. Gregerson (eds.), *Tonality in Austronesian Languages*, pp. 75–89. Honolulu: University of Hawaii Press.

Makarova, V. (1999a). Perception of intonational contrasts by Japanese and Russian listeners. In *Proceedings of the 14th International Congress of Phonetic Sciences*, 3, pp. 1945–1948.

Makarova, V. (1999b). Pitch peak alignment in Russian declaratives' interrogatives, and exclamations. In *Proceedings of the 14th International Congress of Phonetic Sciences*, 2, pp. 1173–1176.

Martinet, A. (1962). *A Functional View of Language*. Oxford: Clarendon Press.

Matisoff, J. (1970). Glottal dissemination and the Lahu high-rising tone: A tonogenetic case-study. *Journal of the American Oriental Society* 90, 13–44.

Matisoff, J. (1973). Tonogenesis in Southeast Asia. In L. M. Hyman (ed.), *Consonant Types and Tone*, pp. 71–95. Los Angeles: University of Southern California.

Matsumori, A. (2001). Historical phonology of Japanese dialects. See Kaji (2001), pp. 93–122.

McCarthy, J. J. (1999). Sympathy and phonological opacity. *Phonology* 16, 331–399.

McCarthy, J. J. (2002). *A Thematic Guide to Optimality Theory*. Cambridge: Cambridge University Press.

McCarthy, J. J. and A. Prince (1993). Generalized alignment. In G. Booij and J. v. Marle (eds.), *Yearbook of Morphology*, pp. 79–153. Dordrecht: Kluwer.

McCarthy, J. J. and A. Prince (1995). Faithfulness and reduplicative identity. In J. N. Beckman, L. W. Dickey, and S. Urbanczyk (eds.), *Papers in Optimality Theory*, pp. 249–384. University of Massachusetts, GLSA.

McCawley, J. D. (1978). What is a tone language? See Fromkin (1978), pp. 113–131.

Meeussen, A. (1970). Tone typologies for West African languages. *African Language Studies* 11, 266–271.

Mertens, P. (1987). *L'intonation du français. De la description linguistique à la reconnaissance automatique*. Ph.D. thesis, Louvain.

Mertens, P. (1992). L'accentuation de syllabes contiguës. *I.T.L. Review of Applied Linguistics 95/96*, pp. 145–165.

Mihm, A. (2002). Graphematische Systemanalyse als Grundlage der historischen Prosodieforschung. In P. Auer, P. Gilles, and H. Spiekermann (eds.), *Silbenschnitt und Tonakzente*, pp. 235–264. Tübingen: Niemeyer.

Mol, H. and E. Uhlenbeck (1956). The linguistic relevance of intensity in stress. *Lingua* 5, 205–213.

Monaghan, A. (2000). Null focused item? Linguist List, Subject 11.667. 23 March 2000.

Morton, E. W. (1977). On the occurrence and significance of motivation-structural rules in some bird and mammal sounds. *The American Naturalist* 111, 855–869.

Moulines, E. and E. Verhelst (1995). Time-domain and frequency-domain techniques for prosodic modification of speech. In W. B. Kleijn and K. K. Paliwal (eds.), *Speech Coding and Synthesis*, pp. 519–555. Amsterdam: Elsevier Sciences.

Mountford, K. (1983). *Bambara Declarative sentence intonation*. Ph.D. thesis, Indiana University.

Myers, S. (1998). Surface underspecification of tone in Chicheŵa. *Phonology* 15, 367–391.

Nespor, M. (1999). Stress domains. See van der Hulst (1999), pp. 117–159.

Nespor, M. and I. B. Vogel (1986). *Prosodic Phonology*. Dordrecht: Foris.

Nettle, D. (1998). *Linguistic Diversity*. Oxford: Oxford University Press.

Newman, J. and R. G. Petterson (1990). The tones of Kairi. *Oceanic Linguistics* XXIX, 49–76.

Newman, P. (1974). *The Kanakuru Language.* Leeds: West African Linguistic Society. Institute of Modern English Language Studies, University of Leeds.

Newport, E. (1982). Task specificity in language learning? Evidence from speech perception and American Sign Language. In *Language Acqusition: The State of the Art*, pp. 450–486. Cambridge: Cambridge University Press.

Nolan, F. and E. Grabe (1997). Can ToBI transcribe intonational variation in English? See Botinis, Kouroupetroglou, and Carayannis (1997), pp. 259–262.

Nooteboom, S. G. (1996). Lexical retrieval from fragments of spoken words: Beginnings vs. endings. *Journal of Phonetics* 9, 407–424.

O'Connor, J. and G. Arnold (1973). *Intonation of Colloquial English.* London: Longman. 2nd edn.

Odden, D. (1986). On the Obligatory Contour Principle. *Language* 62, 353–383.

Odden, D. (1997). Domains and levels of representation in tone. In R. Herbert (ed.), *African Linguistics at the Crossroads. Papers from Kwaluseni 1st World Congress of African Linguistics*, pp. 119–146. Cologne: Rüdiger Köppe. Swaziland 18–22 July 1994.

Ohala, J. J. (1978). Production of tone. See Fromkin (1978), pp. 5–39.

Ohala, J. J. (1983). Cross-language use of pitch: An ethological view. *Phonetica* 40, 1–18.

Ohala, J. J. (1984). An ethological perspective on common cross-language utilization of f_0 invoice. *Phonetica* 41, 1–16.

Ohala, J. J. (1996). The frequency code underlies the sound symbolic use of voice pitch. In L. Hinton, J. Nichols, and O. J. J. Ohala (eds.), *Sound Symbolism*, pp. 325–347. Cambridge: Cambridge University Press.

Ohara, Y. (1992). Gender-dependent pitch levels in Japanese and English: A comparative study. In K. Hall, M. Bucholtz, and B. Moonwomon (eds.), *Locating Power. Proceedings of the Second Berkeley Women and Language Conference*, pp. 469–477. Berkeley, CA: Berkeley Women and Language Group.

O'Shaughnessy, D. and J. Allen (1983). Linguistic modality effects on fundamental frequency in speech. *Journal of the Acoustic Society of America.* 74, 1155–1171.

Ostendorf, M., P. Price, and S. Shattuck-Hufnagel (1995). The Boston University Radio News Corpus. Technical report, Boston University ECS Technical Report ECS-95-001.

Palmer, H. E. (1922). *English Intonation with Systematic Exercises.* Cambridge: Heffer.

Peeters, W. and B. Schouten (1989). Die Diphthongierung der westgermanischen î- und û-Laute im limburgischen. *Zeitschrift für Dialektologie und Linguistik LVI*, pp. 309–318.

Peng, S.-H. (2000). Lexical versus 'phonological' representations of Mandarin sandhi tones. See Broe and Pierrehumbert (2000), pp. 152–167.

Peters, J. (2002). Intonation und Fokus im Hamburgischen. *Linguistische Berichte* 189, 27–57.

Pierrehumbert, J. B. (1979). The perception of fundamental frequency declination. *Journal of the Acoustic Society of America* 66, 363–369.

Pierrehumbert, J. B. (1980). *The Phonetics and phonology of English intonation.* Ph.D. thesis, MIT. Published by Garland Press, New York (1990).

Pierrehumbert, J. B. (1990). Phonological and phonetic representations. *Journal of Phonetics* 18, 375–394.

Pierrehumbert, J. B. (1993). Alignment and prosodic heads. In *Proceedings of the Eastern States Conference on Formal Linguistics*, Ithaca, NY, pp. 268–286. Cornell University, Graduate Student Association.

Pierrehumbert, J. B. (2000). Tonal elements and their alignment. See Horne (2000), pp. 11–36.

Pierrehumbert, J. B. and M. E. Beckman (1988). *Japanese Tone Structure*. Cambridge, MA: MIT Press.

Pierrehumbert, J. B. and J. Hirschberg (1990). The meaning of intonational contours in the interpretation of discourse. In P. Cohen, J. Morgan, and M. Pollack (eds.), *Intentions in Communication*, pp. 271–311. Cambridge, MA: MIT Press.

Pierrehumbert, J. B. and S. Steele (1989). Categories of tonal alignment in English. *Phonetica* 46, 181–196.

Pike, E. and K. Wistrand (1974). Step-up terrace tone in Acatlán Mixtec (Mexico). In R. M. Brend (ed.), *Advances in Tagmemics*, pp. 81–104. Amsterdam: North-Holland.

Pike, K. L. (1945). *The Intonation of American English*. Ann Arbor, MI: University of Michigan Press.

Pike, K. L. (1948). *Tone Languages: A Technique for Determining the Number and Type of Pitch Contrasts in a Language, with Studies in Tonemic Substitution and Fusion*. Ann Arbor, MI: University of Michigan Press.

Poser, William, J. (1990). Evidence for foot structure in Japanese. *Language* 66, 78–105.

Poser, W. J. (1984). *The phonetics and phonology of tone and intonation in Japanese*. Ph.D. dissertation, MIT.

Post, B. (1999). Restructured phonological phrases in French. *Linguistics* 14, 965–968.

Post, B. (2000a). Pitch accents, liaison and the phonological phrase in French. *Probus* 12, 127–164.

Post, B. (2000b). *Tonal and Phrasal Structures in French Intonation*. The Hague: Thesus (Subsidiary of Holland Academic Graphics).

Prieto, P., J. van Santen, and J. Hirschberg (1995). Tonal alignment patterns in Spanish. *Journal of Phonetics* 23, 429–451.

Prince, A. (1983). Relating to the grid. *Linguistic Inquiry* 14, 19–100.

Prince, A. and P. Smolensky (1993). Optimality theory. Constraint interaction in generative grammar. Rutgers University and University of Colorado. Technical Report 2.

Pulgram, E. (1965). Prosodic systems: French. *Lingua* 13, 125–144.

Pulleyblank, D. (1986). *Tone in Lexical Phonology*. Dordrecht: Reidel.

Quirk, R., S. Greenbaum, G. Leech, and J. Svartvik (1985). *A Comprehensive Grammar of the English Language*. London: Longman.

Radford, A. (1981). *Transformational Syntax*. Cambridge: Cambridge University Press.

Ramsay, R. (2001). Tonogenesis in Korean. See Kaji (2001), pp. 3–17.

Reetz, H. (1996). *Pitch Perception in Speech: A Time Dimension Approach*. Dordrecht: Foris.

Reetz, H. (1999). *Artikulatorische und akustische Phonetik*. Trier: Wissenschaftlicher Verlag Trier.

Remijsen, B. (2002). Lexically contrastive stress accent and lexical tone in Ma'ya. See Gussenhoven and Warner (2002), pp. 585–614.

Remijsen, B. and V. van Heuven (1999). Gradient and categorical pitch dimensions in Dutch: Diagnostic test. In *Proceedings of the 14th International Congress of Phonetic Sciences*, 2, pp. 1865–1868.

Riad, T. (1998), Towards a Scandinavian accent typology. In W. Kehrein and R. Wiese (eds.), *Phonology and Morphology of the Germanic Languages*, pp. 77–109. Tübingen: Niemeyer.

Riad, T. (2000). The origin of Danish stød. See Lahiri (2000), pp. 261–300.

Rialland, A. (2001). Anticipatory raising in downstep realization: Evidence for preplanning in tone production. See Kaji (2001), pp. 301–321.

Rietveld, A. and C. Gussenhoven (1985). On the relation between pitch excursion size and prominence. *Journal of Phonetics* 13, 299–308.

Rietveld, A. and V. van Heuven (1997). *Algemene Fonetiek*. Dordrecht: Coutinho.

Rietveld, T. and C. Gussenhoven (1995). Aligning pitch targets in speech synthesis: Effects of syllable structure. *Journal of Phonetics* 23, 375–385.

Rietveld, T., J. Kerkhoff, and C. Gussenhoven (forthcoming). Vowel duration in Dutch as a function of word prosodic structure. Phonetica.

Rivera-Castillo, Y. (1998). Tone and stress in Papiamentu: The contribution of a constraint-based analysis to the problem of creole genesis. *Journal of Pidgin and Creole Languages* 13, 297–334.

Rivierre, J.-C. (2001). Tonogenesis and evolution in the tonal systems in New Caledonia. See Kaji (2001), pp. 23–42.

Robert, S. (2000). Le verbe wolof ou la grammaticalisation du focus. In B. Caron (ed.), *Topicalisation et focalisation dans les langues africaines*, pp. 229–267. Louvain and Paris: Peeters.

Römer, R. G. (1991). *Studies in Papiamentu Phonology*. Amsterdam and Kingston: Caribbean Culture Studies. Edited by Norval S. H. Smith and John M. Stewart.

Sagart, L. (1999). The origin of Chinese tones. See Kaji (1999), pp. 91–103.

Scherer, K. (1979). Personality markers in speech. In K. Scherer and H. Giles (eds.), *Social Markers in Speech*, pp. 147–201. Cambridge: Cambridge University Press.

Scherer, K. R. (2000). Cross-cultural investigation of emotion inferred from voice and speech: Implications for speech technology. In *Proceedings of the 6th International Conference on the Processing of Spoken Language*, 2, pp. 379–382.

Schmerling, S. F. (1974). *Aspects of English Sentence Stress*. Austin: Texas University Press.

Schmidt, J. E. (1986). *Die Mittelfränkische Tonakzente (Rheinische Akzentuierung)*. Stuttgart: Franz Steiner.

Schmidt, J. E. (2002). Die Sprachhistorische Genese der mittelfränkischen Tonakzente. In P. Auer, P. Gilles, and H. Spiekermann (eds.), *Silbenschnitt und Tonakzente*, pp. 201–233. Tübingen: Niemeyer.

Schubiger, M. (1965). English intonation and German modal particles: A comparative study. *Phonetica* 12, 65–84. Reprinted in Bolinger (1972), pp. 175–193.

Selkirk, E. (1978). On prosodic structure and its relation to syntactic structure. In T. Fretheim (ed.), *Nordic Prosody* II, pp. 268–271. Trondheim: TAPIR.

Selkirk, E. (1980). The role of prosodic categories in English word stress. *Linguistic Inquiry* 11, 563–605.

Selkirk, E. (1984). *Phonology and Syntax: The Relation Between Sound and Structure*. Cambridge, MA: MIT Press.

Selkirk, E. (1986). On derived domains in sentence phonology. *Phonology Yearbook* 3, pp. 371–405.

Selkirk, E. (1995). The prosodic structure of function words. In J. Beckan, L. Walsh Dickey, and S. Urbanczyk (eds.), *Papers in Optimality Theory*, pp. 439–470. Amherst, MA: GLSA.

Selkirk, E. (2000). The interaction of constraints on prosodic phrasing. See Horne (2000), pp. 231–261.

Selkirk, E. (2002). Contrastive *FOCUS* vs. presentational *focus*: Prosodic evidence from English. See Bel and Marlien (2002), pp. 643–646.

Selkirk, E. (2003). How autonomous is prosodic structure. Handout presentation, 7 March, MIT.

Selkirk, E. (forthcoming). Bengali intonation revisited: An optimality-theoretic analysis. In *Papers in Optimality Theory* 2. University of Massachusetts Occasional Papers 26 (2003).

Selkirk, E. and T. Shen (1990). Prosodic domains on Shanghai Chinese. See Inkelas and Zec (1990), pp. 313–337.

Seuren, P. A. (1998). *Western Linguistics. An Historical Introduction.* Oxford: Blackwell.

Shattuck-Hufnagel, S. (1989). Stress shift as the placement of phrase-level pitch markers. *Journal of the Acoustic Society of America 86*, S493.

Shattuck-Hufnagel, S. (1995). Pitch acccent patterns in adjacent-stress vs. alternating stress words in American English. In *Proceedings of the 13th International Congress of Phonetic Sciences*, 3, pp. 656–659.

Shattuck-Hufnagel, S., M. Ostendorf, and K. Ross (1979). Stress shift and early pitch accent placement in lexical items in American English. *Journal of Phonetics 22*, 357–388.

Shattuck-Hufnagel, S. and A. E. Turk (1996). A prosody tutorial for investigators of auditory sentence processing. *Journal of Psycholinguistic Research 25*, 193–246.

Shen, X. (1990). *Prosody of Mandarin Chinese.* University of California at Berkeley.

Shi, C. (1997). Decrination in Mandarin. See Botinis, Koroupetroglou, and Caryannis (1997), pp. 293–296.

Shimizu, K. (1996). *A Cross-Language Study of Voicing Contratsts of Stop Consonants in Asian Languages.* Tokyo: Seibido.

Silverman, K. E. (1984). F_0 perturbations as a function of voicing of prevocalic and post-vocalic stops and fricatives, and of syllable stress. In E. Lawrence (ed.), *Proceedings of the Autumn Conference of the Institute of Acoustics* 6, pp. 445–452.

Silverman, K. E. (1985). Perception of intonation depends on vowel intrinsic pitch, *Journal of the Acoustic Society of America Supplement 1*, 79, S38,

Silverman, K. E. (1990). The separation of prosodies: Comments on Kohler's paper. See Kingston and Beckman (1990), pp. 139–151.

Silverman, K. E. and J. B. Pierrehumbert (1990). The timing of pre-nuclear high accents in English. See Kingston and Beckman (1990), pp. 72–106.

Silverman, K. E., M. E. Beckman, J. Pitrelli, M. Ostendorf, C. Wightman, P. Prica, J. Pierrehumbert and J. Hirschberg (1992). To BI: a standard for labeling English prosody. *Proceedings of the 2nd International Conference on the Processing of Spoken Language*, pp. 867–870.

Slis, I. H. and A. Cohen (1969). On the complex regulating the voiced–voiceless distinction. *Language and Speech 12*, 80–102 (Part I), 137–155 (Part II).

Sluijter, A. (1995). *Phonetic Correlates of Stress and Accent.* The Hague: Holland Academic Graphics.

Sluijter, A. and V. van Heuven (1997). Spectral balance as an acoustic correlate of stress. *Journal of the Acoustic Society of America* 101, 312–322.

Smiljanić, R. and J. I. Hualde (2000). Lexical and pragmatic functions of tonal alignments in two Serbo-Croatian dialects. In A. Okrent and J. Boyle (eds.), *Proceedings from the Main Session of the 36th Regional Meeting of the Chicago Linguistic Society*, 36(1), pp. 469–482. CLS.

Snider, K. (1999). *The Geometry and Features of Tone*. Arlington: Summer Institute of Linguistics and The University of Texas at Arlington.

Snider, K. L. (1990). Tonal upstep in Krachi: Evidence for a register tier. *Language* 66, 453–474.

Snider, K. L. (1998). Phonetic realisation of downstep in Bimoda. *Phonology* 15, 77–101.

Soukka, M. (2000). *A Descriptive Grammar of Noon: A Cangin Language of Senegal*. LINCOM EUROPA.

Steedman, M. (1991). Structure and intonation. *Language* 67, 260–296.

Steele, J. (1775). *An Essay Towards Establishing the Melody and Measure of Speech to be Expressed and Perpetuated by Peculiar Symbols*. London: Privately printed. Also listed as *Prosodia Rationalis*. Microfiche reproduction published by Scolar Press, London (1974).

Stevens, K., J. Keyser, and H. Kawasaki (1986). Toward a phonetic and phonological theory of redundant features. In J. Perkell and D. H. Klatt (eds.), *Invariance and Variability in Speech Processes*, pp. 426–449, Hillsdale, NJ: Erlbaum.

Stewart, J. M. (1966). The typology of the Twi tone system. *Bulletin of the Institute of African Studies* 1. Preprint.

Strik, H. and L. Boves (1995). Downtrend in f_0 and P_{sb} *Journal of Phonetics* 23, 203–220.

Sugahara, M. (2002). Conditions on post-FOCUS dephrasing in Tokyo Japanese. See Bel and Marlien (2002), pp. 655–658.

Sundberg, J. (1979). Maximum speed of pitch changes in singers and untrained subjects. *Journal of Phonetics* 7, 71–79.

Svantesson, J.-O. (2001). Tonogenesis in South East Asia: Mon-Khmer and beyond. See Kaji (2001), pp. 45–58.

Swerts, M. G., R. Collier, and J. Terken (1994). Prosodic predictors of discourse finality in spontaneous monologues. *Speech Communication* 15, 79–90.

't Hart, J. and R. Collier (1980). *Cursus Nederlandse Intonatie*. Louvain: Acco.

't Hart, J., R. Collier, and A. Cohen (1990). *A Perceptual Study of Intonation: An Experimental-Phonetic Approach to Speech Melody*. Cambridge: Cambridge University Press.

Taff, A. (1997). Intonation patterns in Unangan. See Botinis, Kouroupetroglou, and Carayannis (1997), pp. 301–304.

Thomas, E. (1978). *A Grammatical Description of the Engenni Language*. Dallas, Tex: Summer Institute of Linguistics.

Thorsen, N. (1978). An acoustical analysis of Danish intonation. *Journal of Phonetics* 6, 151–175.

Thorsen, N. (1983). Two issues in the prosody of Standard Danish. See Cutler and Ladd (1983), pp. 27–38.

Trager, G. L. and H. L. Smith Jr (1951). *An Outline of English Structure*. Norman, OK: Battenburg Press. Reprinted by the American Council of Learned Societies, Washington (1957).

Trim, J. (1959). Major and minor tone groups in English. *Le Maître Phonétique* 112, 26–29.

Truckenbrodt, H. (1995). *Phonological phrases: Their relation to syntax, prominence and focus.* Ph.D. thesis, MIT.

Truckenbrodt, H. (1999). On the relation between syntactic phrases and phonological phrases. *Linguistic Inquiry* 30, 219–255.

Truckenbrodt, H. (2002a). Upstep and embedded register levels. *Phonology* 19, 77–120.

Truckenbrodt, H. (2002b). Variation in p-phrasing in Bengali. *Linguistic. Variation* 2, 257–301.

Uldall, E. (1960). Attitudinal meanings conveyed by intonation contours. *Language and Speech* 3, 223–234.

Uldall, E. (1964). Dimension of meaning in intonation. In D. Abercrombie, D. B. Fry, P. A. MacCarthy, N. Scott, and J. L. Trim (eds.), *In Honour of Daniel Jones: Papers Contributed on the Occasion of his Eightieth Birthday*, pp. 271–279. London: Longman. Reprinted in Bolinger (1972), pp. 250–259.

Uwano, Z. (1999). Classification of Japanese accent systems. See Kaji (1999), pp. 151–178.

Vaissière, J. (1983). Language-independent features. See Cutler and Ladd (1983), pp. 53–66.

Vallduví, E. (1992). *The Informational Component.* New York: Garland.

van Bezooijen, R., T. de Graaf, and T. Otake (1995). Pitch stereotypes in the Netherlands and Japan. In *Proceedings of the 13th International Congress of Phonetic Sciences*, 3, pp. 680–683.

van den Berg, R., C. Gussenhoven, and T. Rietveld (1992). Downstep in Dutch: Implications for a model. See Docherty and Ladd (1992), pp. 335–359.

van der Hulst, H. (1999). Word accent. See van der Hulst (ed.) (1999), pp. 3–115.

van der Hulst, H. (ed.) (1999). *Word Prosodic Systems in the Languages of Europe.* Berlin: Mouton de Gruyter.

van der Hulst, H. and N. Smith (1988). The variety of pitch accent systems: Introduction. See Hulst and Smith (1988), pp. ix–xxiv.

van der Hulst, H. and K. Snider (eds.) (1993). *The Phonology of Tone: The Representation of Tonal Register.* Berlin, and New York: Mouton de Gruyter.

van Heuven, V. J. and J. Haan (2002). Temporal distribution of interrogativity markers in Dutch: A perceptual study. See Gussenhoven and Warner (2002), pp. 61–86.

Vance, T. J. (1987). *An Introduction to Japanese Phonology.* Albany: State University of New York Press.

Vanderslice, R. and P. Ladefoged (1972). Binary suprasegmental features and transformational word-accentuation rules. *Language* 48, 819–838.

Varga, L. (2002). *Stress and Intonation: Evidence from Hungarian.* Basingstoke: Palgrave.

Verluyten, S. (1982). *Recherches sur la prosodie et la métrique du français.* Ph.D. dissertation, University of Antwerp.

Vismans, R. (1994). *Modal Particles in Dutch Directive: A Study in Functional Grammar.* Amsterdam: IFOTT.

Vogel, I., T. Bunnell, and S. Hoskins (1995). The phonology and phonetics of the Rhythm Rule. In B. Connell and A. Arvaniti (eds.), *Phonology and Phonetic Evidence: Papers in Laboratory Phonology IV*, pp. 111–127. Cambridge: Cambridge University Press.

Vogel, I. B. and I. Kenesei (1990). Syntax and semantics in phonology. See Inkelas and Zec (1990), pp. 339–363.

Voorhoeve, J. (1973). Safwa as a restricted tone system. *Studies in African Linguistics* 4, 1–22.

Warner, N. (1997). Japanese final-accented and unaccented phrases. *Journal of Phonetics* 25, 43–60.

Waugh, L. R. and C. Van Schooneveld (eds.) (1980). *The Melody of Language*. Baltimore: University Park Press.

Wedekind, K. (1983). A six-tone language of Ethiopia. *Journal of Ethiopian Studies* 16, 129–156.

Wells, J. C. (1990). *Longman Pronunciation Dictionary*. London: Longman.

Welmers, W. E. (1959). Tonemics, morphotonemics, and tonal morphemes. *General Linguistics* 4, 1–19.

Whalen, D. H. and A. E. Levitt (1995). The universality of intrinsic f_0 of vowels. *Journal of Phonetics* 23, 349–366.

Wichmann, A. (2000). *Intonation in Text and Discourse. Beginnings, Middles and Ends.* Harlow: Longman.

Wichmann, A., J. House, and T. Rietveld (1997). Peak displacement and topic structure. See Botinis, Kouroupetroglou, and Carayannis (1997), pp. 329–332.

Wichmann, A., J. House, and T. Rietveld (2000). Discourse constraints on F_0 peak timing in English. See Botinis (2000), pp. 163–182.

Wiesinger, P. (1975). Strukturgeographische und strukturhistorische Untersuchungen zur Stellung der bergischen Mundart zwischen Ripuarisch, Niederfränkisch und Westfälisch. In J. Göschel and W. Veith (eds.), *Neuere Forschungen in Linguistik und Philologie*, pp. 17–82. Wiesbaden: Steiner.

Wightman, C. W., S. Shattuck-Hufnagel, M. Ostendorf, and P. J. Price (1992). Segmental durations in the vicinity of prosodic boundaries. *Journal of the Acoustic Society of America* 91, 1707–1717.

Willems, N. J. (1984). *English Intonation from Dutch Point of View*. Dordrecht: Foris.

Winston, F. (1960). The 'mid tone' in Efik. *African Language Studies* 1, 185–192.

Xu, Y. (1998). Fundamental frequency peak delay in Mandarin. *Phonetica* 58, 26–52.

Xu, Y. (2002). Articulatory constraints and tonal alignment. See Bel and Marlien (2002), pp. 91–100.

Xu, Y. and X. Sun (forthcoming). Maximum speed of pitch change and how it may relate to speech. *Journal of the Acoustic Society of America*.

Yip, M. (1980). *The tonal phonology of Chinese*. Ph.D. thesis, MIT, Cambridge, MA.

Yip, M. (1989). Contour tones. *Phonology* 6, 149–174.

Yip, M. (2002). *Tone*. Cambridge: Cambridge University Press.

Zhang, J. (2000). The phonetic basis for tonal melody mapping. In *Proceedings of the West Coast Conference on Formal Linguistics* 19, pp. 603–616. Somerville, MA: Cascadilla Press.

Zoll, C. (1997). Conflicting directionality. *Phonology* 14, 263–286.

Zonneveld, W., M. Trommelen, M. Jessen, C. Rice, G. Bruce, and K. Árnason (1999). Wordstress in West-Germanic and North-Germanic languages. See van der Hulst (1999), pp. 477–603.

Zubizarreta, M. L. (1998). *Prosody, Focus, and Word Order*. Cambridge, MA: MIT Press.

Index

Subject index